Johann Most

Johann Most

Life of a Radical

TOM GOYENS

UNIVERSITY OF
ILLINOIS PRESS
Urbana, Chicago, and Springfield

Cataloging data available from the Library of Congress

ISBN 978-0-252-04691-9 (hardcover)
ISBN 978-0-252-08903-9 (paperback)
ISBN 978-0-252-04847-0 (ebook)

It is no secret to the rich and powerful that mankind can only be enslaved and exploited when the necromancers of the churches ingraft sufficient servility into the hearts of the masses of the people to make them look upon the earth as a vale of tears, to imbue their minds with the justness of the godly decree; "Serve ye your master" (those in authority), and to buy them off with an alleged "spare-rib" of which the people will get the soup in that home beyond the skies, the "Nobodyknows."

—John Most, The God Pestilence (1887)

Contents

Acknowledgments

This biography could not have come to life without the contributions, wisdom, and encouragement of many remarkable individuals. Although my name graces the cover, this book is, at its core, a collective achievement. It is my privilege to acknowledge the collaboration, support, and friendship that made it possible.

First and foremost, I owe a debt of gratitude to the late Paul Avrich, Ronald Creagh, and Paul Buhle. Their mentorship ignited my passion for the history of anarchism and their influence continues to guide my work to this day.

Over the years, I have been fortunate to be surrounded by a community of scholar-friends who have served as both an intellectual compass and a wellspring of inspiration: Bert Altena, Allan Antliff, Constance Bantman, Marcella Bencivenni, Spencer Beswick, Morris Brodie, Christopher J. Castañeda, Peter Cole, Andy Cornell, Raymond Craib, Geoffroy de Laforcade, Kathy Ferguson, Montse Feu, José Antonio Gutiérrez, Robert Helms, Steven Hirsch, Andrew Hoyt, Ruth Kinna, Ole Birk Laursen, Carl Levy, Dieter Nelles, Kirwin Shaffer, David Struthers, Anna Elena Torres, Lucien van der Walt, and Kenyon Zimmer. Their groundbreaking research, thoughtful insights, and unflagging encouragement are interwoven into every page of this book.

I am equally indebted to those scholars from adjacent fields who generously offered their time, knowledge, or shared invaluable research materials, many of which found a home within these pages: Thomas Adam, Franz Adlgasser, Jesse Cohn, Pietro Di Paola, Federico Ferretti, Lars Fischer, Elun Gabriel, Benno Gammerl, Robert Goodrich, Andreas Graf, Jennifer Guglielmo, Dirk Hoerder, Rachel Hui-Chi Hsu, Nathan Jun, Jeremy King, Susanne F. Kohl,

Mark Lause, Timothy Messer-Kruse, Folkert Mohrhof, Barry Pateman, Nunzio Pernicone, Michael Rudloff, Raffael Scheck, Jürgen Schlimper, Anna L. Staudacher, Peter Teichert-Köster, Davide Turcato, and Marcel van der Linden.

A special thanks goes out to the librarians, archivists, and technicians who have tirelessly preserved and curated the very sources on which this biography stands. Their quiet but vital work is the foundation of historical scholarship. I am especially grateful to the teams at the International Institute of Social History in Amsterdam, Amsab-Institute for Social History in Gent, Landesarchiv Berlin, the city archives of Augsburg and Chemnitz, the public library of Chemnitz, the Rudolfsheim-Fünfhaus district museum in Vienna, the German Bundesarchiv, the State Library in Berlin (Preußischer Kulturbesitz), the John F. Kennedy Institute at the Free University Berlin, the Labadie Collection at the University of Michigan, the New York Municipal Archives, the New York Public Library, and Yale University Library.

Finally, my deepest thanks are reserved for my family. My loving partner, Heather Harvey, has been my steadfast companion and comrade, while my son, Mathijs, has patiently watched this manuscript take shape. Their love and unwavering support have sustained me. I must also thank my colleagues at Salisbury University for their moral and financial backing, which has been a pillar of my research endeavors.

I am honored to have the University of Illinois Press as the publisher of this work. Their talented editors and creative artists have transformed my research into something truly special.

Tom Goyens
Easton, Maryland

Johann Most

Introduction

AT 10:30 P.M. ON MAY 11, 1886, New York police inspector Thomas Byrnes, accompanied by four detectives, made their way into a tenement building at 198 Allen Street on Manhattan's Lower East Side. The structure contained four cramped apartments, and Byrnes wasted no time informing the landlady, Mrs. Brown, that they were there to arrest Johann Most. For the past eighteen days, Most had been in hiding, evading authorities after delivering a fiery speech brandishing a rifle. His incendiary rhetoric came on the heels of a deadly bombing at an anarchist rally in Chicago, and suspicions had fallen on him. The detectives discovered Most in the third apartment, swiftly arrested him, and hauled him off to the station.

However, the daily newspapers spun a more salacious tale. Reports claimed Most had been captured in a brothel, found cowering under a bed. Even though he protested and tried to set the record straight, the sensationalist version persisted. Most would later accuse the police of intentionally fueling these lies. On May 16, the *New York World* ran a two-part illustration by artist Walter McDougall titled "The Hero of the Anarchist Legion," which depicted Most as a manic, wild-eyed figure brandishing a rifle in a beer hall. In the second image, he's shown trembling under a bed, surrounded by dynamite and gunpowder. The image stuck, and just six days later, the famed cartoonist Thomas Nast featured Most in *Harper's Weekly*, further cementing his image as the archetypal anarchist rabble-rouser. Most's physical appearance only added fuel to the mockery. His unkempt, wild hair was seen as a mirror of his chaotic radicalism, and a childhood illness had left his jaw permanently askew—a feature he attempted to conceal beneath a tangle of beard, yet one that only made him easier to caricature in the public eye.[1]

This enduring stereotype is a key reason why Johann Most (1846–1906) remains an enigma in the histories of German socialism and American anarchism. The caricature of Most as a fanatical, one-dimensional agitator has long overshadowed the true complexity of a man who wielded words like weapons. His limited proficiency in English has only added to the distortion, obscuring the intellectual depth and human vulnerability behind his fiery public persona. To fully understand Most's life and legacy—a transnational revolutionary with a deeply human side—we must strip away the layers of myth that have settled over his memory. Born in 1846 in Augsburg, Bavaria, Most endured a series of personal hardships as a child, traumas that would shape his rebellious spirit. His early life took him across Central Europe, with stints in Switzerland, Austria, and Germany, before he was forced into exile in London. After spending thirty-two years in Europe, Most embraced anarchism and moved to New York City at the end of 1882. Over the next four decades, he became a magnetic figure in the revolutionary movement, rousing workers with speeches and writings that combined the passion of an actor, the bite of a satirist, and the precision of a rhetorician.

By the time he passed away in Cincinnati in 1906, Most had edited four influential radical periodicals, produced four collections of revolutionary songs, authored thirty-three original pamphlets, and penned an untold number of fiery editorials. His public defiance led to nine years behind bars in Austria, Germany, England, and the United States. Yet in all his tireless activism, Most sought no personal gain. Material wealth meant little to him; his true wealth lay in the power of ideas, which he shaped and reshaped depending on the political climate around him. Emma Goldman, who knew him intimately, once described Most as "one of the most picturesque and unique characters of our time." His ideological foundation was as eclectic as his journey through life—a man constantly adapting, constantly evolving but always driven by a fierce belief in revolution. It is time to rediscover the real Johann Most, a figure far more complex, creative, and yes, deeply human than the enduring caricature would have us believe.[2]

The life and legacy of Johann Most remain deeply significant today for a number of reasons. As a key figure in the history of German socialism in the 1870s and American anarchism in the decades that followed, Most's contributions to revolutionary thought have often been overshadowed by stereotypes and distortions. The historiography of German socialism has been particularly unkind to Most, largely due to the harsh criticisms of his former colleagues and subsequent socialist historians. Figures such as August Bebel, Wilhelm Liebknecht, Eduard Bernstein, and Franz Mehring attacked Most's character and downplayed his role in the movement after he embraced revolutionary socialism, a shift that led to his expulsion from the Social Democratic Party in 1880. Although Most never positioned himself as an intellectual on the same level as Marx, Bebel, or Bernstein, he possessed a rare ability to inspire militancy among the proletariat.

It was not until Rudolf Rocker's 1924 biography that an important corrective emerged, challenging the socialist establishment's efforts to erase or misrepresent him. In 1976, the radical German writer Horst Karasek echoed Rocker's sentiments, sharply criticizing the "official historians of Social Democratic or bourgeois origin" for their attempts to either silence Most or distort his image to the point of inhumanity. By the mid-1980s, political scientist Volker Szmula had further advanced Most's rehabilitation, publishing and annotating four volumes of his socialist writings.[3] Szmula argued that Most had functioned as the "unofficial publicist" of the Social Democratic Party and that much of what the German public knew about the party came through Most's efforts as a communicator.[4] Yet, despite these efforts, old critiques persisted. In his 2000 interpretation of the early German socialist movement, historian Thomas Welskopp revived Bernstein's derision, dismissing Most as overly emotional, a mere "haranguer and buffoon."[5] Nonetheless, the tide began to turn with a 2003 academic workshop in Berlin, which sought to reevaluate Most's contributions to the German labor movement of the 1870s. This workshop culminated in a special 2005 issue of the journal *Internationale wissenschaftliche Korrespondenz zur Geschichte der deutschen Arbeiterbewegung*, titled "Johann Most, an Underestimated Social Democrat?" edited by Andreas Graf and Heiner Becker. Becker's extensive archival research further illuminated Most's overlooked contributions.[6]

Johann Most—who changed his name to John after emigrating to the United States—was a central figure in the development of American anarchism despite the conventional imagery. The early anarchist movement in the United States is difficult to fully understand without considering Most's impact. Alongside the Haymarket affair, Most helped shape the enduring caricature of anarchism as violent and chaotic. His ideas and leadership, though controversial even within anarchist circles, left a profound mark on immigrant radicals during an era of fierce labor struggles. One of the most significant legacies of the German anarchist movement, driven in large part by Most, was its influence on Yiddish-speaking radicals. These radicals helped carry anarchist and unionist ideals into the twentieth century.

Most's courage in the face of ridicule and repression inspired dedication to anarchist principles in others, including Emma Goldman and Alexander Berkman, two of the most important figures in Jewish American radicalism. Given the Jewish Left's profound impact on American radicalism after 1900, understanding Most's role in shaping this intergenerational transfer of ideas is crucial.[7] However, Most's influence remained largely confined to ethnic enclaves of German, Czech, and Yiddish-speaking radicals. One key reason for this was his bleak view of America, which he saw as a country consumed by violence, greed, and a shallow materialism. This harsh perspective, combined with what he saw as the absence of idealism in American politics and culture, limited his broader appeal. Most's disdain for the methods of native-born radicals—whether anti-monopolists, populists, socialists, or progressives—further isolated him from the radical wing of the Progressive movement. His legacy was eventually overshadowed by figures such as his protégé Emma Goldman and native-born labor leader "Big Bill" Haywood.[8]

One cannot help but admire Johann Most's unwavering dedication to his cause, regardless of one's stance on his politics. Whereas many of his older comrades eventually withdrew from activism, Most continued editing, traveling, and speaking until his last breath. Allegedly, his final words, uttered in a delirious state, were, "Let me go out—I must go out to speak."[9] Friends and adversaries alike remarked on his relentless commitment to the anarchist movement. American-born anarchist Voltairine de Cleyre lauded his "courage and fortitude," while Emma Goldman observed that a "truly extraordinary tenacity" defined Most's character, a quality "the defenders of the old order could not forgive." Anarchist historian Max Nettlau echoed this sentiment, calling it an "uncompromising tenacity of purpose."[10] Even an obituary in a Milwaukee socialist paper acknowledged that the world had profoundly wronged a man like Most, who stubbornly defied it. The paper observed that "this peculiar man possessed extraordinary qualities: immense, tireless perseverance; enormous capacity for work; significant oratory skills; and originality in his forceful language."[11] Yet Most's achievements were not the result of individual effort alone. Behind his public persona stood a network of friends and comrades who were as devoted and self-sacrificing as he was—though he did not always recognize their contributions. None was more crucial than his anarchist partner, Helene Minkin. Not only did Minkin share Most's ideological convictions, but she also took on the burdens of household and child-rearing. Most's much-praised resolve and resilience in his later years were made possible, in large part, by Minkin's quiet strength and personal sacrifices.

Equally inspiring for today's activists is the fact that Johann Most never neglected the aesthetic and artistic dimensions of life—a common sacrifice for many revolutionaries absorbed in their cause. At his core, Most was a Romantic, envisioning a revolution that embraced both bread *and* roses. He was an avid lover of theater, poetry, music, chess, and good wine. Emma Goldman remembered Most not only as her teacher of social ideas but also of "new beauty in art and music." As she wrote, "Most loved both intensely, and helped me to learn to love them."[12] Beyond his fiery rhetoric and militancy, Most could be a charming and excellent companion. De Cleyre remarked on his "courtly manners," calling him the "personification of grace in his movements."[13] A colleague from Buffalo confirmed that, for all his militancy, Most was "an extremely pleasant and entertaining companion; he could spin yarns and anecdotes effortlessly." Most's Romantic spirit also extended to his deep connection with nature. As a young man, he hiked extensively across Central Europe, and even after settling in cities like Berlin, London, and New York, he often longed for nature walks. Despite his revolutionary fire, he had a gentle aversion to hunting and fishing. If he caught a fish, he would return it to the water.[14]

Johann Most possessed an extraordinary mastery of the German language, wielding it with precision to explain complex theories, satirize the privileged, inspire workers, and challenge authority. This linguistic prowess set him apart from his contemporaries, turning every speech or written piece into a verbal spectacle. Anyone who encountered his words was met with a barrage of witty twists, clever phrases, and inventive wordplay—punctuated by humor, biting satire, and double meanings. It is an irony of history that such a gifted wordsmith became synonymous with revolutionary violence despite never having committed a violent crime himself. His talent for language was appreciated only by those who could understand him, a limitation that sometimes worked against him in his adopted country. The Jewish anarchist Saul Yanovsky once observed, "Since the German language did not give him enough words, he often creates them himself."[15] For Most, German literature and language were like a bottomless arsenal from which he unleashed his satire, denunciations, and theoretical musings. He only spoke in English when specifically requested by comrades, admitting that it was "a hard job for me."[16] Most's talent for the German tongue—combined with his humor and razor-sharp invective—was most vividly on display in his speeches and the four newspapers he edited. Of these, *Freiheit* was his life's work. He often referred to it as his daughter in need of protection, convinced that rivals and meddlers were always lurking to destroy or steal it. As Helene Minkin poignantly observed, "He did not publish *Freiheit* so he could live; rather, he lived so that he could publish *Freiheit*." This close relationship with *Freiheit*, which began in 1879, is crucial to understanding both Most's temperament and many of his actions. It also fed into his reputation for being controlling, rigid, and at times, vengeful. Emma Goldman recalled his "impatience with opposition" and his occasional intolerance, which manifested in his stark attitude: "Who is not with me is against me." When Most passed away in 1906, Minkin found solace in the fact that *Freiheit* had outlived him, continuing its run until 1910.[17]

Johann Most is also relevant for critique of religion and his defense of science within the context of emancipatory movements. He was a significant figure in the history of free thought, an area often overlooked by historians of labor and radicalism. Most believed that discarding religious beliefs and dismantling clerical authority were crucial first steps toward genuine liberation. Long before he embraced socialism, Most had already become a fervent atheist, and throughout his life, he never separated his critique of religion from his critique of capitalism and oppression. By the late 1870s, Most had emerged as one of Germany's most outspoken atheists, boldly linking religious dogma to the subjugation of the masses—a mission he carried with him to the United States. His relentless atheism and sharp critique of all forms of worship informed his worldview and fueled his drive for freedom. Most's widely read pamphlet *Die Gottes-Pest und Religions-Seuche* (The God pestilence), published in 1883, was translated into more than a dozen languages. In it, he argued that atheism and anticlericalism were essential components of any direct action against capitalism and oppression, as religion paralyzes the masses in the face of economic exploitation. While Most could be intolerant of different opinions, he frequently warned against a workers' movement becoming too dogmatic. He believed that Social Democrats in both Germany and the United States had become too institutionalized. Max Baginski, who briefly took over the editorship of *Freiheit* after Most's death, credited him with preventing the establishment of a "Socialist Vatican" in America.[18]

Johann Most's life unfolded amid two significant developments: the maturation of industrial capitalism and the rise of nationalism in Europe and the United States. To revolutionaries like Most, these forces were not just abstract concepts; they were profoundly destabilizing, radical in their impact on human life and well-being. Nationalism, cloaked in rhetoric of expansion and destiny, followed in the wake of the American Civil War and Bismarckian war and diplomacy during the 1860s and 1870s, ultimately leading to the formation of the German Empire in 1871. Industrial capitalism, meanwhile, unleashed relentless pressures on millions of working people, becoming the "mediating factor" for agitation and discontent that shaped Most's life. Far from being irrational or impulsive agitators, radicals like Most channeled their activism in response to the economic despair and staggering inequality of their time. By 1890, the census laid bare the stark reality: the wealthiest 1 percent earned more than the combined income of the bottom 50 percent.[19] Calls for reforms were largely ignored or actively suppressed, even as the economy faltered through a constant boom-and-bust cycle. Radicals like Most saw a peculiar form of violence embedded in this system. Indeed, violence perpetrated by employers, vigilantes, and law enforcement far exceeded the sporadic outbursts attributed to radicals or workers. The industrial workplace itself was rife with danger, as historian Beverly Gage points out: American industry "killed an estimated 35,000 workers in accidents each year at the turn of the century."[20]

Retracing the life of Johann Most reveals a journey through various geographic and ideological landscapes, reflecting the shifts in his worldview as he encountered a spectrum of left-radical ideas across different countries. From Switzerland and Austria to Germany, England, and the United States, the political climate in each place shaped his opportunities for propaganda and his ideological evolution. His transformation—from a republican rooted in popular sovereignty and individual rights, to a social democrat, and finally to an anarchist—spans four decades of complex political engagement. Most's conversion to socialism in 1867, followed by his involvement with the German Social Democratic Workers' Party, occurred in a period before the dominance of Marxist thought. Most believed in the transformative power of secular education, propaganda through speech and the written word, and the ballot box as tools to revolutionize the proletariat and establish a "people's state" modeled after the Paris Commune of 1871. However, Otto von Bismarck's repressive anti-socialist laws in 1878 pushed Most into exile in London, where he renounced parliamentary socialism for a more radical, revolutionary approach. This biography aims to shed light on Most's intellectual trajectory and his influence on the broader socialist movement, highlighting how the political environments he navigated shaped his evolving views on revolutionary action and social change. It emphasizes the nuance in his journey—how his experiences of repression, exile, and the limitations of institutional politics spurred his break with social democracy and cemented his commitment to anarchism as a means of liberation for the working class.

Johann Most's entry into the social revolutionary movement was initially not aligned with anarchism, and it took several years before he fully embraced anarchist principles. Throughout the 1870s, anarchism was marginalized within Germany's socialist ranks, which were firmly focused on the parliamentary path to social change. However, during his time in London, Most found himself increasingly drawn to the anarchist movement. The Russian revolutionary Mikhail Bakunin had earlier championed anarchism as an alternative to Marx's vision of state socialism, advocating for insurrectionism and conspiratorial action to ignite social revolution. This advocacy contributed to the development of the concept of "propaganda by the deed," a phrase that gained currency in 1877, a year after Bakunin's death. The idea originated in the context of armed rural and urban insurrections in the early 1870s, demonstrating the potential of direct action to galvanize support for revolution—something mere pamphleteering and speeches had struggled to achieve. The increasing repression of radicals by state authorities further pushed anarchists, including Most, toward clandestine and violent methods. The appeal of revolutionary terrorism grew, aided by the recent invention of dynamite, which seemed like the only viable method left. As one historian noted, "Political terrorism constituted a desperate attempt on the part of the anarchist movement to escape the isolation which parliamentary socialism had sidetracked it into."[21] At the 1881 London Congress of Social Revolutionary, these tactics were formally endorsed, along with the study of chemistry for manufacturing explosives. Although Most was imprisoned in London at the time, he was kept informed of these discussions. Many anarchists drew inspiration from groups fighting imperial oppressors, such as Russian nihilists and Irish nationalists. As historian Zoe Baker points out, the congress's adoption of these tactics just months after the assassination of the Russian czar using explosives was no coincidence.[22]

Sometime in late 1882, Most embraced revolutionary anarchism, though he still focused primarily on "propaganda by the deed." He rejected the state, religion, and electoral politics, adhering to the principles of antiauthoritarianism, individual autonomy, and grassroots liberation of the working class without the intervention of political parties or governments. Historian Max Nettlau has suggested that during the early 1880s, Most did not fully grasp the tenets of anarchism, though his readers believed that *Freiheit* was presenting the latest version of anarchist thought. The Haymarket affair of 1886–87, during which four anarchists were executed for their alleged role in a bomb attack, marked a significant turning point for the American anarchist movement. In response, Most distanced himself from revolutionary terrorism while still advocating for the proletariat to arm itself in self-defense. It was not until after 1887, when Most's ideological stance began to shift more toward communist anarchism, that he demonstrated a deeper understanding of anarchist philosophy and an increasing engagement with the social dynamics of Gilded Age America.[23]

It is indeed ironic that the stereotype of the anarchist bomb thrower emerged during 1870–1920, despite the fact that discussions of ideologically motivated violence have often been marginalized in American historiography to support an exceptionalist interpretation of the nation's past.[24] Revolutionary violence and terrorism did exist in the United States, as Johann Most's life illustrates. Most fervently championed class warfare and the use of terror, including explosives, as weapons in the struggle for social revolution. His infamous handbook, *Revolutionary War Science*, discussed during the Haymarket trial, offered meticulous guidance—from safety precautions to determining explosive size based on the intended target. While his incendiary rhetoric fueled the stereotype of anarchists as violent fanatics, Most's embrace of these tactics was surprisingly brief, spanning roughly from 1882 to 1886. In the final two decades of his life, he stepped back from advocating violent revolution, opting for a more measured and thoughtful stance, particularly as he adjusted to the complexities of the American political landscape. This evolution mirrored a broader shift within the anarchist movement itself, as it wrestled with balancing revolutionary zeal against the moral and practical consequences of violence.[25]

Upon arrival, Most found himself in a society where violence was not monopolized by state institutions like the military or police, as it often was in Europe. Instead, violence in America was diffuse, embedded in the fabric of everyday life and carried out by various segments of civil society. Historian Richard Hofstadter, writing in 1970, famously remarked on the "sheer commonplaceness" of American violence, highlighting the tension between the country's violent reality and its cherished image of moral exceptionalism.[26] This broader context is key to understanding how Most's early promotion of revolutionary tactics fit into America's cultural landscape of violence. The so-called cult of dynamite, a phenomenon among a fringe group of anarchists in the 1880s, can only be fully understood when viewed against this backdrop of a nation that both glorified and denied its violent undercurrents. An 1875 Chicago newspaper editorial declared,

> If the Communists in this country are counting upon the looseness of our police system and the tendency to proceed against criminals by due process of law, and hope on that account, to receive more leniency than in Europe, they have ignored some of the most significant episodes in American history. There is no people so prone as the American to take the law into their own hands when

the sanctity of human life is threatened and the rights of property invaded in a manner that cannot be adequately reached and punished by the tortuous course of the law. Judge Lynch is an American by birth and character. The Vigilance Committee is a peculiarly American institution. Every lamp-post in Chicago will be decorated with a communistic carcass if necessary to prevent wholesale incendiarism or prevent any attempt at it.[27]

The treatment of Johann Most in American courts, where he was repeatedly convicted for his incendiary speeches and writings, starkly exposes the double standard at play in Gilded Age America. Whereas Most was punished for his radical rhetoric, industrialists, politicians, and the mainstream press routinely unleashed violent and hateful language against marginalized groups with impunity. During times of labor strikes and social unrest, newspapers and pundits openly called for brutal actions against workers and minorities. In 1877, the *Chicago Times* suggested that "hand-grenades should be thrown among these union sailors . . . as by such treatment they would be taught a valuable lesson, and other strikers could take warning from their fate." This shocking statement prompted Albert Parsons, one of the Haymarket defendants, to label the newspaper the "first dynamiter in America."[28] Even respected public figures could incite violence without fear of retribution. Philanthropist and nurse Mary Livermore once declared, "Tramps have no claim on human sympathy. . . . The hand of society must be against these vagrants; they must die off, and the sooner they are dead and buried the better for society."[29] In 1883, the year Most was touring the United States for the first time, the South saw some of the most heinous crimes, reported by the *New York Times* with headlines like "Terrorism in South Carolina" and "A Revival of Kukluxism."[30] Yet the same newspaper called Most a "detestable and odious scoundrel" and suggested not only torture but murder: "If anyone should be moved to wring the neck of this wretched blackguard MOST, the proceeding would be irregular, but nobody would call it unjust."[31] By 1914, progressive sociologist Robert Hunter would go so far as to assert that "the history of terrorist tactics in America largely centers about the career of Johann Most," conveniently ignoring the far more egregious and systematic terrorism of the Ku Klux Klan, founded in 1866.[32] This selective application of justice reveals a broader, disturbing pattern: radical violence was vilified as foreign and dangerous, while state-sanctioned or vigilante violence was rationalized as necessary for maintaining order. Most and other anarchists became convenient scapegoats, allowing the capitalist system to deflect attention from its own structural injustices. As historian Jeffory Clymer sharply observes, the specter of terrorism became "an important hegemonic prop in the maintenance of America's capitalist order."[33]

The earliest biographical sketches of Johann Most were penned by his fellow anarchists, such as Max Baginski (1906, 1911), Max Nettlau (1906), Emma Goldman (1926), and Max Nomad (1939). In 1924, Rudolf Rocker, another prominent anarchist, published the first full-length biography of Most. Although sympathetic, Rocker's account lacks rigorous citations and remains accessible only in German. His work provides limited insight into Most's early life but offers a detailed exploration of the radical movements Most engaged with in Austria, Germany, England, and the United States. Rocker also sought to correct what he saw as misunderstandings about Most and the German anarchist movement, misconceptions that had taken root even within radical circles. More recently, Frank Harreck-Haase self-published a useful but dense and unwieldy two-volume biography in German, spanning over a thousand pages. Frederic Trautmann's *The Voice of Terror* (1980) remains the only biography of Most in English, but its sensationalist title and flawed structure do little to enhance our understanding of Most's life, making it unsuitable as a scholarly work. A recurring issue in Most historiography, likely due to language barriers, is the tendency for European scholars to focus on his activities in Europe and American scholars to emphasize his exploits in the United States. This has created a fragmented narrative that separates his socialist and anarchist phases. My biography aims to bridge this divide, offering a cohesive account of Most's life that traces his ideological evolution across different continents and political environments. I strive to let Most speak for himself, while providing context and maintaining a clear narrative. As a historian, my guiding principle is evidence, but no biographer is entirely free from bias. A measured degree of empathy is essential to grasp a historical figure's worldview, yet it must always be balanced by a critical examination of their beliefs and actions.

1 A Wild Desire for Wander

IN NOVEMBER 1889, forty-three-year-old John Most invited twenty-year-old Emma Goldman, whom he had just met, to share one of his greatest passions: the theater. He took her to the Amberg Theatre on Irving Place in Lower Manhattan to see *The Merchant of Venice*, starring Ernst Possart, one of Germany's most renowned actors. Most often sacrificed basic necessities to experience the ecstatic pleasure of an excellent performance. During the play, Goldman noticed how intensely absorbed Most was, captivated by every word and gesture of Possart. His silence as they left the theater struck her as unusual. Then, suddenly, Most grabbed her arm. "The cruelty of it, the bitter cruelty!" he cried. "To think I could have been in Possart's place, perhaps even greater than he, but for my dreadful face. The blind cruelty of it!" Once he had calmed down, Most began recounting the story of his childhood in Bavaria and the event thirty years earlier that led to his facial disfigurement—what he regarded as "the deepest tragedy of his life."[1]

Augsburg, where Most grew up, is one of Germany's oldest cities, rich in history and a vibrant commercial center connecting Italy with northern Europe. After the Napoleonic wars, the city experienced significant growth, with its population rising from 29,469 in 1812 to over 49,000 by 1864, driven largely by rural migrants seeking work in its burgeoning factories and mills. By the 1830s, Augsburg had harnessed its waterpower potential through canals, sluices, and turbines, fueling urban development. Forward-thinking citizens invested in industries like textiles while also improving public infrastructure. The 1840s brought major modernization efforts, including public wells, sewer lines, parish schools, a children's poorhouse, and a hospital. The city's connection to Munich by railway in 1840 marked its entry into the industrial era, with gas lighting illuminating the streets by 1847, followed two years later by the establishment of the kingdom's first volunteer fire brigade.[2] Augsburg was also home to the widely circulated *Allgemeine Zeitung* newspaper. In the eastern district of the city lay Jacobtown, a residential area housing a mix of day laborers, artisans, domestic servants, and lower middle-class households. Jacob Street served as the main road connecting the eastern gate to the city center. This neighborhood was characterized by narrow, winding streets and foul-smelling canals. Catholic residents knew the area as the St. Maximilian parish, with the solid St. Max Church at its heart.[3]

Johann Joseph Most, known as Hans, was born on February 5, 1846, at 225 Langes Sächsen-Gäßchen in Jacobtown, an alleyway that housed artisans, day laborers, milkmen, brewers, spice merchants, and a spinning mill.[4] Johann's birth was out of wedlock, a fact he later humorously noted as being "contrary to police regulations."[5] Given the high infant mortality rate of the time, his parents, Viktoria Hinterhuber and Anton Joseph Most, were fortunate that Johann was among the 965 live births in a city of more than 38,000 inhabitants.[6]

The house where Johann was born belonged to his grandparents, Joseph Sr., a bricklayer from Augsburg, and Maria, the daughter of a schoolteacher from a nearby village.[7] At the time of Johann's birth, both grandparents, possibly along with his uncle Lorenz, lived there.[8] Despite their financial struggles, Johann's parents valued education and the arts. His father, Joseph, born in the same house in 1820, had initially pursued a career as a traveling musician and stage actor before settling into a low-paying clerk position at a law firm.[9] In early 1845, Joseph met Viktoria Hinterhuber, a Munich native two years his senior, and the daughter of an army officer.[10] Although Viktoria's family appears to have been more financially stable than Joseph's, she also faced hardships. She lost a brother at a young age, and by the time she was eight, her father had become the family's sole breadwinner.[11] Viktoria attended a school for needy students in Munich, where she graduated top of her class.[12] Described by Most as "well-educated and liberal-minded," she found work as a governess, teaching music, singing, needlework, and either French or Italian to her employer's children—a typical occupation for respectable, unmarried middle-class women.[13] Her employment ended in the summer of 1845 due to her pregnancy.

Because the municipal authorities deemed Joseph unfit to support a family, they refused to issue him a marriage license, which meant that Joseph and Viktoria had to endure the stigma of an illegitimate birth. At the time, it was illegal for unmarried couples to live together. In an attempt to circumvent this, Joseph's father devised a plan in which Viktoria was hired as a servant and Joseph moved in as a "chamberlain," but this arrangement failed.[14] The couple endured societal condemnation for over two years before finally being able to marry legally. About a year after Johann's birth, Viktoria gave birth to a daughter, Katharine. In anticipation of the arrival of their second daughter, Viktoria, in January 1848, Joseph purchased his father's house. Tragically, shortly after Johann's second birthday, Katharine passed away.[15]

In the spring of 1848, widespread demonstrations erupted across Germany, with protesters calling for liberal reforms and an end to autocratic rule. Initially, the middle and working classes joined forces, but this alliance fractured when workers and artisans began demanding more radical economic changes. In Bavaria, the political unrest led to the king's abdication, and in Augsburg, a new municipal council was elected, which may have helped Joseph and Viktoria finally secure a marriage license. They solemnized their union in St. Max parish on October 9, 1848.[16] Most recalls with some humor a childhood memory of inadvertently disrupting his parents' wedding celebration by chasing after the nuptial carriage at the age of two, much to the amusement of the neighbors.[17]

Figure 1. Anton Joseph Most, father of Johann, in Most, *Memoiren*, I–IV (New York, 1903–7).

15

Poverty cast a long shadow over the Most household. Joseph's modest salary afforded no luxuries, and there were times when even food was scarce.[18] Starting in 1849, both grandparents received a weekly allowance and food rations from makeshift soup kitchens throughout the city.[19] That July, Viktoria gave birth to another daughter, Pauline, who survived into adolescence. However, Pauline faced difficulties later in life, being arrested for prostitution in Würzburg at twenty-six, before eventually marrying and returning to Augsburg.[20] Viktoria had three more children—two boys and a girl—but tragically, the boys did not live past their first birthdays.[21] Determined to save her surviving son, Johann, from a life of poverty and aimlessness, Viktoria made his education a priority, nurturing his early literacy. Despite her progressive views, she enrolled him in a convent school to prepare him for elementary education the following year.[22]

Corporal punishment was common in Most's early schooling, with teachers using methods like whipping to enforce discipline.[23] Bavarian regulations also required teenagers to attend Sunday Bible lessons, which Johann found starkly at odds with the irreverent, freethinking atmosphere at home, where his parents openly ridiculed religious teachings.[24] During his first year of school, his father's new position with the district government's accounting office prompted the family to move to 179 Unterer Lauterlech.[25] Despite the struggles they faced, Most remembered his family as affectionate, finding comfort in their acceptance of him amid his inner turmoil.[26]

On New Year's Day, 1854, seven-year-old Hans Most awoke with a swollen left cheek after catching a cold during his parents' New Year's Eve celebration. What began as a minor illness quickly spiraled into a five-year ordeal. Despite seeking treatment from over a dozen healers—ranging from swallowing pills and herbal teas to undergoing painful procedures like tooth extraction—his condition only worsened. Festering ulcers soon developed, leaving him in constant pain and discomfort. Doctors eventually diagnosed him with incurable cancer, leading to his withdrawal from school.[27] In the fall of 1854, as the new school term began, Augsburg was gripped by a cholera outbreak. The first deaths were reported in August, and medical understanding of the disease was still rudimentary, with conflicting theories about its transmission.[28] Whereas some believed cholera spread through contaminated water, others, like Munich physician Max von Pettenkofer, had alternative explanations, resulting in ineffective emergency measures in Augsburg, such as distributing hot soup and advising people to wear flannel cloth as protection.[29] The epidemic claimed 1,236 lives in the city, including Most's grandparents.[30] Augsburg's streets were deserted, and a visitor at the time recalled, "One could see only people clad in black—here and there a doctor or a priest; I also encountered a wagon loaded with coffins."[31] Although the outbreak subsided over the winter, it resurged in the spring, claiming the life of Most's two-year-old sister, Franziska, and tragically, his mother, Viktoria, who succumbed to a disease related to cholera at the age of thirty-seven.[32] The family was left shattered, with only Hans, his father, Joseph, and his sister Pauline surviving. A year after Viktoria's death, Joseph remarried, taking Maria Lederle as his wife. However, her relationship with the children was strained from the beginning.[33] Most harbored deep resentment toward his stepmother, describing her with venomous disdain in his later writings. He never used her real name, instead referring to her as "a lousy good-for-nothing," a "shifty arch-Catholic," or simply, "a crafty bitch." This period marked a time of profound emotional turmoil and psychological abuse for the young Johann.[34]

Meanwhile, Most's infected jaw posed a life-threatening risk due to misguided treatments he had received until Dr. Georg Agatz intervened.[35] At thirty-four, Dr. Agatz and his wife, Ernestina, had moved to Augsburg to assist in combating the cholera outbreak.[36] On March 18, 1859, at age thirteen, Most underwent a daring operation performed by Agatz and a team of four surgeons to remove the gangrenous bone in his jaw. They made an incision from the left temple to the corner of the mouth and extracted a three-inch section of bone. Since artificial bone replacements did not exist at the time, the surgeons shifted Most's jawbone from right to left to reattach it. Even though the operation saved his life, it left him permanently disfigured—a trauma he later described to Emma Goldman as the "deepest tragedy of his life."[37] Goldman believed that this experience instilled in him a lifelong "inferiority complex."[38] It would be many years before a full beard could obscure the deformity. Despite the emotional and physical toll, Most credited Dr. Agatz as the savior of his life and a skilled surgeon.[39]

After completing elementary school, Most's father enrolled him in the District Industrial School in Augsburg (now the Holbein-Gymnasium) in February 1858.[40] Housed in a former monastery, the school had been established in 1833 and produced notable alumni, including engineer Rudolf Diesel. Passing the entrance exam was a significant achievement for Most, given his previous school absences. These secondary-level industrial schools prepared students for careers in various trades and served as feeders for polytechnic, engineering, and veterinary schools. Students were divided into two tracks: industrial and commercial. While Most excelled in subjects like natural sciences, history, and mathematics, he showed little interest in art and foreign languages and was not shy in voicing his discontent.[41] He even pulled pranks on his teachers and once violated the school's honor code by bringing snuff tobacco to class. After orchestrating a class strike against his French teacher, he faced expulsion.[42]

Fearful of confessing his expulsion to his family, Most pretended to attend school for two weeks, until his stepmother discovered the truth from a classmate. His father, determined that Most should acquire a trade, confronted him and gave him three days to choose an apprenticeship. "I wanted the best for you," his father said, "but I've exhausted my patience with your empty tricks."[43] Despite Most's passion for theater, his father dismissed it as a career option, believing Most's disfigurement would make it impossible. Reluctantly, Most settled on an apprenticeship in bookbinding, hoping it would still allow him time to pursue his love for theater.[44] Augsburg's main theater, with its newly renovated 1,200-seat auditorium, stood conveniently across from St. Jacob's Church, just a short walk from Most's home. Although Augsburg was a minor stop on the theater circuit, Most found solace in the performances, which ranged from operas and Shakespearean works to light comedies.[45] He was especially drawn to Friedrich Schiller's plays, such as *Die Räuber* (The robbers), which depicted revolutionary violence and harshly criticized the pretensions of class and religion. He dreamed of one day playing the lead characters in these powerful dramas.[46]

In the spring of 1860, fourteen-year-old Hans Most began his apprenticeship under Johann Jakob Weber, a master bookbinder who lived halfway between Most's home and the town hall square.[47] At that time in Bavaria, apprenticeships followed medieval traditions and were a common path for young men seeking to become independent artisans. Although the specific terms of the three-year contract between Joseph Most and Weber are lost, it likely included training, food, and lodging for a fee of one hundred guilders. In return, Most would have agreed to obey his master's rules, assist with household chores such as laundry, provide his own bedstead, and complete menial tasks like sweeping, scrubbing floors, carrying water, chopping wood, and rocking the baby to sleep. Masters had the right to use corporal punishment to discipline their apprentices. Most's transition from a difficult home life to an attic room in a new neighborhood did little to ease his burdens.[48] His days were long and exhausting, often starting at dawn and continuing until dusk in the summer or late into the night during winter. He later recalled working up to sixteen hours a day.[49] The craft of bookbinding demanded skill with various materials, including cloth, leather, millboard, glue, and paste. Each client's printed sheets were carefully arranged, pressed, perforated for stitching, and guillotined at the edges. Depending on the commission, the book might be gilded and then bound in hardcovers made of cardboard and leather. In addition to binding books, artisans like Weber also produced leather goods such as placards, briefcases, wallets, and gloves to supplement their trade.[50]

Although Most viewed the apprenticeship as a temporary step toward a future in the theater—once his full beard could hide his facial disfigurement—he took every chance he could to attend theater performances. Often defying Weber's curfew, he sneaked into shows, leading to frequent clashes with his employer.[51] His true solace, however, came from the books he worked on, especially those critical of religion, echoing his mother's influence. Most's defiance of religious practices began early, as he regularly skipped confession and church services. His resistance culminated in an incident where he was apprehended by the police for avoiding religious duties. In another version of events, a priest dragged him into the street and forced him to kneel in prayer on the sidewalk. Most later described this moment as the one that freed him from the clutches of religion.[52] Religion, and the clergy in particular, became "themes of provocation and attack" throughout his life, as noted by historian Heiner Becker, well before Most's eventual turn to socialism.[53] Most completed his apprenticeship in April 1863 and transitioned to the status of a journeyman, which required him to travel from town to town, gaining further experience in his trade.[54] Yet, as he embarked on this new phase, he was soon confronted by the encroachment of mechanization in the trades, which displaced artisans and eroded their autonomy as they became wage laborers. This early encounter with the industrial transformation of skilled labor would shape Most's later political views and actions.

Over the course of five and a half years, Johann Most worked across Germany, primarily as a bookbinder and in related trades. Each of his work stints typically lasted eight to nine months, allowing him to spend the remaining time traveling extensively through German-speaking Europe, the Austro-Hungarian Empire, and northern Italy. By the end of 1868, he had covered more than 5,500 miles on his journey.[55] Since a unified Germany did not yet exist, Most encountered significant variations in laws, customs, and practices across different states, principalities, and independent cities. These differences contributed to a long-standing tradition of particularism in the German heartland, which was culturally distinct from cosmopolitan centers like Berlin or Munich.[56]

On April 21, 1863, a slender teenage Most departed from the Augsburg train station, bound for Stuttgart, a city renowned for its bookbinding industry, located about one hundred miles to the west. He was eager to explore the wider world, expressing his desire to "get out afar."[57] With some money and a travel book, which served as both his passport and résumé, Most navigated the bureaucratic hurdles of police and guild authorities, who meticulously recorded his job performance and moral standing. Without proper documentation, a journeyman could be classified as a vagrant, risking fines or expulsion.[58] A journeyman had the right to terminate a contract under specific conditions, such as abuse, severe illness, or the death of a parent. Otherwise, there were strict penalties for runaway workers or participants in strikes. Although men like Most were expected to register for military service upon turning twenty-one, adherence to such rules was inconsistent, and many journeymen, like Most, struggled with the tension between fulfilling these obligations and pursuing personal freedom. Most later reflected on how he prioritized his "right to enjoy life" over conforming to societal expectations.[59] After a short while in Stuttgart, Most arrived in Frankfurt, where he found work in Syrus Aloysius Ewald's bookbinding workshop near the cathedral. By June 1863, he had secured a position with a leather goods manufacturer in the nearby town of Bornheim. Despite the long and demanding work hours, Most carved out time for intellectual enrichment, such as visits to museums, libraries, and the theater.[60]

Here, Johann Most first encountered labor politics, though his primary focus remained on self-education rather than adopting a strict ideological alignment. The journeyman associations he encountered, mostly religious in nature, adhered to the economic philosophy of Hermann Schulze-Delitzsch, a liberal economist whose advocacy of credit unions and cooperative banking was well regarded among German craft workers and small merchants. Schulze-Delitzsch promoted an economic program of self-improvement that rejected state intervention. Whereas this appealed to many, Most, as an atheist, was reluctant to engage deeply with these associations. Instead, Most gravitated toward the local *Arbeiterbildungsverein* (Workers' Educational Association), where he attended lectures by liberal and early socialist reformers. One of the most influential speakers was Ferdinand Lassalle, a key figure in German socialism, who addressed the Frankfurt association in May 1863. At the time, Most was unfamiliar with socialist ideology and initially uninterested. However, in retrospect, he regretted his dismissive attitude, later writing, "I believed myself to be one of those half-intelligent people . . . who ridicule everything that doesn't fit their world."[61] Lassalle, who had emerged as a revolutionary during the 1848 uprisings and reentered the political stage after his release from prison, offered a stark contrast to the bourgeois liberalism of Schulze-Delitzsch.[62] He critiqued the liberal notion of self-improvement, arguing that it did not address the structural inequalities perpetuated by the "iron law of wages." Instead, Lassalle advocated for state-supported producer cooperatives and universal suffrage, proposing that only an independent workers' party could secure true emancipation through legal reform. This approach diverged from the self-help philosophy of Schulze-Delitzsch and rejected any reliance on liberal patronage. Lassalle's ideas were met with opposition from Karl Marx and Friedrich Engels, but he was instrumental in founding the Allgemeine Deutsche Arbeiterverein (ADAV), Germany's first independent labor party, in May 1863. Unfortunately, Lassalle's life and political career were cut short when he died in a duel in August 1864.[63]

By the spring of 1864, after ten months of labor in Bornheim, Most felt a "wild desire for wander" and set off on an ambitious journey to Venice, covering over five hundred miles across the Alps. "It wasn't clear to me then or later what drew me so irresistibly to the City of Lagoons, but," he assured readers in 1878, "I know this much: no one was going to dissuade me from my plans." This journey took him through the Black Forest at remarkable speed, into Switzerland, and east to Austria, eventually crossing the Brenner Pass into Italy. At the time, the provinces of South Tyrol and Venice were under Austrian rule despite their Italian-speaking populations. Along the way, Most received financial help from his father, which allowed him to continue despite being swindled by an Italian companion who had stolen his travel funds. Undeterred, he pressed on to Venice, where he spent two days enjoying the city's unique scenery before heading to Trieste to receive more money from his father. Three weeks later, Most arrived in Vienna but found the job market severely lacking. His search for work led him back to Munich, where he reconnected with former colleagues from the Bornheim factory, who were now working as flatboat men transporting logs down the Danube to Vienna. Eager for employment, Most joined them. From there, his travels took him north through Moravia and Bohemia, visiting Prague, where he faced rejection due to his facial disfigurement. This experience left him embittered, as he wrote later, "Such statements were very painful for me and filled me with hatred for an Exploitation not simply content with buying the labor of wage slaves for a pittance, but also with a need to indulge in a taste for certain faces."[64] His facial deformity, the result of his earlier lifesaving surgery, became a persistent source of emotional pain as it not only hindered social acceptance but also job prospects.

In November 1864, Most returned to Frankfurt, rejoining a factory where he had previously worked. Although the work was monotonous, it provided him with stability and the opportunity to improve his material conditions and resume his self-education. He later wrote, "I had thoroughly satisfied my urge to travel, and it became necessary to bring order to my material condition and to resume my autodidactic studies." Despite this sense of stability, Most refused to work overtime, which led to a dispute with a supervisor and ultimately his dismissal. Undeterred, Most traveled north in December 1865, walking along the frozen Rhine River in search of new employment. After weeks of hardship, he finally secured a position with a bookbinder in Beckum, Westphalia. However, Most's defiance of religious norms soon led to his dismissal. He refused to attend church and even delivered a provocative speech in a local tavern, which earned him the ire of his employer. His rebellious streak continued when he found work at the Mission Institute in Hermannsburg, a seminary for missionaries. Most disdainfully referred to the institution as an "apostle factory" due to its mass production of proselytizing literature. In the bookbindery, where Most worked, he and his fellow workers played pranks, including one day sounding the fire alarm during mass, a clear expression of his ongoing rebellion against religious piety.[65]

In April 1866, weary of rural conservatism, Most turned his attention to the port city of Bremen, sixty-two miles to the west. Overwhelmed by what he called "Europe fatigue," he resolved to emigrate to the United States but was held back by a lack of funds. Reflecting on this decision, he wrote, "My turning back from emigrating . . . at that time was of utmost significance for my later life because America would surely have broken me morally if not physically."[66] His words suggest that he wanted his 1903 audience to understand that his turbulent life as a European socialist had steeled him for the challenges of capitalist America. Most's frustrations deepened when he failed to find work in Bremen or Hamburg, realizing that artisanal opportunities were still more common in small towns and villages. Although he enjoyed the cultural amenities of the city, he begrudgingly acknowledged the charm of rural life. In Tessin, a village near the Baltic Sea, he found a temporary reprieve, spending May and June working for a friendly bookbinder.[67] Their camaraderie, playing chess and reading in the garden after work, soothed Most's discontent with provincial life. "Indeed, the coziness grew so much," he recalled, "that I completely forgot about small-town provincialism and intended to stay in Tessin for the time being."[68]

However, this peaceful interlude was soon interrupted by the outbreak of civil war between Prussia, allied with North German states, and Austria, backed by South German forces. Orchestrated by Otto von Bismarck to curb

Austrian influence, the war plunged the economy into recession, particularly hurting demand for luxury goods. As a Bavarian subject in northern Germany, Most faced increasing hostility, especially in places like the Grand Duchy of Mecklenburg, where his South German roots made him a target of regional chauvinism. Narrowly escaping violence in Berlin after insulting the king and Bismarck, he fled the city.[69] As Prussian victories mounted, Most witnessed the war's toll firsthand. Traveling from Berlin to Frankfurt, he saw residents struggling under the demands of occupying forces—horses and weapons were confiscated, and the local liberal newspaper's editors, despite their building flying an American flag, were briefly detained.[70] Frankfurt's citizens also had to pay six million guilders to support the Prussian war effort, draining the city's treasury.[71] Most undoubtedly sympathized with the people of Frankfurt, a city where he had spent considerable time. The war ended in August 1866, with the formation of the North German Confederation under Prussian leadership, marking a major step in Bismarck's campaign to unify Germany. Like many South Germans, Most's father opposed Bismarck's push for Prussian dominance.[72] By 1867, a new North German parliament (Reichstag) and constitution had been established, granting voting rights to men over twenty-five. Citizens could now travel freely within the confederation using a single passport, supported by an integrated postal system. Executive power rested with King Wilhelm I, assisted by Chancellor Bismarck.

After the war ended, economic conditions remained dire. Throughout the fall and winter of 1866, Most wandered aimlessly across southern Germany, Switzerland, and Austria in search of work. His journey eventually brought him to Stuttgart, the capital of Württemberg, an emerging industrial hub. There, Most immersed himself in the city's cultural life and formed a close friendship with Ignaz Auer, a fellow Bavarian who would later become a key figure in the Social Democratic Party. Both men shared similar backgrounds, having grown up in poverty and lost parents at a young age, and they had spent years traveling as discontented journeymen. A friend of Auer's would later claim that it was in Stuttgart that Auer "received from Johann Most his first political ideas."[73] Their collaboration extended beyond political discussions, as they also teamed up to stage "evening entertainments" in exchange for food.[74] Most specialized in comedic and classical performances, while Auer amused audiences with witty limericks. The two parted ways in early 1867 but would meet again in the future.[75]

With the arrival of spring, Most's restlessness returned, prompting him to set off for Switzerland. After a challenging hike through the Swiss Alps, he reached Bern and faced a pivotal choice: return to familiar territory in

Germany or venture into the French-speaking regions of Switzerland, where he would encounter a new language and culture. Drawn by the watchmaking communities in the Jura district, particularly in Le Locle and La Chaux-de-Fonds, Most saw an opportunity for growth. These fiercely independent artisans, known for their political activism, worked in small workshops and cottages, producing an impressive 85,000 watches annually.[76] Most discovered that one of the side industries in the area was the production of leather cases and that few bookbinders knew about it. He quickly learned the trade, enjoying better pay and sustenance than he had found in Germany. He also welcomed the chance to immerse himself in French language and culture. Moreover, the local workers' associations' radical philosophy on labor and revolution deeply resonated with him, further shaping his evolving worldview.[77]

2 Lost in a World of Ideals

ON SEPTEMBER 28, 1864, the International Workingmen's Association (IWA) was founded at St. Martin's Hall in London to unite working-class organizations and promote international labor solidarity. The IWA's General Council handled administrative tasks, while labor groups around the world were encouraged to form independent sections and affiliate with the international. All sections shared a common goal: the belief that the liberation of labor could only be achieved through collective struggle. Karl Marx, a German scholar, provided the IWA with a cohesive philosophical framework and a practical program, advocating for the emancipation of the proletariat and the seizure of political power. After the failed revolutions of 1848, Marx, alongside Friedrich Engels, had coauthored *The Communist Manifesto*, which championed class struggle and critiqued the flaws of capitalism. They argued that economic exploitation was the root cause of oppression and that economic emancipation, rather than mere political reform, was the path to true freedom. In Germany, two rival socialist factions emerged: the Lassalleans (ADAV) and the internationalists. Although both groups used the newly established manhood suffrage under the Constitution of the North German Confederation, their political ideologies differed sharply. The ADAV, led by Ferdinand Lassalle, focused on countering the influence of the liberal bourgeoisie, even seeking support from Otto von Bismarck to advocate for state-sponsored producer cooperatives.[1] Lassalle saw the state as an agent of justice, essential to implementing a socialist agenda. In contrast, internationalists like Marx and Engels rejected Lassalle's reliance on the state, viewing it as a tool of capitalist structures rather than a means of achieving socialism. Wilhelm Liebknecht, a university-educated journalist and veteran socialist, along with August Bebel, a turner by trade and prominent socialist orator, became the leading voices of anti-Prussian internationalist socialism, opposing Lassalle's ideas.

The Swiss Jura region, where Most lived, became a center of internationalist activity, especially among French-speaking artisans. In the summer of 1867, Most attended a workers' festival in La Chaux-de-Fonds, organized by the local section of the IWA. The event, attended by artisans from the thriving Swiss clock and watchmaking industry, had a profound impact on him.[2] The passionate speeches promoting class consciousness, solidarity, and social revolution struck a deep chord, igniting a fervent commitment to socialism. For Most, discovering socialism was a life-changing experience, giving him a sense of purpose and humanity he had not felt before. "I became a different person having just entered the realm of socialism; I wished I could've won over the whole world," he later recalled. "In short, I was on fire."[3] This clarity of purpose stayed with him throughout his life, as he reflected in his memoir, written in his later years: "I lost myself in a world of ideals. I was inspired by a certain urge to fulfill a higher mission."[4] Most was captivated by the ideals of socialism, which he found far more compelling than any liberal self-help program he had encountered before.[5] He also admired the IWA's ability to foster solidarity among workers across national borders, as seen in the coordination of labor actions and mutual support between workers from different countries. This newfound dedication led him to seek out socialist literature, setting him on a lifelong path of activism and advocacy for social justice.

Most's embrace of socialism had a direct impact on his economic situation in Switzerland. Serving as the corresponding secretary for a local educational association, he worked to incorporate socialist principles into its activities, which led to a significant increase in membership.[6] This rise is corroborated by a letter from Le Locle to the General Council of the IWA, suggesting that the educational association was affiliated with the International and that Most was actively recruiting new adherents to socialism.[7] However, his employer confronted him about his socialist involvement during the winter of 1867–68, which led to his dismissal or voluntary departure.[8] After a brief excursion through the Alps, Most relocated to Zurich, the country's primary manufacturing center, where he found work as a hatter and briefly started his own hat-making business.[9] He soon joined Eintracht (Unity), a prominent workers' club in Zurich founded by liberal intellectuals. Within Eintracht, discussions on socialism grew more intense, driven by figures like Karl Bürkli, a pioneer of consumer cooperatives, and Herman Greulich, a journeyman bookbinder turned socialist advocate. Greulich played a pivotal role in shaping Most's socialist education, equipping him with both the theoretical foundations and the practical communication skills needed to engage blue-collar audiences. Greulich often spoke passionately about a ten-hour workday and the importance of propaganda.[10] To the German socialist Eduard Bernstein, Greulich had "the gift of rapid and orderly expression."[11] Under Greulich's mentorship, Most participated in gymnastics, discussions, and dramatic performances, all of which helped him hone his oratorical skills.[12] A shy, beardless Most once auditioned to recite a humorous piece. "The youth rose and recited a bawdy poem with inimitable hilarity," Greulich recalled, "and was thus added to our roll."[13] Most made significant contributions to the Drama Club, producing Johann Gottfried Seume's play *Miltiades* and delivering a memorable performance as the blind Epicelos.[14] In January 1868, Bavaria instituted compulsory military services, forcing Most to return to Augsburg, where he visited his father. Although declared unfit and exempt from service, he was required to pay a fee, which his father, despite their profound political disagreements, agreed to cover. Shortly after, Most returned to Zurich to continue his activities.[15] Driven by an insatiable thirst for knowledge, Most frequented the club's library, immersing himself in radical literature and periodicals. By April 1868, he was elected as the association's librarian, granting him broader access to socialist texts.[16] He also became actively involved in a thriving consumer cooperative, pooling resources with fellow members to procure goods to sell without profit in cooperative stores.[17] In August 1868, Eintracht formally voted to embrace socialism and affiliate with the IWA.[18]

Regional political developments had a profound impact on Most, deeply shaping his evolving ideas about socialist mass politics. Canton Zurich had long been dominated by Alfred Escher, a liberal whose vast entrepreneurial empire granted him immense influence across various sectors. However, growing discontent among the middle and working classes, exacerbated by economic hardships stemming from credit restrictions and a downturn in the textile industry due to the American Civil War, fueled a movement against the entrenched "Escher system." Led by figures like Bürkli, this left-liberal, democratic movement gained momentum. By December 1867, the movement achieved a significant victory, ousting Escher from power through the electoral process. In April 1869, Zurich adopted a new constitution, ushering in sweeping reforms that included the establishment of a representative government, the abolition of the death penalty, and the implementation of progressive policies such as a property tax, the creation of a national bank, and the development of a state-run railway system. Most found these events particularly instructive and inspiring, seeing them as a model of bloodless revolution. He was especially impressed by how mass demonstrations had forced political change "over the heads of the oligarchs."[19] Historian Heiner Becker argues that these regional political upheavals were crucial in shaping Most's understanding of socialist mass mobilization—an aspect that has often been overlooked by earlier scholars.[20]

In the autumn of 1868, Most resumed his wandering lifestyle, seeking both work and leisure. His travels eventually led him to Vienna, where he became involved in the city's growing labor movement. Curiously, Most's two accounts of this period diverge significantly. In his 1878 narrative, which seems more authentic, Most describes how he and a companion journeyed through the mountains toward Tyrol, entertaining guests in local inns before reaching Vienna. However, in his 1903 narrative, he presents Vienna as a key turning point in his radical career, entirely omitting the Alpine trek.[21] Regardless, Most's entry into the Austrian labor movement proved transformative, marking a shift from his carefree life as a journeyman to more serious political activism. "While I never sought a life for myself in the party," he wrote in 1878, "so many urgent requests for leading this or that intellectual enterprise were made by numerous comrades that I willy-nilly took it upon myself to fulfill these duties."[22] Yet, it is important to recognize that Most's explorations of natural and cultural landscapes also played a critical role in shaping his worldview. His encounters with the grandeur of nature instilled in him a romantic sensibility and a passion for the natural sciences and history, further informing his view of industrial bourgeois society as an artificial construct that stifled the free spirit of humanity. This perspective was further solidified by his discovery of socialism, which offered a powerful critique of exploitation, greed, and the religious dogma prevalent in contemporary society.

*   *   *

Johann Most's time in Austria, from the fall of 1868 to May 1871, was a pivotal chapter in his life. During this period, he honed his propaganda skills and emerged as a prominent socialist activist. His involvement in the nascent Austrian labor movement, including a treason trial and eventual expulsion, laid the foundation for his later ascent in the German labor movement of the 1870s. Most looked back on his Vienna years as a noble and pure time, "so absent of corrupt, intriguing politicians," underscoring the significance of this phase in his political development.[23] His biographer, Rudolf Rocker, even described this period as "the most beautiful chapter in Most's stormy life."[24] Yet Most's rise from an unassuming youth to an influential socialist was not predetermined; rather, it was shaped by a complex interplay of events, personalities, and social dynamics.

Most understood that politics and power were deeply tied to place, mobility, and territoriality. Having navigated the fragmented geography of German principalities and Swiss cantons throughout his life, Most now found himself settled in Vienna, the imperial capital of the Austro-Hungarian Empire. This multicultural empire was undergoing significant political reforms after its defeat in 1867, transforming into a dual monarchy where a liberal-leaning bourgeoisie gained political clout. The new constitution limited the monarch's authority and guaranteed civil liberties. Austria now had a minister-president, a cabinet, and even a parliament with a House of Lords and a House of Deputies. As historian A. J. P. Taylor observed, an Austrian citizen after 1867 "had more civic security than the German and was in the hands of more honest and more capable officials than in France or Italy."[25] Nevertheless, European liberals were not democrats, and Austria did not institute universal suffrage until 1907. In response to this limited political enfranchisement, a vocal labor movement sought to mobilize the growing industrial proletariat, which numbered around three hundred thousand in Vienna alone.[26] These workers faced grueling twelve-hour workdays, meager wages, and lived in overcrowded, unsanitary conditions in districts like Mariahilf, Floridsdorf, and Fünfhaus.[27] Although the economic downturn of the 1860s intensified their struggles, workers were initially barred from forming unions or participating in strikes, out of fear that such activities might "spill over into subversive politics."[28] The passage of the Association and Assembly Act in 1867, however, legalized workers' associations, albeit under stringent government oversight. Organizations deemed subversive could be swiftly shut down, every meeting had to be cleared with authorities twenty-four hours in advance, and political groups were required to submit their bylaws and membership lists to the police.[29] Despite these limitations, workers began forming nonsocialist self-help organizations, consumer cooperatives, and educational associations. At a rally on December 1, 1867, approved by authorities, some six thousand workers gathered without incident.[30] Within the labor movement, divisions emerged between those advocating for self-help initiatives in collaboration with liberals and those championing socialism, who stressed the importance of an independent working class. Despite the challenges posed by state repression, socialist voices in Austria grew louder, advocating for workers' empowerment and autonomy.[31]

In December 1867, the Workers' Association Gumpersdorf, Austria's first socialist organization, was established under the leadership of Hermann Hartung, a carpenter from Hannover.[32] The association aimed to empower workers through self-initiative. "Workers must try to participate in the force of the state through the achievement of universal suffrage," Hartung argued, adding, "the one who has shown this way forward is Ferdinand Lassalle."[33] With nearly a thousand members, the group included both Lassalleans and internationalist socialists, marking the genesis of the Austrian labor movement. At this early stage, the movement lacked fully developed ideas of militant class struggle or social revolution, as labor leaders remained focused on achieving goals through legal means. The association's 1868 "Manifesto to the Working People of Austria" clearly outlined its demands, which included universal suffrage, the emancipation of the working class, unrestricted freedom of association, assembly, and press, the abolition of a standing army, separation of church and state, and the establishment of producer cooperatives with state support. Additionally, the manifesto called for resolving the divisions between Austria's nationalities—a particularly delicate issue in Austrian politics.[34] The socialists emphasized the importance of transcending national borders, both in labor solidarity and commerce: "The time of isolating nationalities is over," they proclaimed. "The labor market has no state boundaries; world commerce crosses all language borders."[35] Despite these ambitions, Liberal interior minister Carl Giskra dismissed the workers' demand for universal suffrage, fearing that expanding voting rights to the masses would result in "mob rule." At the time, only about 6 percent of Austria's population could vote for the lower legislative chamber.[36] Nevertheless, the association continued to expand, recruiting members and increasing its cultural influence through libraries and reading rooms stocked with socialist literature. In response to this growing momentum, the authorities banned all political meetings, creating an atmosphere of impending repression. Many feared that a large-scale government crackdown was imminent.[37]

It was against this backdrop of both hope and apprehension that Johann Most arrived in Vienna in October 1868, returning after four years.[38] The city had changed dramatically: a new tree-lined ringway, flanked by the new parliament and criminal court buildings, had replaced the old ramparts. This grand panorama contrasted sharply with the sprawling working-class districts beyond the manicured parks. Most rented an apartment at 28 Wiesengasse in the Alsergrund district northwest of the city center.[39] Most quickly immersed himself in the socialist movement, which had grown to over 5,500 members. He also joined the Union of Bookbinders, Leather Workers, and Case Makers, a prominent Vienna trade union.[40] However, Most's time in Austria was fraught with economic challenges. He lost his factory job after his public speeches were reported in newspapers, and his subsequent employers either fired or blacklisted him. On one occasion, he was dismissed after threatening a strike over long work hours. Most briefly attempted to run his own shop, producing leather and felt items, but the venture likely failed.[41]

In Austria, Johann Most encountered socialism not as a mere abstract concept or club activity but as a vibrant mass movement deeply embedded in the everyday lives of the working class. He witnessed the power of opposition within a hostile empire, attending meetings and demonstrations where the sight of workers rallying under the socialist flag filled him with excitement and hope.[42] Although he was initially reserved during these gatherings, contributing to debates sparingly and avoiding confrontations over academic disputes, Most's presence became increasingly felt in the movement.[43] Historian Heiner Becker observed that Most often refrained from taking hardline stances against fellow socialists, preferring to adopt a more conciliatory approach to preserve unity within the movement.[44] Despite Most's enthusiasm, he and his fellow activists faced growing government repression. The police frequently disrupted meetings, and in April 1869, several labor leaders were arrested and convicted.[45] Yet, even under these pressures, the socialist movement in Vienna persevered. The launch of *Volksstimme* (Voice of the people), the party's organ, marked a significant step forward. The paper boldly declared the socialists' ambition to establish a democratic *Volksstaat* (people's state) should the government refuse to move "forward on the road to progress and freedom."[46] At a time when nationalist fervor was rising across Europe, what set the socialist movement apart—and alarmed authorities—was its commitment to international working-class solidarity. *Volksstimme* frequently published statements and minutes from the General Council of the IWA, signaling the movement's allegiance to the broader global struggle of labor, consciously distancing itself from the patronage of liberal elites.

By 1869, when Most was just twenty-three years old, his influence in Vienna's labor movement began to rise sharply. He formed a close friendship with Andreas Scheu, a fellow socialist and Viennese gilder, who shared his passion for oratory, poetry, and theater. Together, they pioneered efforts to bring the "social question" to the stage, writing four theatrical pieces performed at festivals attended by thousands.[47] One of their plays, *Die Reise nach Amerika, oder: Das Wiedersehen* (The journey to America, or: The reunion), garnered critical acclaim, with reporters praising it as "a zany, skillfully made burlesque."[48] Most's talent as an actor was also recognized, earning him a reputation as a "great theatrical talent."[49] Most's contributions to political theater and poetry during his time in Austria were not only celebrated in his own era but continued to resonate well into the twentieth century. His role in shaping Austrian socialist culture, particularly through political theater, was acknowledged in retrospectives of the socialist movement that extended into the 1940s, underscoring his lasting influence on both the artistic and political dimensions of the labor struggle.[50]

In May 1869, Johann Most took his talents beyond theater and began delivering public speeches, quickly establishing himself as a forceful and charismatic orator within Vienna's burgeoning socialist movement. His speeches, addressing crowds of thousands of workers, were noted for their candid, down-to-earth delivery, laced with satire and sharp wit. As Most himself reflected, his speeches were "drastic, folksy, original, from the heart," emphasizing his ability to connect directly with working-class audiences.[51] He embraced the role of a *Volkstribun* (people's tribune), a title befitting his advocacy for the oppressed, and became known as "the satirist at the Vienna workers' gatherings" due to his biting critiques of the political establishment.[52] One particularly memorable rally saw Most speak to nearly ten thousand workers, delivering a fiery condemnation of social injustice and calling for universal suffrage.[53] In a speech brimming with passion, he proclaimed, "So far, they have withheld education from the worker; they have often brought [the worker] to despair, driven him to criminality because of hardship, and made him a cripple!" His words were met with loud cheers. He called on workers to remain loyal to social-democratic principles, urging them to "win or die" in their fight for justice. Most's rhetoric, which condemned the judicial system as a scam, the clergy as deceivers, and the bourgeoisie as executioners, electrified the crowd but also drew sharp criticism from conservative circles.[54] This speech, along with others, put Most directly in the crosshairs of the authorities. Identified by name in the conservative press, Most lost his job, was evicted from his apartment, and arrested on charges of incitement and disparagement of public institutions.[55] Sentenced to three months in prison—later reduced to one—Most narrowly avoided exile.[56] His imprisonment, however, did little to quell his enthusiasm for the socialist cause; instead, it gave him time to read and write, further solidifying his ideological commitment.

Most's oratory skills were nothing short of remarkable, as noted by those who witnessed his speeches. Despite his slender build, when he took the stage, he transformed into a commanding figure, blending the roles of actor, satirist, rhetorician, and revolutionary. His ability to weave humor and satire into his political speeches made him a compelling speaker. One famous example occurred during a speech to the bookbinders' union, where Most, when reminded by a police officer to focus solely on trade matters, cleverly employed the imagery of bookbinder's paste to subtly address political issues. For nearly an hour, as Andreas Scheu recalled, Most "stirred, stroked, and glued so many jokes about 'the [political] situation,'" engaging

Figure 2. Johann Most in
Vienna in 1869 or 1870.
Courtesy of International
Institute of Social History,
Amsterdam.

and entertaining his audience while maintaining a veneer of compliance with
the officer's warning.[57] Heinrich Scheu, another socialist, similarly lauded
Most's quick-wittedness and humor, calling him "a popular speaker by the
Grace of God." On one occasion, Most "surpassed himself" as he skillfully
blended humor and political commentary, settling accounts with his critics
in the press. Most's unique oratorical style, combining satire, humor, and
political insight, made him an unforgettable presence in the socialist movement and left a lasting impact on those who heard him speak.

Johann Most's imprisonment coincided with Wilhelm Liebknecht's visit
to Vienna to invite delegates to a convention in Eisenach, Saxony, where the
German Social Democratic Workers' Party (SDAP) was founded in August.
Recognizing the importance of this new party and its commitment to internationalist principles, Most understood it posed a serious threat to the Habsburg
government, especially when aligned with Austrian labor groups. The Eisenach
program, adopted by the SDAP, outlined an ambitious platform that included
universal suffrage for German men, direct legislation by the people, a militia
instead of a standing army, free education, a ten-hour workday, restrictions on
women's labor, the abolition of child labor, progressive income taxes, and state
support for cooperatives.[58] The party's structure featured an editorial office for

its new newspaper, *Der Volksstaat* (The people's state), a control committee, and annual congresses to debate and pass resolutions. The Vienna government quickly responded by banning all social-democratic groups and severing ties with foreign political organizations.[59] Constitutional rights to speech and assembly were granted only at the government's discretion, sparking opposition from liberal factions concerned about a conservative backlash. Despite the ban, socialist organizing continued, with Most actively recruiting members and participating in an international conference that ratified the Eisenach program.[60] Most's socialism was reflected in his personal style and behavior. He and others adopted Jacobin symbols, wearing caps, red shawls, and gray trousers and addressed each other as "citizens."[61] Decades later, a Viennese journalist remembered him as the "Marat of Augsburg," a testament to his lasting influence and revolutionary fervor.[62]

Government repression only strengthened socialists' resolve to defend civil liberties. On December 1, Most joined thousands in supporting a resolution demanding an end to arbitrary censorship and the suppression of assemblies.[63] Liberal city council members also criticized the national government for violating constitutional rights out of an unfounded fear of the working class. Even mainstream liberal newspapers, like the *Morgen-Post*, endorsed the resolution.[64] The government defended its actions by labeling social democracy as subversive, but Most argued that the real subversion was the existing economic system, marked by corrupt plutocracy and the arbitrary cruelty of authorities toward workers.[65] In response, the administration invited labor representatives to present their grievances to a ministerial council. Labor leaders agreed to do so at a mass demonstration scheduled for December 13, 1869, the opening day of parliament. Police were instructed to discourage workers from attending, and troops were put on alert. A circular sent to all labor groups emphasized that the demonstration was "not an act of violence but an impressive show of how many workers there are in Vienna."[66]

Monday, December 13, a day that would be remembered as the day "the working classes stepped onto the world stage," began cold and overcast.[67] Around eight in the morning, workers from factories, train yards, and workshops put down their tools and made their way to the city center. Most, along with fifty other socialists, aware of the potential repercussions of any incident, helped manage the swelling crowds.[68] By nine o'clock, despite the freezing temperatures, between fifteen thousand and twenty thousand men and women had gathered in the square.[69] A delegation of workers prepared to deliver a petition demanding the restoration of press and assembly freedoms, the institution of universal suffrage, and the replacement of the standing army with a militia as a "guarantee for peace and freedom." The petition warned that if parliament ignored these demands, the people would continue to express their will through repeated, larger demonstrations.[70] However, unrest spread through the crowd when news broke that the legislature had postponed its session until the following day. The petition was delivered to Count Eduard Taaffe, the Conservative minister-president, who declared the demonstration illegal.[71] Even though he promised to discuss the petition with his cabinet, he made no concrete commitments. Despite the disappointment, the crowd remained peaceful, marching in columns to Zobel's on Mariahilfer Street.

Two days later, Count Taaffe took two decisive actions. First, he introduced a bill in parliament concerning the right of coalition, provoking consternation among deputies who accused him of capitulating to a mob. Second, he handed the signed petition to Vienna's state prosecutor, Hermann Schmeidel, for further investigation. Meanwhile, the upper house applied pressure on the cabinet to take a harsher stance against labor. Two delegates who had met with Taaffe were arrested on charges of "dangerously threatening" the government.[72] At the same time, the prosecutor's office began preparing to arrest all known socialist organizers, editors, and speakers. House searches yielded substantial evidence for a large-scale trial aimed at dismantling the movement. Despite the looming threat, Most refused to go into hiding, continuing to speak at meetings in and around Vienna.[73] Some sections of the press blamed foreign agitators for the unrest, suggesting that expelling them might resolve the crisis.

In January 1870, Johann Most was summoned by the police to verify his employment status, a necessary step to avoid expulsion.[74] He urgently needed official documents from Augsburg but was met with silence when he pleaded for help from his father.[75] Their ideological differences had long strained their relationship. Joseph Most, a member of the Bavarian Patriotic Party—a conservative Catholic group with anti-modern and ultramontanist views—stood in stark opposition to his son's radical politics.[76] Adding to Johann Most's frustration, a newspaper in Augsburg reported on his troubles with the police, further widening the rift between father and son.[77] The only surviving letter between them, dated January 13, 1870, was confiscated and later used as evidence. In it, Most voiced his disappointment in his father's silence, attributing it to their political and religious disagreements. He reminded his father that he had never concealed his views and recalled how, at one time, his father had tolerated them. "At that time, you didn't have many objections," Most wrote. "So I don't see why I should play the prodigal son just because I didn't trade my republicanism for your ultramontanism." Most refused to abandon his principles to satisfy his father, asserting his identity as a "tribune of the people." He emphasized that he would rather choose his political beliefs over material comfort, famously declaring that he preferred the "dry bread" offered by comrades over a lucrative position with a hostile party.[78] This letter circulated widely in Germany, leaving a strong impression on many, including August Bebel, who praised Most's unwavering character and highlighted the "dry bread" passage in his own memoirs.[79]

In March 1870, the Austrian government launched a crackdown, arresting Johann Most and thirteen others. Rumors spread that they could be charged with high treason, a crime punishable by death—though executions in Austria were typically reserved for the most serious, unrepentant offenders. During his detention, Most and his fellow prisoners were denied access to reading and writing materials. Despite these restrictions, Most ingeniously devised a pulley system using rope and stones to communicate with a fellow socialist in the cell above. He smuggled dispatches out of the prison and received updates from the outside world.[80] Remarkably, Most also created a satirical newsletter, *Nußknacker* (Nutcracker), filled with humorous stories about inmates and guards, witty poems, and absurd announcements like fictitious marriages and deaths of flies. In one section on "Strange Natural Phenomena," he humorously described "petrified insects" discovered in prison food. Most distributed the newsletter by tucking folded sheets under a large rock in the prison courtyard.[81] Eventually, the guards discovered and confiscated the newsletter, but Most continued his creative work. During his solitary hours, he composed "Die Arbeitsmänner" (The workingmen), one of the most enduring proletarian songs in the German-speaking labor movement, which has since been translated into multiple languages and is still recited in some circles today. In June, Most and the others were formally charged with high treason and disturbing the peace, facing potential sentences of up to twenty years in prison. The authorities even used the *Nußknacker* newsletter as evidence against them.[82] The treason charge stemmed from the involvement of some socialists in the Eisenach congress and the Austrian socialist movement's endorsement of its program, which advocated for a republican democracy and was seen as a direct threat to the imperial state.

* * *

The treason trial of Johann Most and his associates began on July 4, 1870, at the criminal court in Vienna, drawing considerable media attention. Major newspapers covered the proceedings extensively, with liberal outlets advocating for civil liberties and urging the government to respect due process. For example, the *Morgen-Post* described the trial as "of European importance," expressing sympathy for the workers' demands while condemning republicanism.[83] Public opinion in Vienna appeared to favor the defendants, with one historian noting widespread support for them.[84] The trial's impact extended beyond Vienna, reaching places like Augsburg, where local newspapers highlighted "the journeyman bookbinder Johann Most, son of the well-known ultramontanist agitator Joseph Most."[85] The courtroom allowed only a limited number of spectators, while the fourteen defendants were represented by two defense attorneys. Most of the accused were young, the oldest being fifty, and several had families. Four of them—Heinrich Oberwinder, Most, Johann Schönfelder, and Heinrich Gehrke—were Germans. Outside the courtroom, thousands of workers gathered, chanting slogans such as "Long Live Our Traitors!" and "We Want the Right of Association!"[86] These demonstrations continued for nine days, but tension mounted when rumors circulated that troops might be deployed to disperse the crowds.[87] The prosecution argued that the defendants sought to subvert the state by spreading the socialist ideals of the Eisenach program and inciting Austrian workers against the government. They aimed to convince the jury that the socialists were advocating for republicanism and a "democratic people's state," which they framed as an attempt to overthrow the monarchy. A key element of the prosecution's case was the alleged danger posed by foreign radicals influencing Austrian workers, which they portrayed as more threatening than the domestic workers' movement itself.

When Johann Most was cross-examined, observers were quick to comment on his physical appearance. Heinrich Scheu, sitting in the press box, remarked on Most's distorted features. "His young beard was still too sparse to embellish the poor facial structure," he noted, "and his sand-colored hair stood up like the bristles of a boar."[88] Despite this seemingly unassuming appearance, Most's demeanor and sharp-witted responses during questioning revealed a serious and astute individual. A journalist made the following observation:

> Anyone watching him in his harmless, drab summer outfit, with his face shifted to the left by some grotesque whim of nature, may at first believe him to be a comic figure. A closer observation of the way he listens attentively to the questions . . . , his head forward with sparkling eyes, of the way he answers with a rare quick-wittedness, instinctively reminds you of the convention speeches during the first French Revolution, and one must admit that this seemingly insignificant man must be taken very seriously.[89]

Most was accused of knowingly joining a subversive party and spreading socialism among various groups, including farmers and soldiers. Evidence against him included SDAP membership cards found in his residence and his involvement in the December 13 demonstration, which highlighted his reputation as a powerful speaker and made him a prime target. Most admitted to being a member of the SDAP and reaffirmed his republican beliefs, which he had held since his youth. When questioned about whether republican ideals could be achieved without violence, he responded enthusiastically that they could. "When the republican idea permeates the people, when the great masses are willing to put it into effect," he explained, "what force could stop the republic's formation?" The judges confronted Most with an essay he had written that called for fighting "to the knife." He dismissed it as a figure of speech, meant for the amusement of fellow inmates rather than for public consumption. Defending the idea of a "free people's state," Most argued that a truly free state must serve the people's interests over class privileges. "I don't know anything in a state other than the people," Most reasoned. "So I cannot distinguish between a 'free state' and a 'free people's state' unless one views a 'free state' as a place where class privileges still exist." The accusation that Most was attempting to recruit farmers and soldiers into the socialist movement was even more serious. The judge cited a circular addressed to the rural population and a resolution from a socialist congress advocating the distribution of pamphlets to the military. He also referenced an entry from Most's now-lost diary in which Most wrote that soldiers had assured him they would not fire on workers. Most explained this diary entry as the result of a chance meeting with two socialist soldiers rather than part of a broader subversive campaign. He maintained that even if he were in the military, he would not change his opinions, and he suggested that many soldiers shared his opposition to violence against unarmed people. "As a party man, I was delighted," Most told the judge, "and I wrote about it in my diary."[90]

During the trial, the defense argued that the socialist movement's inquiries into the social question were legitimate and not subversive, emphasizing the need to improve working and living conditions through international labor solidarity. They advocated for civil liberties for all citizens, including workers, drawing parallels to previous political movements like liberalism, which had similarly been repressed by reactionary governments. However, defending Most's inflammatory language—particularly his use of the phrase "fighting to the knife"—proved to be a significant challenge. The defense characterized Most's prison writings as "harmless, if indelicate, fun," asserting that he had never expected his casual remarks to be used against him. To the prosecutor, however, Most's intemperate words added a hint of insurrection to ideas already deemed dangerous. Sensing the likely outcome of the trial, Most decided to address the court—and the nation—candidly. He rejected the notion that foreign agitators were manipulating the working class and defended the moral integrity of both himself and his fellow socialists. "I have never let myself be seduced into anything," he declared. "My actions came from my deepest convictions and my own initiative; no one tempted me, no one put words in my mouth." Despite being repeatedly reprimanded for his ironic tone, Most remained defiant, boldly proclaiming his allegiance to social democracy.

> I confess that I am a social democrat; I confess that I will remain one as long as I live, pay homage to it in the highest degree, and hold up its banner no matter what the verdict may be. I deny, however, that I ever did something unlawful while in Austria. I have always operated on legal grounds; I spoke only at authorized public meetings and in the presence of official commissars. You may not attribute more to me. That was all that lay within my weak powers and that I did. I deny that it ever occurred to me to achieve anything through acts of violence or even to participate in such actions, and I am not aware that a violent act was ever planned in any form. I should also hope, councilors, that your judgment will be based on the law, not on a party, and that you won't let the government influence you.[91]

Most's impassioned defense resonated with working-class readers, with a labor paper in Budapest praising his classical eloquence, sharp logic, and "rare candor."[92] Even the judges acknowledged his remarkable wit and "determined character."[93]

On July 19, 1870, Johann Most, along with Oberwinder, Andreas Scheu, and Johann Pabst, was convicted of high treason, leading to a commotion in the courtroom. Most received a sentence of five years, which included one mandatory fast day each month, and he faced expulsion upon completing his term. The grounds for his conviction included his intention to distribute Socialist Party membership cards, his use of inflammatory language, and his knowing involvement in a subversive group.[94] Most later acknowledged that while the Austrian socialist movement outwardly appeared social-democratic and peaceful, it was imbued with a revolutionary spirit, calling the defense's denial of this "nonsense."[95] He noted that every influential figure within the movement "had a rock-solid conviction that revolution would come in a relatively short time."[96] The other defendants were found guilty of public disorder, with Oberwinder receiving a ten-month sentence, while Andreas Scheu and Pabst received two-month sentences. The high court agreed to reduce Most's sentence from five to three years due to the absence of violence in the treasonous activity and his lack of prior convictions; however, his appeal was denied.[97]

The verdict sparked unease among Austrians, many of whom considered the sentences too harsh. Outraged workers responded with public protests, particularly after several workers' associations were disbanded by decree on the day of the verdict. Vienna experienced a general strike lasting three days as a result of the public outcry. Karl Kautsky, who was a high school student at the time, recalled the widespread perception of a blatant miscarriage of justice, noting that "the entirety of Vienna's bourgeois democrats stood on the side of the accused."[98] Whereas much of the Austrian press refrained from criticizing the government directly, German newspapers extensively covered the trial proceedings. One German publication even reprinted the chief judge's opinion of Most, praising his "unusual wit and energy."[99] Heinrich Scheu's published trial transcript became a popular source of information, particularly within labor circles.[100] For Most, the trial was "one of the significant events in [his] life," and he felt flattered by the attention it garnered. "To what do I owe the honor of being taken so seriously?" he reflected in 1903. "You're just an ordinary journeyman with a big mouth, as they say." In his eyes, being branded a traitor by the imperial government was a badge of honor for a "genuine proletarian rebel."[101] Just three years after embracing socialism, Most found himself catapulted into prominence as a leading figure in the Austrian socialist movement.

In late September 1870, Most was transferred to the prison at Suben, located in a small village on the border of Austria and Bavaria, overlooking the Inn River. Originally an Augustinian monastery, the facility had been converted into a detention center in 1865 (and still serves this purpose today) and could accommodate up to three hundred inmates. Conditions at Suben were relatively comfortable compared to other prisons. There was no hard labor, and prisoners had access to newspapers and books. Most was pleased to discover that inmates were not required to shave, allowing him to grow a fuller beard during his time there. He shared a large cell with Pabst and spent much of his time studying, referring to his stay as his "Suben vacation." Most continued to compose poems and songs, some of which were smuggled out of prison. Radicals often used time behind bars as a welcome educational interlude before returning to the movement. It was upsetting for Most to learn that his father had attempted to secure his release by seeking a pardon from the emperor. Joseph Most allegedly gained access to Duke Maximilian Joseph of Bavaria, the father of Empress Elizabeth ("Sisi") of Austria. However, Most was indignant at the idea of requesting mercy, especially since it would require admitting guilt or wrongdoing: "I have to beg for mercy when I suffered injustice? Never!"[102]

The men convicted of treason did not serve their entire sentence; they were released due to the instabilities of Austrian politics. The Liberal government had been facing challenges, with the nobility showing disdain for what they saw as a "lawyer's club," the church alarmed at the rise of free thought, and Slavic minorities fearing for their autonomy. In February 1871, a new government issued a general amnesty for political prisoners.[103] Most, along with Oberwinder, Andreas Scheu, and Pabst, were among those amnestied. Remarkably, Most was released after serving only four months and was permitted to remain in the country, which was an unexpected turn of events.[104] Upon their release, the four men were greeted by a large crowd at the Vienna train station. "When Oberwinder entered, all jumped off the grain sacks and huddled around him as they did with Scheu, Most, and Pabst," one reporter wrote.[105] The enthusiastic reception deeply affected Most, who viewed it as a testament to the positive outcomes of the trial ordeal. "I was immediately convinced," he remembered, "that the previous persecutions have yielded delicious fruits."[106] Following his release, Most actively participated in socialist gatherings and discussions despite continued repression. He addressed audiences of thousands, sharing his recent experiences and criticizing censorship and the mainstream press.[107] Heinrich Scheu, who heard Most speak for the first time after his release, described him as a charismatic and popular orator.[108] Socialists continued to advocate for universal suffrage, parliamentary representation, and an end to press censorship. Party members chose Most to embark on a spring speaking tour into the provinces, aiming to inspire workers to join associations and subscribe to the party's newspaper.[109] He lectured in numerous locations, including as far as Trieste on the Adriatic coast, with his speeches drawing large crowds and making a significant impact.[110] For example, on March 12, he spoke in three towns and still found time to perform in short theatrical pieces.[111] This itinerant style of agitation became a hallmark of Most's career, continuing until the end of his life.

While Johann Most's lectures primarily centered on Austrian politics, civil liberties, and universal suffrage, he could not overlook the significant events unfolding around him. One notable occurrence was the conclusion of the Franco-Prussian War, which culminated in the proclamation of a new German Empire in Paris on February 11, 1871. However, it was a more immediate and consequential event that drew Most's attention: on March 18, during his travels through the Carinthia province, a civil war erupted in France. Parisian workers and artisans resisted disarmament efforts by Adolphe Thiers's government troops, leading to a violent conflict. Soldiers began to fraternize with the workers, compelling Thiers to retreat to Versailles, which ultimately resulted in the establishment of the Paris Commune. The commune enacted measures to ensure public services, food distribution, and social legislation. It adopted the red flag, guaranteed the separation of church and state, abolished night work for bakers, and implemented progressive measures regarding pensions, rent control, school reform, and debt relief. Despite its radical actions, the commune leaned more toward social democracy than a full-blown social revolution. In a speech, Most expressed hope that France's "fake republic" would be replaced by "a truly radical and socialist one," suggesting that the commune embodied the ideals socialists had long advocated.[112] However, the events in Paris sparked fear and alarm among the middle and upper classes throughout Europe, who viewed the armed uprising as a direct threat to their social order. Vienna journalist Karl von Thaler noted that socialists, including Most, wholeheartedly embraced the commune, openly expressing sympathy for the insurgents. "The horrific business of the commune is completely to their taste," he wrote, "and they admit without shame their sympathy for the Reds of Montmartre and Belleville. . . . There is a certain Most who is traveling the interior Austrian provinces, giving lectures to workers where he rants inimitably against Germany and extols the general Republic based on ideas still being promulgated from the Paris city hall." Thaler criticized the Left's internationalist stance, lamenting, "They grope about in a cosmopolitan haze that prevents them from grasping healthy political views; most of them neither feel Austrian nor German, but rather as 'mere humans.'"[113] The situation in Paris remained tense and uncertain, with escalating violence, reprisals, and assassinations reflecting the complex and volatile nature of the times.

In early April 1871, Johann Most was arrested for allegedly inciting a riot by preaching "communism" in Austria. He was given a strict ultimatum: leave Austria "forever" by May 11.[114] Never one to back down, Most responded with characteristic wit and defiance. "Forever?" he asked. "Yes, forever," answered the official. "It is by no means certain that Austria will exist forever," he retorted, stunning the officials present. His friend Andreas Scheu would later be expelled from Austria, but the two men would reunite. On the eve of his departure, Most addressed his friends, reaffirming his allegiance to their cause: "I must leave you now, but I'll stay in your ranks; our party doesn't end at the Austrian border."[115] Hundreds of workers accompanied Most to the train station, demonstrating the profound impact he had made on the Austrian labor movement.[116] As he departed Austria, Most reflected on the transformative journey he had undertaken since his arrival in 1868. He had evolved from a novice activist to a battle-tested leader, witnessing firsthand the power dynamics between the state and the working class. He saw industrial workers organize for a common purpose and embrace a new, modern vision of the world. Above all, Most cherished the friendships and camaraderie he had found among fellow proletarians. Crossing into the new German Empire, Most resolved to continue his activism with renewed vigor. No longer a stranger in Bavaria and Saxony, he embarked on a mission to spread his message throughout these regions.

3 A Smithy's Hammer

JOHANN MOST'S ACTIVITIES IN AUSTRIA significantly influenced the local labor movement and had broader implications for the socialist movement in Germany. His prosecution and subsequent expulsion from Austria unleashed a new force in the German labor scene, where he emerged as a prominent figure within the Social Democratic Party, making substantial contributions to the development of German socialism. During Most's time in Germany from 1871 to 1878, the Social Democratic Party was characterized by a lack of a unified economic ideology; it primarily shared "principles of political democracy," as Vernon Lidtke argues.[1] The ideas of Karl Marx and Friedrich Engels were not yet dominant or fully understood within the party, and it was not until 1891 that the party officially adopted a Marxist program. Most espoused a pragmatic and gradualist philosophy, emphasizing the importance of agitation, which he promoted through numerous pamphlets, articles, and speeches. Although he was part of the Eisenacher wing of the party, he was not anti-Lassalle. Although he disagreed with Ferdinand Lassalle's pro-Prussia stance, he was drawn to Lassalle's conception of the state and his critique of liberal do-gooders. This nuanced approach reflected the ideological landscape of German socialism during this period.[2] Notably, Most did not advocate for a violent and immediate revolution in the 1870s; instead, he believed that society was in a "transitional phase" toward socialism, where agitation and education were essential precursors to significant social change.[3]

The geopolitical landscape in Germany underwent considerable shifts during this time, particularly with the proclamation of the new German Empire in January 1871, following the Franco-Prussian War. Hostilities between the two powers began around the time of the treason trial in Vienna. The Battle of Sedan on September 1, 1870, led to a French capitulation the following day, igniting nationalist fervor and presenting a dilemma for socialists, as many German workers supported the war effort. Despite the party's general statement in favor of defending Germany "against Napoleonic or any other despotism," several of its leaders were vehemently anti-Prussian.[4] Figures such as Wilhelm Liebknecht and August Bebel openly opposed the annexation of Alsace-Lorraine by Prussia, leading to their condemnation as "traitors to the fatherland."[5]

Most's expulsion from Austria only served to elevate his status within the German socialist movement, as his reputation preceded him during his speaking tour of Bavaria in May 1871. News of his expulsion spread through various German newspapers, with *Der Proletarier* hailing him as the "bookbinder from Augsburg made famous by the Vienna workers' trial." Even *Volksstaat*, a socialist publication, expressed gratitude to the Austrian government for inadvertently strengthening the ranks of socialist agitators by expelling Most.[6] During his lectures, Most addressed the current political climate and predicted the impending collapse of Austria. Despite the serious subject matter, he infused his speeches with humor that even amused police officers in attendance.[7] His lecture in Augsburg attracted a diverse audience, including not only socialists but also Catholic activists—his father may have been among them—despite the historical animosity between the two groups. They found common ground in their opposition to Otto von Bismarck and Prussian influence. When Most expressed the hope that the "united Romance people would end the Germanness of his time," he warmed the hearts of everyone in the audience. However, his praise for the Communards in Paris shocked the Catholic activists present.[8] Reports of violence in Paris, where government troops faced heavy resistance from the Communards, painted a grim picture of the situation. As soldiers advanced through the city, they murdered civilians suspected of aiding the Commune, and reports emerged of summary executions and reprisals by the Communards, including the execution of the archbishop. The subsequent suppression of the Commune was marked by extraordinary brutality, with thousands of Communards killed by firing squad or forced into exile or penal colonies. As many as forty thousand may have been murdered in what *Volksstaat* referred to as a "blood orgy."[9] The fortunate few fled to Belgium, London, or the United States. The events in Paris underscored the ongoing struggle for social justice and the lengths to which authorities would go to suppress dissent.

The Paris Commune represented a profound shift in the dynamics of class struggle, leaving a lasting impact on both the elite and the Left. For the elite, it instilled fear of an armed urban working class seizing control of a European capital and seeking retribution against the privileged classes. For the Left, however, the Commune symbolized a courageous uprising for a popular republic that was tragically crushed in a wave of bloodshed. March 18, the day Parisians expelled the government troops, became a significant date on the radical calendar, often referred to as the "birthday of the social revolution."[10] Many on the Left, including Most, viewed the Commune as "a crossroad in the historic struggle of the labor movement against the bourgeoisie."[11] Lassalleans and Eisenachers expressed solidarity with the Communards, and even in the Reichstag, the socialist deputy August Bebel shocked his fellow lawmakers when he declared that the Commune's cry "War on the Palaces, Peace for the Cottages, Death to Hardship and Idleness" would eventually become the battle cry of the proletariat in the decades to come.[12]

In late May 1871, Most traveled to Leipzig, the headquarters of the SDAP, to meet with Liebknecht and Bebel. However, the local party was grappling with financial difficulties and internal strife between the Lassalleans and Eisenachers.[13] Despite these challenges, the party maintained a dual strategy for liberating the working classes: one focused on political engagement to secure socialist representation in the Reichstag, and the other on fostering sustainable trade unions and newspapers for socioeconomic progress. A significant milestone was the establishment of the *Chemnitzer Freie Presse* (Chemnitz free press) in the industrial city of Chemnitz, south of Leipzig. As one of Germany's oldest local social democratic publications, it played a pivotal role in raising class consciousness in the region.[14] Ethnographer Ernst Hofmann described its founding as a "decisive break" in the history of the Chemnitz labor movement, which had previously relied mostly on oral communication.[15]

What role could Most play in a swiftly industrializing region like Saxony, home to the largest concentration of socialist and union activists in Germany?[16] His encounter with Liebknecht, who was twenty years his senior, did not go as expected. Liebknecht, who had been arrested and charged with treason during the 1848 upheavals, returned to Germany in 1862 after meeting Marx in London. He briefly collaborated with Lassalle but found Lassalle's pro-Bismarck stance unacceptable. After settling in Leipzig, Liebknecht was elected to the parliament of the North German Confederation (the precursor of the Reichstag) and became editor of the newly founded *Volksstaat*.[17] "So you are Most." Liebknecht asked, "What do you want here in Leipzig, then?" Most's goal was to continue spreading the ideals of socialism, but recalling Most's fiery rhetoric in Austria, Liebknecht warned him, "Here in middle Germany, scientific socialism has been introduced. One cannot operate here with talk of revolution."[18] He suggested that Most might find better success working with the Lassalleans in Berlin, but Most refused. He later described the encounter with Liebknecht as "beneath contempt." This moment marked the beginning of a complex relationship between two men divided by nearly a generation.[19] Most's meeting with Bebel, however, was far more productive. Bebel saw potential in Most and believed his arrival in Saxony came at an opportune time.[20] Most likely knew of Bebel's recent controversial speech in the Reichstag, where he had praised the Paris Commune. Moreover, both men shared a militant atheistic worldview.[21]

Bebel successfully persuaded Most to join him and Liebknecht in addressing a public demonstration scheduled for June 24 in Chemnitz. Frustrated by the failure of their petitions for a ten-hour workday, the workers aimed to show their collective strength. Around 15,000 people gathered in one of Chemnitz's large squares.[22] "Citizens of Chemnitz," Most shouted, "let me introduce myself. I am Most, the traitor from Vienna, and I have been living in this new German Reich of godliness and pious customs for a few days."[23] The crowd erupted in enthusiastic cheers. Most delivered his speech with remarkable energy, leaving the audience awestruck by the force and passion coming from his slender frame. He urged them to see the futility of relying on parliament for improvements and instead rallied them around the demand for a ten-hour workday, igniting excitement and energy throughout the square. The impact of his speech reverberated across the region. Following the demonstration, Most was charged with inciting a riot and promptly arrested in Leipzig. Authorities, citing an 1850 law, informed him that "agitation" would not be tolerated and ordered him to leave the town within twenty-four hours.[24] Official records show that during his custody, Most was paraded in front of police officers so they could familiarize themselves with his features in case he returned to Leipzig. In response, Most took legal action against the police department, resulting in the Ministry of Justice nullifying both the expulsion order and the prohibition on his public speaking in Leipzig in December 1871.[25]

* * *

After the success of the market square demonstration, Most was offered the editorship of the *Chemnitzer Freie Presse*, a daily socialist newspaper. After some careful consideration, he accepted the position.[26] It was a significant milestone in his career, providing him with a relatively stable job aligned with his passion for educating and agitating through the printed and spoken word. His salary slightly exceeded that of a skilled machinist, one of the highest earners among factory workers.[27] Despite lacking the academic background typically favored by the party for editors, Most's witty, unpretentious proletarian style effectively broadened the paper's readership.[28] The role demanded a rigorous schedule: all editorial work had to be completed in the morning to ensure the timely publication of six four-page issues.[29] Afternoons and evenings were dedicated to lectures and other activities, as socialist newspapers were seen as an "extension of popular oratory."[30] Chemnitz, Saxony's third largest city and a major center for machine and textile production, had over seven thousand workers employed in large, fully mechanized factories. Workers commuted to this industrial hub, often referred to as the "Manchester of Saxony" because of its "veil of smoke and soot."[31] This bustling industrial backdrop provided the foundation for sustaining a daily labor paper, a rarity in the early 1870s.[32] Most settled into a third-floor apartment at 11 Obere Hainstrasse in Sonnenberg, a growing working-class suburb near the train station.[33]

Most understood the importance of using vernacular expressions, idioms, and relatable styles to connect with the working class, avoiding dry philosophical debates and factional polemics.[34] He infused the local party with new energy and focus, earning praise from socialist historian Ernst Heilmann, who remarked that Most's "formidable ability for work and agitation created an entirely new, incomparably stronger and livelier party life in Chemnitz."[35] Within a year, subscriptions to the *Chemnitzer Freie Presse* had increased tenfold, due in part to Most's "rousing and irresistible" tone, which a colleague compared to the force of a "smithy's hammer."[36] Although Liebknecht criticized Most for his fiery and sometimes intemperate language, historian Heiner Becker argued that Most's editorial style was more nuanced, blending "mockery, irony, satirical distortions, and ridicule."[37] Most defended his approach, claiming that his spicy language helped foster lasting class consciousness. He contrasted this with Liebknecht's more restrained tactics in Leipzig, famously quipping, "If Liebknecht wants to cook a pauper's broth" in Leipzig, let him, but here in Chemnitz, "we serve paprika schnitzel."[38] Most believed in the liberating power of creative and unorthodox language, echoing the sentiments of twentieth-century anarchist writer Paul Goodman, who viewed everyday speech as a form of resistance. "Authority imposes format on speech because it needs speech, but not autonomous speech," Goodman wrote in 1972, "format is speech colonized, broken-spirited."[39] Most denounced the capitalist bourgeois state as a system of "organized violence," sustained by what he called an "interdependent trio of church, school, and military." He emphasized the role of religion in keeping the masses subjugated through ignorance, obedience, and fear.[40] However, his preference for spicy language often led to accusations of insult, particularly under Germany's repressive press laws, which allowed authorities to enforce censorship. A free press did not truly exist in Europe before 1914.[41] Between the summers of 1871 and 1872, Most faced forty-three indictments for libel or insulting the emperor, although he frequently escaped conviction, sometimes with hefty fines.[42] Despite his legal troubles, Most remained defiant. Eventually, he was arrested in his office in Chemnitz. This time, he served a one-month sentence, unable to pay the fines imposed on him. Adding to the indignity, he was billed for services like barbering, heating, and even hay during his detention.[43]

Socialists like Most envisioned a government elected by the people as the steward of the means of production, directing output according to the needs of the people. "Legislation," Most wrote vaguely, "is practiced directly by the people."[44] In his ideal socialist society, civil liberties would be safeguarded, gender equality ensured, and both state-sanctioned marriage and religion abolished. All producers, he believed, would share equally in the enjoyment of life. For Most, democracy was the vehicle to achieve socialism, and he asserted that "pure popular rule is the precondition for socialism."[45] Recognizing the entrenched and undemocratic nature of the current political structure, Most advocated relentless propaganda to sway public opinion before a socialist commonwealth could be established. Most's views were articulated at the party congress in Dresden in August 1871, where he represented several Bavarian groups.[46] When asked to deliver the keynote address in Liebknecht's absence (due to the birth of his son Karl), Most proposed full cooperation with the International Workingmen's Association (IWA).[47] Despite police warnings not to mention the Paris Commune, Most defiantly declared, "If the reaction is uniting internationally, then it is self-evident that the revolution must also unite internationally," prompting thunderous applause.[48] The congress also resolved to push for a legal ten-hour workday, with Most emphasizing closer ties with the Austrian movement, which had been peacefully organizing and striking for reduced working hours.[49] However, the debate about socialist agitation in rural areas was much more contentious. Many believed only industrial workers, whom Most regarded as the "spearhead" of the movement, could achieve class consciousness.[50] Most feared that conservative farmers could become "dangerous" counterrevolutionaries, potentially thwarting progress toward socialism.[51] Nevertheless, he urged peasants and rural workers to combat the "stultification of the people" and gradually "oust the ruling parties."[52] His ideas drew attention at an academic conference in Berlin, where a preacher criticized his pamphlet for promoting "seductive illusions."[53]

Figure 3. Clara Franzisca
Hänsch in Leipzig, 1870s.
Courtesy of International
Institute of Social History,
Amsterdam.

Shortly after he arrived in Chemnitz, Most met Clara Franziska Hänsch, a nineteen-year-old police officer's daughter whom he described as "one of the prettiest girls in town."[54] Hänsch expressed an interest in socialism, and it is likely that Most first noticed her during one of his speeches, "smitten by a pair of black eyes."[55] Their acquaintance soon developed into a deeper relationship, culminating in their engagement—the first serious romantic involvement for both.

For years, Most had struggled to find confidence and initiative in pursuing romantic relationships, blaming his difficulties on his stepmother and his facial disfigurement, which he could not conceal until he was able to grow a full beard. He confessed to Hänsch that "my heart was nailed shut regarding the fair sex," believing that flirting and dating were beyond his reach.[56] At times, Most harbored resentment toward women, feeling they shunned him because of his appearance. The absence of a beard made him feel particularly rejected, especially when he saw his comrades in Zurich easily socializing with women. This frustration led him to adopt a defensive stance, which sometimes earned him unwarranted accusations of being a "Don Juan."[57] Once, in Vienna, when he learned that a woman he quietly admired was engaged, Most vented his frustration and self-loathing in his journal. He lamented his physical shortcomings compared to her fiancé: "He was a strapping lad; I, a weak fellow. He was handsome; I, ugly as sin. Since I could not yet grow a beard, I most likely made . . . a mere repulsive impression on the eternal feminine."[58] These experiences reveal a man grappling with deep insecurities and societal pressures regarding appearance and romantic pursuits.

*　*　*

In October and November 1871, a major strike by metal workers brought the Chemnitz region to a standstill, attracting national media attention. The workforce in machine production had surged from 750 in 1846 to nearly 8,000 by 1875.[59] These workers were now demanding a reduction of the workday from twelve to ten hours, without any loss in pay or existing holidays. The manufacturers' early offer of a 10.3-hour workday, coupled with the elimination of ten holidays, was swiftly rejected. With no existing maximum hour law in Germany, employers dismissed further demands, and some large firms even reorganized as publicly traded corporations to shift responsibility for worker grievances onto shareholders.[60] Despite the limited strength of the International Union of Metal Workers in Chemnitz, workers persisted in their campaign through petitions and public demonstrations, echoing the mass gathering where Most had initially addressed Chemnitz workers in June. While some factions advocated for an immediate walkout, the socialists argued that a strike should only be called "when an imperious necessity is present and when funds are available."[61] However, Most believed that immediate reforms were essential as a precursor to deeper social transformation. He argued that wage increases and shorter hours could mitigate the problems of overproduction and underconsumption. Using a metaphor, he once said that we dress our wounds to relieve pain "in order to hold out until the radical cure is implemented."[62]

Most threw himself into organizing the workers and raising funds to support their cause. He set up a central coordinating committee and arranged public lectures to galvanize support. He also called on Theodor Yorck, leader of the Union of German Woodworkers, to come to Chemnitz and help organize the factory carpenters.[63] Workers' morale received a boost when news spread that one textile manufacturer had implemented a ten-hour workday and granted a wage increase. In his first popular pamphlet on the subject, Most chastised the bourgeoisie for advocating education as the only remedy for workers' problems while simultaneously depriving them of the time needed to pursue it. He condemned piece-rate work as a tactic employed by employers to dissuade workers from demanding a shorter workday. Expressing skepticism about the potential for legislative action, Most issued a veiled warning to employers: "Against the pressure of capital, a counterpressure can be applied; we will prove that you are not all-powerful. . . . If you remain obstinate, which we hope you won't, the consequences may be more adverse than you think." He concluded with an impassioned call to the workers: "Down with servility, bootlicking, and cowardice! Show them you have a sense of honor, that you are awakened!"[64]

Despite Most's organizing efforts, he believed the union was too weak to go on strike, but his caution was ultimately disregarded. On October 15, the union's central committee formally presented its demand for a ten-hour workday without any loss of pay or holidays to Hartmann's Saxon Machine Works, the region's largest firm, which employed 2,700 workers. While most employees supported the union's demands, management swiftly rejected the proposal. A week later, the union voted to give the company three days to accept or face a city-wide strike. The manufacturers' association countered with a proposal for a sixty-two-hour workweek, including reduced overtime—an offer the workers decisively rejected. As a result, around eight thousand machine workers, iron molders, and carpenters initiated what became Germany's largest walkout. With the strike in full swing, Most called for solidarity, distributing flyers titled "To the Proletarians of All Nations," which were printed in socialist papers as far away as Brussels. In a striking display of unity, workers donned blue shirts, gray trousers, low blue caps, and red shawls—a nod to Most's past initiatives in Vienna. Concerns soon arose about the potential deployment of the Chemnitz garrison, recently returned from France, to suppress the strike. The mayor had already requested assistance from the garrison commander in case of riots. To prevent conflict, labor organizers advised strikers to maintain good relations with the soldiers, considering them "fellow workers in uniform." This solidarity campaign proved effective, as contributions to the strike fund poured in from workers across Saxony. Groups affiliated with the IWA from Austria and Belgium collected roughly 3,600 thaler. Metal workers in distant cities like Dortmund and Frankfurt staged sympathy strikes. Despite prohibitions, Most continued delivering speeches in surrounding towns, often using false names to evade authorities, and even traveled to Bavaria to rally further support.[65]

A week into the strike, the industrialists and the city government, with backing from the bourgeois press, ramped up efforts to pressure and intimidate the strikers. The conservative *Chemnitzer Tageblatt* (Chemnitz daily news) launched a relentless smear campaign against the strike's central committee and Most. False allegations surfaced, with a Dresden paper accusing Most of embezzling funds when he traveled to Bavaria.[66] Despite these challenges, the strike persisted until Saxon Machine Works issued a final ultimatum: any employee who failed to return to work by November 7 would be terminated. Reluctantly, a portion of the strikers began reporting back to work. Shortly thereafter, Most was assaulted by hired thugs in a local restaurant. A week later, the strike officially ended, with another four thousand workers returning to their jobs. Strike leaders and committee members faced immediate dismissal and were blacklisted by employers. In the aftermath, industrialists implemented their original compromise: a sixty-two-hour workweek with reduced pay and ten fewer holidays. To consolidate their power and prevent future labor actions, employers formed a national manufacturers' association and lobbied lawmakers to strengthen "breach of contract" provisions and other control measures.[67]

Johann Most became the scapegoat for the failed metal workers' strike, with industrialists and the press singling him out as the chief instigator. He was subjected to multiple successful libel lawsuits.[68] The prevailing narrative painted him as the firebrand who incited workers into a premature and destructive strike, only to abandon them when it collapsed. Even within his own party, some members criticized his confrontational rhetoric, arguing that it may have hindered the chances of a favorable agreement. However, the historian of the Chemnitz labor movement Heilmann disputes this version of events, asserting that "the employers had wanted the strike" in order to break the labor movement, regardless of Most's language.[69] Socialist Party historian Franz Mehring also defended Most, noting that "up to the last moment [Most] sought to prevent the . . . strike."[70] Most, in his own defense, explained in the socialist press that he had believed the strike was premature and had tried to deescalate the situation. However, once thousands of workers were involved, he felt it was his "duty to support them, and that's what I did with all my power."[71] Contrary to the accusations of inciting unrest, Most consistently advised against rioting and violence, and the strikers followed this advice.[72] Shortly after the metal workers' strike ended, Most played a pivotal role in helping secure a major victory for a carpenters' strike, which resulted in a substantial 15 percent wage increase.[73]

* * *

By 1872, Johann Most had emerged as one of the most compelling and innovative voices in the German socialist movement. What made him stand out was his insistence that socialism was not merely an intellectual endeavor but a way of thinking and living that demanded both thought and action. For Most, socialism was a comprehensive challenge to social norms and conventions, requiring radical critique through irreverence, satire, and revolutionary engagement. This belief took shape in his creation of *Nußknacker* (Nutcracker), a satirical supplement to the *Chemnitzer Freie Presse*.[74] Reviving a title he had previously used in Vienna, *Nußknacker* became known as "the first political-satirical organ of German social democracy," earning praise as one of Most's "outstanding performances" during his time in Chemnitz.[75] The supplement became a platform for Most's fiery brand of satire, featuring political poems, sharp-edged short stories, and parodies that typically pit noble workers against disdainful bourgeois figures. These writings resonated deeply with his working-class audience. At the same time, Most carved out a pioneering role as a creator and publicist of revolutionary songs, a contribution that often goes unacknowledged in the historiography of German socialism. In May 1871, he published his *Austrian Songs* and attempted to smuggle the booklet into Austria, leading the imperial government to ban all printed material bearing his name.[76] His most enduring work, "Die Arbeitsmänner" (Workingmen), continued to be sung by labor movements into the twentieth century. In 1872, he also published a collection of fifty proletarian songs, including his own, which became a best seller across several editions.[77] Although the socialist songbook tradition was not new, Most's collection stood out for its militant tone and its ability to rally the working class.[78] Songbooks played a vital role in the labor movement before modern means of communication. Anyone attending a socialist meeting was reminded to bring their songbook.[79] Singing together fostered camaraderie and a sense of righteousness, with traditional tunes often infused with new revolutionary lyrics, sometimes with humorous twists. As Jesse Cohn noted, socialists like Most would "use the old songs as a fulcrum for their own ideological work" to better connect with working-class audiences.[80] Despite Most's significant contributions to revolutionary songwriting, his name gradually faded from memory, particularly after his break with the Social Democratic Party. In 1924, Rudolf Rocker, Most's first biographer, lamented that many young radicals were unaware of his role in shaping their favorite songs.[81]

In his public lectures, Johann Most frequently undertook historical analyses that culminated in a vigorous critique of the legitimacy of the bourgeois state. The atmosphere in 1872 was particularly charged, with Liebknecht and Bebel imprisoned for nine months following a treason trial due to their outspoken views on the recent Franco-Prussian War and the Paris Commune. Feeling the weight of responsibility, Most believed he had to step up, stating,

"The essential agitation for all of Saxony now rested on my shoulders."[82] Although the trial dealt a blow to the movement, Most sought to uplift his audiences by dismantling the concept of treason.[83] He argued that the charge of treason was not inherent but rather a product of historical circumstances, functioning as a tool of power discourse, to borrow a phrase from Michel Foucault. Consequently, he contended that socialists should not succumb to intimidation from such charges. Most asserted that the weakness of Bismarck and his supporters became evident whenever they targeted the socialists, proclaiming to his audience, "When the ruling power shows no anxiety and fear, and when a party is not being persecuted, then such a party does not amount to much." Most also launched scathing criticisms against the mainstream press, accusing them of forsaking their independence and capitulating to the ruling classes in their coverage of the socialist movement. He urged workers to reject bourgeois newspapers and support socialist publications like the *Chemnitzer Freie Presse*.[84]

Most's unabashed editorializing against officials and institutions often landed him in the crosshairs of numerous libel suits, resulting in a two-month stint in jail. Rather than allow his struggling paper to fold, he opted to step down as editor, hoping to find new leadership.[85] Historian Heilmann attributed the paper's financial woes to Most's "tempestuous" nature, suggesting that Most lacked "the practical ability to preserve the financial health of a printing business" despite rising subscriptions.[86] His successor, Julius Vahlteich, stood in stark contrast in temperament and approach, viewing Most's tenure as detrimental to the cause in Chemnitz. In turn, Most doubted Vahlteich's ability to galvanize the movement, remarking that he had turned the factory workers into "pure sleepyheads."[87] The discord between Most and Vahlteich illuminates their differing personalities and tactics. Whereas Most cultivated a proletarian identity characterized by militant irreverence, humor, and theatricality, Vahlteich favored education and a more reserved bourgeois lifestyle.[88] Heilmann believed that Vahlteich, being less enamored with illusions of proletarian victory, downplayed the enthusiasm sparked by Most's hopeful and passionate rhetoric.[89] Although Most demonstrated a pragmatic side, Heilmann's analysis echoed sentiments from moderates like Liebknecht, who had earlier expressed reservations about Most's approach. However, in a movement still relatively free from hierarchy and bureaucracy, individuals like Most could ascend based on the power of their words, occasionally drawing criticism from fellow socialists, some of whom accused him of speaking without fully understanding the issues at hand.

During his eight-week sentence in the Chemnitz city jail in the summer of 1872, Johann Most experienced relatively lenient treatment. He was allowed to read, stroll around town, and visit friends under the watchful eye of a guard. This leniency can be attributed in part to the politics of particularism, as many German states sought to maintain their regional identity in opposition to Bismarck's Prussian nationalism. As long as socialist activities remained peaceful, Saxon civil servants were willing to collaborate with socialists against Prussian nationalism.[90] However, it is important not to overstate this goodwill toward socialists, as higher authorities still targeted socialist activists. For instance, the Saxon Interior Ministry prohibited Most from engaging in "work for periodicals" within the kingdom. Following his release in August, Most secured a suspension of previous judgments against him, enabling him to attend both the upcoming Sedan celebrations and the party congress in Mainz.[91]

On September 2, Sedan Day had transformed into a jubilant celebration of Germany's victory over France in 1870, rather than a solemn remembrance of the human toll of the battle. Across the country, Germans erected victory monuments in their city squares, demonstrating their patriotism. In Chemnitz, the atmosphere was described as "emperor-loyal, German-nationalistic, militaristic."[92] The day was marked by school closures and a day off for workers, showcasing the burgeoning phenomenon of national commemorations of war and fallen soldiers in 1870s Europe. The Franco-Prussian War was the first conflict to be memorialized in both Germany and France. Recognizing the fervor surrounding Sedan Day, Johann Most believed it warranted a counterweight, particularly in a city with a significant working-class population. He urged metal workers to abstain from the festivities organized by what he termed "murder patriots," a phrase that could be construed as an affront to the German military or the emperor.[93] The *Chemnitzer Freie Presse* declared, "For us social democrats, September 2 is a bloody day that awakens sorrow, not joy."[94] Most did not limit his protest to words alone. Instead of displaying the national flag, working-class residents showcased a collage of tax receipts—an idea put forth by Most. The facade of the *Freie Presse* office was adorned with a red flag flanked by two black ones. During the parade, socialists distributed a "Festival Newsletter" containing anti-war songs to unsuspecting onlookers.[95] Later, some three thousand workers, chanting proletarian songs, marched to the central market square where the official torchlight parade was scheduled to commence. At the forefront of the procession, a banner bore a grim reminder of the human cost of war: "40,881 Dead on the German Side, Even More on the French Side, Countless Crippled! And

You Celebrate to Glorify Such Outrage." Upon reaching the square, workers encircled the official gathering, replacing the original lyrics of "Die Wacht am Rhein" with an anti-war rendition. They then proceeded to a different square where Most addressed the crowd.[96]

The following day, fearing imminent arrest, Most traveled to Mainz to participate in the fourth Socialist Party Congress as one of fifty-one delegates.[97] The atmosphere among attendees was subdued due to increased state repression in many regions. With Bebel and Liebknecht still incarcerated, Most was elected to speak on the "Principles of Social Democracy."[98] He lifted spirits by reminding his colleagues that increased persecution did not signify weakness but rather indicated the growing strength of socialism. "If the movement amounted to nothing," he reasoned, "they would leave us alone." He emphasized the urgency of accelerating socialist agitation in Germany, lamenting the comparative lethargy of the populace in embracing ideals of freedom, equality, and fraternity, contrasting it with the swift adoption of these ideas by the "vivacious" French.[99] Most called for transcending factionalism between Lassalleans and Eisenachers, emphasizing the common struggle against bourgeois exploitation.[100] A central tenet of the socialist platform, according to Most, was the establishment of a free peoples' state through collective and international action by workers, without regard to "nation or skin color."[101] Despite the 1871 constitution's guarantee of universal suffrage for men aged twenty-five and older, Most criticized Bismarck's deliberate choice of this age, which coincided with completing military service and thus the indoctrination into the bourgeois state. When a police officer threatened to shut down the meeting unless Most moderated his language, he retorted with characteristic sarcasm. "I'm astonished," Most sneered. "Did I speak excitedly? I believe I was quite moderate. Anyway, I will continue and endeavor to moderate my moderation."[102] The delegates also debated Bebel's proposal to remove "Workers" from the Social Democratic Workers' Party name for the sake of inclusivity. Most opposed the change, arguing that the party was primarily composed of workers and did not need those who shied away due to the name: "If men of science and others shy away from membership just for that reason, we don't need them."[103] Most's hostility toward the liberal bourgeoisie was shared by many of his colleagues, reflecting a broader political schism in Germany between workers and the bourgeoisie. The motion to change the name was ultimately defeated.

The ideological split within the IWA, culminating in the congress in The Hague in September 1872, served as a significant backdrop to the Socialist Party Congress in Mainz, although it was not explicitly discussed there. This division stemmed from fundamental differences between the state socialist followers of Marx and the antiauthoritarian socialists led by the Russian anarchist Mikhail Bakunin. Marxists, advocating for the proletarian seizure of political power and centralized organization of workers, believed that social revolution could only occur in advanced capitalist societies. On the other hand, Bakuninists argued for spontaneous revolution initiated by workers and peasants, rejecting all forms of centralization as oppressive. They accused the Marxists of authoritarianism and sought to establish a decentralized, federated society. They believed the IWA ought to be "an embryo of the human society of the future" and, as such, "is required in the here and now to faithfully mirror our principles of freedom and federation."[104] The split reached a head with Marx's maneuvering to expel Bakunin from The Hague congress, further solidifying the divide between the camps. While Marx moved the General Council to New York after the split, the antiauthoritarians continued to hold congresses, primarily in Switzerland, exerting influence over German workers sympathetic to anarchism.

* * *

The period following September 1872 was tumultuous for Johann Most as he embarked on a speaking tour across central Germany and the Rhineland. Instead of solely promoting socialism, he found himself caught in the middle of reconciling differences between various socialist factions.[105] Back in Saxony, while staying with a friend, Most came across a wanted ad in a Chemnitz newspaper: "Most, 26 years of age, of small stature, with blond hair and a full beard, and a deformed mouth covered by a thick beard, stands out only when speaking; he wears dark clothes, including a single-breasted coat with a stand-up collar."[106] Most was aware that charges were pending against him, but he objected to being labeled a fugitive. In response, he published an announcement in the *Chemnitzer Freie Presse*, explaining that he was finishing his speaking tour and that the authorities "would have to be patient for a few more days."[107] He was arrested the next day on charges that included insulting the monarch, inciting violence, obstructing the police, and insulting the court and prosecutor during the Leipzig treason trial. He was also charged with insulting the Chemnitz City Council.[108] Most was convicted on most counts and, in December 1872, sentenced to eight months in the Zwickau state prison.[109] This period also saw the conviction and sentencing of several other socialist editors for publishing allegedly offensive articles or editorials.[110] A month before his release, Most was banned from Saxony, further complicating his future.[111]

During his imprisonment, Most made the best of his circumstances, using his privileges to read, write, and study in private. He even attempted to learn French. One Chemnitz newspaper complained that he was receiving such "luxurious" treatment.[112] Decades later, Most humorously credited Bismarck and the Austrian emperor with unwittingly funding his education.[113] Most's most significant project during his time in prison was writing a popular summary of Marx's *Capital*. Having previously struggled with the dense, theoretical nature of Marx's text, Most aimed to make its ideas more accessible to a working-class audience.[114] His booklet, titled *Capital and Labor: A Popular Summary of "Capital" by Karl Marx*, completed in October 1873, condensed Marx's voluminous work into a more digestible sixty-page format. Most simplified complex concepts and focused on the most relevant labor-related issues, replacing the formal structure of numbered headings and sub-headings with twelve chapters on key labor questions.[115] Understanding that his heavy revisions introduced some errors and inaccuracies, Most sought Marx's assistance in reviewing the summary. A clear and accurate summary of Marxism was especially valuable as the Lassalleans and Eisenachers united at the Gotha congress in 1875 to form the Socialist Workers' Party of Germany (SAPD). Along with Liebknecht and Vahlteich, Most implored Marx to revise the summary.[116] With Marx's revisions, the corrected edition of *Capital and Labor* was published in 1876, becoming the "first scientifically sound guide to Marxian political economy for a wider audience."[117] It was later serialized in English translation in the American Labor Standard.[118]

4 Awaken the Mind of the People

THE EXPULSION FROM SAXONY MARKED a crucial turning point in Johann Most's life. He and Clara relocated to Mainz, where he was offered the editorship of the struggling *Süddeutsche Volksstimme* (South German voice of the people).[1] From the outset, Mainz did not sit well with him—a small garrison town lacking an industrial proletariat.[2] His new editorial office proved equally dispiriting, riddled with factionalism. "I found a business in disarray," he lamented to Wilhelm Liebknecht, "though the terrain is good, if poorly tilled."[3] One contributing issue was the lack of a printing cooperative to reduce costs, a problem Most sought to resolve as he had done in Chemnitz. Despite the severe economic downturn causing unemployment and dislocation, his optimism about socialism's prospects remained undiminished. "I tell you," he wrote to August Bebel, "with just 1,000 men like you, or even like me (without hubris), Europe, not just Germany, would be socialist in five years."[4] To further socialist ideals and maintain his ties to Chemnitz, Most ran for a seat in the Reichstag, Germany's lower house. He received party and *Volksstaat* endorsements as the socialist candidate for the Chemnitz district. Liebknecht praised Most for revitalizing the local movement and its paper with unmatched "energy and selflessness."[5] On January 10, 1874, Most won a three-year Reichstag term representing Chemnitz, capturing 57 percent of the vote and defeating liberal economist Wolfgang Eras by over 2,600 votes. Nationally, socialists garnered a modest 6.8 percent of the vote, a 3.6 percent increase since 1871, holding just 9 out of 397 seats. The first legislative term was set to begin on February 5—Most's twenty-eighth birthday—prompting his journey to the capital. But before that, just eleven days after the election, Johann and Clara married in Bischofsheim, a small town east of Mainz.[6]

Most quickly grasped the Reichstag's complex rules. Members could not simply rise and speak at will; instead, a speakers' list was prepared in advance, favoring prominent factions controlled by the Caucus of Elders. As a young member, Most spoke only twice during the forty-one meetings of the first session. On one occasion, he questioned the secretive nature of the speakers' list, pointing out that decisions were made behind closed doors, with factions coordinating amendments and votes beforehand. Debates in the assembly felt theatrical. While members were prohibited from directly criticizing the emperor, they could question the government through interpellation, provided it was submitted in writing and had at least thirty cosigners. Additionally, fifteen members had to endorse a bill for it to be considered on the floor, though many bills passed by the Reichstag often met their end in the upper house.[7] Perhaps due to these limitations, Most advocated a "protesting position" for socialists rather than active legislating. "We will hurl the unvarnished truth in the faces of the bourgeois representatives," he promised his constituents.[8] He urged social democrats to carefully observe their opponents' tactics, essential for the party's extra-parliamentary struggle.[9] However, since social democracy aspired to a people's state, which was largely synonymous with parliamentary democracy, it was logical to pursue substantive policy matters.[10] For instance, they opposed a bill reducing parliament's authority over the military budget and rejected a restrictive press bill.[11] On the other hand, they strongly supported a bill granting MPs free first-class rail passage—a move that directly benefited Most by easing his commute between Berlin and Mainz on nightly express trains.[12]

In 1874, Most addressed a policy matter only once, during a debate on a vaccination bill, which he vehemently opposed. The bill proposed mandatory vaccination against smallpox for every child before the age of two and again at twelve, with penalties including fines and imprisonment for noncompliance. Smallpox was a well-known threat in Europe, particularly following the Franco-Prussian War. Edward Jenner's discovery of using cowpox to protect against smallpox had significantly shaped public health policy. Britain had made vaccination compulsory in 1853, and several German states had already implemented vaccination programs before 1874.[13] However, strong opposition arose, driven by concerns over religious beliefs and personal liberty. Most argued that the scientific consensus was not conclusive and condemned the suppression of dissenting views. He likened mandatory vaccination to state-sponsored "blood poisoning" and instead advocated for improving living conditions, building public baths, and giving workers time off to use them. His proposals were met with ridicule and were ultimately rejected.[14] In hindsight, Most's stance on the issue was misguided. After the Vaccination Law was passed, smallpox mortality rates plummeted, and widespread epidemics ceased in the country.[15]

Shortly after the legislative session ended, Most was arrested in his editorial office in Mainz and taken back to Berlin. The arrest was instigated by a warrant from state prosecutor Hermann Tessendorf, who harbored a personal vendetta against Most and was determined to prosecute as many socialists as possible.[16] Most's arrest marked the beginning of a broader campaign of persecution and surveillance. In Prussia alone, over a hundred trials were held in 1874, leading to the imprisonment of seventy-eight socialists.[17] Most faced charges of inciting violence and insulting the military, which he had referred to as a "worthless institution" in two speeches. In these speeches, he defended the Commune and criticized the military bill under debate in the Reichstag.[18] He maintained that his remarks on the Commune were a historical analysis rather than an incitement to violence, noting that even Otto von Bismarck had compared the Paris Commune to a "German municipal ordinance."[19] Despite Most's defense, Tessendorf secured a conviction, and Most was sentenced to one year and eight months in prison.[20] This turn of events brought significant hardship for both Johann and Clara. Most not only lost his job and legislative privileges, but Clara, who was eight months pregnant and in poor health, also faced difficulties. She received financial support from the Socialist Party and moved to Chemnitz, where she gave birth to a baby boy who tragically died shortly after birth.[21]

On October 13, 1874, Most arrived at Plötzensee, the largest prison in Germany, built to house over a thousand inmates. His requests for better food, exemption from forced labor, and access to books were initially denied. However, after several months, thanks to a friend's intervention, he was granted access to books and nonsocialist newspapers. This allowed him to engage in scientific, philosophical, and economic studies. Reflecting on the importance of constant reading to prevent intellectual stagnation, he remarked to Bebel, "You have to read so much these days just to avoid becoming a blockhead."[22] To ease the pain of separation from Clara, Most crafted a miniature model of his cell, including a figure of himself, which he sent to her as a Christmas gift.[23] During his imprisonment, Most formed a friendship with dramatist Paul Lindau, who was serving a fourteen-day sentence. They bonded over a shared love of theater, satire, and skepticism toward religion. Lindau described Most as "a staunch social democrat" who remained unwavering in his convictions, and remembered him as "a kind, highly talented man" whose self-education had given him a formidable intellect.[24] Both Liebknecht and Most petitioned the Reichstag for the separate treatment of political prisoners and common criminals, but the justice and interior ministers ignored the request.[25]

When Most was released from prison in June 1876, a crowd of over six thousand gathered to welcome the "champion and martyr of socialism," an event organized by his friends Paul Grottkau and August Heinsch.[26] Sharing the stage with Most was Julius Hoffmann, a socialist physician from New York who became a lifelong friend. Among the messages of support was a letter from Aaron Lieberman, a typesetter for the London paper *Vpered!* (Forward!).[27] Soon after, Most was appointed coeditor of the *Berliner Freie Presse*, a newspaper feared by the police as the "most influential daily paper of the party."[28] Historian Heiner Becker described Most's writing style as "dismissive mockery" and "ironic unmasking," which quickly endeared him to readers and established him as one of the wittiest and most prolific writers in the socialist press. Becker noted Most's knack for repurposing passages in different contexts, employing "scissors and glue" in his editing process.[29] Under Most's leadership, subscriptions to the *Berliner Freie Presse* soared from 1,800 to 14,000 by October 1878.[30] Karl Kautsky regarded the paper as "a dreaded power in the state," with Most emerging as one of its most prominent voices."[31] Johann and Clara settled in a second-floor apartment at 47 Pücklerstrasse on the eastern end of town south of the Spree River.[32] Most thrived in the vibrant and cosmopolitan socialist community. Over the next two years, he gave lectures to audiences ranging from three hundred to two thousand, often in beer halls and restaurants, where undercover agents meticulously documented his speeches. His charismatic oratory, blending wit with righteous anger, made him an exceptionally effective speaker. His lectures resembled a stand-up comedian's mix of biting humor and impassioned politics. "Mr. Most has missed his calling; he should have gone into the theater instead of being an agitator," observed a liberal newspaper. "His comedy is rather captivating. . . . He ripped to pieces the politics of Prince Bismarck, scattering the whole edifice like a house of cards." To this reporter, Most was the "Demosthenes" of the socialist movement.[33] Most also forged connections with foreign activists traveling from Russia to Western Europe. Aaron Lieberman, a Russian Jewish socialist, arrived in Berlin from Vilna after authorities discovered an underground socialist circle he had helped organize. Most facilitated collaboration between German and Yiddish socialists by establishing a Berlin section of Jewish socialists, marking the beginning of his enduring ties with Yiddish-speaking radicals.[34]

More of a clever and outspoken popularizer than a scholarly purist, Johann Most avoided rigid ideological dogma, preferring instead to explore diverse ideas from various thinkers. Like many of his contemporaries, he held a firm belief in human progress. "In human society, as in nature, we find a continuous development driven by a constant change of forms," he wrote in 1875.[35] Most viewed the drive for progress as an inherent creative force within nature rather than as the will of a divine being. He found support for this perspective in Henry Thomas Buckle's *History of Civilization in England* (1857–61), which he read while imprisoned. Buckle's work, though presented scientifically, was, as one historian noted, essentially a form of "political theology," offering a grand narrative of social progress.[36] Most saw society as an organic entity, similar to nature, where old forms naturally decay and new ones emerge. Liberalism, he believed, gradually replaced conservatism, and socialism, the final stage, was already beginning to assert itself, though it was not yet mature enough to completely replace older structures.[37] Despite his socialist convictions, Most and his fellow socialists still adhered to fundamental principles of philosophical liberalism, such as belief in progress, human agency, and the potential of science and reason to improve society for all. He embraced Jeremy Bentham's utilitarian principle of maximizing pleasure and minimizing pain as a central mission of socialism: building an egalitarian society aimed at maximizing happiness for the greatest number.[38] According to Most, three main forces were propelling history toward socialism: mass production, the capitalist state based on property rights, and a shift from self-interest to a focus on the common good. While the French Revolution planted the seeds of liberty, equality, and fraternity, Most argued that socialism was the next necessary step in human evolution, as the ideals of the revolution had remained "bourgeois in form" during the 1790s, lacking the framework of mass production and true societal equality.[39]

To tackle the social question, socialists like Most believed that workers needed to gain political power and awaken the exploited masses. "The more political rights the masses win for themselves," Most emphasized, "the closer they get to their social goals."[40] By expanding civil liberties and reducing the workday, the proletariat would gain more time and resources to engage politically. However, political democracy alone would not be enough to end exploitation. Prioritizing the "establishment of economic equality," as Bebel eloquently expressed in articles endorsed by Most, was crucial.[41] Through gradual economic emancipation and the extension of political rights, the state would transform from a defender of capitalism into a mediator between social classes, eventually evolving into a proletarian state. Most envisioned that a socialist state would meet the people's material, mental, and intellectual needs. As he expressed in 1875, "Once people feel physically well, the most careful education continuously refines their spirits; in a word, when they are truly human, they can strive toward unlimited idealism."[42]

Throughout his time in Germany, Johann Most consistently advocated for a carefully planned, gradual transformation of society, rejecting the idea of an immediate, violent revolution. In 1876, he emphasized that the era of coups and conspiracies was a thing of the past.[43] He differentiated between revolution and reform, arguing that revolution involves replacing existing circumstances with a new principle or paradigm, while reform only modifies the current conditions. He insisted that changing the status quo is a fundamental human right, even if authorities deem such actions illegal. However, he admitted, "it remains a sad fact that the vast majority of working people are either indifferent . . . or help empower the ruling classes in enslaving the masses."[44] Most envisioned a two-stage transformation. The first stage, a "Revolution of Minds," aimed to cultivate an alternative working-class culture to dispel the illusion "that the present is unchangeable." In this initial phase, he saw himself as a tribune of the people. The second stage, a "Revolution of Things," would follow, unfolding without physical violence, as the popular will would become irresistible.[45] Emphasizing the importance of peaceful methods, Most assured his readers, "We do not want to rouse wild passions, we don't inflame destructive rage, we don't call for fists! Rather, we raise spirits; we awaken the mind of the people."[46]

* * *

While incarcerated at Plötzensee, Johann Most immersed himself in the works of Eugen Dühring, a blind philosopher and economist from the University of Berlin. Dühring's economic theories, sharp critiques of the establishment, and call for political activism resonated with many socialists, including Bebel and Liebknecht.[47] Although Dühring identified as a socialist, he challenged Karl Marx's Hegelian framework of economic determinism, arguing that it left little room for purposeful political action. He also opposed the idea of state ownership of the means of production, advocating instead for economic and political decentralization. Dühring envisioned a society composed of interconnected communes operating on liberal economic principles within a loosely defined "justice state." Most and others welcomed the intellectual debate Dühring sparked, believing that the socialist movement was "sufficiently flexible to accommodate both [Marx and Dühring]."[48] "They complement each other splendidly," Most responded when asked to choose between Louis Blanc, Marx, Ferdinand Lassalle, or Dühring. He saw such intellectual diversity as an "inexhaustible treasure trove" for the social democrats.[49] Most, in particular, appreciated Dühring's critique of rigid dialectical determinism, favoring more flexible and organic solutions.

Most's efforts to popularize Dühring's ideas led to a brief conflict between Berlin socialists and Marx and Friedrich Engels. In February 1876, Most sent Liebknecht a manuscript designed to make Dühring's concepts more accessible to the working class, hoping to avoid any "tearing down" of the professor.[50] However, under pressure from Engels, Liebknecht rejected the manuscript, warning against spreading unorthodox ideas. "What the hell!" Most retorted. "Are we pushing a personality cult? . . . It sure looks like we're some church." He later assured Liebknecht that Dühring was no fanatic. "Our people," Most insisted, "make their judgments and take the best of all sides, wherever it may be. And so do I."[51] Unfazed by Liebknecht's refusal, Most published the manuscript in the *Berliner Freie Presse*, prompting Marx and Engels to respond with a series of articles later compiled as Anti-Dühring.[52] This controversy highlighted a broader conflict, which historian Thomas Welskopp described as the "ideological self-assertion of the party," championed by Bebel and Most, versus Marx's "claim of unlimited leadership."[53] However, many socialists overlooked Dühring's anti-Semitism, even as he derided social democracy as a "Jewish clan."[54] Eventually, Dühring renounced socialism, and Most distanced himself from Dühring's ideas. Throughout the controversy, Marx developed a particular disdain for Most, viewing him as an inept dilettante who had no business meddling in theoretical matters.[55] "If they [Most and consorts] give up working and become literary men as a profession," Marx grumbled, "they invariably instigate 'theoretical' mischief and promptly join the scatterbrains of the supposedly learned caste."[56]

Despite the controversy, the Dühring affair attracted university students to the socialist movement. They formed the Mohren Club, a debating society named after its street location, where lectures by figures like Paul Grottkau, Ignaz Auer, and possibly Johann Most were held. The club also organized plays, dance sessions, and even established a radical school in 1878.[57] The Berlin socialist movement thus fostered a vibrant, radical milieu of writers, artists, and dissenting intellectuals. Literary critic Heinrich Hart recalled the movement as "alive with idealism," describing it as a "great brotherhood, waiting in ecstasy for the coming reversal of all things."[58] For socialist politician Adolph Hoffmann, Most played a crucial role in shaping the socialist youth movement. Hoffmann remembered how Most captivated young minds during nature hikes, urging them to "rebel against any form of bondage" if they loved nature's beauty. Although Hoffmann and his teenage friends were initially amused by Most's facial appearance, they were soon enthralled by his words during these excursions—an experience they "remembered forever."[59]

In the mid-1870s, Johann Most encountered and ultimately rejected early anarchist philosophy. As a busy editor in Berlin, he began corresponding with the German anarchist August Reinsdorf. In 1876, Reinsdorf wrote, "I see it now, my friend, our desires and hopes can only be realized with a second Bartholomew's Night. . . . Be assured, therefore, that anyone who bangs on about the 'peaceful solution to the social questions' is a wretch and does not take our cause seriously." Most disagreed with Reinsdorf's militant position, but their discussions in Berlin left a lasting impression on him.[60] Despite defending social democracy, Most found Reinsdorf's arguments compelling enough to agree to publish the anarchist's articles in the *Berliner Freie*

Figure 4. Drawing of August Reinsdorf. Courtesy of International Institute of Social History, Amsterdam.

Presse.[61] However, due to the limited understanding of anarchism among socialist activists in Germany, Most insisted that Reinsdorf's contributions be submitted anonymously.[62] The term "anarchist" was seldom used during the 1870s, and the ideology of libertarian or antiauthoritarian socialism entered Germany primarily from Switzerland. Otto Rinke, Emil Werner, and Reinsdorf, all associated with the Swiss Jura Federation of the International, launched the *Arbeiter-Zeitung* in July 1876, the first German-language anarchist paper aimed at spreading anarchism across the border.[63] Influenced by French socialist Paul Brousse and Russian anarchist Peter Kropotkin, these activists played a critical role in introducing anarchist thought to Germany, although their initial success was limited.

In 1914, Wilhelm Blos suggested that Most had already anticipated his "anarchist future" in the late 1870s. Similarly, Rudolf Rocker, Most's first biographer, claimed that Most was a nascent anarchist in his early years, remarking that "his acquaintance with Dühring and his ideas was, in a way, the first step from authoritarian to free socialism, although he was hardly aware of the significance of his development at the time." However, this interpretation is questionable.[64] Max Nettlau disputed the idea that Most fully embraced Dühring's anti-statism, while Karl Schneidt, an anarchist editor who knew Most personally, rejected the notion that Most had harbored anarchist inclinations from the outset.[65] Historian Volker Szmula also challenges the simplified narrative that Most shifted successively from Lassalle to Marx, then to Dühring, and finally to revolutionary anarchism. Instead, Szmula suggests that Most employed a "strategy of obfuscating" the significance of the anarchist movement rather than confronting it as an alternative ideology.[66] For instance, Most attributed the schism within the International Workingmen's Association (IWA) to bourgeois government repression rather than acknowledging ideological differences between Marx and Mikhail Bakunin.[67] He also conspicuously omitted any mention of anarchist involvement in his detailed account of the Paris Commune.[68] Most echoed Marx's criticisms of the French anarchist Pierre-Joseph Proudhon, dismissing him as a "third-tier social quack" and ridiculing his slogans like "Property is theft" and "Anarchy" as mere scare tactics.[69] Most often equated anarchism with chaos, reinforcing this sentiment in 1877 when he declined an invitation to speak about the Paris Commune in Switzerland, fearing association with anarchist agitation. When anarchists clashed with police in Bern, Most avoided the city, concerned that the press might brand him as one of the rioters.[70] Historian Frank Harreck-Haase more recently suggested that Most's eventual adoption of anarchism in the early 1880s had its "roots" during his 1867 sojourn in the Jura region and could have emerged fifteen years earlier had he remained there. This interpretation, however, is overly teleological. While the Jura sections were among the first to advocate federative antiauthoritarian socialism, the term "anarchism" was not widely used at the time. Differentiation within the socialist movement only emerged in the mid-1870s, when Most was deeply embedded in the social democratic fold, with little to no exposure to anarchist literature. Most himself identified his conversion to anarchism as occurring in the 1880s. Furthermore, in his 1903 memoirs, he could have suggested that anarchism had been developing within him since the late 1860s, but he did not. Thus, in the 1870s, Johann Most was not a proto-anarchist; rather, he was focused on expanding the social democratic movement in Germany through legal means.[71]

* * *

Between 1877 and 1878, Johann Most emerged as a prominent and influential socialist speaker and debater, engaging on various platforms. He returned to the Reichstag for a second term, where he frequently faced interruptions from conservative members who objected to his advocacy for a shorter workday and his opposition to criminal penalties for employee contract breaches.[72] Eduard Bernstein recalled Most's "extraordinary restraint and matter-of-factness" as he addressed the chamber. Most also sought to build a coalition between socialists and liberal democrats within parliament, though his efforts were unsuccessful.[73] Beyond the legislative sphere, he eagerly engaged in public debates with bourgeois liberals and intellectuals. One notable encounter was with Karl Birnbaum, a professor at the University of Leipzig, who aimed to refute socialism through five theses. Most's articulate arguments against the wage system were so compelling that Birnbaum asked to continue the debate privately.[74] In the summer of 1877, Most delivered seven lectures on social movements in ancient Rome, drawing on studies he conducted while in prison. His critique of Theodor Mommsen's acclaimed 1856 work on Roman history drew attention; Most detected a bourgeois bias in Mommsen's portrayal of the Roman Empire's consolidation under the Caesars as a "natural and inevitable manifestation."[75] Most argued that Mommsen's support for Bismarck's unification of Germany influenced his interpretation of ancient history, potentially justifying contemporary authoritarian practices. This critique sparked backlash from the bourgeois press, which often misquoted him. Some of his socialist colleagues felt his public criticism of the esteemed historian was unwarranted and regrettable. As Franz Mehring put it, "All too often, Most spoke of things he didn't understand."

While acknowledging that Most's critique of Mommsen was not as extreme as the bourgeois press suggested, Mehring noted that it still "left much to be desired."[76]

The socialist movement's burgeoning influence among urban crowds in the late 1870s worried middle-class Germans and law enforcement. In response to escalating persecution, Most played a crucial role in founding the Association for the Protection of the Interests of Working People in Berlin in November 1877, which quickly became a target for police harassment.[77] The funerals of two prominent activists highlighted the socialist movement's expanding power. The funeral of August Heinsch saw around fifteen thousand individuals adorned with red carnations in attendance. Most and other deputies delivered speeches amid a somber procession led by a brass band playing Beethoven's Funeral March.[78] Whereas one mainstream paper commended the "admirable discipline" of the social democrats in managing the large gathering, another described it as a display of "worker battalions."[79] Tensions escalated following the death of Paul Dentler, a close associate of Most, who died of tuberculosis while in police custody after being charged with lèse-majesté (defaming a ruler) and insulting police officers. His funeral turned into a political rally, with women activists like Bertha Hahn and Pauline Stägemann mobilizing the Berlin Working Wives and Girls Association. Approximately ten thousand workers took part in what Bernstein described as "the first political street demonstration by Berlin workers," with Most again delivering a eulogy. While Bernstein viewed these politicized memorials as enhancing the party's reputation, Tessendorf and possibly Bismarck himself recognized that their suppression tactics were ineffective. The popularity of socialist street demonstrations raised concerns that it could translate into electoral success in the Reichstag.[80]

Social democracy instilled fear in many sectors of German society, as it was seen as contrary to the nation's values. In the 1870s, socialists were marginalized as dangerous outsiders, a critical context for understanding Most's balance between militancy and moderation. Whereas most Germans celebrated the unification of the Reich, socialists praised the radical democratic ideals of the Paris Commune. As nationalism prevailed among Germans, socialists championed international solidarity and condemned the annexation of Alsace-Lorraine. While Christianity remained dominant for most Germans, leading socialists, including Most, were vocal atheists who denounced the clergy for oppressing the masses. To one socialist writer, religion was "the most powerful enemy of socialism, . . . the main bastion of anti-socialism, reaction, the breeding ground of all social evil," a view Most fervently shared.[81] In early 1878, Most launched a public campaign urging workers to formally leave the church (*Kirchenaustritt*) and stop providing financial support. Traditionally, German children were baptized into their parents' church for life, but by the 1870s, several states allowed individuals to register as "dissidents," as Most did.[82] The catalyst for this campaign was the rise of the Christian Social Workers' Party, led by the anti-Semitic chaplain Adolf Stöcker, an advocate of the Christian Social Gospel movement. Most and Stöcker engaged in public debates on Christian socialism and religion's role.[83] When Stöcker claimed the socialist motto "freedom, equality, fraternity" originated from the Gospels, Most countered with a history lesson on religious atrocities. An audience member recalled that Most "possessed a terrifying eloquence and swept the largely nonjudgmental crowd along with him like a whirlwind."[84] He clearly outshone Stöcker, leading the *Allgemeine Zeitung* to concede, "The social democrats achieved a complete triumph; in his eagerness to save religion and monarchy, the court chaplain has handed a win to social democracy in the capital."[85] Encouraged by this victory, Most and his fellow socialists distributed forms for leaving the church at debate venues. He also challenged Stöcker's allies, such as Hermann Theodor Wangemann, director of the Berlin Mission Society. Most advocated for a secular education system and ridiculed religious dogma, promoting a materialist, Darwinian worldview.[86] When Wangemann joked that he could not have evolved from living apes, Most curtly corrected him, stating that humans and apes share a common ancestor.[87]

For a time, the leave-your-church campaign, led by socialist activists across the country, attracted significant media attention and concern from cautious politicians. According to Bernstein, even the aging emperor expressed alarm and urged authorities to intervene.[88] The campaign faced backlash from church officials, who filed complaints against Most for insulting the clergy. In April 1878, Most was convicted and sentenced to two months in prison. Despite its eventual decline, the campaign left a lasting impression, especially in Berlin.[89] In later years, some socialists criticized the campaign as a result of Most's perceived tactlessness. Mehring, for instance, attributed the initiative to Most's "careless zeal" during what he called "spectacles of oratorical competitions," arguing it contradicted party tactics. Mehring's critique, however, overlooked the fact that the 1872 Mainz congress had approved the campaign. Moreover, prominent figures like Bebel, known for his militancy, shared Most's atheistic stance, with even Liebknecht formally leaving his church.[90] Whether futile or not, the free thought and anticlerical movement held deep significance for Most, who had long abandoned faith and religion.

"In my opinion," he wrote in 1885, "the truly logical mind cannot exist until all religious filth has been removed." Years later, in conversation with Russian anarchist Peter Kropotkin, Most asserted that atheism was the precursor to communism and anarchism.[91] By May 1878, Most had accumulated a combined five-month prison sentence from various jurisdictions, though his incarceration was postponed until the end of the Reichstag session.[92]

Johann Most's intense public activism strained his relationship with Clara. Sparse records provide only a partial glimpse into their dynamic. A significant blow occurred in October 1874 when Most, imprisoned at Plötzensee, received the news of their first child's death. Clara returned to Chemnitz but occasionally visited her husband in prison. Rumors circulated about her alleged infidelity during Most's incarceration, but these remain unverified.[93] Upon his release in June 1876, the couple settled in Berlin, though Clara resented Most's ban from returning to Chemnitz. Municipal records show she traveled between the two cities. After the 1877 election, they reunited, with Clara becoming pregnant again. On May 9, 1878, she gave birth to a daughter, Melita Clara Johanna, in their Berlin home.[94] In later years, Most openly acknowledged the unhappiness in their marriage, describing it as a "cat and dog existence." He seemed unable or unwilling to balance family life with his political movement. Reflecting on their tumultuous history, Most wrote, "Three times—in Chemnitz, in Mainz, in Berlin—I set up a family abode, but the hailstorms unleashed by my political struggles destroyed them all."[95] In his memoirs, he confronted the question, party or family? Ultimately, he confessed, "One had to come before the other. I sacrificed my family."[96]

Before the 1890s, the German socialist movement was predominantly male dominated, partly due to legal restrictions preventing women from joining political organizations as well as reluctance among many male socialists to include women. Although the party professed gender equality in principle, many male leaders still adhered to Victorian ideas about gender roles.[97] However, Most's views on gender dynamics evolved during the 1870s. In 1871, he criticized the factory system for disrupting traditional gender roles. "Today, a woman is torn from the family," he wrote, forced to become a wage earner "instead of dedicating herself to her natural, noble, and sublime vocation of child-rearing and running an orderly household."[98] Four years later, he questioned, "Why should men do less and women more within the family." Confining women to domestic duties, he argued, amounts to "family tyranny." He advocated for a more equitable partnership where both genders shared the benefits of labor. He foresaw technological advancements liberating women from household chores and envisioned day-care centers alleviating the burden of child-rearing.[99] Most criticized his colleagues for internalizing bourgeois ideals that confined women to menial and unfulfilling tasks, insisting that such practices had no place in a socialist society. He warned that perpetuating gendered domestic roles could lead men to assert special privileges, undermining the socialist vision.[100] Despite his personal struggles, he envisioned relationships built on "real affection and mutual respect" without a "servant of the state or heaven getting involved."[101]

* * *

On May 11, 1878, a twenty-one-year-old plumber named Max Hödel fired two shots at Emperor Wilhelm I while the latter was seated in an open carriage in downtown Berlin. Fortunately, no one was injured, and Hödel was swiftly apprehended. During the investigation, authorities found photographs of prominent socialists—Liebknecht, Bebel, and Most—in Hödel's possession, along with a membership card for the Association for the Protection of the Interests of Working People in Berlin and a pamphlet from Stöcker's social reform party.[102] Socialists quickly condemned the attack, calling Hödel a "lunatic" who had been expelled from the party shortly before the incident.[103] Records show that Hödel had been involved in the socialist movement as a newspaper peddler from 1875 to 1877 and had attended lectures by Liebknecht. By early 1878, he was in contact with Werner and Reinsdorf, who were known for their recruitment efforts for the anarchist cause. It remains unclear, however, to what extent Werner may have influenced Hödel's assassination attempt.[104] Nevertheless, Bismarck seized on Hödel's brief association with socialists to push for a harsh anti-socialist "attentat bill." Although the measure ultimately failed, it allowed Bismarck to blame lawmakers for any further political violence.[105] Meanwhile, Most was arrested again for discussing the Hödel affair and, along with his previous convictions, faced a total of five months in prison.[106] While in custody, he learned of a second assassination attempt on June 2, carried out by Karl Nobiling, a thirty-year-old office worker who seriously wounded the emperor with a shotgun. Although Nobiling admitted to attending socialist lectures, he adamantly denied being part of any socialist conspiracy. Nonetheless, politicians used this second attempt to discredit the socialist movement as a whole.[107]

In the weeks that followed, a red scare swept across Germany. Most's residence, where Clara and Melita lived, was thoroughly searched by authorities. During the raid on the offices of the *Berliner Freie Presse*, police confiscated numerous documents, including Most's correspondence and subscription lists. By early July, Most was secretly transferred from a prison in Chemnitz back to Plötzensee to begin his five-month sentence. Despite the grim circumstances, Most remained resilient.[108] Socialist Philipp Wiemer noted that Most's humor remained intact and that he saw the red scare as a potential catalyst for purifying and strengthening the labor movement. "The efforts by police to destroy socialist aspirations," he assured Wiemer, "are futile."[109] Meanwhile, Bismarck pressured the upper house to dissolve the Reichstag and called for fresh elections, favoring the reactionary faction.[110]

On October 19, 1878, the Reichstag passed a Law against the Publicly Dangerous Endeavors of Social Democracy, commonly known as the Anti-Socialist Law. This legislation took effect just three days later, causing alarm and despair among socialist activists. The law posed a significant threat to the grassroots movement. It outlawed any association attempting "to overthrow existing political or social order through social-democratic, socialistic, or communistic endeavors" was outlawed. Police were granted authority to disband gatherings, processions, or public events suspected of promoting such aims. All socialist newspapers, whether published domestically or abroad, were banned, and authorities were empowered to seize printing equipment. Distributing banned publications carried penalties of fines or imprisonment, although mere subscription was not criminalized. Additionally, fundraising or providing meeting spaces for organizations seeking to overthrow the political and social order was forbidden. Local authorities could declare a "minor state of siege" when public safety was threatened by individuals considered "dangerous," who could then be expelled from their residence.[111] Notably, the nine socialist deputies in the Reichstag, known as the party faction, retained their seats under the law, and individuals could still run for office on a socialist ticket. In response to the imminent threat of expulsion or imprisonment, the Socialist Party's executive committee dissolved the party two days before the Anti-Socialist Law went into effect. The socialist deputies in the Reichstag, now serving as the de facto leadership, signaled compliance with the law, as did the editors of *Vorwärts* (Liebknecht and Wilhelm Hasenclever). This strategy of acquiescence was aimed at preventing socialism's total destruction and to portray Bismarck's law as an excessive measure that would eventually backfire. Liebknecht confidently predicted that within three months, the law would be seen as "Bismarck's greatest stupidity."[112] However, many rank-and-file members were unaware of this strategy. To them, it became clear that the law aimed not only to suppress socialism but also to dismantle the entire German labor movement.[113]

The final months of 1878 were especially challenging for Most. He lost his job when the *Berliner Freie Presse* was shut down, and all his pamphlets were banned and removed from circulation. For a decade, he had devoted his energy to socialist journalism and organizational activities, the very foundations that were now being systematically dismantled. Speculation arose that Most might seek refuge in the United States after his release.[114] Tragedy struck on November 25 when he received the heartbreaking news of the death of his six-month-old daughter, Melita.[115] He was finally released on December 9, but by then, Berlin had declared a minor state of siege, resulting in the expulsion of over sixty socialists. Most was given just twenty-four hours to leave the city.[116] With barely enough time to gather his belongings and bid farewell to Clara and his comrades, he boarded a train to Hamburg by eleven that night. In Hamburg, the atmosphere among socialists was one of uncertainty and resentment.[117] News of Most's arrival sparked anxiety among his comrades, as another court had just sentenced him to six months' imprisonment.[118] There were concerns that his presence in Hamburg might provoke local authorities to impose a minor state of siege. The Berlin police president had already informed his Hamburg counterpart that Most was "one of the most fanatical and most outstanding leaders of the Social Democratic Party with formidable influence over the masses as an orator, who invariably represents the most extreme line."[119] Shunned by colleagues, facing a lack of job prospects, and evading the law, Most saw no alternative but to leave Germany. "When I was chased out of Plötzensee and Berlin," he wrote to Georg von Vollmar, "people in Hamburg avoided me so as not to compromise themselves. They were determined to push me away to America at once."[120] Using an alias, Most sailed for England sometime between December 11 and 22.

5 Exile in London

THE RECENT TUMULTUOUS EVENTS THAT "sent [him] off to London by
storm and weather—literally and morally" had a profound impact on the
thirty-two-year-old Johann Most.[1] In just three months, he faced the heart-
break of losing a child, his job, his Berlin apartment, and a crucial subscription list. To make matters worse, his relationship with Clara and many of
his party comrades grew increasingly strained. Twenty-four party leaders,
including longtime comrades like Ignaz Auer, issued a statement urging
members to comply with the law and avoid violence, warning of severe consequences if anyone misstepped and "gave the reaction a justification for their
violence."[2] Most was incredulous that the executive committee had capitu-
lated without a fight, especially when he believed resistance was imperative.
He was determined to champion the socialist cause with the same fervor
he had shown in Austria in 1869 when the movement defiantly confronted
government repression.

Possibly on December 18, Most arrived in London and reunited with his
friend and fellow socialist Franz Josef Ehrhart, whom he had known since 1871.[3]
Ehrhart, who had left Germany a year earlier, was serving as secretary of the
Communistischer Arbeiter-Bildungsverein (CABV, or Communist Workers'
Educational Association), the oldest German workingmen's association outside
Germany, located at 6 Rose Street near Soho Square (now Manette Street).[4]
"It was one of my most joyous surprises," Ehrhart recalled, "to find my dear
friend so unexpectedly in our clubhouse at lunchtime."[5] During their meeting,
Ehrhart proposed that Most become the editor of a new German-language
socialist weekly newspaper to be printed in London—an idea that had been in

discussion since June 1878.[6] Most readily accepted the offer. A seven-member press commission was formed to oversee the production of the weekly newspaper, named *Freiheit* (Freedom), which featuring four pages and four columns. The inaugural issue was scheduled for publication on January 3, 1879.[7] Among the members of the commission was Johann Christoph Neve, a cabinetmaker who had lived in Paris and the United States. Neve, who became Most's closest associate and lifelong friend, "devoted all his energy to the administration of *Freiheit*."[8] The mission of *Freiheit* was to "independently illuminate the most important events of state and society from a radical point of view and discuss republican and socialist principles in larger essays."[9] Most settled into two garret rooms at 22 Percy Street, just off Tottenham Court Road, while the second floor served as the editorial office and meeting room.[10] Clara Hänsch joined Most in London sometime in the second week of January.[11] To supplement their income, Most opened a "school of oratory."[12]

Initially, *Freiheit*'s subscribers, estimated at around a thousand, were primarily Germans living in Britain, France, Belgium, and Switzerland.[13] The ultimate goal was to expand the paper's influence into Germany and Austria despite the bans in those countries. Achieving this was a significant challenge and required ingenuity, discretion, and courage. Sending the newspaper by mail was risky, and German secret agents were dispatched to London to surveil and potentially infiltrate the CABV and the *Freiheit* office. Most's English tutor, Heinrich Sachs, was revealed to be a spy, providing the majority of intelligence on Most's activities.[14] "Since Most took over the reins," reported one spy, "the CABV has become livelier than ever. [He] is the soul of it all, editor of '*Freiheit*' and permanent speaker at all major gatherings."[15] To circumvent the obstacles, the distribution of *Freiheit* was meticulously planned. With Most's old subscription list confiscated, the newspaper was shipped in bulk to trusted addressees, who were instructed to find additional readers and rebuild the mailing list. Most used fake titles like "Bismarck" or "Tessendorff" to evade detection by German authorities.[16] However, port cities like Hamburg were targeted by law enforcement, leading to occasional package interceptions and arrests.[17] Another strategy involved sending packets to border locations in the Netherlands, Belgium, or France, with individuals carrying them across the border, albeit with inherent risks. Despite the challenges, the smuggling operation was largely successful, prompting frustration from the Berlin police chief: "Most keeps finding ways to get it across the border from various points and in an inconspicuous manner."[18] At one point, Otto von Bismarck pressured the British government to act against Most, leading Scotland Yard to share intelligence on his activities.[19]

Amid these developments, socialist leaders in Germany expressed disapproval of launching a new periodical outside their control, fearing that authorities could use *Freiheit* and any perceived incendiary language as justification to tighten repression at home. Consequently, socialist deputies urged members not to support foreign papers. However, Most argued that the time called for defiance against censorship, leading to a year-and-a-half-long intraparty dispute over tactics and ideology, ultimately resulting in a permanent rupture. In subsequent years, party leaders such as August Bebel and Franz Mehring accused Most of founding *Freiheit* without consulting the party leadership despite the executive committee's dissolution.[20] However, records indicate that at the time, figures like Wilhelm Liebknecht, Karl Marx, and Friedrich Engels recognized the necessity of a socialist paper abroad. Marx and Engels even subscribed to *Freiheit* without raising objections when it was published.[21] After nine issues, Engels reported to Liebknecht that *Freiheit* "seems to be going well. . . . Of course we wish him [Most] good luck."[22] Another criticism, often made in hindsight, was that the paper's tone and content were inappropriate and dangerous. However, Most's editorial style during the first year of *Freiheit* mirrored that of his time at the *Berliner Freie Presse*, which had been widely read by party leaders.[23] Nonetheless, personal animosities and power struggles played a central role in the leadership's opposition to *Freiheit*. Some viewed it as another of Most's impractical ventures, akin to his 1878 leave-your-church campaign, which some socialists believed had contributed to support for anti-socialist legislation. The fact that the rank-and-file consistently saw Most as one of the most effective advocates for socialism likely added to the irritation among his colleagues.

In March 1879, during a speech to the Reichstag, Liebknecht distanced himself from Most, referring to him as a "former colleague" and asserting that social democracy had nothing to do with him. "Many influential party members," he continued, "have vigorously disapproved of the founding of newspapers abroad by German party members." He further assured lawmakers that the Socialist Party was strictly reformist: "I most emphatically deny that our efforts are aimed at overturning the existing state and social order."[24] In response, the CABV released a manifesto advocating for propaganda efforts from abroad and "secret agitation" within Germany rather than compliance with a legislative system that had recently outlawed socialism. "What is needed," the Londoners proclaimed, "is not a tactic of prudence under the Anti-Socialist Law but one of cunning against it."[25] The manifesto garnered support from exile socialists in Brussels and Paris.[26] Most rejected Liebknecht's binary view of socialist tactics—violence or compliance—and instead proposed continued agitation from abroad through smuggling as an illegal yet nonviolent alternative.[27] "If we're only allowed to fumble in the dark for ten years," he wrote to Georg von Vollmar, "how will workers retain even a vague idea about socialism?"[28] Most was baffled by the treatment he received from his colleagues and offered to step down as editor. However, some of his associates, including Andreas Scheu, who had taken refuge in Britain since 1874, encouraged him to stand firm. Scheu reminded Most of the freedom he enjoyed in London to express his views without the constraints imposed by Bismarck's regime.[29]

* * *

The conduct of party leaders and the ongoing repression in Germany led Most to adopt a social-revolutionary stance in the late spring of 1879, a sentiment increasingly shared by socialists across Europe. Many began to doubt the viability of achieving change within the legal and institutional frameworks of conservative monarchical states. Incremental reforms through parliamentary channels no longer seemed capable of delivering true liberation; instead, they appeared as distractions that benefited the bourgeois class.[30] Isolated from mainstream party activities and immersed in the diverse intellectual environment of London, Most explored alternative strategies beyond parliamentary tactics. His shift toward social-revolutionary politics found support from Russian exiles, who shared their experiences of resisting oppression under one of Europe's most repressive regimes. Faced with such conditions, extreme underground methods emerged as the only viable option for advocates of radical change, sparking a wave of revolutionary terrorism that shook the country. In January 1878, there was an attempt on the life of the harsh governor of St. Petersburg, and six months later, the chief of Russia's secret police was assassinated. In April, Alexander Soloviev made a failed attempt to assassinate the czar. These tactics were then adopted by Narodnaia Volia (The People's Will), an organization founded in October 1879. Most drew inspiration from the actions of Russian radicals who refused to submit to repression. Undercover agents reported that Most had been connected to Russian "nihilists" even before he arrived in London.[31] With no Russian-language socialist publication in London during the late 1870s and early 1880s, *Freiheit* occupied a unique position, serving as a platform for various international revolutionary movements.[32] In the German context, Most proposed sustaining socialist agitation through a network of decentralized groups, believing that the autocratic regimes in Germany and Russia could be "unhinged only by a revolutionary act."[33] He argued that socialists had the right to defend themselves: "What could be more natural," he wrote in October 1879, "than the conviction that no other salvation is possible here than through violence."[34] Rejecting the notion of waiting for a majority to embrace revolutionary ideals, Most asserted that a committed minority could lead the way for change. In response to accusations of terrorism, he highlighted the true perpetrators of terror—the powerful and oppressive forces that enforced draconian discipline and subjected millions to slavery and brutality throughout history.[35]

Exiled French Communards also contributed to the discussions on revolutionary tactics within London's vibrant network of pubs and eateries. "The cafés are quite unlike the ordinary London tea- or coffee-shop," wrote Howard Wheeler. "They usually begin to get busy in the late hours of the evening. . . . Men and women of every nationality sit at little tables talking and drinking coffee. They rarely seem to eat."[36] To immerse himself in these discussions and absorb new ideas, Most chose to frequent Audinet's restaurant on Charlotte Street rather than the CABV clubhouse. This establishment, run by the Belgian widow Elizabeth Audinet and her two sons, served as a gathering place for French Communards and other radicals. It was here that Most reconnected with an old acquaintance, the revolutionary physician Édouard Vaillant, whom he had befriended during his time in Vienna in 1869 alongside Scheu.[37] During the Paris Commune, Vaillant had embraced the teachings of Auguste Blanqui but was later forced to seek refuge in England, where he crossed paths with Marx. Vaillant advocated for a working-class movement that rejected all bourgeois parties and candidates, even those considered progressive. His studies in Germany had given him proficiency in the language and a nuanced understanding of German politics.[38] By May 1879, Vaillant expressed his satisfaction in a letter to Scheu, noting that Most had distanced himself from parliamentary politics. The correspondence between Most and Vaillant remained frequent, reflecting their shared commitment to revolutionary ideals.

During the summer of 1879, Most traveled to Paris and Brussels to rally German exile socialists to support revolutionary resistance and increase *Freiheit* subscriptions. In Paris, his comrades resolved to align themselves with *Freiheit*'s stance on party strategy.[39] However, his trip to Belgium encountered unexpected obstacles. Despite Franz Ehrhart's efforts to organize lectures for Most, he was arrested upon arrival. Authorities promptly escorted him onto a train bound for the seaside town of Ostend and then put him on a boat back to England. These expulsions sparked widespread condemnation, not only from Belgian socialists but also from most liberal newspapers, which argued that such actions tarnished Belgium's reputation as a tolerant nation.[40] The growing support for *Freiheit* came at a crucial time, as socialist leaders launched *Der Sozialdemokrat* in Zurich in the fall of 1879 to compete for the allegiance of German workers both at home and abroad. Bebel candidly remarked that *Sozialdemokrat* would serve as "an appropriate weapon against Most," though he also suggested that it might be more prudent to "fashionably ignore" *Freiheit* rather than directly confront it.[41] In Berlin, *Freiheit* did experience a decline in influence compared with *Sozialdemokrat*, largely due to Most's favorable portrayal of Max Hödel and Karl Nobiling.[42]

The arrival of Leo Hartmann and Victor Dave in London in March 1880 further enriched Most's philosophical and political circle. Hartmann, who spoke German, was a Russian revolutionary and member of Narodnaia Volia's executive committee, involved in a failed attempt on the czar's life. After fleeing to France, he was arrested and expelled before finding refuge in London.[43] Most also formed connections with Russian Jewish socialists like Aaron Lieberman, who had undergone radicalization through their transnational experiences.[44] Dave, a Belgian anarchist editor and journalist, arrived in London along with sixteen German revolutionaries following their expulsion from France. With a background in philosophy and history, Dave had

Figure 5. Victor Dave in Paris. Courtesy of International Institute of Social History, Amsterdam.

been active in radical and free-thought circles, notably within the Belgian sections of the International Workingmen's Association (IWA) from 1868 to 1873. Energetic and erudite, Dave had a talent for presenting social questions clearly.[45] He played a key role in the early anarchist movement, delivering the declaration of the minority against Marx and the "centralists" at the fifth congress of the IWA in The Hague in 1872. This statement asserted the "principles of federative autonomy as the basis of the organization of labour."

Dave further immersed himself in the anarchist movement when he met Mikhail Bakunin at the subsequent congress in Geneva. Dave and Most's paths crossed in Paris in 1880, leading to a close friendship grounded in their shared interests in history, philosophy, free thought, and the labor movement.[46] Despite Most's limited access to reliable information on anarchism, Dave became an invaluable mentor outside the German movement, offering insight into Bakuninist or collectivist anarchism.[47] However, there was little time for study; together with Neve, they focused their efforts on expanding *Freiheit's* influence in German-speaking Europe.[48]

* * *

In 1880, the ongoing debate within the socialist movement over tactics— whether to pursue revolutionary resistance or parliamentary reform—evolved into a significant philosophical rift, with Most emerging as a central figure. In an open letter to his estranged Berlin constituents in May 1880, he boldly declared, "Modern society can no longer be improved; it must be overthrown." He continued, "My solution is down with the throne, down with the altar, down with the moneybag." At this point, Most had not yet fully embraced anarchism. While he still supported the objectives of social democracy, including the concept of a "red republic," he no longer endorsed conventional means to achieve them.[49] Most's new outlook was well received by *Freiheit's* publishing committee and the majority of the CABV, as demonstrated by their overwhelming support for renewing his contract and the Paris comrades' endorsement of the new principles.[50] Drawing inspiration from the revolutionary traditions of France and Russia, Most rooted his vision in the belief that the Paris Commune represented the "fighting form of the social revolution." He argued that a society upheld by violence must be overthrown by force.[51] In May 1880, the socialist MP Wilhelm Hasselmann stunned his colleagues by declaring himself a social revolutionary and voicing support for the Russian anarchists. "The time for parliamentary chatter has passed," he proclaimed, "and the time for deeds begins."[52] During the same Reichstag session, lawmakers extended the Anti-Socialist Law for several years. Hasselmann eventually departed for New York in September 1880 but maintained his connection with *Freiheit*, occasionally sending reports for publication.[53]

Amid the internal strife, the socialist leadership devised a strategy to distance themselves from Most and Hasselmann. While Hasselmann faced expulsion from the party, dealing with Most proved more complicated due to his considerable international support.[54] Led by Bebel, the plan aimed to confront Most directly during a party congress scheduled for May 16, 1880, in Rorschach, Switzerland. "Most knew nothing of our staging of the matter," wrote Julius Motteler, another party leader. "It was important to us to have him at the congress and bring him to his senses."[55] Most agreed to attend and traveled to Switzerland, only to find that the congress had been abruptly canceled due to security concerns. Bebel later claimed that there had not been enough time to notify delegates, particularly those traveling from afar—a claim historian Frank Harreck-Haase has challenged. Most, however, argued that the real motive behind the cancellation was the party leaders' realization that up to thirty radical, pro-Most delegates were expected to attend, making it difficult to secure a consensus against him.[56] Instead of returning to London, Most took the opportunity to engage with Swiss workers and promote *Freiheit*.[57] In Fribourg, he joined forces with August Reinsdorf, who promised to assist in distributing *Freiheit* and contribute original articles to the publication.[58]

The party leadership hastily organized a new meeting to publicly reprimand Most before his return to London. Eduard Bernstein and Julius Dolinski, both former colleagues, persuaded him to attend an open gathering on May 17 in Zurich, presented as a tribunal. Most anticipated a constructive "exchange of ideas," but upon entering, he faced a hostile crowd of 250 people demanding evidence for his accusations against party leaders.[59] Notably, three individuals identified as "oppositional" were forcibly removed by the organizers. After enduring minutes of verbal abuse, Most defended himself without backing down. Eventually, a resolution was passed, threatening "excommunication" if *Freiheit* continued its revolutionary rhetoric and polemical stance. Motteler, who launched personal attacks against Most, later recalled that Most stood "deathly pale and with water in his eyes."[60] What made the experience particularly painful was that several of the interrogators had once been close colleagues in Vienna and Berlin. This dramatic confrontation marked an irreparable rupture between Most and social democracy. "Ties were severed, and any settlement would be in vain," concluded historian Harreck-Haase.[61]

This rift also extended to the CABV in London, which oversaw the publication of *Freiheit*. According to Most, a minority faction within the CABV, loyal to *Sozialdemokrat* and led by Heinrich Rackow and Wilhelm Wentker, initiated a systematic campaign against *Freiheit*. Their efforts included failed attempts to seize *Freiheit*'s subscriber list and account books. Rackow even went as far to establish a separate section within the CABV to serve as a platform for anti-*Freiheit* agitation. He also published his version of events in *Sozialdemokrat*, falsely claiming that two weeks after the Zurich meeting, Most and party leaders had agreed to a "truce" and would cease all hostilities.[62] Most vehemently denied this, dismissing the story as a fabrication intended to portray him as a "malicious disturber of the peace."[63] Reports from police agents suggest that Most formed a clandestine League of Propagandists (*Propagandistenbund*), consisting of around twenty members, to promote revolution through international agitation. The plan involved setting up sections in various countries, with representatives convening in a central committee to coordinate theory and practice. The report concluded that Most's ongoing efforts, and any further successes, would "have to be subjected to careful observation."[64]

On August 22, 1880, Most and Hasselmann were expelled in absentia from the German Socialist Labor Party during a congress held at Wyden Castle near Ossingen, Switzerland. The congress excluded exile groups believed to be sympathetic to the social-revolutionary faction, allowing only delegates "living in Germany" to participate in the vote.[65] Most was accused of launching *Freiheit* without consulting party leaders, though several delegates acknowledged the contentious nature of this accusation.[66] The motion to expel, introduced by Bernstein, also included a baseless and unnecessary allegation that Most had "encouraged" police agents. In response to his expulsion, Most released a scathing pamphlet outlining his vision for social revolution, which garnered considerable support during his lecture circuit appearances.[67] His expulsion from the party, coupled with his eventual adoption of anarchism, led some historians of social democracy to reevaluate or discredit his role as the party's "unofficial publicist," as one biographer had described him.[68] For instance, in 1898, Mehring wrote that Most's "eccentric character" had caused trouble for the party even before the Anti-Socialist Law of 1878, impairing his "awareness of political responsibility."[69] More recently, Vernon Lidtke portrayed Most and Hasselmann as the primary troublemakers who were "intentionally disloyal to the party, slandered many respected leaders, and generally showed a total disregard for party discipline."[70] However, this assessment is one-sided and misleading. Heiner Becker's careful analysis shows that Most initially exercised restraint and did not instigate hostilities.[71] Most's departure from the Socialist Party coincided with another significant personal separation: his divorce from Clara Hänsch in the summer of 1880, after six tumultuous years of marriage. Becker suggests that the tipping point in their relationship occurred when Hänsch became involved with Wilhelm Wentker, a cofounder of the anti-*Freiheit* faction in London. Shortly after the divorce, Hänsch and Wentker married.[72] Most then moved out of the Percy Street residence and rented the front parlor of a house at 101 Great Titchfield Street, where he set up a backyard workshop as a printing and editorial office.[73] He also began a relationship with Marie Roth, a Swiss-born teacher.[74]

* * *

Most's political evolution in London was so profound that one historian described it as a "paradigm shift."[75] He embraced the idea of immediate revolution, even if it required violence, prioritizing individual actions or revolutionary group endeavors over gradual, collective efforts to emancipate the working class. He began to view the state as an outdated and ineffectual entity.[76] His experience of exile played a pivotal role in this transformation, disconnecting him from the Austrian and German socialist movements that had once grounded him. "It was Most's misfortune of being chased out of his native land, the only one in which he was grounded," wrote Rudolf Rocker, "and then to develop his revolutionary effectiveness on foreign soil, where he never felt at home."[77] Historian Volker Szmula explained that exile altered Most's perspective by forcing him to express his dismay indirectly, given the absence of familiar reference points such as language and culture.[78] Most's new vision was eclectic, shaped by conversations with charismatic figures like Hartmann, Dave, Vaillant, and Reinsdorf, all of whom spoke German. He was not fully committed to anarchism, as Dave's influence was limited due to the immense task of delivering revolutionary propaganda into Germany. "It was not Most who was anarchistically influenced by Dave," observed Max Nettlau. "Rather it was Dave who adapted to the German social revolutionary movement, which seemed lively and energetic to him at the time."[79] However, Most did open *Freiheit* to anarchist ideas. In one instance, he added a footnote to an article by Reinsdorf, clarifying that the publishing committee did not endorse anarchism.[80] In September 1880, the paper published Sergei Nechaev's *Catechism of a Revolutionary*, mistakenly attributed as Bakunin's *Revolutionary Catechism*. Nettlau has argued that *Freiheit* did not express a coherent anarchist outlook at the time, but unfortunately, many of its German readers and the public believed that revolutionary terrorism equaled anarchism.[81]

Most and other social revolutionaries rallied around the principles of combative propaganda, secret organization, and exemplary revolutionary deeds, even if they involved violence. The concept of "propaganda by the deed" traces back to Italian anarchists of the 1870s who engaged in agrarian protests. Influenced by Bakunin, these Italians envisioned insurrection rather than political assassination. "Reinforcing socialist principles through deeds," wrote Errico Malatesta in 1876, "is the most effective means of propaganda." As the anarchist IWA disintegrated and state repression intensified in the late 1870s, "propaganda by the deed" took on a more urgent and encompassing character. By December 1880, another Italian anarchist, Carlo Cafiero, wrote, "Our actions must be a permanent revolt, in words and writing, with fists, guns, and bombs. . . . We will use any means to carry out insurrection."[82] Most was probably not yet familiar with these ideas, as the phrase "propaganda by the deed" rarely appeared in *Freiheit* in 1879 or 1880. He envisioned a Jacobin-style revolutionary army to "exterminate" bourgeois society and destroy "all existing instruments of 'order.'" He justified this approach by referencing the brutal tactics used by reactionary Versailles troops during the suppression of the 1871 Commune. Most was particularly drawn to Blanqui's concept of small groups of professional revolutionaries preparing the way for total transformation, although Dave opposed this idea.[83] Most proposed establishing a network of secret affinity groups or cells within Germany to distribute printed material and carry out Russian-style revolutionary deeds to inspire the masses. Many European revolutionaries drew inspiration from the radical struggle against the Russian czar, closely monitoring events in Russia where several attempts on the czar's life had occurred in recent years.[84]

In the midst of it all, the smuggling and distribution of *Freiheit* became increasingly costly and perilous. In March 1880, Germany's highest court declared the circulation of prohibited literature within closed groups illegal.[85] While a detailed examination of the distribution network is beyond the scope of this book, a brief overview highlights the challenges faced by radical exile editors. Key figures such as Neve and Theodor Eisenhauer constantly devised creative methods to smuggle literature across borders, from stuffing bundles of paper into tin cans or bamboo canes to sewing them inside garments.[86] Once inside Germany, a clandestine network ensured that the materials reached subscribers. However, the relative success of police infiltration and occasional oversights by Most are notable. Despite Rocker's dismissal of these missteps, police files reveal spies frequently outmaneuvered Most. Andrew Carlson observes, "By nature, Most was not a careful or cautious man," while historian Jürgen Jensen agrees that Most's lack of suspicion made him vulnerable to manipulation by spies.[87] In the autumn of 1880, a visibly shaken Most confided to Scheu over lunch that a subscription list had gone missing. Scheu reprimanded Most for leaving the Percy Street office unlocked, divulging too much information to strangers, and leaving correspondence on his desk. Both men suspected Oskar Neumann, a *Freiheit* distributor later exposed as a spy.[88] Most urgently sent Dave to Germany to alert cell leaders about the security breach and arrange a meeting of group representatives in Darmstadt in December. However, their efforts proved futile. In December, police dealt a severe blow to *Freiheit* and the revolutionary movement by arresting forty-four cell members, including Dave, who was found carrying letters from Most and coded travel plans. Although the trial did not begin until October 1881, Dave and fourteen others were charged with treason. Two months later, police arrested fourteen socialists in Vienna for distributing illegal literature. Despite these setbacks, Neve remained undeterred, heading to Belgium to resume the smuggling operation.[89]

*　*　*

On March 13, 1881, European capitals were flooded with telegrams announcing the assassination of Czar Alexander II by revolutionaries in St. Petersburg. Although the act was widely condemned, the *Times* of London offered context, citing Russia's despotism and backwardness.[90] The paper editorialized, calling the assassination a "terrible illustration of the perils surrounding despotic authority," while noting the prevalence of political conspiracy and Russia's late entry into the "race of civilization."[91] Indeed, a significant portion of the British public despised Russian despotism. Historian Luke Kelly argued that in Britain, Russian terrorists were viewed as liberals operating under "exceptional circumstances." Michael Hughes, in his study of British public opinion, observed that many believed "the use of violence to bring about change in an autocratic political system was qualitatively different from resorting to terror in a constitutional system where other avenues for non-violent change were available."[92] Social-revolutionaries on both sides of the Atlantic celebrated. In New York, activists gathered in beer halls, unfurling a banner that read, "Sic Semper Tyrannis" (Thus always to tyrants). In London, Most delivered multiple speeches commemorating the Commune and praising the assassination of the czar.[93] He published a version of his speech titled "Endlich!" (At last) in the March 19 issue of *Freiheit*, bordered in red. In it, Most lauded the perpetrators, vividly describing the bloody scene and concluding, "At last, he died like a dog." He also warned the ruling classes that every successful act of resistance instilled respect and inspired imitation. "From Constantinople to Washington," he claimed, "they tremble for their long-since forfeited heads. This fright is a high enjoyment

for us." Most lamented that tyrannicide was too rare and proposed dispos-
ing of a "crowned wretch" every month.[94] The article sparked widespread
discussion among radicals, with some newspapers publishing translated
excerpts.[95] A week later, Charles Edward Marr, a middle-aged teacher of
modern languages who had lived in Russia and Germany, bought several
copies of *Freiheit*. Troubled by its contents, he sent one copy, likely with a
translation, to his MP, Lord George Hamilton, inquiring about possible legal
action against Most. Hamilton replied that the matter was under investigation following a foreign embassy's alert, which had prompted British police
to obtained a copy.[96]

On March 30, around three in the afternoon, Most was arrested at his
office by detectives from Scotland Yard, charged with "conspiring or solicit-
ing to commit murder" under section 4 of the Offenses against the Person
Act of 1861.[97] Bail was denied, and Most spent April and May in detention
awaiting trial. During this time, news outlets and some MPs criticized the
police for unlawfully confiscating composition materials, financial documents, photographs, and address lists, which were then secretly shared with
foreign powers in their campaign against dissidents.[98] Documents revealed
that the Home Office had allowed representatives from the courts of Berlin,
Vienna, and St. Petersburg to inspect these papers "so that they might take
such measures as they th[ou]ght fit to defeat these criminal plots."[99] In May,
it emerged that recent arrests in Vienna were linked to Most's detention in
London, as encrypted correspondence and a decoding key found among
Most's papers had been "transferred to the Vienna police authorities."[100] When
questioned in Parliament, Home Secretary William Harcourt denied these
reports, presenting a memo from the Austrian ambassador that claimed the
"arrests had not derived from the information given to the Austrian authorities from Most's paper."[101]

The trial at the Central Criminal Court began on May 25, 1881. Contributions for Most's legal defense came from the CABV and comrades in New
York.[102] Leading the defense was Alexander Martin Sullivan, an Irish MP who
had previously been imprisoned for publishing an incendiary article.[103] Sullivan's strategy was for Most to deny authorship of the unsigned article, but
Most refused to disavow his beliefs. He argued that putting an editor on trial
set a dangerous precedent and was an attack on freedom of the press. "This
charge is not meant for me alone," Most declared in court, "but is an attack on
the liberty of the press in England."[104] Confident that an English jury would
not convict him for writing a newspaper article, he maintained his stance.
Prosecutor Harry Poland countered, arguing that Most's article went beyond

Figure 6. "The 'Freiheit' Prosecution—Trial of Herr Most at the Central Criminal Court" in *The Graphic: An Illustrated Weekly Newspaper*, June 4, 1881. Most is seated at far left.

expressing opinions on assassinations; it incited others to commit such acts. He contended that this amounted to incitement to murder, punishable by up to ten years in prison.[105] Sullivan expressed concerns about the implications for the British press and argued that the law applied to actual conspiracies, not to a general newspaper article not directed at a specific individual. Despite Sullivan's appeals for leniency, citing Most's foreign status and lack of prior offenses, the jury returned a guilty verdict.[106] A higher court later upheld the verdict, sentencing Most to sixteen months of hard labor.[107] "We might as well be in Russia," Most lamented as he was led out of the courtroom.[108] Whereas some newspapers supported the guilty verdict, many criticized the "vindictive and outrageous" sentence.[109]

The British government's decision to proceed with the trial of a relatively obscure German immigrant editor like Most raises questions about their motivations.[110] While one might speculate that the trial aimed to uphold public morals, other factors likely influenced their decision.[111] Foreign powers, particularly Russia and Germany, may have pressured the British government to prosecute Most and his newspaper, *Freiheit*. This action sparked outrage among a significant portion of the British public, described by Bernard Porter as "popular radical patriotism." Many argued that if despotic regimes wanted to quell unrest, they should adopt more liberal policies instead of pressuring liberal England to prosecute foreign dissidents. "The venomous rubbish and bluster of the *Freiheit* will cease," editorialized the *Weekly Times*, "when Czars and Kaisers let a healthy public opinion grow."[112] Despite the Home Secretary's denials of foreign pressure, documents reveal otherwise, showing efforts to conceal such influences. A particularly incriminating letter from the German ambassador to the Foreign Secretary, dated March 21—just two days after the *Freiheit* article—expressed Germany's desire for Most's prosecution.[113] Porter has argued that one of the "chief motives behind the prosecution" was to avoid pressure by gaining favor and sympathy with foreign powers.[114] Additionally, Most's trial coincided with an unrelated bombing campaign against British government sites launched by Irish Republican revolutionaries, funded by Fenians in the United States, including Jeremiah O'Donovan Rossa. Between January and July 1881, seven bombs either detonated or were defused.[115] This situation presented a dilemma for Britain, which had historically resisted joining international efforts to suppress political opposition. It would be hypocritical for Britain, now facing revolutionary violence, to request that the American government act against the Fenians while refusing to prosecute *Freiheit*. Most's trial resolved this issue as shortly after his conviction, the British government formally requested that the Americans prosecute a Fenian publication. Home Secretary Harcourt privately believed that Most's conviction had positive implications "both at home and abroad."[116] Moreover, Most's trial marked the introduction of police surveillance of the radical community, a practice previously uncommon in Britain.[117]

*   *   *

On July 5, Most was transferred to Coldbath Fields prison, shackled as prisoner number 300.[118] His cell, while similar in size to those at Plötzensee, offered markedly different and harsher living conditions compared to his experience in Germany.[119] Prisoners only received full food rations after four months. During the first month, they slept on plain boards; in the second month, this discomfort was reduced to eight nights, and in the third month, to four. Most was allowed to send or receive one letter and meet visitors only once every three months. Much of the day was spent mending inmates' garments, a monotonous task. When not working, prisoners sat alone in their cells, and their single hour of daily courtyard "exercise" was conducted in complete silence. Most's appeals for better treatment went unanswered, as English prisons did not recognize the category of "political prisoner."

Although there was a prison library, the *Freiheit* Defense Committee's efforts to send him books and newspapers failed. When supporters proposed petitioning the government for a reduced sentence, Most firmly opposed the idea.[120] Two months into his sentence, a journalist reported that Most was "comparatively cheerful, and was in fairly good health, but complained about having access only to religious tracts and being denied the use of pen and paper."[121]

Despite the prosecution's attempts to silence *Freiheit*, the determination and sacrifices of the social-revolutionary members of the CABV's Section I ensured the paper's survival in Most's absence. Frank Kitz and Neve established the *Freiheit* Defense Committee, and both visited Most in prison.[122] The English Section of the CABV, formed in 1877 by Kitz, played a crucial role in organizing support. Members like Joseph Lane and John Lord raised funds for Most's legal defense. In New York, Justus Schwab, a radical saloonkeeper and friend of Neve, sent $200 to keep the paper running.[123] The committee even produced seven English-language issues between late April and early June with the subtitle *A Journal for the Diffusion of Socialistic Knowledge amongst the People*. Subscriptions surged as activists from various backgrounds rallied for press freedom and protested against illegal police confiscations. However, without Most's prolific writing, the issues published by the Defense Committee lacked the same intensity and militancy. An undercover agent noted, "The editorial committee has neither Most's energy nor skillfulness and imagination."[124] Neve reached out to Josef Peukert, an Austrian radical and longtime supporter of *Freiheit*, asking him to contribute articles. However, Peukert, still holding a grudge from past rejections, refused to write for Most again.[125] Despite these challenges, Most found ways to write articles using chalk, toilet paper, and a sewing needle as a pen, even bribing guards to smuggle these fragments out of prison. According to some, including Rocker, Most may have authored the entire March 18, 1882 issue through these clandestine efforts.[126]

Nine days after Most's imprisonment, forty-five delegates convened in Cleveland Hall near Fitzroy Square for an International Social-Revolutionary and Anarchist Congress from July 14 to 20.[127] The idea for such a gathering had been proposed by Belgian social revolutionaries in 1880 and actively promoted by Most, who had established connections with Russian, French, and Italian exiles.[128] The primary objective was to unite social revolutionaries and discuss revolutionary tactics and organization. For six days, some of the most prominent figures in European revolutionary politics gathered under one roof, including Peter Kropotkin, Malatesta, Louise Michel, Emile Gautier, Peukert, Saverio Merlino, Nikolai Tchaikovsky, Neve, and Gustave Brocher.

The only notable absence was John Most, though delegates like Neve, Kitz, and Sebastian Trunk kept him informed. Among the discussion topics, insurrectionary methods and the use of chemistry gained widespread support. However, disagreements arose over tactics, with figures such as Kropotkin objecting to indiscriminate violence. Despite these differences, delegates agreed to revive the International Working People's Association, adopting federalist principles. Meanwhile, in Chicago, revolutionary groups founded the Revolutionary Socialist Party, which advocated for a dual strategy of anti-parliamentarism and revolutionary unionism.[129]

In the wake of the London congress, *Freiheit* faced several significant setbacks. In September 1881, Reinsdorf was arrested in Munich and sentenced to four and a half months in prison. Disruptions to *Freiheit*'s distribution network had already begun the previous year with the arrest of key operators like Dave, Max Metzkow, and Joseph Breuder. Following their convictions and sentences at the Leipzig treason trial, the network suffered a severe blow. All but four of the defendants received sentences of at least two years in prison, with Dave sentenced to two and a half years.[130] The network never fully regained its strength or reach. Andrew Carlson estimates that no more than fifty cells, with a combined membership of about three hundred, remained operational for the next decade. Interestingly, police allowed these cells to continue operating to gather intelligence.[131] In May 1882, after the murders of Lord Frederick Cavendish and Undersecretary Thomas Henry Burke in Dublin's Phoenix Park by Irish nationalists, *Freiheit* published an unsigned article (written by Karl Schneidt) in support of the assassins. In response, the paper's compositors, William Merten and Friedrich Schwelm, were swiftly arrested, tried, and sentenced. Police once again resorted to illegally confiscating composition materials to prevent further production.[132] With publishing *Freiheit* in England and distributing it across the continent becoming increasingly difficult, Most faced a dire situation. As a temporary solution in June 1882, Neve and the Defense Committee secretly arranged with Hermann Stellmacher and Karl Schröder (later exposed as a police spy) to print eight issues, with two thousand copies each, in Switzerland.[133]

On October 25, 1882, John Most was released from prison, one day ahead of schedule to prevent potential disturbances. Radical groups in Europe and the United States had already extended invitations to support his revolutionary mission.[134] However, since his expulsion from Belgium, France, Austria, and Germany, Most found Europe increasingly restrictive. With limited options available, he considered three possible paths forward. The first was to accept an invitation from the New York Social-Revolutionary Club to embark on a lecture tour across America.[135] The second was to relocate to Zurich, where revolutionary action still seemed possible. However, this plan was complicated by the dismissal of Stellmacher from the *Freiheit* team amid accusations of self-dealing.[136] A third and least favorable option was to remain in London. Even his closest associate, Neve, had fled to Paris, and the typesetting materials for *Freiheit* were locked away in a police station. When Most eventually recovered the materials after repeated requests, he found them damaged and unusable.[137] Ultimately, Most decided that a lecture tour in America presented the best opportunity to gather resources to sustain *Freiheit* and eventually return to England. Schwab agreed to produce the paper in New York while Most was in transit.[138] Most then purchased a second-class ticket on the steamer *Wisconsin* of the Guion Line. As he bade farewell to London, he gave a speech reflecting on four years of struggle and promised to return after three months in America. "I have agreed to return to England," he told an American reporter one week after his arrival, "and I intend to keep my word."[139]

On December 2, 1882, Most, listed as "Moest" and identified as a "traveler," boarded the *Wisconsin* as one of thirty-one intermediate passengers, primarily English and Americans. The ship made a brief stop at Queenstown (now Cobh) in southern Ireland the next day to pick up additional passengers, bringing the total to 144 men, women, and children. Most was the sole German passenger aboard. During the fifteen-day journey, he befriended K. Minami, a thirty-year-old Japanese man traveling to Japan via the United States. However, he found the other passengers "too pious or too closed off" for meaningful interaction. The only respite from the monotony came during the daily musical sessions performed by members of the Salvation Army.[140] While Most was at sea, Clara Francisca Wentker passed away in London.[141]

6　Sturm und Drang

IN THE EARLY MORNING DARKNESS of December 14, 1882, about 250 miles from New York, the steamer *Wisconsin* collided with a bark, causing a jolt that alarmed passengers. Although the bark was eventually repaired, the accident and rough seas caused significant delays.[1] Finally, on December 18, at nine in the morning, with temperatures below freezing, passengers disembarked onto Pier 38 at the foot of King Street in Manhattan. Among them was John Most, wrapped in a blanket and wearing a Derby hat, greeted by a group of about a dozen men, including Justus Schwab, Joseph Kayser, Edmond Mégy, and Victor Drury. Most told a reporter that he planned to embark on a lecture tour of major cities to spread socialism among American workers.[2] A welcome gathering was scheduled for that evening at the Great Hall of Cooper Union. Before the event, Most visited Liberty Hall at 50 First Street on Manhattan's Lower East Side—a small beer hall operated by Schwab that was a popular meeting spot for revolutionaries. Schwab, a mason by trade, had immigrated to America in 1869, joined the German Workingmen's Association, and befriended French radicals Mégy and Drury.[3] Known for his robust demeanor and booming voice, Schwab had a colorful past; he had been arrested for inciting a riot and waving a red flag during a Tompkins Square demonstration in January 1874. The following year, he married and opened a beer hall on Clinton Street, later moving it to 50 First Street, where in 1880, it served the American branch office of *Freiheit*.[4] Schwab, a prominent member of the Socialist Labor Party's (SLP's) New York section, had challenged the party's reformist strategy alongside Moritz Bachmann. Together, they advocated for a decentralized structure to empower the rank and file, but the party expelled dozens of members who then formed the Sozial-Revolutionäre Klub (Social-Revolutionary Club of New York) in November 1880, the first anarchistic organization in the United States. This club supported *Freiheit* and affiliated with the Anarchist International formed at the London congress.

By eight that evening, the chilly basement hall of Cooper Union was filled with some five thousand men, women, and children, eagerly awaiting the appearance of the celebrated editor of *Freiheit*. Hundreds more had to be turned away. Notably, many women occupied seats near the stage, with one even sitting on the platform cradling an infant on a pillow. Edward King of the Central Labor Union presided over the event, introducing John Most, who was seated in an armchair on the platform, as a true "cosmopolitan victim." Victor Drury, a veteran labor activist, hailed *Freiheit's* relocation to New York as a victory over the British government. When Most rose to speak, the audience strained to catch sight of the unassuming man with spiky hair, dressed in gray trousers, a Prince Albert frock coat, square-toed boots, a scarf around his neck, and a red rose pinned to his lapel. He apologized for his broken English before switching to German and began his address by affirming his commitment to the principle of social revolution. Striking an optimistic tone about the prospects of revolution in Europe, he emphasized the responsibility of individuals to be prepared. Most argued that the great powers of Europe were hesitant to initiate another war, fearing that socialists would seize the opportunity to incite a social revolution. He predicted that militarism would eventually bankrupt Europe, asserting that the spirit of revolution had already taken root among the oppressed masses, who were only waiting for the signal to overthrow the old order.[5]

The Cooper Union meeting concluded with three resolutions recognizing Most as "the fearless representative and apostle of anarchism" and pledging support for his "mission to revolutionize the people of the United States."[6] Even before leaving England, Most had written, "It is anarchism that makes the world tremble."[7] He had abandoned the idea of a "people's state" and the peaceful means to achieve it, embracing Bakuninist anarchism instead. This ideology envisioned a federated network of autonomous consumer and producer associations and other communes based on solidarity and respect for individual freedom. He described a state as "a circle with a strongly marked center around which numerous smaller circles (communes) are grouped and, as it were, coupled to one another." An anarchist society, he suggested, would resemble "a network whose threads crisscross in all imaginable directions, forming a thousand nodes."[8] Following both Karl Marx and Mikhail Bakunin, Most advocated a labor theory of value, proposing that the unit of value would be determined by measuring the "hourly necessary labor embodied in a commodity" to prevent fraud.[9] This stance contrasted with Peter Kropotkin's communist anarchism, which argued for distributing the fruits of labor according to need—an idea Most ridiculed at the time.[10] However, during the early 1880s, Most focused on tactics more than theory.

As he would later discover, the revolutionary struggle in the United States was different from that in Europe. After the upheaval of the Civil War, the nation expanded commercially, industrially, and geographically, reaching continental proportions. Despite a wave of postwar nationalism, divisions along class, racial, and regional lines persisted. The benefits and burdens of expansion were unevenly distributed. Most recognized that the American socialist movement was primarily composed of German and French immigrants, echoing the division between social democrats and social revolutionaries he had seen in Europe. However, he did not fully grasp that the origins of a social revolutionary movement in Europe differed from those in North America. In Europe, state repression and debates over appropriate responses had led to the emergence of a radical faction. In contrast, in the United States, where a secret police force was absent, it was the conversation around capitalist-driven violence and political corruption that led radicals to break away from the Socialist Party. During the depression of the 1870s, widespread labor unrest radicalized many socialists in New York and Chicago, prompting them to establish self-defense groups known as Lehr-und-Wehr Vereine (Educational and Defense Associations), much to the dismay of party leaders. Tensions further escalated during the 1880 presidential election year. When socialist leaders sought cooperation with the middle-class Greenback movement, trade unionists and other radicals rejected electoral politics outright. The exclusion of the only socialist council member by Chicago Democrats further eroded faith in the ballot box among Chicago socialists. Radicals also accused party leadership of disregarding the autonomy of local chapters, sparking what historian Paul Avrich termed a "secessionist movement."[11] A minor regional divide emerged between Chicago and East Coast radicals. In Chicago, figures like Albert Parsons and August Spies advocated for revolutionary unionism, viewing labor unions as the foundation for a new society. Both came from middle-class backgrounds and became editors and labor activists—Parsons, originally from Alabama, had been orphaned at a young age and fought in the Civil War, while Spies, born in Hesse, had immigrated in 1872 and became an upholsterer. On the East Coast, radicals like Schwab and eventually Most distrusted labor unions, focusing instead on small groups and insurrectionary actions.

Most's highly anticipated lecture tour commenced on December 22, 1882, marking his most extensive effort yet. The initial leg from New York to Chicago covered a distance equivalent to that from Hamburg to Munich. Chicago, a booming industrial city and a center of socialist activity, was where he stayed with Dr. Ernst Schmidt, a former socialist mayoral candidate, Civil War veteran, esteemed physician, and staunch supporter of the socialist cause.[12] Most delivered three lectures, each attracting thousands, held in various Turner (gymnastics) halls across the German district.[13] Confident in the proletariat's readiness for revolution in Germany and the United States, Most declared that the time for revolution was near. He envisioned the United States undertaking its third great struggle: after defeating foreign imperial rule and racial slavery, it was now poised to abolish wage slavery. Notably, he emphasized that the Civil War had abolished property relations without compensation. Rejecting electoral politics, Most proclaimed that a new society could only be achieved through revolutionary means—"powder, lead, petroleum and dynamite, poison and dagger" and armed with rifles, "Congreve rockets, and dynamite bombs." At one Chicago lecture, attendees resolved to combat the capitalist system "by all means that can lead to its downfall" in the pursuit of human justice.[14] Throughout January 1883, Most continued his tour, speaking in Milwaukee, Louisville, Cincinnati, Cleveland, Detroit, Buffalo, and Pittsburgh, where local socialists honored him with a banquet. He even visited the small coal-mining town of Salineville in Ohio. His appearances drew the attention of Thomas Nast, one of the country's foremost cartoonists, who caricatured him as a comically small, wild-eyed, and disheveled figure—an image that would persist in the popular imagination.

By February 3, Most had reached Philadelphia, sharing the stage with labor leaders Victor Drury and Peter McGuire. During a meeting with the Russian revolutionary Leo Hartmann, rumors circulated in the press about another assassination attempt on the czar being planned.[15] A week later, addressing an audience in Baltimore, Most reiterated his belief that workers were oppressed whether under a monarchy or a republic, where "railroad barons and money lords" held sway. "This country, America, has not made a good impression," he told a reporter. "I found it exactly as I thought it would be." Before returning to New York, he made a brief visit to the nation's capital on February 13 without holding any public events.[16] Covering three thousand miles in two months, he had spread his message of social revolution to thousands across twelve major urban centers.

Following consultations with his associates in London, Most embarked on a second lecture tour in April 1883, extending beyond the Mississippi River.[17]

HERR MOST'S ADDRESS.

CHICAGO.

"ALL institutions must be obliterated from the face of the earth.... You must kill every one now ruling over the people. .... Take everything you can get. Money must be bad. Use petroleum and dynamite. Keep on killing.... You must open banks and stores, and help yourselves to what you want."

Figure 7. Cartoon by Thomas Nast in *Harper's Weekly*, January 13, 1883.

This time, he aimed to mobilize activists into "societies" that would send delegates to a future social revolutionary congress.[18] Recognizing the influence of American newspapers in shaping public opinion, he chose a more academic lecture topic—capital and labor—while continuing to denounce monopolists like Cornelius Vanderbilt.[19] When asked by journalists about violent revolution, he cautiously stated that he supported only "what is necessary to secure those inherent rights of the working classes." He suggested that American workers might follow their European counterparts in breaking the power of monopolists through "their votes, the legislature of the country, or by violence if it is forced upon them."[20] However, he had long rejected the ballot box in discussions with his followers. Throughout April, he revisited the same cities as earlier in the year. In May, he traveled westward, speaking in St. Louis, Kansas City, St. Joseph, Omaha, and Denver, culminating in his westernmost stop at the foot of the Rockies. The next day, he took the long train ride back to Chicago. In Milwaukee, he addressed a crowd of five hundred, drawing comparisons between American factories and European prisons, criticizing American journalists and police, condemning the prison system, and deriding American politicians for their perceived willingness to "prostitute" themselves. Following a brief stop in Boston, he concluded his tour, returning to New York in early June to resume his editorial duties.[21] As Most's influence among radical workers grew, he faced sharp criticism from social democrats for his brand of insurrectionary anarchism. For instance, the socialist Wilhelm Fritzsche debated him in Philadelphia. In St. Louis, socialists organized an anti-Most gathering, and Philip Van Patten, a leader of the SLP, questioned Most's exaggerated claim of his proximity to Marx.[22]

Most's final objective during his American tour was to establish an American anarchist federation, a concept he deliberated with key supporters such as Spies of Chicago. A convention was scheduled for October 1883 in Pittsburgh, strategically located between Chicago and New York.[23] Most urged delegates to prioritize organization and unity over theoretical disagreements, although some warned against a centralized structure that might infringe on group autonomy. A blueprint, primarily drafted by Most, emphasized self-defense, cooperation, and solidarity among revolutionary workers. While advocating for a militant labor movement, he cautioned against focusing on issues such as wage increases or working hours, which he saw as distractions. Delegates from Chicago, including Parsons and Spies, envisioned the revolutionary labor union as "an autonomous commune in the process of incubation," a precursor to a future free society. They believed that short-term gains could attract mass support for a broader revolutionary agenda through an armed uprising—a strategy referred to as "the Chicago idea."[24] The task of drafting the final proclamation was assigned to an elected committee consisting of Most, Drury, Parsons, Spies, and the St. Louis editor Josef Reifgraber, ensuring a balanced representation of ideologies.

The Pittsburgh proclamation, unveiled on October 16, 1883, bore a strong influence from Most's ideas. A blend of Bakuninist and Blanquist ideologies, it served as an antiauthoritarian blueprint for the International Working People's Association's (IWPA's) fledgling American federation. The proclamation called for resistance against oppression and class rule "by all means" and advocated cooperative production, free exchange, secular education, and equal rights for all sexes and races. It also promoted the "regulation of all public affairs by free contract between the autonomous (independent) communes and associations, resting on a federalistic basis." It concluded with a foreboding yet eloquent warning: "Tremble, oppressors of the world! Not far beyond your purblind sight, there dawns the scarlet and sable light of Judgment Day!"[25] Authored by immigrants, the proclamation invoked the spirit of the Declaration of Independence, calling for overthrow of a despotic government following "a long train of abuses and usurpations" because the current circumstances demanded it. As historian Ronald Creagh observed, the revolution was framed as "a desirable, possible, and American ideal."[26]

The lecture tours and the Pittsburgh congress cemented Most's status as the leading advocate of anarchism in the United States. A Chicago anarchist publication reported that the number of anarchist groups in the country increased from thirty in August 1883 to eighty by 1885, with an estimated membership of three thousand individuals and an additional four thousand sympathizers.[27] This rapid growth did not escape the attention of German authorities, who viewed the rise of anarchism with alarm. One police report warned that "given the zeal of Most and his followers, it can be assumed that the Social-Revolutionary Party will very soon gain the upper hand over the social democrats everywhere." The report also identified the social-revolutionary clubs in New York as "dangerous for the old world," highlighting that members from various countries gathered there and were willing to use "criminal methods" to accelerate the overthrow of state and society.[28]

After a year in the United States, Most observed that the American daily press was more aggressive and unscrupulous than its European counterpart. In 1881, many Americans first heard of Most through coverage of his London libel case. While some editorials dismissed his political views, they defended his right to express them. As one American reporter noted, Most had gained "temporary notoriety" by presenting himself as a "martyr to the cause of Socialism."[29] Similar to how the Austrian government's prosecution of Most for treason in 1870 inadvertently gave him publicity, the British government's actions did the same. In 1883, the American press often portrayed him as an amusing curiosity, frequently using "blatherskite" as a favored insult. Since Most rarely responded in English to correct or clarify erroneous reports, falsehoods often persisted for days as newspapers aimed to satisfy the public's appetite for sensational stories. However, not all coverage was dismissive. One popular magazine described him as "one of the best-known Socialist leaders in the world" with a "natural aptitude for public speaking."[30] Despite this, Most recognized that balanced coverage of radicalism, anti-labor, or racial violence was almost nonexistent.

* * *

From 1883 to 1885, John Most lived a precarious and unsettled life in New York City, as the prospect of returning to Europe gradually faded. In August

1884, he expressed to Victor Dave, his only trusted correspondent, that he intended to return once it became possible to publish *Freiheit* there again. However, his optimism diminished six months later: "The way things stand right now is that I'm essentially banned from the entire European continent."[31] Feeling disconnected from his colleagues in London and Germany, he lamented, "I've often felt quite unhappy and ill-humored [in America] because the conditions here don't allow me to be as active for the cause of the working people as I think desirable."[32] Socialist Karl Kautsky once commented that New York German radicals like Most "lost an appreciation for German conditions, without gaining an appreciation for American conditions, and are living in an imagined world without solid ground to stand on."[33] Most's understanding of the United States was limited, and he made little effort to learn English, either in writing or speaking.[34]

Despite the challenges, Most managed to piece together a livelihood through speaking engagements, selling his newspaper, and the support of an unnamed "well-to-do friend" (likely Schwab).[35] With "dogged persistence," he steered *Freiheit* back to financial stability.[36] The first American edition was released on December 9, 1882, with the new subtitle *Organ of the Revolutionary Socialists. Against Tyrants All Means Are Lawful.* Subscriptions increased following his speaking tours, and the number of vending agents rose from one in 1880 to thirty-six by December 1883, with circulation reaching a respectable five thousand to eight thousand.[37] By the middle of 1885, Most was paying himself a modest $5 a week, when the average daily wage for a New York compositor in 1884 was $2.65.[38] The European operations, however, presented a different picture. For each issue, a smaller batch was distributed in the United States, while a larger batch was sent either to London or directly to smugglers in Switzerland and Belgium.[39] Payments for these London shipments were erratic; in 1883, only half of the postage expenses were reimbursed, and no payments were made for the paper itself. As a result, Most was forced to cut the number of copies sent to London from 1,700 per week to just 350, with no compensation. The compositors of *Freiheit* worked for reduced wages, attributing their difficulties to the London operations.[40]

The 1880s marked a period of growth for German international anarchism, but internal conflicts over leadership and ideology simmered beneath the surface. These disputes culminated in a feud that significantly hindered the movement's progress, involving figures like John Most and consuming precious years of their lives. Most's relocation of *Freiheit* to America gave him full control over its format and content, a departure from its previous management by a publishing committee in London.[41] This raised questions: Should one person wield such influence over a major radical publication? And why was a paper primarily read by Europeans being published in America? The Social-Revolutionary Club of New York argued that *Freiheit* should have remained in Europe, but Most and Schwab contended that the conditions in England or Switzerland were unsuitable for its publication. Unfortunately, what began as a legitimate debate devolved into petty squabbles, as demonstrated when club members used funds meant for *Freiheit* to publish an anti-Most pamphlet.[42]

Josef Peukert, a prominent Austrian anarchist, believed that a socialist paper should be an independent, "open and free tribune" managed by a rotating editorial committee rather than a single, permanent editor.[43] Most dismissed these concerns as driven by jealousy and ambition on Peukert's part. In October 1883, Peukert and his associate Otto Rinke launched *Der Rebell* in London. Initially, Most welcomed the new publication but worried that the movement could not support two papers. Peukert and Rinke argued that *Freiheit* had become too Americanized and that German-speaking anarchists in Europe needed their own publication. Tensions escalated in May 1884 when Most's close friend Dave arrived in London and began undermining *Der Rebell*, fearing it would threaten *Freiheit*'s survival. John Neve, agreeing with this concern, sought to prevent the movement from splitting into factions. However, Dave and Most were unwilling to relinquish control of the European terrain to *Der Rebell* without a fight. "I think Peukert is a very bad character," Most wrote to Dave. "We can expect more trouble from him in London because he has surrounded himself with bootlickers. His only aspiration is to be a paid editor."[44] The stakes increased when it became clear that Peukert and Rinke, as communist anarchists, opposed Most's adherence to Bakuninism. This ideological divide further intensified what was already a *Bruderkrieg* (fratricidal war). Intrigues continued throughout 1884, jeopardizing the smuggling network that distributed anarchist literature. Most's possessiveness and control over *Freiheit* were evident.[45] In May 1885, *Freiheit* openly criticized *Der Rebell*, accusing Peukert's smuggling connections in Europe of being unreliable. Consequently, Peukert and his associates were expelled from the Communistischer Arbeiter-Bildungsverein, leading them to establish Club Autonomie, a communist-anarchist faction advocating propaganda by the deed and rejecting formal organizations and leaders.[46] To the autonomists, both Most and Dave, as Bakuninists, embodied the perceived flaws of international anarchism. Meanwhile, Neve remained neutral and, in November 1885, traveled to Belgium to stabilize the smuggling operation for both *Freiheit* and *Der Rebell*, serving as a crucial link between New York, London, and Germany for distributing printed material.[47]

* * *

John Most's advocacy for revolutionary terrorism and armed insurrection to bring about a new society reached its peak in the United States. His aim was to accelerate the revolution through propaganda by the deed, whether through collective actions or individual acts, with Europe as the primary target.[48] From 1882 to 1886, he spread these ideas through pamphlets and lectures, with four of the six pamphlets translated into English.[49] Excerpts of his violent rhetoric occasionally appeared in newspapers, selectively translated by German American reporters, cartoonists, or detectives. As a result, his ideas significantly influenced how Americans perceived anarchism during this period. Even as Most's views evolved after 1885, he struggled to shed the terrorist image he had helped create.

The fascination with dynamite in the 1880s was not unique to John Most and his anarchist supporters. Since the Civil War and Alfred Nobel's invention of dynamite in 1866, Americans from various backgrounds had shown growing interest in military technology and scientific warfare. Experimenting with explosives became common, and popular magazines like *Scientific American* and *Van Nostrand's Eclectic Engineering Magazine* frequently featured articles on the uses of dynamite, explanations of explosive devices, and even instructions for making them. Most, lacking formal training in chemistry or engineering, likely relied on this literature to write his own articles from a left-revolutionary perspective. He also drew inspiration from the Fenians, a revolutionary group that had long discussed skirmishing, dynamite bombs, and even the aerial bombing of British military targets from hot air balloons. Arguments for this type of modern warfare regularly appeared in O'Donovan Rossa's *The United Irishman*. The Fenian pamphlet *Dynamite against Gladstone's Resources of Civilisation* published in 1883 by Professor Mezzeroff—who also wrote for *Freiheit*—provided further inspiration.[50] For Most, the relative ease with which oppressed groups could access firepower to rival that of their oppressors presented a revolutionary opportunity. Dynamite, in his view, became an effective means to wage class war and was central to his analysis of modern capitalist society.

One of Most's central arguments, shared by many radicals, was the fundamental incompatibility between industrial capitalism and democratic republicanism. Immigrants, drawn to the promises of political democracy, were disillusioned by the lack of democracy in the workplace. Most identified an untamable "beast of property" as the root cause of social evils, fueling class antagonism, greed, and corrupting human behavior. He advocated for the "extermination" of this beast to restore justice and happiness.[51] The conflict between labor and capital, he argued, stemmed from this fundamental source but manifested differently in Europe and America. Whereas European workers faced oppression under monarchies and militarism, American workers endured the greed of monopolists and their political allies. Most viewed the representative systems in Germany, England, and the United States as mechanisms to obscure the tyranny of the beast of property, likening elections to "valves on a steam engine" that temporarily released accumulated pressure.[52] This explained why he rejected the idea that the working class could peacefully acquire political power. Instead, he called for armed resistance, urging workers to arm themselves in self-defense and expropriate the propertied classes. Citing historical events like the French Revolution, the American Civil War, and the Paris Commune, he argued that armed conflict would be necessary.[53] Most further contended that overcoming asymmetrical warfare required violent means, including poison, daggers, pistols, and dynamite—the weapon of the oppressed. He praised Russian revolutionaries for pioneering the use of dynamite in their campaign against the czarist regime, describing it as a "new Messiah" capable of combating military oppression.[54] Robbery and arson were also justified, he claimed, since bourgeois wealth had been acquired at the expense of the working class.[55]

In one of his most violent passages, Most advocated for anarchists to pursue the total destruction of the existing order "through the indiscriminate use of violence" against any representatives of the old regime. When faced with objections about the futility of targeting individuals, Most responded, "it would certainly be better to eradicate the whole reactionary brood (the whole family) at once like a poisonous weed, but for the time being, isolated executions are not without benefit." He even went so far as to recommend "lynch justice" as a tactic for revolutionaries, seemingly oblivious to the grim reality that, in 1883 alone, fifty-one Black Americans had been publicly lynched.[56] Ethical considerations in Most's rhetoric were either absent or ambiguous, as shown by statements like, "We do not recommend acts of cruelty, only what is necessary."[57] These chilling directives were primarily aimed at European rulers and officials who ruthlessly persecuted radicals.[58] Despite such extreme language, even a firebrand like Most did not glorify violence for its own sake. "We are revolutionists, not from love of gore, of bloodshed, or of the frightful scenes that must accompany a revolution," he told an audience, "but because there is no other way to free and redeem mankind."[59]

Although Most cannot be held directly responsible for every action taken by his readers or followers, several controversial incidents are associated with him. He used *Freiheit* as a platform to promote and solicit donations for propaganda by the deed.[60] His involvement with his old friend August Reinsdorf was particularly significant. In 1883, Reinsdorf planned to detonate the Niederwalt Monument near Rüdesheim, which commemorated the unification of Germany. Most was aware of this plan and praised Reindorf's capacity to "hate out of love."[61] Reinsdorf corresponded about practical details of the plot, including the use of "self-igniting fluid," and set the date for September 28, 1883, coinciding with the official opening of the monument, when the emperor and high officials would be present.[62] However, Reinsdorf was injured, leaving the execution of the plan to two inept accomplices. The plot failed when the dynamite stored in a drainage pipe became wet, preventing the explosion. The public remained unaware of this failed attempt until seven months later.[63] Shortly after, an explosion damaged the Frankfurt police headquarters, targeting Karl Rumpf, the police superintendent who had disrupted the smuggling operation in the area.[64] Although Rumpf suspected Reinsdorf, the latter provided an alibi. The socialist press accused Rumpf of staging the attack, while *Freiheit* eagerly claimed credit for the anarchists, referring to it as a successful "blasting test."[65] Four days later, the Frankfurt police received a threatening letter after they posted a reward for catching the perpetrator.[66] Then, on November 24, 1883, *Freiheit* cleared up any confusion: "To verify the quality of the dynamite produced by us, one of our own has let off a dynamite bomb on the main staircase of the Klesernhof [police building] in Frankfurt." This was followed by a threat: "If on this occasion Rumpf and the other criminals who dwell in that nest escaped uninjured . . . rest assured that before long, they won't escape."[67] Reinsdorf was arrested in Hamburg in January 1884, but Most believed he was not responsible.[68] During the ensuing trial, several conspirators admitted to reading *Freiheit* but shifted blame onto Reinsdorf. For Most, what he saw as "the most glorious event in the history of our century" was thwarted by betrayal.[69] Rumpf was later murdered by another activist, Julius Lieske, although there is no evidence linking Most to this act.[70] Reinsdorf, whom Most regarded as the father of German anarchism, was executed in February 1885 at the age of thirty-six.[71]

A series of robberies and homicides committed by anarchists sent shock waves through Austria, triggering a crackdown with far-reaching consequences. The first incident occurred on December 15, 1883, when police inspector Franz Hlubek was shot dead while returning home from a workers' meeting he had attended for surveillance purposes. The perpetrator, later identified as Anton Kammerer, a fervent believer in anarchist propaganda by the deed and a collaborator in smuggling *Freiheit*, initially evaded capture. Months earlier, *Freiheit* had published a threatening letter, purportedly from Kammerer under a pseudonym, targeting undercover police inspectors.[72] On January 10, 1884, another attack occurred at a currency exchange office. Two men assaulted the owner, Heinrich Eisert, with an axe, resulting in his death a few days later. They also brutally murdered Eisert's two young sons and assaulted their tutor, leaving her critically injured. The assailants fled with a substantial sum of money in gold and bonds, some of which were later traced to support families of incarcerated activists and fund the anarchist press. The investigation into these crimes was interrupted by yet another murder on January 25, 1884, when detective Ferdinand Blöch was shot dead in Vienna on his way to work. The perpetrator, identified as Hermann Stellmacher, a former editor of *Freiheit* in Switzerland who had been dismissed by Most, was found carrying a cache of weapons and explosives.[73] Subsequent trials revealed that Kammerer and Stellmacher were associates who adhered to anarchist propaganda by the deed and were involved in all the murders. Both were executed in 1884. The shocking crimes prompted a state of emergency in Austria and sparked widespread public outrage against anarchists. The radical movement in Austria suffered a significant blow and never fully recovered, leading many activists to flee abroad, including to the United States.

Two weeks after the murder of Detective Blöch, John Most and around five hundred others gathered at Manhattan's Irving Hall for a meeting organized by German anarchists. The purpose was to laud the "glorious deeds" of the anarchists and terrorists in Vienna. Speeches, delivered in multiple languages, including English, German, Czech, French, and Italian, defended the violent tactics of the anarchists. However, there was a conspicuous absence of any mention or condemnation of the Eisert bloodbath. Victor Drury, referring to Stellmacher as "our valiant comrade," captured the sentiment of the evening by declaring, "There are only two kinds of people in the world: workers and idlers; the latter have no right to exist and must ultimately disappear. Anyone who eliminates one of them is not a criminal but a benefactor to humanity." Most echoed these sentiments, expressing his satisfaction at the swift demise of individuals like Hlubek and Blöch. He also advocated eliminating figures like Vanderbilt and Jay Gould, suggesting they should be hanged from the nearest lamppost.[74] Despite subsequent revelations confirming Kammerer and Stellmacher's guilt, Most and many anarchists in New York continued to glorify them, depicting them as martyrs during a second commemorative meeting held at the Germania Assembly Rooms.[75] This stance drew widespread repulsion from socialists and many rank-and-file anarchists. Several sections of the anarchist IWPA denounced Most, with some members potentially aligning with the SLP, whose executive committee labeled the tributes to Stellmacher as a "reprehensible and barbaric farce."[76] Bachmann, an early New York anarchist, expressed horror at the fanatical atmosphere within Most's group, recounting instances where members "earnestly advocated for the murder of all children of capitalists," believing them to be the offspring of tyrants.[77]

In the summer of 1884, unfazed by criticism and convinced of the necessity of a violent revolution, Most devised a plan to obtain explosives by gaining access to a manufacturing facility. Only Schwab and Dave were aware of his plan to acquire enough materials to ship to Europe. Operating under the alias Henri Germain, he took up residence at 64 Bowers Street, a property owned by Maurice and Arabella Wirths in Jersey City Heights, just across the Hudson River from Manhattan. Developing a close relationship with the Wirths family, Most relied on their discreet lodging multiple times.[78] The safe house was located two blocks from the Palisades, a cliff overlooking the town of Hoboken and offering a view of Manhattan. "With a few dozen cannon or dynamite throwers," he wrote to Dave, "you could blow up anything from these heights; this will happen one day sooner than many think." With the help of a comrade who was a foreman at a nearby factory, Most gained entry and began pilfering substances, accessories, and instruction manuals to ship to Europe for revolutionary purposes.[79] He shared his newly acquired expertise with *Freiheit* readers in a series of articles during the first half of 1885.[80] "Just one man, acting under good instruction and with circumspection," he assured Dave, "could easily perform 5 to 6 acts in as many different places without danger."[81] However, there were more supporters than actual actors. Most complained to Dave that potential revolutionists often took the money and fled.[82] He even contemplated sending explosives within the United States, particularly to aid striking miners in Ohio's Hocking Valley. When Spies, who visited the region in October 1884, was threatened by the Pinkertons, Most planned to send twenty to twenty-five pounds of "medicine" but never followed through.[83]

Most compiled his findings from the New Jersey factory and all the *Freiheit* articles into a red-covered manual titled *Revolutionäre Kriegswissenschaft* (Revolutionary war science), published in July 1885.[84] It contained detailed instructions on the use of dynamite, nitroglycerin, guncotton, and other explosives, as well as information on poisons and invisible ink. He recommended purchasing or stealing dynamite rather than producing it privately. Consequently, much of the book focused on the handling and effects of explosives. Like the Fenians, Most predicted explosives would be "the decisive factor in the next stage of world history" and encouraged revolutionaries to obtain funds through any means necessary, even suggesting the use of dynamite. "The money is in other people's pockets," he quipped. "How it can be gotten will always remain the crux of the matter." His manual also criticized the romantic image of the self-sacrificing rebel. "A revolutionary who recklessly endangers his life without the absolute necessity for the success of the intended action," he wrote, "acts against the interests of the revolutionary cause."[85] Copies of the manual circulated at anarchist gatherings nationwide, and police raids uncovered its influence. In one notable raid in San Francisco, police found not only the handbook but also dynamite and a hit list targeting prominent figures like Senator Leland Stanford. Similarly, Chicago police discovered a copy of the manual along with weapons and explosives in the home of a Bohemian worker in March 1886.[86]

The uncritical promotion of revolutionary terrorism by a small faction of anarchists inevitably led to harm to innocent people and internal divisions within the movement. Although some individuals unconnected to anarchism may have exploited its name for criminal activities, there is undeniable evidence that committed anarchists engaged in or condoned such acts when they served to finance revolutionary efforts.[87] One such example is Gruppe Schlüsselbein (Group Collarbone), a clandestine anarchist organization recalled by Carl Nold, which engaged in robbery, arson, and prostitution to fund propaganda efforts.[88] During 1883 and 1884, members of New York Group I and the Social-Revolutionary Club resorted to insurance fraud to finance their activities. Their preferred method involved renting a tenement, insuring their possessions for inflated values, then secretly removing the belongings, setting fire to the property, and claiming losses to collect insurance payouts.[89] These schemes occurred repeatedly over several years, resulting in significant profits. While John Most eventually distanced himself from these arson schemes, there is no evidence to suggest that he directly ordered or directed such criminal activities.[90]

The militant faction of Mostians created significant discord within the German anarchist movement, leading to the expulsion of veteran activist Bachmann from New York Group I. Bachmann, who opposed propaganda by the deed, found himself at odds with the increasingly radical direction of the group. Unable to reconcile his principles with the group's trajectory, he left. "The members of the New York German Group . . . have become rude and devoid of all refined qualities of mankind," he lamented. "Day by day, the spirit of rudeness and a fanatical desire for cruelty grows."[91] As early as 1884,

Schwab, another prominent figure in the movement, demanded that Most publicly disavow the arsonists. However, Most, known for his stubbornness, refused. The situation escalated in 1885 when Robert Reitzel, editor of the anarchist literary magazine *Der arme Teufel* and a close friend of Schwab's, also called for Most to condemn the criminal elements publicly.[92] In November 1885, a tragic incident occurred when a tenement fire set by cigar maker Henry Kohout, allegedly a member of a secret anarchist club associated with Most, claimed the lives of a mother and her two daughters. Despite mounting pressure, Most refused to publicly denounce this horrific act.[93] The rift deepened when Schwab banned the criminals from his saloon and resigned from the management of *Freiheit*. This forced Most to find a new composition room. Schwab issued an ultimatum, stating that their friendship would end unless Most publicly condemned the criminal elements. Most, however, chose to sacrifice a friendship. By January 1886, Reitzel reported that Most "did not have the courage to disavow those dishonest elements publicly" and was no longer seen in Schwab's saloon.[94]

Pressure on Most reached new heights in March 1886 when Benjamin Tucker, editor of the individualist anarchist periodical *Liberty*, decided to expose the arson affair, feeling that "the time has come to speak." Informed by Bachmann, Tucker believed that transparency was essential. "It is only fair to John Most . . . to say that he had nothing to do with originating the plots of those criminals," he granted, "but it is nonetheless true that, after he was made aware of these acts, he not only refused to repudiate them but persisted in retaining as his right-hand men some of the worst of the gang." Tucker urged other media outlets to report the facts, emphasizing the importance of redeeming the name and philosophy of anarchism.[95] The *New York Tribune* and *New York Sun* subsequently picked up the story in the spring of 1886, providing additional details and naming individuals involved.[96] Around the same time, Most faced another embarrassing incident when Carl Willmund was arrested and found in possession of weapons, bomb-making materials, and a note addressed to Most: "If you need anything, just drop me a few lines. I am always ready to act for our cause, even to the knife."[97]

Years later, Most expressed regret over his estrangement from Schwab and offered two reasons he could not publicly disavow the arsonists. First, he adamantly refused to act as an informant against anyone. Second, Most viewed petty criminals as primitive rebels. "I saw in every criminal a 'wild' anarchist, whether I liked him or not," he wrote, "because such a person is only a product of his time, even if he acts on his initiative and for personal gain."[98] Although it is unclear if these arguments completely mended the relationship between Most and Schwab, the two eventually appeared together at events, suggesting some reconciliation.

Most's outspoken advocacy for propaganda by the deed deepened the divide between anarchism and social democracy during that era. Despite different strands of socialist thought, Most's prominent role as an editor made him the de facto figurehead of anarchism at the time. German-language socialists and anarchists vied for the support of workers and artisans, prompting the Chicago groups of the IWPA to organize a public debate between Most and Paul Grottkau in May 1884. The two men had been socialist coeditors of the *Berliner Freie Presse* in the mid-1870s. Although the event was titled "Anarchism or Communism?" Grottkau, who was not a member of the SLP, represented a form of libertarian socialism, while Most advocated Bakuninist anarchism. Grottkau, who resented Most's stature as a radical leader, argued that anarchism and communism were incompatible because the former emphasized the autonomy of small groups, whereas the latter promoted solidarity and collective property. He also criticized anarchist tactics as arbitrary and akin to the law of the jungle. In response, Most contended that anarchism and communism were complementary rather than opposites. He criticized Grottkau's rigid model for the future, warning that blind solidarity and majority rule could suppress individuality and human happiness. The debate was substantive enough to warrant the publication of its proceedings in a pamphlet.[99] In the end, Most could not help but question Grottkau's motives for engaging in the debate, accusing him of trying to sow discord within the movement. "Grottkau turns out to be a scoundrel," he wrote to Peukert (who sided with Grottkau), "whose only reason for fighting with me is to split the organization and bring at least a part of it over to the blue camp [SLP]. . . . He's quite isolated with his views and has to get out. Our people will hang him out to dry."[100]

The SLP consistently denounced the growing advocacy for violent propaganda by the deed, particularly championed by Most and his followers. In February 1885, following several Fenian dynamite attacks in London, the New York socialists organized a public meeting to clarify their stance on the Irish cause and its methods. While they expressed support for Irish activists and attributed the violence to oppressive conditions, they firmly condemned the use of dynamite, warning that such tactics would only serve to divide the working classes along national lines. "We beseech [the Irish people] to direct every blow only against the common enemy of labor of both nations," one resolution stated, "and to avoid any act that will turn your English brothers and comrades in arms against you; let's not sacrifice humanity for nationality."

Most and several other anarchists were also in attendance. Insisting on reading a statement representing the anarchist viewpoint, he proclaimed, "With all our hearts, we call out to the fighters: Good luck, you sons of Ireland! Forward with dynamite and all means of destruction!" He criticized the socialist position as hypocritical and accused them of failing to take a clear stand in favor of all revolutionary actions.[101] The meeting quickly devolved into chaos, culminating in a physical altercation between the anarchists and socialists. According to one newspaper account, a socialist named John Ritter grabbed Most and was ready to pounce when others pulled them apart. The police eventually cleared Concordia Hall, wielding their clubs indiscriminately. Schwab was arrested and charged with assault.[102] Most narrowly escaped the police cudgels by jumping out of a window, only to be beaten by individuals who blamed him for instigating the chaos. A socialist newspaper later described the event as "a dark day in the history of the New York labor movement."[103]

7 Facing America

IN 1885, JOHN MOST SHIFTED HIS FOCUS from Germany to the American labor and revolutionary movements. He believed that capitalism caused harm on both sides of the Atlantic and saw the United States as fertile ground for anarchist propaganda. This change was partly driven by the increased stability of *Freiheit* in America, which eased the logistical and financial challenges of coordinating with comrades in London. Most expanded the newspaper's format and saw a substantial rise in American subscriptions. *Freiheit* now carried the subheading *Organ der Anarchisten deutscher Sprache* (Organ of German-speaking anarchists). According to historian Heiner Becker, *Freiheit* had a circulation of between eight thousand and twelve thousand during this period, with fewer copies being sent to Europe over time.[1] By late 1885, Most established *Freiheit*'s new editorial and composition office at 167 William Street in downtown Manhattan, located in the financial district east of city hall, an area known as Newspaper Row. The office occupied two rooms on the third floor, where volunteers handled typesetting, folding sheets, and preparing packages.[2] Most worked at a standing desk in one of the rooms, surrounded by portraits of anarchist figures like Peter Kropotkin and Louise Michel, along with newspaper clippings.[3] Additionally, on January 15, 1886, Most rented a furnished room under a false name at 198 Allen Street in Little Germany, near Justus Schwab's saloon.[4] This space offered him a quiet retreat for writing, editing, and correspondence. He used a courier service via the elevated railroad between Allen Street and city hall to maintain communication between the two locations. The compositors at William Street would receive his drafts, ready for typesetting, and prepare them for the printer.[5] Despite his prominent role as the voice of revolutionary anarchists in America, Most led an isolated, likely lonely, life in New York City. Letters from Marie Roth, an old friend from London, were among his few personal connections, as he had little time for romantic relationships. His closest companion was *Freiheit*, which he saw as an extension of himself. "My heart is '*Freiheit*,'" he once wrote. "She's not just a piece of my life; she's my second (or rather first) self. Anyone who reaches for her touches the root of my life. Whoever is hostile toward her is my enemy."[6]

Starting in 1886, Most moved away from promoting terroristic propaganda by the deed, instead emphasizing workers' self-defense, readiness, and collective revolutionary action. Like many revolutionaries, he believed violent revolution was necessary for social change and saw arming workers as crucial for the American labor movement.[7] In one article, he suggested a "house and factory war" where men would occupy their workplaces while their wives defended the homes with boiling water or oil. This, he argued, would allow the men to "make short work of the manufacturers, traders and their clan, while [the women] settle accounts with the landlords."[8] These ideas were not new; Most had long championed an armed proletariat and urban guerrilla warfare, drawing from the defense strategies of the Paris Communards. However, he was also influenced by a domestic tradition of armed resistance. Since the 1870s, a radical faction within the socialist movement had been advocating for armed self-defense, although their rhetoric was mild compared to the alarming statements from business leaders and the media during the economic depression of 1873. Wealthy Americans, oblivious to the deep inequalities in their society, grew increasingly fearful of the working class and the unemployed, who roamed the country seeking work and food. Newspapers stoked class hatred, portraying the unemployed as a "tramp menace." One Chicago gun manufacturer advertised a new lightweight pistol as a "TRAMPS TERROR" suitable for police officers or home defense when "Tramps, Burglars and Thieves Infest[ed] Every Part of the Country."[9] The *Chicago Tribune* even suggested contaminating food supplies given to tramps with "strychnine or arsenic" to kill them and serve as "a warning to other tramps to keep out of the neighborhood."[10]

Hard times reached a peak with the Great Railroad Strike of 1877, when a spontaneous protest against wage cuts escalated into the first national labor uprising in American history, involving over one hundred thousand workers. Initially, the strikers received widespread public support, but the mainstream press soon painted them as rioters or worse. The actions taken by business leaders, law enforcement, the militia, and employer-backed private forces like the Pinkerton Detective Agency during this period remain shocking even today. Tom Scott, the president of the Pennsylvania Railroad, notoriously suggested that the militia put strikers on a "rifle diet for a few days" to teach them a lesson.[11] Chicago millionaire Marshall Field funded the construction of city armories, while the Citizens' Association provided the police department with a cannon, a Gatling gun, nearly three hundred rifles, and ammunition. The *Chicago Tribune* called for a shoot-to-kill policy by the police.[12] On July 26, 1877, Chicago police, armed with guns and batons, forcefully entered the Vorwärts Turner Hall where German union members were meeting to discuss the eight-hour workday. They fatally shot one man and brutally beat others as they tried to flee. As historian James Green wrote, "Sent out to suppress rioters, the police became rioters themselves." In the days that followed, thirty people died in Chicago, with no police casualties. In Baltimore, a dozen protesters, including women and children, were killed, and over twenty people lost their lives in Pittsburgh. These brutal acts provoked violent reprisals and left behind "toxic fumes of animosity."[13]

John Most learned about these events through the firsthand accounts of anarchists like Schwab, Albert Parsons, and August Spies, who had all been deeply affected by the upheaval. He strongly supported efforts to bolster workers' self-defense and urged all members of the International Working People's Association (IWPA) to acquire rifles and practice their shooting skills.[14] Participation in groups like the Lehr-und Wehrvereine (Education and Defense Associations) and other rifle clubs steadily increased, with many aligning themselves with the IWPA. These groups purchased rifles, ammunition, and uniforms, conducted drills and shooting practice, and even held public demonstrations in full gear. In response, the state of Illinois passed a law in 1879 banning unauthorized paramilitary groups and prohibiting the public assembly of armed individuals without official approval—a measure upheld by the Supreme Court in 1886. Some groups disbanded as a result, while others continued their activities in secret. John Most himself acquired a Winchester rifle and may have helped establish or joined the Internationaler Schützenbund New York (International Defense League New York). Although he dismissed the feasibility of universally arming the working class in Europe, he saw potential for such efforts in the United States: "Proletarians of the world, arm yourselves! Arm yourselves however you may; the hour of battle is near!"[15]

*   *   *

By late 1885, parts of the labor movement in Chicago and beyond had revived the demand for an eight-hour workday without a reduction in pay, setting a firm deadline of May 1, 1886. A newly formed Eight-Hour Association gained substantial support, even attracting middle-class Americans who hoped this modest reform would promote labor harmony and economic stability. In November, trade unions in New York City also pledged their support for the eight-hour cause, authorizing the Central Labor Union to pressure employers for its adoption.[16] Anarchists typically dismissed short-term reforms as superficial. "Shortening the hours of labor is no real remedy," wrote Spies in 1885. "It still leaves people in the condition of masters and servants."[17] However, some in Chicago saw the propaganda value in the renewed eight-hour campaign and embraced revolutionary unionism. Parsons persuaded figures like Spies and others to join the movement. Initially skeptical, Most saw an opportunity to promote the idea of arming workers within this context. "Although I did not believe in the eight-hour movement of the time," he remembered, "it seemed to me that it created the right mood to encourage at least a section of radical workers to arm themselves, without which nothing can be done against capitalist rule." To Most, the eight-hour movement was merely a diversion, a "lightning rod against the electricity of *truly* revolutionary movements." Despite Spies's attempts to convince him otherwise, Most held firm, arguing that workers should not waste time on short-term goals and should never enter a fight unprepared.[18]

On April 23, 1886, the anarchist rifle club International Schützenbund held a meeting at the Germania Garden on Second Avenue. The gathering aimed to address the rising violence against striking workers, such as the April shooting of six people in East St. Louis by guards during a railroad strike. A day earlier, three thousand sugar refinery workers in Brooklyn had walked out when the Havemeyer company refused to negotiate. Approximately five hundred individuals attended the rifle club meeting, including several uniformed and plainclothes police officers. Adolph Schenck, a printer and Most's neighbor, placed a rifle on the platform table and opened the proceedings. Most then took the stage, delivering a fiery speech advocating for arming and self-defense instead of begging for eight hours. "Arm yourselves now!" he thundered. "Arm yourselves before it is too late and they shoot you down." He invoked the citizen soldiers of the American Revolution and argued that the violence in East St. Louis and Brooklyn could have been avoided if the workers had been armed. He then picked up the rifle on the table and held it up: "This is the protection of the workingman." Following his speech, Richard Braunschweig, another rifle club member known for his volatile temper, confronted the police officers present, narrowly avoiding a physical clash.[19] One of the undercover agents present took detailed notes, which were later presented to a grand jury. On April 28, Most was indicted for unlawful assembly and inciting to riot, marking his first confrontation with the American legal system. The next day, Recorder Frederick Smyth, an Irish American Tammany Democrat, issued a bench warrant for Most's arrest. However, when Inspector Thomas Byrnes arrived at Most's residence on William Street, he found only typesetters at work. Schenck and Braunschweig were arrested, but Most remained hiding at his Allen Street apartment, continuing his editorial work.[20] Meanwhile, the Eight-Hour demonstration on May Day brought twenty thousand people to Union Square and proceeded without incident.[21]

While Chicago newspapers speculated that Most had fled the city—a claim unlikely to be true—he managed to evade detection for two weeks.[22] During this time, a series of explosive events unfolded. On May 3, the *New York Sun* published a detailed article on the anarchist arsonists, building on an earlier exposé in *Liberty*. However, the real drama was in Chicago, the epicenter of the revolutionary movement. In the lead-up to May 1, enthusiasm for the eight-hour day movement surged, with thousands of workers joining unions and striking for improved working conditions. Fearing unrest, Chicago's middle and upper classes pressured the mayor to appoint Inspector John Bonfield, a known hardliner against strikes, which only escalated tensions. Meanwhile, anarchists like Parsons and Spies advocated for armed resistance, even promoting the use of dynamite bombs as a defense against anticipated police violence. For over a year, Chicago's English-language anarchist paper *The Alarm* had been publishing articles on explosives and revolutionary tactics, often translated directly from *Freiheit*, and advertising Most's pamphlet on warfare.[23] On May 1, with tensions high, over three hundred thousand workers nationwide went on strike, including tens of thousands in Chicago.[24] Two days later, news of a violent clash at Chicago's McCormick Reaper Works between strikers and Bonfield's police, resulting in the deaths of two workers, spread quickly. In response, Spies distributed flyers urging workers to arm themselves, while insurrectionary anarchists like Adolph Fischer and George Engel, who were indifferent to union matters, met to plan armed retaliation against police attacks. After reading Spies's leaflet, they organized a protest meeting for May 4 at Haymarket Square, drawing around three thousand attendees to hear Spies, Parsons, and Samuel Fielden speak about the McCormick incident. The mayor, initially present and seemingly reassured by the peaceful nature of the gathering, instructed Bonfield to dismiss his officers. However, later reports from detectives claimed that the speeches had become inflammatory, prompting Bonfield to deploy a small force to Haymarket Square. By the time they arrived, only a few hundred people remained, and rain had begun to fall, leading some to suggest moving the meeting indoors. As the police ordered the crowd to disperse, Fielden initially resisted but eventually complied. At that moment, a dynamite bomb was thrown into the police ranks, instantly killing one officer and injuring many others. In the ensuing chaos, police fired indiscriminately, killing and wounding an untold number of civilians.

In the following weeks, the first red scare in American history prevented any thorough investigation or pursuit of accurate information. The role of the police that night was ignored, and it was widely assumed that an organized anarchist assault was to blame. The bomb thrower—who was never identified—was presumed to be an anarchist, and it was believed that stray bullets came from anarchist guns. Egged on by the press, the police launched a witch hunt: they illegally entered and searched homes, beat suspects, and bribed others to testify for the state.[25] The hysteria surrounding the event hindered any careful investigation into the identity of the perpetrator, as the authorities (and much of the public) showed little interest in the truth. "Public justice demands," opined the *Chicago Times*, "that the European assassins, August Spies, Michael Schwab, and Samuel Fielden, shall be held, tried, and hanged for murder."[26] The *New York Times* directly implicated Most: "The villainous teachings of the anarchists bore bloody fruit in Chicago to-night, and before daylight at least a dozen stalwart men will have laid down their lives as a tribute to the doctrine of Herr Johann Most." The newspaper also called for barring the entry of "anarchists, criminals, and paupers" into the country.[27] Inspector Byrnes capitalized on the post-Haymarket atmosphere in New York, aggressively targeting anarchists while ignoring the widespread corruption within his ranks. Eventually, he was forced to resign amid public backlash. As historian Frank Donner noted, Byrnes was "ferocious in dealing with labor unrest and radicals" but "tender in his toleration of grafters and boodlers under his command."[28]

Holed up in his apartment, Most received news of the arrests of Spies, Fielden, Fischer, and others, as well as the suppression of anarchist and socialist publications. In the May 8 issue of *Freiheit*, Most celebrated the Haymarket incident as a bold act of anarchist resistance and issued a fervent call to arms. One editorial questioned whether the freedom of the press "is not strained beyond the limits of prudence and toleration."[29] Inspector Byrnes, tracking Most's courier shuttling materials between the apartment and the William Street office, traced his location to 198 Allen Street. On the evening of May 11, 1886, four detectives arrested John Most, confiscating books, newspapers, his rifle, and a briefcase containing $180 in subscription funds. Most later discovered that the police fed gross falsehoods to the press, claiming they had apprehended him in a brothel, hiding under a bed in a room belonging to a woman named Lena Fischer. "I have experienced much slander against me," he wrote several days later, "but I have never encountered such an amount of falsehoods, such systematic lying from sentence to sentence as took place there." It is likely that the police were inspired by an illustration that had appeared ten days *before* his arrest in the *Evening Telegram*, which depicted him under a bed; they added the brothel detail for extra sensationalism.

Inevitably, several major newspapers spread this misinformation, prompting Most to issue a correction, stating that he had been arrested standing up in the middle of his own room.[30] On May 16, the *World* published a cartoon depicting Most brandishing a rifle at a meeting alongside an image of him hiding under a bed, his "model weapon" hanging on the wall. The theme was echoed by the famous cartoonist Thomas Nast, who published his unflattering illustration in *Harper's Weekly* on May 22.

LOOKING FOR HERR MOST.

Figure 8. "Looking for Herr Most," *Evening Telegram*, May 3, 1886.

THE HERO OF THE ANARCHIST LEGION.

Only a Simple Step from the Sublime to the Ridiculous.

Figure 9. Cartoon by Walter McDougall in *New York World*, May 16, 1886.

Lena Fischer, a close confidante of Most, had indeed been living with him under false names since May 1, using the name "Mary Georges" while Most went by "West."[31] She might have been related to the German socialist Richard Fischer, a former housemate and colleague of Most in Berlin during the late 1870s.[32] Lena Fischer informed reporters that they rented from a "Mrs. Brown." En route to the police station, Most stated that the landlords were not anarchists but rather a "poor tailor" and his wife.[33] Following his arraignment, Most was held at the House of Detention on Centre Street, known as the Tombs, until his editorial assistant Moritz Schultze posted bail two days later. Most appointed Schultze as interim editor and instructed the staff to destroy all recent letters and other materials.[34]

The trial of Most, Schenck, and Braunschweig took place from May 26 to 28. Several police officers and detectives testified that during the April 23 rifle club meeting, the defendants had urged workers to arm themselves, form companies, and equip their spouses with petroleum bombs. A defense witness argued that Most's call to arms was meant to make the May Day marchers appear more impressive. On the final day, the wives of Schenck and Braunschweig testified to their husbands' good character. Defense counsel William F. Howe, known for his flamboyance, managed to get one count dismissed. Surprisingly, he allowed Most to address the jury. In broken English, Most condemned the smear campaign against him and criticized the police for failing to return the confiscated funds from his apartment. He referenced

WHEN HIS SKIN IS NOT IN DANGER, AND—

WHEN IT IS.

Figure 10. Cartoon by Thomas Nast in *Harper's Weekly*, May 22, 1886.

recent labor unrest incidents where men, women, and children were killed, arguing that workers should be armed to defend themselves. "The servants of the capitalists are armed," he reasoned, "and why should not workingmen be armed?" He maintained that the April meeting was orderly and protected by the Constitution. "My conviction," he concluded, "would mean the downfall of free speech! Then will come the downfall of the freedom of the press and the end of the Republic!"[35] The jury deliberated for one hour before returning a guilty verdict for all defendants on June 2. Recorder Smyth sentenced Most to one year of hard labor at the penitentiary on Blackwell's Island (now

Roosevelt Island) and imposed a $500 fine. At one point, the judge addressed Most directly: "A more wicked and atrocious scoundrel than you are does not disgrace the face of this earth!"[36] Most's trial coincided with the aftermath of the Haymarket bomb attack and the subsequent red scare. In Chicago, dozens of anarchists were indicted for murder and conspiracy. Many Americans viewed the Haymarket tragedy as a limit on free speech, with some arguing that Most had crossed that line, particularly when he displayed a rifle and encouraged a volatile assembly to arm themselves, "when precisely similar counsel had been followed on May 3 in Chicago by an attack on the police."[37] Regardless of the circumstances, as Frank Harreck-Haase observed, Most, like in his London trial, was prosecuted and imprisoned not for any committed action but for his spoken or printed words. He saw himself as a "victim of a barbaric violation of freedom of speech."[38]

For John Most, Blackwell's Island was a more degrading experience than anything he had endured in Austrian or German prisons. This narrow, one-and-a-half-mile-long strip of land in the East River housed various public buildings, including hospitals, a lunatic asylum, almshouses, workhouses, and a formidable four-story granite penitentiary erected in 1832. Schenck, Braunschweig, and Most arrived on a picturesque summer day on June 2, 1886. The prison was overcrowded and understaffed. Most was one of 1,005 inmates in a facility designed for 800, managed by only seventy-one officers.[39] To supplement their income, corrections officers occasionally permitted afflu-ent tourists to observe the anarchist inmates as though they were specimens in a zoo. The most humiliating moment for Most came when his beard, untouched his entire life, was shaved for the first time, exposing his facial deformity. He raised his objection to the new warden, Louis Pillsbury, who eventually allowed Most to regrow his beard during the final four months of his incarceration.[40] Good behavior could potentially reduce his sentence by two months. Cell 16, located on the first floor, was dark, damp, and claus-trophobic. Light and fresh air filtered through a grated opening in the door and a narrow window offering a glimpse of passing excursion boats on the East River. Heating was limited to the hallways.

Each cell contained only essential amenities: a drinking vessel, a toilet bucket, and an iron frame that served as a bed when folded down from the wall. There was no table or chair. "Not in all the dominions of European despotism," wrote Most, "had I ever seen, let alone be enclosed, in anything like this hole that the henchmen of a Republic put me in."[41] Daily life followed a regimented routine. Prisoners woke at five, washed, and marched to the river to empty their toilet buckets before proceeding to the mess hall for bread and coffee. Clad in a

Figure 11. "Prisoners' Cells in the Penitentiary, Blackwell's Island," in Campbell, *Darkness and Daylight* (1897), 367.

striped uniform, Most toiled in the blacksmith's shop from seven to six, with only a brief interruption for a meager lunch of bread and soup. There was scant time for exercise or socializing, and access to newspapers or writing materials was only possible through bribery of the guards. Prisoners were permitted one visit and one letter per month. As a former inmate poignantly remarked, "[The convicts'] lives have but three elements—hard work, harder loneliness, and, hardest of all, monotony."[42] Left to his own ruminations, Most grappled with "a feeling of immense bitterness, mixed with hatred for those who put me in this situation, exacerbated by a sense of absolute powerlessness made further unbearable by the impossibility of exchanging thoughts with another human soul."[43] After two months, his sense of humor returned: "I'm also learning to drill in my old age despite my great aversion to all militarism. There is a parade every morning, but we hold a toilet bucket instead of a gun."[44]

Two weeks later, shocking news reverberated from Chicago: the Haymarket defendants, including Most's friends Spies and Fischer, were convicted of murder and sentenced to death. From his cell, an incensed Most penned scathing words denouncing the trial and verdict as a "monstrous crime" unparalleled in the annals of judicial murder, perpetrated by "twelve carefully selected, bribed scoundrels" who were manipulated by the lackeys of the ruling elite and influenced by the sensationalist press.[45] There was hope. The Illinois Supreme Court granted a stay of execution to hear oral arguments in March 1887. "It seems almost certain," he wrote in February, "that they will not dare to hang our comrades."[46] To his great dismay, he learned that his old adversary Wilhelm Liebknecht, who had railed against social revolutionaries, had visited the imprisoned Haymarket defendants.[47] As six months passed, boredom and fury consumed Most once more. "My heart is full of poison and gall, mockery and scorn, contempt for the world and love of freedom," he wrote to readers.[48] Days before the release date, a reporter recognized Most, whose prison outfit "hung about him like a closed cotton umbrella about its stick." Most was only physically threatened once by a fellow prisoner who heard about the Haymarket bombing.[49] The warden viewed him as a man of above-average intelligence but also someone who could do great harm.[50]

Nevertheless, Most was granted an early release of two months for good behavior and was discharged on April 1, 1887. "The torment is over," he recalled. "Richer in some experiences, 'unreformed' and with bitter hatred in our hearts, we return to the world. We'll have to resume our duty."[51] Approximately fifty individuals, braving the brisk wind, gathered at the Fifty-Second Street landing to extend a heartfelt welcome to Most, who was dressed in his familiar Prince Albert coat and appeared emotionally touched. Reports noted that Lena Fischer linked arms with Most as they walked to the elevated train station accompanied by friends.[52] He moved from Allen Street to a modest apartment at 464 Second Avenue.[53] During his absence, *Freiheit*'s operations underwent streamlining, prompting Most to temporarily relocate to Hoboken, New Jersey.[54] Gone were the days of producing two distinct editions; instead, a single edition was typeset from which a condensed European version was assembled. The reduction in size to four pages served as a cost-saving measure, with circulation reaching eight thousand by 1887.[55] Three days following his release, a crowd of three thousand people flocked to Cooper Union to hear Most recount his experience of incarceration.

*   *   *

Figure 12. Johann Most addresses a meeting at Cooper Union, 1887, in *Frank Leslie's Illustrated Newspaper*, April 16, 1887. Courtesy of Library of Congress.

The red scare that followed the Haymarket bombing marked a turning point in Most's political perspective. Convinced that anarchists needed to unite with socialists in opposition to exploitation and repression, he began articulating this view while still imprisoned, hoping to inspire his comrades. He urged his fellow anarchists to set aside "petty jealousies, ambitions, and the resulting gossip" and advocated for reorganizing the IWPA now that the Chicago group was disbanded.[56] Most outlined his vision in a pamphlet titled *To the Proletariat*, published upon his release. He acknowledged that although anarchists and socialists differ in tactics, they ultimately pursue the same goal. Anarchists, he argued, should uphold the integrity of their philosophy while engaging in constructive dialogue with socialists. He emphasized that criticism should be based on facts and delivered in a fraternal spirit, adding that through this approach, "some things that previously stood in the way of revolutionary development will be lifted."

I agree that I should also improve in this respect, and from now on, I'll tone down the infighting within our circles. Upon reflection, may I raise another banner: *Be more tolerant!* All anarchists ask of you [the proletariat] is an open door. We, in turn, invite you to our meetings to participate in discussions. . . . Of course, it cannot be expected that proletarians of other faiths should serve anarchism. . . . I do have in mind a relationship where organized workers, regardless of differences in theory and tactics, form an unbroken chain in opposition to the capitalist world.[57]

Many within the movement welcomed Most's call for cooperation amid the post-Haymarket repression. In April 1887, the Social-Revolutionary Club, previously critical of Most's leadership, pledged to collaborate with New York Group I.[58] Despite some comrades cautioning against excessive "flirting" with socialists, Most reiterated his advocacy for increased cooperation at a meeting of New York anarchists a few months later.[59]

Most found himself a target of the red scare, as many blamed him as the intellectual author of the violent events at Haymarket. Julius Grinnell, the chief prosecutor in the Haymarket case, sought to bring him to trial in Chicago, and reports surfaced that a grand jury was considering indicting him.[60] However, Most's conviction and imprisonment in New York likely protected him from further legal threats. Authorities wondered if Most could be provoked into criminal acts or incendiary statements. Years later, he recounted encounters with suspicious visitors at the William Street office. One man, dressed in an army uniform, claimed to be a deserter and asked to join a secret society. Another offered money for the cause and inquired about secret anarchist meeting places, even suggesting he could avenge the Haymarket defendants alone. Yet another sought a letter of recommendation from Most to act against Bonfield and Judge Gary. Most, suspecting them to be agents provocateurs, promptly dismissed them.[61] A month after Most's release, on the anniversary of the Haymarket bombing, the Illinois legislature passed a conspiracy law that criminalized advocating revolution or overthrowing the existing order, effectively barring Most from conducting any lecture tours in Chicago, at least for the foreseeable future.[62]

The Haymarket affair sparked a contentious debate over immigration and naturalization laws. Several *New York Times* editorials advocated for denying citizenship to immigrants with socialist or anarchist beliefs, arguing that such individuals could not genuinely uphold the Constitution and laws of the United States. There were even proposals to revoke the citizenship of known radicals like Schwab and Sergei Shevitch, a prominent New York socialist critical of electoral politics, accusing them of perjury during their naturalization process. John Most, vehemently opposed to such measures, announced his intention to challenge the laws by becoming a test case.[63] On

September 12, 1887, accompanied by friends and reporters, Most presented himself at the courthouse to declare his intent to become a citizen. During the standard interview, the clerk asked, "Do you believe in the Constitution of the United States?" "Yes, sir," Most responded. "Do you believe in obeying the laws as they are passed by the proper authorities of the state of New York?" "Yes, if they are good laws," Most replied, asserting his duty to resist laws infringing on the rights of the people, even if it meant resorting to force. When the clerk pressed further, asking if he had been punished for violating laws, Most retorted, "I have, but those laws were unconstitutional." Consequently, the clerk declined to administer the oath but allowed Most the option to appeal to a judge.[64]

* * *

The events of 1886 and early 1887 deeply reinforced the belief among anarchists like John Most that the liberal American republic offered no greater freedom than a European monarchy despite its professed commitment to civil liberties and small government. Initially, he harbored "a certain affection for a land of republicanism" and its civil liberties, but he soon came to view these as mere illusions, particularly concerning freedoms for working people.[65] In his view, freedom of the press and assembly was meaningless when used by the working class. He decried the undermining of the Second Amendment, the corruption of elections, and how jury selection and rules of evidence were disregarded in criminal trials. He also criticized the prison system, claiming it was harsher than those in monarchies. "Liberty is a lie," he declared in Philadelphia. "I prophesied the fall of the eight-hour law and was its first martyr. The American prisons are the worst. . . . Your government is an infamous swindle." To him, the United States had become a "North American Monopolist's Republic."[66] One reporter noted that Most, in a moment of rage, even told the press they would hang for what they had done to him.[67] Most believed that the press's scorn and hostility toward him were disproportionate, given the limited influence he had. He also held a dim view of the American populace, accusing them of lacking idealism and being driven solely by greed. For "a riffraff so numerous and corruptible as the great majority of the American masses," he saw little hope for redemption.[68] Throughout his time in the United States, Most never felt entirely at ease. "I was always impatient," he reflected in 1887, "for the moment that would make it possible for me to shift my field of activity back to Europe."[69] Max Baginski, a fellow anarchist who knew Most well, commented that Most was "out of his element" in the United States, lacking the "inspiration and impetus" derived from the "life and struggle of the masses."[70]

As the fate of the Haymarket defendants awaited the Illinois Supreme Court's ruling, the frustration among anarchists like Most only grew. In response, anarchists in New York and New Jersey organized weekly events—lectures, concerts, dances, and picnics—to raise funds for the defense committee.[71] Beyond these efforts, Most publicly denounced the judicial system's injustices and initiated a monthly pamphlet series titled *Internationale Bibliothek* (International library), providing a platform for exploring various topics. Despite a slight easing of antiradical hysteria, nonradical voices questioning the trial's fairness could not sway the outcome. On September 13, the Illinois court upheld the previous decision, scheduling the execution of the seven defendants for November 11, 1887. The announcement sparked widespread protests. Four thousand men and women wearing red ribbons attended a unity protest at Cooper Union, where its great hall adorned with a black-and-red flag. Most condemned the death sentences as "premeditated murder" and "a crime against civilization." He reiterated his belief that authorities would not dare proceed with the executions, warning of uprisings if they did.[72] The U.S. Supreme Court agreed to hear an appeal but ruled unanimously on November 2 that any constitutional violations were only relevant in federal cases. That night, at a somber meeting in a restaurant near the *Freiheit* office, Most, Schwab, and Shevitch set aside their differences to strategize. Schwab expressed optimism for a full pardon, while Shevitch aimed to mobilize all labor groups to send petitions for clemency. Most proposed a mass rally on the execution day, but Schwab feared the possibility of riots.[73] As the scheduled execution date drew closer, public outcry intensified, and petitions gained over one hundred thousand signatures. Then Louis Lingg, one of the defendants, committed suicide in his cell. The governor commuted the sentences of two defendants to life imprisonment, but the four remaining faced the gallows. On November 11, 1887, shortly after noon, Parsons, Fischer, Spies, and Engel were publicly executed by hanging in the Cook County jail. In New York, authorities dispatched detectives to East Side beer halls, anticipating potential anarchist protests.

During a routine club meeting at Krämer's beer hall on East Seventh Street, Most sought to lift the spirits of his comrades in the somber aftermath of the Haymarket executions. He began by passionately criticizing the flaws of the judicial system, blaming the hangings not only on Judge Gary but also on the relentless calls for blood and revenge from the press. When a member of the audience shouted for revenge, Most quickly intervened, urging restraint and asserting, "Not now. It is not time."[74] He also criticized figures such as Terence Powderly, leader of the Knights of Labor, and Henry George, a reformist politician, for their perceived inaction during the Haymarket ordeal. Most then eulogized the Haymarket defendants as martyrs for the cause, firmly proclaiming the imminent arrival of the social revolution. "Anarchism lives!" he declared. "It will thrive, and it will triumph!"[75] Despite the energy of his address, Most refrained from overtly incendiary rhetoric. One daily noted, "He [Most] isn't very wild about it and doesn't dabble in blood."[76] The *New York Tribune* quipped that the "meeting was carried through to a successful end, that is to say, if peace and quiet may be regarded as success from an anarchist point of view."[77] Even police inspector Thomas Byrnes remarked, "I do not think there is the same ground for arresting Most for his utterances Saturday night as there was on the previous occasion."[78] However, Solomon Dreyfuss, attending as a reporter, felt differently. While Most was still speaking, Dreyfuss rushed to a nearby police station, wrote down his version of the speech, and handed it to two German American detectives, Louis Roth and John Sachs.[79] Consequently, Byrnes reversed his decision, leading to Most's indictment for unlawful assembly and incitement to riot. Dreyfuss also gave a copy to his brother, a reporter for the *World*. Most was arrested at his William Street office on November 17.[80]

Convinced he had been framed, Most sought the legal expertise of the renowned duo William Howe and Abraham Hummel, who had previously defended Schwab in 1885. Multiple witnesses challenged the prosecution's portrayal of Most's speech, testifying that he had not made any inflammatory remarks. Hummel, himself of German descent, questioned the language skills of Detectives Roth and Sachs. At one point, Dreyfuss admitted that a significantly different version of the speech published in the *Sun* was accurate. In fact, most mainstream newspapers did not distort the speech and even argued against a conviction. Most presented his prepared notes but acknowledged he may have deviated slightly while speaking. As a last-ditch effort, the prosecution attempted to sway the jury by citing passages from Most's 1884 manual on revolutionary warfare and reciting his views on religion until Judge Cowing intervened. Before the jury deliberated, the judge emphasized that even though freedom of speech must be jealously guarded, it could not extend to slander or inciting riot. He explicitly stated he found nothing in Most's speech that violated any statutes. Nonetheless, the jury, after deliberating for over twelve hours, returned a guilty verdict on November 29.[81] While in custody, Most issued a statement condemning the *New York World* for spreading distorted and false information, a tactic he claimed was common among mass media editors. The journalist William Salisbury recalled that after the Haymarket executions, reporters and editors lamented that the "excitement died down for a while. . . . We had to do some thinking to keep the dear public interested." Salisbury recounted an incident where a reporter, too lazy to attend an anarchist meeting where Most was scheduled to speak, invented a speech from whole cloth for publication.[82] On December 8, 1887, Most was sentenced again to one year at Blackwell's Island penitentiary. While upholding the verdict, Judge Cowing acknowledged the conflicting evidence on the central issue. He told Most that his radical rhetoric had put him "into direct conflict with the great mass of the people; so much so, that I apprehend you have alienated [them. . . .] You have yourself from your avowed sentiments made the American people believe that you are an enemy to their institutions, that you are an enemy to their Government, and, in the main, I believe, that the people of this country love their country."[83] Most's old friends Dr. Julius and Ida Hoffmann posted bail while his defense team appealed his case to the state's Supreme Court, which, in New York, serves as an intermediate appellate court.[84]

Meanwhile, the feud between John Most and the autonomists, led by Josef Peukert, continued to drain the movement's energies during a time of crisis.[85] This state of affairs both angered and saddened Most, though he often downplayed or ignored his own role in the conflict. While the animosity was most intense between Victor Dave and Peukert in London, the dispute spread to the United States when the autonomists established the Radikale Arbeiterbund (Radical Workers' League) in New York, challenging what they perceived as Most's autocratic behavior as an editor. Since November 1886, the London autonomists had also published a biweekly paper, *Die Autonomie*, which competed directly with *Freiheit* for subscribers. Most saw *Freiheit* as "a vehicle for the exchange of ideas, a chronicler of the movement, and a binding agent between the individual parts of the party."[86] The feud soon escalated into a toxic rupture when devastating news broke in February 1887: John Neve had been arrested in Belgium, halting the smuggling of literature. Most learned from Dave that Peukert had visited Neve, accompanied by Charles Reuß, a known police spy exposed by Dave. Despite warnings, Peukert continued to associate with Reuß, which ultimately led to Neve's arrest. Although Peukert was not a spy and had no intention of getting Neve arrested and extradited to Germany, the news convinced many anarchists that foul play was involved. Contrary to Peukert's claim in his memoirs, Most did not immediately accuse him of being a police spy; instead, he "merely accused him of having gone to Neve with a man rightly regarded by many as a tool of the police" and, through this "incomprehensible act," of exposing Neve to great danger.[87] Neve was sentenced to fifteen years in prison despite Most's appeals to Reichstag deputies for his release.[88] As a result, the distribution of *Freiheit* into Germany and Austria dwindled, and by 1888, Most had to cede European territory to *Die Autonomie*. Most then made bitter accusations against the Londoners, alleging theft of subscription lists and collusion with the Berlin police. However, an impartial committee of anarchists, including Kropotkin, dismissed these charges and called for a truce to prevent further damage to the movement. Indeed, historian Andrew Carlson noted that the "German government itself could not have done a more efficient job of destroying the German anarchist movement."[89] Rudolf Rocker, who wrote Most's biography in the 1920s, argued that this "fratricidal war" stunted the development of a freedom movement in German-speaking Europe, with its effects lingering even into Rocker's own time, when German workers displayed a "desperate faith in authority."[90] In the aftermath of the Haymarket and Neve affairs, Most appeared poised to seek new directions and allies.

8 Land of the Future

THE YEAR 1887 MARKED ANOTHER SIGNIFICANT turning point in John Most's mental and intellectual outlook. The tumultuous events surrounding the Haymarket affair, his struggles for civil liberties, the degrading experience of incarceration, the decline of journalism, and the setbacks of the American labor movement all deeply disillusioned and embittered him. Rudolf Rocker described this period as "one of the most agonizing" in Most's militant life.[1] Despite being admired by many, Most found himself increasingly isolated, with more adversaries than allies. He lived a solitary existence—surrounded by comrades but lacking true companionship—delivering lectures but devoid of personal affection. A similar low point had occurred in 1878 when Most was forced to flee Germany and faced rejection from his socialist comrades. This had prompted him to rethink his revolutionary tactics and philosophy. Nearly a decade later, Most once again engaged in introspection and reevaluation. He questioned the feasibility of implementing revolutionary politics in post-Haymarket America, recognizing the vast differences between European and American conditions. The diverse ethnic and linguistic makeup of the United States presented a unique challenge for anarchists: how to disseminate their message effectively without provoking repression. "I'm tired of nurturing illusions for myself and others," he wrote. "It's high time that we see the true state of affairs." This reflection led to a serious effort to reconcile an international proletarian perspective with the complexities of the American context. Unlike in Europe, where revolutionary interests often aligned with those of the working class, Most observed that in America, the laboring masses viewed revolutionaries with suspicion or disdain. "In America," he wrote, "we are a voice in the wilderness. . . . Socialism here is German, and anarchism is a violet that flourishes in obscurity." Nonetheless, he believed it would be a mistake for the movement to retreat into isolation. He advocated for the continued dissemination of ideas, envisioning anarchism as an avant-garde force pushing the boundaries of societal norms.[2]

With this vision, Most significantly revised his anarchistic principles to better fit the American context. He abandoned his former advocacy of propaganda by the deed, which included the use of dynamite and assassinations.[3] Instead, he embraced a strategy focused on propaganda through the spoken and written word. Notably, he chose not to publish a revised edition of his manual on revolutionary warfare. Even though he recognized the legality of self-defense, he stressed that discussions concerning arms should remain private. Most argued that revolutionary education, or propaganda through speech and writing, should be the public face of the anarchist movement.[4] During this transition, he never explicitly admitted the errors of his previous views. However, in 1889, he expressed regret over the prevailing image of anarchists as knife-wielding bomb throwers, an image he had helped create.[5] He envisioned the intellectual development of the proletariat through verbal propaganda by "awakening and sharpening common sense" to grasp revolutionary principles.[6] Most believed that in the United States, "*all* immigrant forces must be drawn into a single *international* propaganda party if they want to instill respect in the native element and persuade them to join."[7] He continued to advocate for anarchists to establish small clubs where "the more intelligent and influential persons" from the organized working class could "clarify ideas, sharpen minds, and build character." He argued that multilingual oral propaganda and literature were the only ways to build an American revolutionary labor movement from the ground up and, eventually, have existing anarchist organizations join it.[8] To further this effort, Most launched the *Internationale Bibliothek* pamphlet series.[9] He urged all radical immigrants to familiarize themselves with the American culture, conduct propaganda in English, and support English-language publications. He believed that revolutionizing the American labor movement must be led by American workers, warning that militant foreigners could inflame American prejudices and derail the entire organizing effort.[10] This shift echoed his earlier 1874 concept of the "revolution of minds." He argued that anarchists and socialists should engage with the latest advancements in the natural and social sciences to accurately assess societal conditions. He lamented how religion had stifled critical thinking, particularly among Americans, describing it as "the scourge of religion" that had left minds "gelatinous" (*verkleistert*).[11]

In 1887, John Most shifted from Mikhail Bakunin's collectivist anarchism to communist anarchism, aligning himself with a philosophy more fully developed by geographers Peter Kropotkin and Elisée Reclus, whom he admired as "one of the greatest inspirers since I became an anarchist."[12] This shift marked a significant change for Most, who redirected his focus from tactical considerations to a renewed engagement with anarchist philosophy. Communist anarchists advocated for the abolition of wage labor and promoted a system where property would be collectively held, rooted in principles of solidarity. They envisioned a society in which goods and services would be distributed according to each individual's abilities and needs. Most seemed eager to signal his shift in philosophy by giving his first communist-anarchist text (August 1887) the same title, *Die freie Gesellschaft*, as his 1884 pamphlet, which had espoused a Bakuninist anarchist vision.[13] Additionally, he published Kropotkin's works, *An Appeal to the Young* and *Law and Authority*, as a pamphlet in his *Internationale Bibliothek* series (October and November 1887). Most echoed Kropotkin's assertion that anarchism was a scientifically and ethically grounded philosophy, free from utopian speculations about the future. "Anarchism is not and cannot be an end goal of human cultural development," he wrote in 1888. "Only a condition under which a steady, undisturbed progress of civilizational perfection is conceivable, the consequences of which, of course, are impossible to foresee."[14] In April 1890, Most further clarified his stance in a lecture titled "Why Am I a Communistic Anarchist?" delivered in English at Cooper Institute as part of the National Debating Club's lecture series. He argued that communism, wherein wealth is held collectively, was not opposed to anarchism but rather formed its essential foundation. "Without the abolition of private property there is no equality possible," he wrote, "and without equality no real independence, while independence is the first condition of liberty, of anarchism."[15]

In August 1888, Most had a unique opportunity to discuss his ideas with representatives of the American government when he was summoned to testify about radical immigration. A House Select Committee, led by Congressmen Melbourne Ford, a Democrat from Michigan, and Richard Guenther, a Republican from Wisconsin, was dispatched to New York in response to revelations of abuses against immigrants at Castle Garden, the immigrant depot administered by New York State but governed by federal laws. The *New York World* had exposed corrupt practices by immigration, steamship, and railroad officials, as well as potential violations of the 1882 law prohibiting the importation of paupers, convicts, contract laborers, "lunatics," and those likely to become public charges.[16] Since debates over excluding anarchists and other radicals had been ongoing since the Haymarket affair, the committee sought insights from John Most and the Russian Jewish socialist Gregory Weinstein. They aimed to understand the reasons socialists and anarchists were emigrating, whether this migration was substantial or minor, and whether American radicals actively encouraged their European counterparts to join them. These inquiries revealed a common assumption among many Americans that anarchism was a foreign ideology unlikely to take root in the United States. Most explained the impact of the 1878 Anti-Socialist Law but disputed its role in triggering mass migration. He acknowledged that persecuted dissenters naturally gravitated toward a republic offering civil liberties. When asked by Congressman Ford to estimate the number of socialists and anarchists worldwide and in the United States, Most gave an exaggerated figure of fifty million globally and two million in the United States, likely to make an impression on the assembled reporters.[17] Ford then asked, "Are socialists not granted more tolerance in this country than in any other?" Most responded, "You have as severe laws against socialism and all efforts of organized labor as you have in any other country, but you don't use them so often." Despite the committee's recommendation, the Immigration Act of 1891 did not yet list anarchists among the excluded groups.[18]

In 1889, the immigrant anarchist movement in New York experienced a resurgence following the post-Haymarket red scare. *Freiheit*'s circulation rebounded to eight thousand, with plans to expand to eight pages the following year.[19] As spring approached, anarchists and socialists prepared to unite around the centennial of the storming of the Bastille on July 14. With Most's support, New York anarchists seized the opportunity to convene a conference of all eastern International Working People's Association (IWPA) groups, aiming to discuss propaganda efforts and demonstrate unity. The conference attracted 150 delegates from northeastern cities and towns, representing diverse ethnic communities, including Jewish, Bohemian, and Italian groups. The agenda featured four main topics: a general discussion on agitation and organization, the establishment of a permanent agitation committee, and the expansion of *Freiheit*. Most successfully proposed replacing the ineffective Information Bureau (a remnant of the 1883 conference) with a new Agitation Committee tasked with coordinating propaganda efforts, particularly in English. All approved propaganda materials would bear the IWPA signature. Additionally, the decision to enlarge *Freiheit* to eight pages was reached after several groups pledged donations.[20] However, the autonomists criticized the conference, viewing it as an attempt at centralization. In response, they launched their own American-based paper, *Der Anarchist*, edited by the young German anarchist Claus Timmermann in St. Louis.[21] Despite internal conflicts, Most remained cautiously optimistic about the potential for revolutionary politics in America. He argued that whereas the oppressed masses in the Old World had long viewed a popular republic as a beacon of freedom and opportunity, the American Republic, as it matured, had revealed gross inequalities, corruption, greed, and violence present in Europe. Most reasoned that the fundamental issue lay in authority itself, regardless of its political guise. Given the growing disillusionment among American intellectuals and artists with statism, he believed anarchism could gain traction in the United States.[22]

*　*　*

The rise of a vibrant and youthful Jewish radical movement in New York and other eastern cities gave Most further reason for optimism regarding anarchism's prospects in America. This movement was predominantly composed of thousands of garment workers who would later play pivotal roles in shaping some of the nation's most dynamic labor organizations. Notably, the Jewish movement included a greater number of women activists compared with its German counterpart.[23] In contrast, the German movement was largely comprised of skilled male artisans such as carpenters, machinists, printers, brewers, cigar makers, and bakers. Many of these men eventually withdrew from activism or remained involved primarily for social and recreational purposes.[24] The early Jewish anarchists, primarily Yiddish speakers with basic knowledge of German, lived and congregated in the southern portion of the Lower East Side fostering a sense of interconnectedness with the older German movement due to their "geographical and linguistic proximity," as historian Kenyon Zimmer describes.[25] Both German and Yiddish immigrant radicals shared a critical stance toward assimilation, striving to preserve their cultural identities while advocating for a multicultural political resistance against class and cultural domination.[26] Many Jewish immigrants held a deeply rooted and "exaggerated respect for German culture," as evidenced by their understanding of German and subscription to German American radical publications, including Most's *Freiheit*. The anarchist Yisroel Kopeloff thought *Freiheit* "had no equal perhaps in the entire history of the radical press."[27] Most's passionate oratory left a lasting impression not only for its educational qualities but also for his fervent zeal. Recollections from those who witnessed his speeches depict Most as a mesmerizing figure, captivating listeners, opponents, and friends alike. "The giant of the revolution rages and roars," remembered Kopeloff, "his fiery words almost bring froth to his lips.

. . . The audience was as if in a hypnotic spell."[28] Etta Byer remembered his voice erupting "like a volcano against the terrors of the capitalistic system." For many younger activists, it was Most's unbridled passion and genuinely rebellious spirit that proved irresistible.[29]

The founding of the first Jewish anarchist group in the United States, the Pionire der Frayhayt (Pioneers of Liberty), occurred in response to the announcement of death sentences for the Haymarket defendants. Swiftly aligning with the IWPA, the group began offering financial support to *Freiheit*.[30] On Christmas Day 1889, Most and Sergei Shevitch were invited to open the inaugural annual convention of the United Jewish Anarchist Groups of North America at the Essex Market building on the corner of Ludlow and Grand in New York. This convention marked a significant milestone in the development of Jewish anarchism in the United States and likely served as inspiration for Most. Its primary aim was to foster closer collaboration between anarchists and socialists and to fund a new Yiddish periodical. In his report, Most praised the Jewish anarchists as an example for his German readers. "The Russian Jewish proletarians," he raved, "are the most enthusiastic. In only a few years, a handful of agitators managed to help build viable associations in a host of cities."[31] *Freiheit* actively promoted Yiddish anarchist club activities, and Most later extended his support to the Yiddish anarchist press.[32] The Pioneers of Liberty was an organization that "works wonders in its circles, as evidenced by the groups that are emerging everywhere in Jewish neighborhoods. Other clubs should take it as an example of what can be achieved through perseverance, energy, and honesty."[33] When *Freiheit* covered a well-attended meeting of the Paterson Jewish group in August 1891, it humorously noted that "the Germans were brilliant in their absence."[34] Most observed a close bond between Jewish anarchists and trade unions, contrasting it with the insular and male-dominated German movement. The militancy displayed by Jewish women in the garment industry challenged Most's conventional view of women in the movement, which held that they cared more about romance than revolution.[35] The mutual affinity between Most and the Yiddish anarchists can be encapsulated in two fundamental principles: anticlericalism and anti-bourgeois sentiments.

Militant atheism formed the cornerstone of the bond between Most and Jewish anarchists in the United States. Most had embraced atheism long before discovering socialism, consistently condemning religion and the clergy for their detrimental impact on society. His influential 1883 pamphlet *Die Gottespest* (The God pestilence) sold over one hundred thousand copies, portraying the monotheistic God as a tyrant who imposed servitude on

humanity "under divine police supervision." He argued that religious doctrines and rituals served the interests of the ruling elites: "It is no secret to
the rich and powerful that humankind can only be enslaved and exploited
when the necromancers of the churches implant sufficient servility in the
hearts of the masses."[36] In 1889, inspired by their London counterparts, Jewish
anarchists in New York organized a ball on Yom Kippur, the holiest day in
the Jewish calendar, when observant Jews fast and engage in introspection.
Most enthusiastically participated in this act of counter-observance, defying
religious norms and openly challenging the authority of religious institutions.
Freiheit explained that on this "long day," the Pioneers of Liberty will "do the
opposite of what is supposed to be done according to the rotten laws of Moses
and his accomplices."[37] Historian Elias Tcherikower argued that anarchist
anti-religious propaganda deserves "serious consideration" because of its
profound impact on Jewish immigrants.[38] The staging of Yom Kippur balls
by anarchists certainly stirred controversy especially among religious Jews.
In 1890, the Pioneers of Liberty were forced to hold their ball in Brooklyn,
but local rabbis petitioned the police commissioner to prevent it. "I shall
talk upon this long day of theirs and give my opinion of it," Most assured a
reporter. "The police have no right to interfere with me, and they know it."[39]
Five hundred anarchists and sympathizers showed up at the entrance blocked
by police, acting on the order of Mayor Alfred Chapin. Most, tipped off about
the situation, stayed in Manhattan, while the crowd in Brooklyn lingered
for a while before dispersing.[40] Radicals and middle-class citizens roundly
criticized the mayor for violating civil liberties. Anarchists and socialists
seized the opportunity, organizing protest meetings and gaining generous
press coverage. These Yom Kippur balls became "a very popular institution
among the people," according to Jewish anarchist historian Joseph Cohen,
who disputed Kopeloff's claim that this type of entertainment contributed
to the decline of anarchism in Jewish life. Indeed, historian Kenyon Zimmer
writes that the inaugural ball drew two thousand people and another two
thousand showed up to protest against repression.[41] Anarchists thus played
a crucial role in promoting free thought during the late nineteenth century.
Most gained recognition as one of New York's prominent atheists, alongside
figures like Robert Ingersoll and Hugh O. Pentecost.[42]

* * *

During one of his lectures in the summer or fall of 1888, John Most noticed
a young woman standing against the wall, her eyes wide with curiosity as she
strained to hear every word. "You captured my attention immediately," he

Figure 13. Helene Minkin,
ca. 1907. Courtesy of
International Institute of
Social History, Amsterdam.

later confessed to Helene Minkin. "She looked like a Russian girl," he thought, deciding to introduce her to his circle. Despite Most's facial disfigurement, his piercing blue eyes and unruly head of hair made an impression. "Most looked like the crucified Jesus with a crown of thorns on his head," Minkin recalled, and she understood enough of the speech to leave her deeply enthralled. To her surprise, Most approached her after the lecture, offering to teach her German and provide her with literature. At just sixteen, Minkin had recently immigrated to America with her older sister Anna and their father, Isaac, settling into a modest two-room apartment.

Despite her grueling work at a corset factory, she was drawn to anarchism, influenced by the tumultuous events surrounding the Haymarket affair, which she described as her "first blow in this free country." Even though her factory job consumed much of her time, Minkin eagerly engaged in activities like selling pamphlets and posting handbills, and she read books at the *Freiheit* office on William Street. However, she yearned for a more active role in the movement and pleaded with Most to become her mentor. Despite being charmed by her youthful zeal, Most believed Minkin was too young and fragile for greater involvement: "It's enough that you continue to remain loyal to our ideal and do what you do now," he advised. Minkin's upbringing mirrored that of countless Jewish families living under the oppressive rule of the Russian czars in the Pale of Settlement, a region in western Russia where Jews were relegated to second-class status. Born in Grodno (now Hrodna in Belarus) on June 11, 1873, she and her sister were raised by strict grandparents in Bialystok, Poland, after their mother died in 1883. Exposure to dissident ideas, possibly including socialist literature, came from hired tutors and young Russian students. Their decision to immigrate to America in 1887 or 1888 followed their uncle, who sought refuge from military conscription, marking the beginning of the first wave of Eastern European immigrants fleeing czarist Russia.[43]

Alexander Berkman, a seventeen-year-old Russian Jewish activist fluent in Russian and German, entered the ranks of the Pioneers of Liberty, eager to work with Most. The two first crossed paths in the spring of 1888, with Berkman recalling Most's "forceful, outstanding personality," while Most recognized in Berkman a steadfast militant ideal for the movement. Historian Paul Avrich described Berkman as admired by friends for his "earnestness and independent spirit, his sharp intellect and lucid intelligence, and his eagerness to toil for the cause." Berkman's extensive education had equipped him with a profound understanding of scientific works, making him a valuable asset to the movement.[44] Berkman quickly forged a friendship with the Minkin sisters and collaborated with them to organize the inaugural Haymarket commemoration at Cooper Union, featuring prominent socialist and anarchist speakers. The event began with a vibrant parade, as six hundred members of German craft unions, led by the Carl Sahm anarchist marching band, marched along First Avenue and Houston Street. They were adorned in red union badges and ribbons, carrying flags and banners. A reporter noticed one bystander mistaking the celebration for the recent election of Republican Benjamin Harrison to the presidency. Joining the procession were Jewish activists from the Pioneers of Liberty, adding to the spectacle as they made their way to Cooper Union. The venue was packed with 3,500 attendees, donning red hats or black bonnets with red strings. Most and Shevitch, two of New York's esteemed orators, delivered impassioned speeches in both English and German. In his first major appearance since his sentencing and pending appeal in December 1887, Most argued that the unidentified bomb thrower had acted in self-defense and denounced the American Republic as nothing more than "a colossal swindle."[45] In accordance with his recent writings, Most avoided incendiary rhetoric during his speech, surprising even the *New York Times* reporter with the "commonplace" nature of his address.[46]

In August 1889, a young activist named Emma Goldman arrived in New York, inspired by the Haymarket defendants. At twenty, she left behind an unhappy marriage in Rochester, seeking a new purpose within the anarchist movement. Her first encounter with a copy of *Freiheit* at a friend's house left her captivated by its bold and irreverent style. She later wrote that the language "fairly took my breath away; it was so different from what I had heard at the socialist meetings. . . . It seemed lava shooting forth flames of ridicule, scorn, and defiance." From that moment, Goldman became a regular reader and eagerly sought out the anarchist literature advertised within its pages. She was eager to meet John Most in New York, believing he could "help me prepare myself for my new task." According to her memoir, Goldman arrived in New York on August 15, 1889, where she was introduced to Berkman and the Minkin sisters, who kindly offered her lodging. Together with the artist Modest Aronstam, they formed a sort of intellectual commune, creating an environment that nurtured radical ideas and activism. That evening, they attended a lecture by Most. "My first impression of him was one of revulsion," Goldman recalled. "He was of medium height, with a large head crowned with greyish bushy hair, but his face was twisted out of form by an apparent dislocation of the left jaw. Only his eyes were soothing; they were blue and sympathetic." However, as soon as Most began to speak, his physical imperfections seemed to disappear, revealing a "primitive power, radiating hatred and love, strength and inspiration." Goldman was captivated by "the rapid current of his speech, the music of his voice, and his sparkling wit." She came to appreciate his mastery of rhetoric, honed over many years—a skill she herself would later adopt. "I marvelled how he could talk and drink until the last moment before going on the platform," she later wrote, "and then speak with such fire and abandon."[47]

Although we rely solely on Emma Goldman's recollection of her encounter with John Most, it remains a significant moment for both individuals. Most, then forty-three years old, met Goldman at the *Freiheit* office on William Street sometime in August 1889. Impressed by her enthusiasm and thirst for knowledge, he lent her several books and invited her to assist with producing *Freiheit* the following week, to which she eagerly agreed.

Their collaboration continued into the evening as they worked tirelessly in the noisy composition room. Later, Most invited Goldman to dinner and proposed attending Johann Strauss's operetta *Der Zigeunerbaron* (The Gypsy

Figure 14. Emma Goldman
in New York, 1892. Courtesy
of International Institute of
Social History, Amsterdam.

baron) at Terrace Gardens on East Fifty-Eighth Street—a departure from the
downtown scene. Over wine, Goldman observed a different side of Most,
noting his graciousness and attentiveness as a host, in contrast to his fiery
public persona. Most, in turn, admired Goldman's passion and eagerness
to engage intellectually. "There is great need in our ranks of young, willing
people—ardent ones, as you seem to be," he remarked, adding, "and I have
need of ardent friendship." Goldman, puzzled by how such a renowned orator
could feel lonely, recorded Most's poignant reflection: "Yes, little girl, idolized
by many, but loved by none. One can be very lonely among thousands—did
you know that?" At the end of the evening, Most took her hand and said, "This
was my first happy evening in a long while." Their friendship soon developed
into a deeper intellectual and physical connection. Goldman found herself
immersed in a new world of music, literature, and theater, drawn to Most's
"rich personality . . . the alternating heights and depths of his spirit, his hatred
of the capitalist system, his vision of a new society of beauty and joy for all."
Most recognized in Goldman an authentic and courageous spirit, believing
she had the potential to carry on his legacy, that she could "take my place
when I am gone."[48] In January 1890, Most played a pivotal role in arranging

a lecture tour that launched Goldman's career as an anarchist speaker. Her dynamic delivery, according to one listener, was "wholly free of affectation and mannerism," and her emphasis on equality and empowerment appealed to a broad segment of working people.[49]

On January 24, 1890, Johann Most received the disheartening news: the New York Supreme Court had upheld his conviction and sentence stemming from his incendiary speech at Krämer's beer hall two years earlier. Anticipating his imminent arrest, he visited Ida Hoffmann, who was on his bail bond, but unfortunately, she had not been notified in time to extend the bail. Consequently, Most was arrested as he left her house the next day. However, he managed to secure a stay of proceedings pending a decision by the court of appeals in Albany, the state's highest court. One unresolved legal dispute in Most's case revolved around whether his speech, which criticized the Illinois judicial system, could be considered a crime under a New York statute. One of the associate justices was skeptical, leading to an extension of his bail and his subsequent release.[50] Around the same time, Most received encouraging news from Germany: for the first time, the German Reichstag rejected a new version of the 1878 Anti-Socialist Law, which had forced him to flee Germany. This decision allowed the law to expire on September 30, 1890, marking a significant victory for German socialists, who were eager to resume their propaganda and electoral activities. Additionally, Emperor Wilhelm II expressed support for protective labor legislation and announced plans for an international conference on labor issues.[51] In the subsequent elections, the German social democrats won thirty-five seats and nearly 20 percent of the vote. This positive momentum continued in March when Chancellor Otto von Bismarck was relieved of his duties. Despite reporters' inquiries about his plans to return to Germany, pending indictments made it impossible for Most to consider such a move.[52] Furthermore, in 1891, the dissident group known as Die Jungen (The Young Ones), expelled from the German Socialist Party, launched a new radical newspaper, *Der Sozialist*, in Berlin.[53]

Throughout 1890, Most found his relationships with Goldman and Berkman increasingly strained. The two Russians had grown closer and were involved in a ménage à trois with Aronstam. Not only did Most hold more conventional views on sexuality, but he also found the idea of elevating free love as an anarchist practice absurd. "[Most] is often prejudiced against new theories of social life," noted one advocate for free love, "as against the question of sex freedom, of which he cannot speak without getting into a frenzy."[54] Years later, Most's son remembered that "he strongly disapproved of the three of them . . . living together as a threesome. 'Degenerates,' he called them. Emma had guts and brains but was lacking in character, he thought. He never forgave her."⁵⁵ Berkman, who admired the austere and uncompromising demeanor of Russian revolutionaries, privately objected to Most's occasional indulgences in restaurants and theaters. In February 1890, Berkman contemplated returning to Russia to join the revolutionary movement. Partly out of jealousy over Goldman, Most supported this idea but persuaded Berkman to learn the printer's trade instead and arranged an apprenticeship with a German paper in New Haven, Connecticut. In the summer of 1890, Goldman and the Minkin sisters joined Berkman in New Haven, where Most was also a frequent visitor.⁵⁶ After a few months, Most hired Berkman as a typesetter for *Freiheit*, but the two men did not get along and tensions escalated. The final rupture in the bond between Most and Goldman (and Berkman) occurred when both young activists began attending meetings of the autonomists in the fall of 1890. This was particularly painful for Most as his archrival Josef Peukert had arrived in New York and become the leading figure in the Radical Workers' League.⁵⁷ Most felt betrayed. Although small in number, the autonomists established themselves as a counterweight to *Freiheit* when their newspaper, *Der Anarchist*, moved from St. Louis to New York. They attacked Most for behaving like an "infallible pope" and the Mostians for being part of a "personality cult."⁵⁸ Berkman's proposal to investigate the Most-Peukert charges further exacerbated tensions, leading Most to lash out at Berkman, calling him "an arrogant young Jew."⁵⁹

Sometime in the winter or spring of 1891, John Most ended his relationship with Emma Goldman. However, conflicting accounts from Goldman and Helene Minkin present opposing reasons for the breakup. Goldman believed that Most desired a conventional, monogamous relationship: "a home, children, the care and attention ordinary women can give, who have no other interest in life but the man they love and the children they bear him—that was what he needed and felt he had found in Helen [Minkin]." In contrast, Minkin took offense at Goldman's portrayal, asserting that she was not a submissive housewife but a committed anarchist activist who "gave herself body and soul to her ideal." "And why would he need a wife to look after him?" she wondered. While Minkin wrote movingly about her devotion to Most, explaining the unique bond that can exist between a young woman and an older man, she envisioned their relationship as a kind of romantic comradeship dedicated to their shared cause. In New Haven, the quiet and reserved Minkin found herself drawn into the interpersonal dramas involving Most, Goldman, and Berkman. Most recognized Minkin's talent for writing and encouraged her to use it in furthering their cause, leading to more frequent visits and letters from him. However, Minkin maintained a distance "not wanting to think that I was throwing myself at him" and because Goldman had conveyed "terrible things" about him.[60] Complicating matters for historians is Most's silence regarding his romantic relationships, along with the mainstream press's tendency to indulge in sexist assumptions about anarchist women associated with him. Various sources also suggest that Most was still in a common-law marriage with Lena Fischer, with whom he lived in an apartment at 266 William Street, just north of the new Brooklyn Bridge ramp and not far from the *Freiheit* office.[61]

On June 16, 1891, the New York Court of Appeals upheld the conviction and sentencing handed down by the trial court.[62] When Most appeared before Judge Rufus Cowing for transfer to the penitentiary, he was accompanied by Goldman, Berkman, and likely Lena Fischer. Standing farther away was Helene Minkin, who had just turned eighteen and had traveled from New Haven. "I greeted him from a distance," she wrote, "fighting back the tears that were about to stream down my face." As Most exited the courtroom, she caught a glimpse of his smile as he returned "an air kiss . . . tipping his hat." Minkin noticed bystanders searching for the intended recipient of his gesture, "but they didn't notice me." She returned to her work at the corset factory in New Haven, leading a "very withdrawn and lonely" life until Most's release. "How I wanted to help him bear the heavy cross!" she reflected. "I would think about it constantly while sitting at the sewing machine."[63] Both Goldman and Berkman put aside their differences with Most and pledged support and admiration. Berkman even accompanied his mentor all the way to Blackwell's Island.[64]

The anarchists and socialists of New York seized on Most's imprisonment as a catalyst for a nationwide battle for free speech that would stir the conscience of America. A defense committee swiftly formed, determined to escalate the case to the U.S. Supreme Court.[65] Departing from the legal duo of William F. Howe and Abraham Hummel, the committee engaged Charles Le Barbier, a prominent defense attorney who pledged to pursue habeas corpus proceedings to secure Most's release. Despite the fervor of their cause, the anarchists encountered limited public support, as they were widely viewed as alien disruptive forces intent on dismantling cherished institutions and freedoms. One New Jersey newspaper distinguished between genuine and false free speech, reserving the former for "the patriotic citizen" while dismissing the latter as the domain of the "political charlatan, the socialist and anarchist."[66] Meanwhile, efforts were underway to support Lena Fischer, who had fallen ill, with a dedicated fund established by Most's supporters.[67]

Changes reverberated within the *Freiheit* office as well. Berkman was fired, although Goldman maintained that he left of his own accord.[68] A press committee assumed the reins in Most's absence, appointing the youthful comrade Lorenz T. Krämer as interim editor, while Most continued to write from prison.[69] The seasoned newspaper peddler Wilhelm Könnecke, an old friend of Most, contributed his time to office duties. However, in September 1891, amid Most's incarceration, the sixty-eight-year-old Könnecke found himself embroiled in a legal dispute with Florentina, who claimed to be married to him and accused him of abandonment for residing with Lena Most at 266 William Street. Wilhelm countered, asserting that he merely sublet the premises and volunteered at *Freiheit*, reasoning that "Mrs. Most, although a highly estimable woman, was hardly capable of conducting the paper in her husban's [*sic*] absence."[70] July 1891 marked the end of Most's legal challenge as the Supreme Court declined to issue a writ of error, consigning him once more to the confines of prison.[71]

Most's second stint behind bars prompted deep introspection regarding anarchist philosophy, propaganda methods, and the movement's vitality. Embracing communist anarchism and dismissing the primacy of violent propaganda, he honed these beliefs into a new declaration just months before his release. This declaration aimed to supplant the outdated 1883 Pittsburgh manifesto and fervently advocated for communist anarchism: "We claim the *right to enjoy life* according to individual needs," he wrote, "made possible by everyone usefully active *according to their inclination, strength, and ability.*" Central to this vision was the relentless opposition to private property, the state, and the church. He cautioned that the social revolution would likely involve a violent struggle given the entrenched resistance of the privileged classes.[72] Shortly after his release, Most expressed frustrations with his colleagues in a piece titled "Musings from the Heart." He acknowledged his evolution in thought, influenced by Kropotkin and Reclus, and emphasized the significance of propagating ideas through discourse. However, this did not mean that he conformed to bourgeois norms. He asserted his right to step outside the breach without comrades questioning his commitment. "No one has the right to abuse me if I were to withdraw from the worst line of fire," he wrote. "And I cannot deny that such an inclination has repeatedly stirred in me." In April 1892, he again repudiated the idea that any violent deed constituted anarchist propaganda:

> There is no greater error than believing that anarchists must only commit *any* act of violence, no matter *when, where,* and against *whom,* to make propaganda.

Such an act must be popular and applauded by a sizable portion of the pro-letariat to have any effect. If this is not the case, or if an act causes general *disapproval* of those sections of the population on which it is supposed to have a stimulating effect, then the result is reversed: anarchism makes itself hated. Instead of gaining followers, many who joined halfway will withdraw. Therefore, anyone wanting to do propaganda by the deed assumes a heavy responsibility and will do well to examine the situation before acting. . . . Propaganda by the deed is *one* means of propaganda, but not the *only* one. First and foremost, disseminating anarchist-communist principles and revolutionary sentiments requires lively verbal and written, private and public *agitation*. In this area, I believe we have plenty to do in America.[73]

Upon Most's release on April 19, 1892, a welcoming gathering was swiftly organized at Cooper Union for the following day. Helene Minkin traveled to New York to see "how he looked and what years of suffering had made of him." Accompanied by her father, they entered the bustling hall, where a sympathetic anarchist musician recognized her and ensured they had seats on stage. Encouraged by Most, Minkin relocated from New Haven to Newark, New Jersey, in the spring of 1892, securing employment at a corset factory and renting an apartment. Her younger sister Rochel, newly arrived from Russia, joined her there. Attending Most's Sunday lectures in Manhattan became a regular pursuit for Minkin, with evenings often spent in each other's company, with Most making visits to Newark. As her involvement in the movement deepened, Minkin began assisting the German anarchists of Newark in organizing meetings and lectures, further immersing herself in anarchist activities.[74]

Shortly after Most was released, the well-known Italian anarchist and law-yer Francesco Saverio Merlino arrived in New York for a speaking tour. Most learned of Merlino's recently published critical pamphlet, which emphasized the need for anarchist organization and critiqued those who advocated in-dividual deeds to advance anarchist propaganda. While the essay stirred debate, Most welcomed it as a "timely and necessary self-critique," viewing it as confirmation of his own ideas by a respected European anarchist thinker. He had the essay translated and published in *Freiheit*. Merlino argued that unpopular individual actions by anarchists were harmful and counterpro-ductive. Most agreed, acknowledging past mistakes in anarchist tactics and urging the movement to "overcome" what he termed its "childhood illnesses." In a surprising turn, this theoretical discussion soon gave way to a tangible test, as the issue of propaganda by the deed became a stark reality, challeng-ing the anarchist movement's identity and allegiances.[75]

*   *   *

On July 25, 1892, Most visited Minkin in Newark, visibly distressed, agitated, and filled with anger. The day before, Berkman had attempted to assassinate Henry Clay Frick, the manager of Andrew Carnegie's Homestead Steel Works, in his Pittsburgh office. Carnegie and Frick had vowed to crush an ongoing strike by a lockout and by sending armed guards against the strikers. At an anarchist gathering the night before, Most learned from Goldman that she knew of the plan to kill Frick. He regarded the assassination attempt as a misguided action, a severe blow to the movement that would likely provoke another round of repression. "Why didn't they consult me?" he shouted furiously. "I would have explained the situation to them. I'm an old veteran in the movement and know that everything has its time and place, and this assassination was inappropriate."[76] Frick survived the attack and proceeded to quash the Homestead strike, dismantling one of the most resilient unions of the period and plunging hundreds of working families into misery. The Homestead strike held significance beyond its immediate impact; it vividly illustrated the anti-capitalist criticisms long espoused by anarchists and socialists. It seemed as though industrialists, judges, and politicians had collectively validated the radicals' critique through their actions. Although many anarchists sympathized with Berkman's desire to avenge Frick's actions, a crucial question remained: Would the steelworkers and residents of Homestead rally behind the radical cause?

The conflict at Homestead erupted on June 30 when the contract between the company and the Amalgamated Association of Iron and Steel Workers expired. Seeking to cut production costs and boost profits, Carnegie, before departing for his Scottish estate, entrusted Frick with the task of creating a nonunion workforce at any cost. Frick wasted no time; he encircled the plant with a wooden fence and insisted on negotiating only with individual workers. He then presented the union with an ultimatum: accept his terms, or the company would no longer recognize the union. Frick had no intention of negotiating. Even before the contract expired, he had engaged armed guards from the notorious Pinkerton Detective Agency to seize control of the plant and bring in replacement workers. Upon learning that three thousand unskilled workers joined the union members to establish picket lines around "Fort Frick," Frick responded with a drastic measure—an unprecedented lockout, dismissing the entire workforce. Meanwhile, Most embarked on a speaking tour in the Pittsburgh region to garner support and subscribers.[77] Although the extent of his discussion on the Homestead events remains uncertain, by July 3, the Allegheny police, wary of unrest, prohibited him from further speaking engagements.[78] As Most returned to New York, tensions escalated at Homestead, with strikers becoming aware of Pinkerton guards approaching on barges via the Monongahela River. On July 6, as the guards attempted to land, a violent twelve-hour confrontation ensued. Two cannons were used against the barges without much success, and dynamite sticks blew holes in the vessels. At one point, strikers pushed a burning railcar down the tracks into the river. Finally, late afternoon, the Pinkertons surrendered and were subjected to beatings and verbal abuse. The exact toll of the conflict remains unclear, but it is estimated that seven strikers and three guards lost their lives, with many more wounded and some perishing later from their injuries.[79] The battle was reported as a defeat for the unpopular Frick, with much of the press siding with the strikers, who retained control of the plant.

To anarchists, the Homestead battle epitomized the start of a revolutionary struggle—a showcase of class consciousness and armed resistance. In response, three Pittsburgh anarchists, allies of Most, ventured to Homestead to gauge the situation and distribute leaflets promoting social revolution and urging workers to "become anarchists!" To their surprise, the workers derided the anarchists and told them to leave.[80] To restore order, the Allegheny County sheriff sought the governor's aid, leading to the dispatch of 8,500 Pennsylvania National Guardsmen, who arrived on July 12. Initially welcomed by the strikers as the "legal authority" after they clashed with private gunmen, the militia soon revealed its bias, becoming a tool for private interests—a development the anarchists had foreseen. The town was occupied for months, martial law imposed, families were evicted, and two thousand replacement workers, protected by the troops, were brought in. Despite resistance, Frick was determined to "fight this thing to the bitter end."[81] Meanwhile, in New York, Goldman, Berkman, and Aronstam greeted the news of the gun battle with immense excitement; they believed a "psychological moment" had arrived, one not for words but for a "supreme deed" now that the nation's attention was on Homestead.[82] They conceived a plan to assassinate Frick using dynamite bombs, later resorting to firearms when bombs proved impractical. Their zeal led to reckless behavior, exemplified by Berkman's decision to manufacture bombs in an apartment building where families lived. Even Goldman was blinded by righteousness. "What if a few [children] have to perish?" she thought. "The many would be made free and could live in beauty and in comfort."[83] Goldman suggested asking Most for help since "he had constantly propagated the doctrine of individual acts."[84]

However, she knew Most had changed his views several years earlier. In any case, Berkman refused to approach Most. Had he been consulted, Most would undoubtedly have advised against the plan. To their surprise, they received no support from Peukert either. Berkman decided to travel alone to Pittsburgh to kill Frick. Most remained unaware of the plot and only later learned of Berkman's presence in Pittsburgh through mutual friends Carl Nold and Henry Bauer.[85]

On July 16, ten days following the battle, Most delivered two lectures on Homestead, still unaware of Berkman's sinister plot. He hailed the July 6 clash as "glorious" and "epoch making," likening it to the heroic acts of rebels throughout history. Most emphasized its spontaneity and lack of leadership, driven by the "revolutionary instinct of the moment," similar to the events of the Paris Commune. In his eyes, the event validated the contentious notion of an armed proletariat capable of resisting capitalist oppression. Since 1889, Most had grown increasingly confident in the revolutionary potential of American workers, and the events at Homestead served as proof. Despite their conservatism, "the American workers trust peace less and less and will at times wield striking (shooting and blasting) arguments against a murderous gang of rulers." It was also significant for Most that Homestead dealt a decisive blow to the Pinkerton agency, revealing its dubious ties to industrialists. The fact that the townspeople treated the militia differently than the Pinkertons appeared to Most as comical and delusional, a sentiment that proved to be correct. He argued that the Battle of Homestead aligned perfectly with anarchist principles; the workers' rejection of anarchism, given their poor understanding of it, did not alter this.[86] Frick seemed to Most the personification of capitalism in its most brutish and greedy form. Significantly, Most called out Americans' hypocritical outrage at anarchist violent deeds at a time when violence and brutality were daily occurrences, such as the terrorism inflicted on Black Americans. "In America, within a year," he wrote, "more acts of violence are committed over the most trivial matters than in the whole rest of the world combined."[87]

Just a week later, on July 23, Most learned of Berkman's attack on Frick while preparing to address a regular meeting of New York Group I attended by Goldman. According to Goldman's memoir, Most questioned whether the newspapers had fabricated the incident or if Frick had orchestrated it for national sympathy. Outraged, Goldman demanded to speak, but the crowd insisted she leave.[88] The following day, an agitated Most visited Minkin in Newark, where it had become public knowledge that Berkman's attempt had failed, landing him in jail while Frick recovered.[89]

Figure 15. Alexander Berkman on September 19, 1892, the day of his sentencing. Courtesy of International Institute of Social History, Amsterdam.

Most not only disavowed individual acts of violence but also believed Berkman's failed attempt tainted the significance and promise of the July 6 battle, potentially inviting further repression. Feeling exposed due to Berkman's previous employment with him and his recent lectures in Pittsburgh, Most was relieved that Nold had destroyed all correspondence regarding Berkman. Although investigators from Pittsburgh came to New York seeking to indict Most, by the end of July, no evidence linked him to a plot against Frick.[90] In an interview with the *Evening World*, Most downplayed the shooting as "a mere scratch" and called Berkman an enemy who betrayed him. "I hate him as much as I do Frick," he told the reporter. "I took him in here and learned [sic] him to be a printer, and then when he got so's he could do some things he turned around and he blackguarded me. . . . He has been a botch all his life, and the botch attack on Frick was just like him." When asked if Berkman's deed advanced the cause of anarchism, Most replied, "Not by the bungling job that was done. All true anarchists hate Frick, but I won't say that he ought to have been killed."[91] Rocker has suggested that Most's attack on Berkman was also fueled by the news that his dear friend John Neve had been transferred to an insane asylum, which surely rekindled his hatred of Peukert and all those who associate with him.[92]

A few days later, Goldman publicly criticized Most in *Der Anarchist* for the first time, accusing him of disparaging Berkman out of personal animosity. She labeled her former mentor "a most pathetic coward, a liar, an actor, and also a wimp," portraying his involvement in the movement as parasitic, driven by "calculation" and "rank ambition." Her article concluded with a thinly veiled threat against Most: "Words are useless with such people; a beating would probably not change this person, but it would shut him up."[93] Goldman's portrayal of Most's stance on propaganda by the deed as a sudden shift motivated by cowardice or jealousy toward Berkman was disingenuous.[94] Most had publicly revised his views in articles and speeches prior to Berkman's arrival in America. Rocker noted that in 1892, no one seemed to remember that Most changed his views in 1887 and that "young comrades like Berkman, Emma Goldman, etc., did not seem to know them at all."[95] Throughout the summer and fall of 1892, Most further elucidated his position through articles and speeches, condemning propaganda by the deed, particularly individual acts of terrorism, as ineffective and detrimental to the movement. "Anyone making a balance of the costs and benefits of this kind of agitation," he wrote, "would face a moral and factual deficit."[96] Furthermore, the assassination attempt on Frick had no propaganda value because native-born Americans could easily turn their initial hatred into sympathy for Frick the moment they realized that the perpetrator was an unemployed Russian Jewish anarchist. "In a country where we are so weakly represented and so little understood," he wrote, "we cannot afford the luxury of attentats. ... In countries like America, where we still need solid ground to stand on, we must limit ourselves to literary and verbal agitation." Americans, by and large, do not believe they live under a despotism, though they "live under the delusion of being free citizens of a free country."[97] Most's analysis was vindicated by the adverse repercussions of Berkman's deed at Homestead, which led to increased arrests, surveillance, and repression. Despite acknowledging Berkman's courage, Most believed Berkman to be "eccentric" and became even more fanatical after joining the autonomists.[98] Most was also genuinely alarmed by the possibility of a conspiracy charge against him that could lead to more prison time. "Whenever anything of this kind is committed [Frick shooting]," one anarchist believed, "it seems the first thing the authorities think of is to connect Most with it and arrest him."[99]

In September, Merlino surprised many by announcing that he no longer aligned with Most's views and opposed Most's stance on Berkman's deed.

Merlino claimed that the shooting of Frick had garnered approval from "many American workers," even though this was inaccurate. He stated, "I have never spoken or written a word that could honestly be interpreted as a declaration against revolutionary actions." But this was misleading. Rocker argued that Merlino had been influenced by the autonomists to support Berkman. Most responded that Merlino was ignorant of American conditions and embarrassed him by quoting his own recent pamphlet in which he argued that anarchists should "completely separate" from "advocates of individual action." The Berkman affair stirred emotions and sparked serious debate within the movement. It led Most to write another essay on propaganda by the deed, a tactic he had deemed inappropriate and ineffective in America for years.

Drawing on history and personal experience, Most argued that assassination attempts as an anarchist tactic had proven suicidal even in most European countries, whereas propaganda through the word had yielded better outcomes. In his critique, Most admitted that he once advocated violent tactics but had revised his views based on facts. He criticized the autonomists' support for Berkman, accusing them of "competing with each other in hero worship that bordered on Catholic martyr worship," even though they had long criticized him for fostering a personality cult.[100]

Goldman was not persuaded and resolved to confront Most at the Pioneers of Liberty meeting on December 18, 1892, where he was scheduled

Figure 16. "Among the Anarchists of New York" drawn by Valerian Gribayedoff in *Harper's Weekly*, August 20, 1892.

to speak. Accompanied by Aronstam and Timmermann, she intended to follow through on her earlier threat.[101] As Most began his speech, Goldman rose from her front seat, demanding evidence for his accusations against Berkman. Dismissing her as hysterical, Most's response further fueled her anger. In a bold move, she leaped onto the stage, brandishing a horsewhip, which she tore into his face before breaking it and hurling it at him. The hall erupted into an uproar with calls to eject her. A week later, two Yiddish groups published a notice in *Freiheit*: "We hereby declare the performance of the infamous Emma Goldman and her accomplices as a vileness that could only have come from the blatant madness of an idiots' clique." In retaliation, Goldman defended her right to publicly "chastise" Most after he insulted her. She criticized his Yiddish supporters, accusing them of lacking courage to oppose him and dubbing them "Cossacks of the Czar Most," a particularly cutting remark. She asserted that Most had always "shown the greatest contempt" for the Jewish comrades to whom "he now clings, like a drowning man to a straw." The Pioneers of Liberty reaffirmed their loyalty to Most and expelled Goldman like a "heretic."[102]

Rudolf Rocker observed in 1924 that the Berkman affair, culminating in Berkman's incarceration in September 1892, marked the conclusion of "one of the most dramatic and eventful chapters in the American anarchist movement."[103] Similar to the Haymarket affair, John Most found himself tangentially involved, fearing the stigma of guilt by association perpetuated by mainstream media and the legal system. In both instances, he witnessed dedicated activists being imprisoned or, in the case of Haymarket, executed. At the age of forty-six, Most grew weary of being the public face of anarchism—repeatedly misunderstood, defensive, and under scrutiny from reporters and law enforcement. Tired of being everybody's "whipping boy," he was prepared to relinquish his leadership role.[104] In a message to the movement in December 1892, Most struck a pragmatic and optimistic tone. He reiterated his firm belief that anarchists in the United States "cannot go beyond the framework of the conditions of the moment" no matter how lofty their ideals, a statement his rivals viewed as too tame. No thoughtful anarchist, he wrote, should succumb to the childish delusion that using explosives constitutes effective propaganda. Instead, it is the distribution and "proclamation of the teachings of communism and anarchy" that will serve the cause in America.[105] Despite stepping out of the limelight, he did not fade into obscurity. Instead, he sought a balance between public activism and family life, a balance he had previously been unable to achieve.

9 Hard Times

DURING THE 1890S, MANY MEMBERS in German anarchist circles were married men, often with children, and their wives frequently participated in commemorative events and recreational outings. There is very little information about John Most's relationship with Lena Fischer. Similarly, details about Most's relationship with Helene Minkin before they lived together are scarce, though insights can be found in Emma Goldman's memoirs, published in 1931, and Minkin's, released a year later. In 1893, when Minkin was nineteen and Most was forty-seven, they shared a deep emotional and intellectual connection despite the significant age gap, which likely led them to be discreet about their relationship at first. Minkin was a passionate anarchist in her own right. She wrote, "The movement which became my life's work was closely tied with Most." Although she did not possess the gift of public speaking, she was one of many tireless, selfless activists often overlooked by history. She had moved to Newark to care for her younger sister Rochel while working at a local corset factory. These circumstances likely made it difficult for her to move to Manhattan, something Most would have encouraged her to do. In early December 1892, Minkin experienced a traumatic incident that may have influenced her decision to relocate to New York City. She received a telegram from her brother-in-law in New Haven, informing her that her older sister Anna was gravely ill. Arriving in New Haven by train at two in the morning, she found no one there to meet her. As she trudged through the snowy streets, a young man pushed her into an alleyway. She fought back with her umbrella, managed to escape, and arrived at her sister's house with her clothes torn. She stayed for two weeks, caring for Anna and her baby.

After returning to New York, she attended a Pioneers of Liberty meeting, where she witnessed Goldman horsewhipping Most.[1]

In early 1893, Most suggested that Minkin leave her factory job to become the bookkeeper and office manager at *Freiheit*, offering her the same salary. "The work will be more interesting for you," he said. "It will strain you less, and you'll be closer to the movement."[2] Initially hesitant due to concerns about how comrades might perceive it, Minkin eventually agreed and rented an apartment in Lower Manhattan. "Most came to see me every night, except when we went to meetings," she wrote, perhaps to avoid raising suspicion among the comrades, "thus gradually it happened that Most and I came together as man and wife."[3] One reason they may not have openly cohabited could have been Most's ongoing relationship with Lena Fischer, who was now known as "Lizzie."[4] In October 1893, news emerged that Lizzie had contracted smallpox and was transferred from their home to Riverside Hospital on North Brother Island. Their apartment was immediately fumigated, bedding was incinerated, and the space was locked and sealed. Although Most was advised to get vaccinated, he refused, holding on to the anti-vaccination views he had held since the 1870s. The fate of Lena Fischer remains unclear, but her relationship with Most ended in November.[5] The exact date of Helene Minkin and John Most's common-law marriage remains uncertain.[6]

In November 1893, Minkin and Most moved into a basement apartment on Skillman Ave in Williamsburg, a German American enclave in Brooklyn.[7] Minkin furnished the space with a bed, a round table, and chairs, while Most brought a couch from the *Freiheit* office. The walls were adorned with pictures depicting scenes from anarchist and labor movements, with particular focus on the Chicago martyrs and a rifle-wielding Louise Michel during the Paris Commune. When Minkin announced her pregnancy, Most was elated. "He never expected that he would again be a father," Minkin wrote. "His past experience brought him terrible pain." For the first time in his life, Most shared with Minkin the trauma of losing two children: "Tears would run down his face when he spoke of them, and I would cry along with him." Minkin stopped commuting to Manhattan but continued to handle the bookkeeping and correspondence for *Freiheit* from home. She worried about raising a daughter in a world where women were "compelled to live in the narrow confines of her four walls while caring for the house and children." Despite her concerns, she hoped the arrival of their child would rekindle Most's "zest for life."[8] However, it soon became apparent that their damp basement room in Brooklyn was unsuitable for raising a child. In the spring of 1894, they relocated to a top-floor apartment at 113 Henry Street in the Jewish quarter of Lower Manhattan, paying nearly double the rent.[9] Around the same time, Most moved the *Freiheit* office to 144 Park Row, where saloonkeeper and former interim editor Lorenz Krämer occupied the first floor. The office was now only a short walk from their apartment. "I wanted him to be able to come home," wrote Minkin of their new apartment, "take a little nap, and see his child every day."[10] John Most Jr. was born on May 19, 1894, after a difficult birth. Most was by Minkin's side and was overjoyed. When Helene's sister Anna arrived from Boston, Most could not contain his excitement: "Sister-in-law, sister-in-law, we have a son! We have a new soldier for our cause!" As atheists, Minkin and Most rejected the religious customs typically associated with the birth of a boy.[11]

Many anarchists loyal to Most expressed concerns that family life would divert his attention from his role as a prominent figure in the movement. "They think . . . the blood in my veins flows only for shouting, speaking," Most complained to Minkin. "They think that my heart beats only for the movement." Implicit in this backlash was the belief that family obligations would distract male activists and weaken their revolutionary resolve. Some feared that it would also divert resources from their activism. This attitude was hypocritical, considering that most rank-and-file German anarchists lived in monogamous relationships and raised children.[12] Minkin noted that some of these men cast doubts about her to Most, leading her to distance herself from his circle. "Now I lived for Most," she wrote, "and for the child I was expecting."[13] Goldman, observing the sexism prevalent among many German anarchist men, became increasingly frustrated and disillusioned with their outdated views on gender. Years later, she remarked, "[The Germans] remain stationary on all points except economics. Especially as regards women, they are really antediluvian."[14]

The severe economic depression triggered by a financial panic in May 1893 deepened the family's financial struggles. With four million Americans thrown out of work and no safety net, New York State's unemployment rate soared to 35 percent. Layoffs began in the summer and continued through the winter, leaving seventy thousand New Yorkers, a quarter of them women, jobless by January 1894.[15] Despite petitions from unions and socialists for direct relief and municipal jobs, state and city governments took little action. Meanwhile, *Freiheit* experienced a decline in subscribers, compounded by rising costs of paper and printing. To make ends meet, Minkin borrowed money from her sister to buy a baby carriage and struggled to obtain fresh milk, although she may have taken advantage of the new pasteurized milk stations in working-class neighborhoods established by Nathan Strauss, the owner of Macy's department store. The subsequent decrease in child mortality led the city to ban raw milk altogether. By the fall of 1894, Minkin found herself pregnant again despite her earlier decision not to have more children. Their second child, Lucifer, was born on July 22, 1895, bringing joy to Most but adding to the family's financial strain. Minkin was less optimistic: "Joy was all he offered them and me; poverty bore down on us even more now."[16] To supplement their income, Most took on bookbinding jobs from his office on Park Row, while Minkin became adept at crafting children's clothes from old adult garments.[17] Despite their difficulties, Most embraced fatherhood wholeheartedly, compensating for the absence of such experiences in Germany; he even spoke English to his children. However, Minkin often found herself alone with the children for extended periods, enduring boredom and loneliness when Most traveled, sometimes for as long as three months.[18] "I felt as if my house was a cemetery, and one could bury the dead there," she recalled. Despite these challenges, she treasured moments of genuine companionship with Most, as they shared stories and laughter late into the night.[19] Minkin captured a domestic scene:

> Most loved his children very much and when they were still babies, he would ask me to put them in bed with him. "I want to have 'office hours' with my boys," he'd say. He would usually come home around lunchtime, and he'd sit in his room and write while I prepared the meal. When the children were home and began to get rambunctious, I'd ask him to help me keep them quiet. He would quickly get himself to work, grabbing a brush and a hand towel, and chasing after the children, beating them with both. They would take all the pillows off the beds and throw them at him. Soon, they would be rolling around on the floor, making so much noise that I would have to shout at them to stop. Because of that they called me "the cop." "Be quiet, children, the cop is here!" he would say. He would laugh until tears ran down his face.[20]

During the summer of 1893, amid the depression, socialists and anarchists in New York engaged in heated debates over how to respond to the perceived failure of capitalism and the alarming rise in unemployment and social unrest. City labor activists and radicals united to organize the unemployed, staging outdoor rallies to show their strength and demand action. Meanwhile, the autonomists, led by figures like Goldman, advocated for direct action by the jobless. On August 21, thousands gathered in Union Square to hear speeches by Goldman and other leaders. Already called the "Queen of the Anarchists" by the press, Goldman emerged as a central figure in the movement for the rights of the unemployed in New York. However, her vocal calls for action led to her arrest on charges of inciting to riot after she urged the predominantly Jewish crowd to "demonstrate before the palaces of the rich. Demand work. If they do not give you work, demand bread. If they deny you both, take bread. It is your sacred right!"[21] John Most, however, was skeptical about the effectiveness of hunger demonstrations and chose not to participate in the rallies, possibly to avoid encountering Goldman. In the columns of *Freiheit*, though, Most echoed Goldman's sentiments, declaring that "every human being has the right to exist" and that looting by starving masses would be "natural, even self-evident."[22]

In August 1894, Minkin and Most briefly feared deportation following the passage of an anti-anarchist bill by the U.S. Senate. Since the Haymarket affair, numerous politicians had sought to amend immigration laws to prevent anarchists from entering the country and to deport those already residing within its borders. These efforts gained momentum after the assassination of French president Sadi Carnot by an anarchist in June 1894, amid concerns that hundreds of anarchist exiles were heading to America. Neither Minkin nor Most were naturalized citizens, though their children were. The 1894 bill, sponsored by New York senator David B. Hill, advanced further toward enactment than any previous measure of its kind. At one point, Senator John Sherman even proposed an amendment allowing the government to deport citizens, although this provision was ultimately discarded. After passing in the Senate, the bill moved to the House but faced a setback. Democratic representative John DeWitt Warner of Manhattan, objected to unanimous consent, citing concerns about the vague definition of "anarchy" and the potential for federal officers to enforce laws against an ill-defined crime. His lone objection led to the withdrawal of the "Hill Bill."[23] Despite the depression and immigration politics, Minkin and Most remained steadfast in their political convictions. Minkin recalls an incident that underscores their principles. After Lucifer's birth in the summer of 1895, the *New York World*, a major newspaper owned by Joseph Pulitzer, approached Most with an offer to write a weekly column for fifty dollars. "What do you have to say about it, Helene?" Most asked. "If I take this on, it would be good for us." However, Minkin knew that Most would never compromise his principles by writing for the bourgeois press. They shared a moment of laughter, affirming their decision. "Bravo, my Helene!" he shouted, "I knew that you would never ask me to do this. Courage, my love! Courage! We will find a way out." "It was better this way," she remembered. "Our souls remained pure."[24]

* * *

By the mid-1890s, American anarchism underwent a transformation, with a new generation of activists, predominantly from Eastern and Southern Europe, rising to prominence. Among these emerging groups, the Jewish radical movement gained significant influence, especially in cities like New York and Philadelphia. This shift did not go unnoticed by the mainstream press, which reported on the changing dynamics. In 1895, a Staten Island paper reported, "It used to be said a few years ago that the rallying point of the red flag socialist in New York was always a German lager beer saloon. . . . But nowadays, one does not look in New York for anarchists among the Germans, but among the Russian Jews on the east side."[25] Goldman, renowned for her powerful speeches in both German and English, became a focal point for both the mainstream press and law enforcement whenever anarchist activities were reported. Despite being only twenty-six years old in 1895, she wielded considerable influence. The relationship between Most and Goldman remained one of mutual avoidance.[26] Most limited his public appearances to historical and philosophical lectures, often addressing Jewish anarchist audiences, and he only attended anarchist anniversaries and events when Goldman was absent. This pattern of avoidance was evident even in January 1899, when over three thousand anarchists, representing all the major languages, gathered at Cooper Union to protest the Anti-Anarchist Conference in Rome. Most refused to attend on learning that Goldman was involved in organizing the meeting. The Italian government had called the Rome conference following the assassination of Empress Elizabeth of Austria by the Italian anarchist Luigi Lucheni on September 10, 1898. Goldman staunchly defended Lucheni and denounced the Rome conference as an imperialist plot aimed at suppressing radical movements.[27]

In the summer of 1894, Most and other radicals found a reason to celebrate. On June 26, 1894, Illinois governor John Peter Altgeld granted pardons to Michael Schwab, Samuel Fielden, and Oscar Neebe, the three Haymarket anarchists who had been imprisoned since 1887. Altgeld, a German-born governor, publicly condemned the prosecution and called the trial a miscarriage of justice. However, his actions faced severe criticism from the press, which accused him of demagoguery and questioned his loyalty and citizenship.[28] Despite this backlash, a monument honoring the Haymarket martyrs was unveiled at Waldheim Cemetery in Chicago the day before, further lifting the spirits of Most and his comrades. "Now that there are signs that we will have justice," he told a reporter, "our sympathizers will become outspoken Anarchists."[29] He compared Altgeld's actions to propaganda by the deed, suggesting that each critique of the trial was like a bomb aimed at the foundations of American "justice."³⁰ Most's fame was such that he was often asked for his opinion on national political issues, though these responses could be exploited by various political candidates. No one wanted any association with "anarchy" or "Herr Most." Altgeld's already troubled political career suffered further when Most publicly praised him as an honest man, clarifying that Altgeld was "not an Anarchist nor a Socialist, but a Democrat who believes in the original principles of the party."³¹ When the Democrats nominated William Jennings Bryan as their presidential candidate and made the "free silver" issue a central focus for the November election, Most found himself drawn into the political fray once again. Despite advocating for the gold standard given the current economic conditions, Most emphasized his vision of a society without money, whether based on silver or gold. However, both parties seized on his comments for their own ends. Republican editors sought to associate "free silver" with "anarchy," while Silver Democrats used Most's support for the gold standard to attack William McKinley's Republican Party. At a Silverite convention in St. Louis, delegates from Minnesota displayed a banner depicting Most and McKinley shaking hands, with McKinley's arm labeled "Trust" and Most's arm labeled "Anarchy." The banner read, "Unite and Down These," with the words "The Modern Herod and Pilate—United to Crucify the Common People" below.³²

Most's primary focus was not on national party politics but on disseminating communist anarchism to a broader English-speaking audience. Despite his discomfort with speaking and writing in English, he supported various initiatives aimed at spreading anarchist ideas through spoken and printed mediums. During the 1890s, he delivered lectures alongside English anarchists Charles Mowbray and John Turner as part of their speaking tours in America. However, Most had mixed feelings about English-language anarchist publications. While he recognized their potential to reach American workers, he worried they would compete with *Freiheit* for younger subscribers. Although his friend John Edelmann once suggested publishing *Freiheit* in English, this idea never materialized.³³ In his endeavor to diversify propaganda efforts, Most turned to a long-standing passion: the stage. Anarchist drama clubs had existed for years; Most had previously been unable to participate due to time constraints. These clubs typically staged farces and light dramas accompanied by music and dance, charging fifteen cents per person for admission. One such club, named Bühnentreu (Stage Loyal), dedicated its proceeds to *Freiheit*.³⁴ In the summer of 1894, about three months after the birth of John Jr., Most established Freie Bühne von New York (Free Stage of New York), an amateur theater company of twenty men and ten women (later expanding to forty-one members). Assuming the roles of business and stage manager as well as principal actor, Most drew inspiration from the independent Free Stage theater in Berlin, which was committed to promoting realist and naturalist drama. He recognized the potential of theater as a powerful tool for propagating revolutionary philosophy as well as a source of income for *Freiheit*. "I believe in the drama as the most effective propaganda," he once told a *New York Times* reporter. "Last but not least, it is a business venture."[35]

The Free Stage of New York debuted with Gerhart Hauptmann's *Die Weber* (The Weavers), a powerful portrayal of the dire working conditions and extreme poverty endured by weavers in Silesia. The play, which depicted street fighting, vandalism, and rebellion, had already drawn the ire of German censors. Although Hauptmann was not writing as an agitator, he based his story on newspaper accounts, according to John Blankenagel.[36] An influential critic noted that the play's focus was not on individual characters or plot intricacies but rather on "the presentation in concrete form of the oppression and struggles of the weavers," making it both innovative and controversial.[37] The first American performance took place on October 8 at the packed Thalia Theatre on the Bowery.[38] The audience initially did not recognize Most, but as soon as he delivered his first line, the crowd burst into cheers. A socialist reviewer criticized Most's alterations to the original text, particularly his addition of explosive lines to Jäger's attack on the industrialist Dreißiger.[39] However, as Jesse Cohn suggests, perhaps anarchists were less concerned with strict adherence to the original text and more interested in exploring its spontaneity.[40] Interestingly, Most did not play Jäger but portrayed Old Baumert, a character instrumental in organizing the weavers against the manufacturer. Baumert, depicted as a "broken old man who despaired of himself and the world" but who becomes agitated by Jäger and schnapps, was well received despite these criticisms.[41]

Overall, the reviews were positive. A Chicago radical paper hailed Most as "the first realist actor in New York."[42] A Brooklyn reviewer remarked, "Oddly enough, Mr. Most made rather a success." A theater magazine called him "an actor of unusual talent, and his performance was received with thunderous applause."[43] The success of the initial performance led to more shows at the Thalia and bookings in New Jersey. However, authorities in Newark prohibited Most's company from performing due to ongoing labor disputes, fearing further agitation. "Therefore," explained the police captain, "I regard it as dangerous to allow an agitator like John Most to incite them even further. If he [Most] dares to come here and speak, I will arrest him." Most was asked to hand over the script to a commission consisting of the police chief, the district attorney, and

Figure 17. Advertisement for *Die Weber* in *Freiheit*,
December 26, 1903.

the mayor, who described Hauptmann's play as "crass and tasteless."[44] Despite this setback, the company found a receptive audience in Paterson, New Jersey, the country's silk manufacturing hub. Despite recent efforts to organize mill workers, there was no interference by the authorities. Six hundred people, nearly all weavers, crowded into Turner Hall to watch the tale of misery and rebellion. The performance moved the audience, who "rose in their seats, waved their hats" but ultimately remained orderly.[45] Most did not resume theatrical activities until May 1896, when the company performed in Brooklyn, Union Hill, New Jersey, and again at the Thalia Theatre.

Keeping *Freiheit* operational remained the paramount concern for Most and Minkin, not only for the sake of the movement but also because it was their sole source of income. The depression years posed significant challenges, including a decline in subscribers and rising expenses, leading to weekly anxiety about meeting publication deadlines.[46] Increased costs for expediting, distribution, heating and lighting, and wages for compositors further strained finances.[47] The total annual expenses for producing the paper in 1893 were 17 percent higher than in 1889. While Most enjoyed a modest surplus of $11 in 1889, he faced deficits of $341 four years later and $455 the following year. The economic downturn also affected *Freiheit*'s readers, as evidenced by the substantial amount of unpaid subscriptions totaling $1,800 in 1895. Theater performances provided some financial relief, with four shows generating $286.70 in proceeds—three at the Thalia and one in Paterson.[48] The paper also underwent stylistic changes. For the June 15, 1895 issue, *Freiheit* transitioned from Gothic to Latin letters, giving it a cleaner look and allowing more lines per page. Most explained that Latin letters "are undoubtedly the international characters of the future and because they make reading German printed matter easier for anyone who is not a native German."[49] Another significant change was the adoption of a typesetting machine to reduce the need for manual typesetting. However, this decision posed a dilemma for Most, who had previously lamented the impact of mechanization on traditional crafts. As the historian Kathy Ferguson notes, anarchist printers were generally hesitant to embrace new technologies, viewing letterpress printing and manual typesetting as an ethical fusion of "mental and manual labor, of art, craft, and collective action."[50] Although Most could not afford a new linotype machine, he likely hired a printer to expedite production. In March 1897, financial constraints compelled Most and Minkin to reduce the paper to three columns to mitigate costs. Historians like Rudolf Rocker have rightfully acknowledged Minkin's indispensable support in managing the paper.[51] Nevertheless, she faced the arduous task of raising two children during challenging times, largely on her own due to Most's annual autumn speaking tours. These prolonged absences eventually strain their relationship. Minkin later recalled moments of melancholic solitude in the park: "Families would go by: a father, a mother, and children. The father helped the mother take care of the children. I felt one hot tear after another roll down my face."[52]

* * *

In the fall of 1897, a potential lifeline for *Freiheit* emerged from Buffalo. Most's friend Lorenz Krämer, who had previously edited *Freiheit* during Most's imprisonment, had taken charge of the Buffalo labor paper, *Buffaloer Arbeiter-Zeitung*, with plans to elevate it to a daily publication. When the previous editor, Richard Baginski, departed, Krämer extended an offer to Most to edit the paper for a weekly salary of fifteen dollars.[53] Most accepted the offer on the condition that *Freiheit* could continue as a weekly supplement. Although Minkin had reservations, Most believed it was the only viable solution to save *Freiheit* from financial ruin.[54] On September 7, 1897, Most traveled to Buffalo to meet with the publishing association and assess living arrangements. However, he quickly realized that the available start-up capital was insufficient and internal disagreements among the associates threatened collaboration. Despite these concerns, Most summoned Minkin and the children to join him in Buffalo, where they rented a four-room apartment at 310 Genesee Street across from the editorial offices.[55] This move marked the first time since his arrival in America in 1882 that Most resided outside New York City for an extended period. Unfortunately, their time in Buffalo proved challenging and disheartening. The socialist and anarchist presence was minimal, and union membership among German workers, aside from brewers, was scarce. Minkin struggled with strenuous domestic duties without the aid of modern conveniences, while Most grappled with an overwhelming workload, obligated to produce a minimum of eight columns daily alongside a coeditor.[56] He did occasionally enjoy leisurely strolls with Minkin and the boys. Most recognized early on that *Freiheit*'s publication in Buffalo was only temporary but resisted the impulse to return to New York, a move he thought was in bad form.[57] A notable highlight during their time in Buffalo was a visit from the esteemed anarchist geographer Peter Kropotkin, whom Most deeply admired, calling him "one of the greatest scholars of this century."[58] An old rumor among autonomists that Most and Kropotkin were adversaries was quickly dispelled when the Russian remarked, "With a few more Mosts our movement would be much stronger."[59] After enduring ten months of hardship, Minkin decided to return to New York with the children to seek alternative means of livelihood despite Most's reluctance to see her leave. She departed under the pretense of visiting her family, leaving Most to confront an uncertain future in Buffalo.

When the Buffalo publishers attempted to exert control over *Freiheit*, demanding changes to its content to avoid offending conservative readers, Most reached his breaking point. He "couldn't sell his soul to them for a bowl of lentils," wrote Minkin. Throughout the summer of 1898, Most and Minkin implored comrades in New York to bolster their support for *Freiheit*. They managed to enlist the help of a typesetter willing to work for free at night and a printer, Frederick W. Heiss, who agreed to defer payment until the paper's financial situation stabilized. On August 6, 1898, after eleven tumultuous months in Buffalo, Most and *Freiheit* returned to New York, establishing headquarters above Hermann Kohle's beer hall at 69 Gold Street. The family secured an apartment at 434 Thirteenth Street in Brooklyn, conveniently located near Prospect Park. However, the strain of their ordeal had taken its toll on Minkin, and she fell ill. Dr. Hillel Solotaroff, an anarchist physician who had introduced Minkin to Goldman nine years earlier, administered electric treatments to aid in her recovery.[60] The Buffalo episode left a bitter taste for Most, who criticized the lack of cultural vibrancy in American cities outside the major urban centers. "In America there are only a few huge cities with any modern-cultural flair," Most grumbled. "The other urban points are nothing more than big villages, and Buffalo is the metropolis of blockheads."[61] Reflecting on this period, Most acknowledged it as *Freiheit's* sole misstep, though he neglected to mention that Minkin had foreseen such challenges.[62] With their finances relatively secure, Most and Minkin steered *Freiheit* toward its twentieth anniversary in January 1899, solidifying its status as one of the longest-running anarchist periodicals. This milestone prompted moments of celebration and pride. "I feel pretty damn young," a fifty-two-year-old Most asserted, "and I still have a few fights in me." He likened himself to an inventor who had successfully conducted a groundbreaking experiment and still possessed the spirit for further struggles.[63]

*　*　*

The depression of the 1890s was a turning point in American history, sparking widespread debate and reform efforts to tackle systemic inequalities, political corruption, monetary policies, and the role of the federal government. For anarchists like Minkin and Most, the repeated failures of capitalism highlighted the urgent need to offer workers an alternative vision for the future. Reflecting on his earlier writings from the 1880s, Most acknowledged a shift in perspective over the following decade. Initially, he believed in the universal applicability of socialism, anarchism, or revolution but later recognized the importance of considering the unique characteristics and idiosyncrasies of the United States.[64] This evolution led to the development of more nuanced and original ideas about America and the possibilities for building anarchism within its context. Unfortunately, the long period from the 1890s until his death—during which he refined his mature ideas—has largely been forgotten or overshadowed by his relatively brief "terrorist" phase of the early 1880s. Most lamented Americans' reluctance to critically examine root causes, especially during economic crises. Instead of challenging capitalism's fundamental structures, many working Americans focused on securing higher wages within the existing system, failing to recognize that monopolies were inherent to capitalism itself. "They ask of the monopolists to pay them higher wages," he wrote, "instead of rejecting monopolism and the wage system altogether." Even in the face of economic depression and increased repression of labor movements, Most observed that Americans maintained a steadfast belief in the inherent goodness and justice of their government. For anarchists and socialists, the economic crisis and the elites' indifference to widespread suffering confirmed their long-held critiques, making the absence of a mass revolutionary movement to overthrow the system all the more frustrating. Most lamented that even the most destitute victims of the depression "refuse to understand why and how they suffer" and seek solace in "all sorts of possible and impossible remedies and can thus be deceived by all imaginable demagogues and charlatans."[65] This faith in the system, coupled with the illusion of control over public affairs, hindered the societal transformations anarchists sought.[66]

Anarchists like Most not only fought against an exploitative economic system but also the pervasive narrative of American exceptionalism. This ideological battle, often overlooked, posed a major obstacle for leftist politics in the United States. Despite the harsh realities of capitalism, Most noted that many Americans stubbornly clung to the belief that their nation was exceptional and morally superior. Public displays of patriotism and religiosity served to reinforce this narrative, complicating efforts to challenge the status quo.[67] Throughout his career, Most skillfully subverted and deconstructed these entrenched ideologies. He criticized official secular and religious holidays as symbols of a society that had abandoned critical thinking, even as principles of freedom and equality were eroded.[68] A history enthusiast, he relished challenging the nation's confidence in its own past. For example, he denounced President's Day celebrations and the construction of the "tasteless" Washington Monument, highlighting Washington's career as a slave owner and elevating figures like Benjamin Franklin and Thomas Paine.[69] In October 1892, long before Howard Zinn wrote *A People's History*, Most attacked Columbus Day festivities surrounding the four-hundredth anniversary of Columbus's first voyage, condemning the Italian explorer for his atrocities against Indigenous peoples. He called Columbus Day a "mad orgy" where the organizers regarded "rape, murder, arson, and theft as the highest among the virtues." As usual, Most pointed to a historical continuity: 1892 was not a moment of celebration but a time to reflect on "a past full of villainy" and a present of "monstrous wretchedness." Even though Most saw the future as bleak, he was not without hope; he believed that only a general rebellion could bring change, even if "at the moment, this is not getting through to Americans." He proposed an Atlantic perspective to dismantle the myth of exceptionalism: "We don't have kings or emperors, but we do have kings of silver, and iron, and gold. . . . Anarchism will sweep away the trusts. Let us send the priests to heaven and the politicians to hell and rule ourselves."[70]

Most extended his anarchist critique not only to America's economic system but also to its electoral politics and political corruption. He warned that the pursuit of power and ambition in the materialistic environment of the United States was undermining the revolutionary spirit of the proletariat.[71] Comparing American and German political systems, Most argued that American politicians were even more corrupt due to the financial gains associated with machine politics. "If it titillates a German parliamentarian (without salary) to put 'MP' behind his name," he wrote a month before the 1894 U.S. midterm elections, "the candidates in an American election campaign get itchy hands because, as everyone knows, victory tends to yield a pretty penny for the most disreputable parasites."[72] Most was part of a group of German American editors and journalists who exposed police corruption before it gained attention in the mainstream press. However, he noted that only those who could read German were aware of this reporting.[73] Despite this, he viewed investigations like the Lexow Committee's probe into corruption as mere political theater—a "Punch and Judy show" and a "clumsy Republican maneuver" aimed at displacing Democrats and placating voters.[74] No fundamental change, he believed, would occur, even if elections resulted in a dramatic power shift. For instance, the Democrats' defeat in the 1894 midterms did not change his skepticism toward the political system. Most argued that such swings only served to reinforce the illusion that elections were genuine mechanisms for change. Most identified a contradiction in American politics: while there was a libertarian call for limited government, there was also an expectation that elections would bring about significant social transformation. "The entire political machinery of the United States," he once wrote, "can be compared to a grandfather clock. Weights hang on the right and left—the democratic and republican weights—and a pendulum in the middle that moves back and forth. This is the reform tail of the machinery and . . . has little to do with progress."[75]

Elections, in Most's view, were not only ineffectual and false comfort but also created the potential for a tyrant to rise by exploiting popular sentiment. Decades before the rise of fascism, he warned of the danger of a demagogue, posing as a champion of the oppressed, gaining power through the manipulation of public opinion.[76] To counter this, Most believed that anarchist propaganda in the United States should focus on "the destruction of the superstition of the ballot box" by urging people to reject the political system altogether.[77] Radicals today continue to grapple with similar questions about the relationship between democracy and capitalism, as well as concerns about the rise of authoritarianism within democratic systems. However, it

Figure 18. John Most,
ca. 1895. Courtesy of
International Institute of
Social History, Amsterdam.

is important to balance Most's pessimism with the recognition that Americans were not entirely without the capacity for righteous indignation and collective action. The economic hardships of the depression of 1893 led tens of thousands of unemployed individuals to take to the streets, demanding jobs and criticizing the existing economic and political order with language rooted in class struggle and radical change. In the spring of 1894, unemployed "armies" marched on Washington—a novel tactic—to demand federal jobs. Jacob Coxey, who led the first such march, accused lawmakers of serving and protecting "idlers, speculators, and gamblers."[78] In Montana, angry miners highjacked a train to make the journey east. Writer Ambrose Bierce, who frequented anarchist saloons, called America a "pickpocket civilization," and Sam Gompers, the country's best-known labor leader, spoke of the "barbarity of capitalism" during the infamous Pullman Strike.[79]

John Most's views on the labor movement, particularly the American one, have often been misunderstood since his departure from Germany in 1878 when he lost direct connections with his working-class constituency.

Although he was associated with revolutionary tactics and propaganda by the deed during the early 1880s, it would be inaccurate to portray him as an opponent of organized labor. Socialists and some anarchists accused Most of undermining trade unions because he opposed the eight-hour-day movement, but this is misleading. His opposition was directed at the centralizing and reformist tendencies within labor organizations rather than the movement itself. Most believed that fighting solely for shorter hours would not fundamentally challenge the exploitative capitalist system. Instead, he argued that labor unions must have a revolutionary basis and work toward the abolition of capitalist exploitation.[80] Most emphasized that unions should be part of a larger struggle for social and international revolution, as seen in continental Europe, where socialists and radicals played a significant role in founding the labor movement.[81] However, he also recognized that the situation in the United States differed from that of Europe. As one of the youngest developed nations, Americans had only recently begun to confront the modern social question. He developed a frontier thesis three years before Frederick Jackson Turner, suggesting that access to western land throughout the nineteenth century allowed many potential proletarians to become farmers and adopt bourgeois values, thus mitigating radicalization. Moreover, Most criticized the influence of English trade unionism, with its conservative outlook, on the American labor movement, particularly within the American Federation of Labor. He believed this conservative influence prevented the American labor movement from achieving revolutionary potential, instead making it vulnerable to manipulation by ambitious politicians and reformers who did not grasp the deeper evils of capitalism.[82] Despite these criticisms, Most saw the potential for trade unions to be established on a revolutionary basis, which could then play a crucial role in organizing a new society. He encouraged anarchists to work within the economic organizations of the workers to spread their ideas and advance the cause of revolutionary change. During the emergence of revolutionary syndicalism in France during the 1890s, Most supported the movement and actively promoted the writings of key figures such as Fernand Pelloutier and Émile Pouget. He viewed revolutionary syndicalism as the organizational form through which communist anarchism could be realized. To him, the general strike by the industrial proletariat held the same historical significance as peasant revolts in premodern Europe.[83] In 1899, Most reaffirmed his belief that trade unions were the natural organization of the proletariat, which would eventually transition from a defensive posture—focused on preserving members' living standards—to an offensive stance aimed at fulfilling their emancipatory role. However, he cautioned that anarchists should not hesitate to criticize trade unions or point out their deficiencies despite supporting them.[84]

From the 1890s onward, Most began addressing American racism and imperialism more frequently, diverging from the tendency of European immigrant anarchists to prioritize class antagonism generated by global capitalism over issues of racial discrimination and colonialism. Initially, he seemed unaware of the virulent racism fueling anti-Chinese sentiments that led to the Chinese Exclusion Act in 1882. However, during the Spanish-American War in 1898, Most argued that the root cause was not a specific national issue but the broader "social question," hoping for the collapse of Spain's autocratic government and an uprising of the Spanish proletariat. He shared letters from tortured Spanish prisoners collected in a German pamphlet with a Buffalo journalist.[85] He predicted the eventual occupation of the Philippines by the United States while advocating for Filipino independence.[86] He was also quick to attribute any excesses at home to Americans' supposedly crude and uncivilized character. In one article, he coined the term "Cowboyania" and the delicious pun *Verunreinigte Staaten* (Polluted States instead of United States, which is *Vereinigte Staaten* in German) to describe his adopted country. Although initially uninformed about the depth of white supremacy and the struggles faced by nonwhite communities, Most—like many radicals of his time—made the careless claim that American chattel slavery had been replaced with a "much more shameful white slavery." Despite never visiting the Deep South, he did occasionally condemn the mistreatment of African Americans by white Americans. In 1899, he described the "unspeakable barbarisms against colored people in the South," which, he wrote, were "cheered by countless eyewitnesses and with the formal consent of those absent, are indescribable, much less comprehensible." He vividly depicted the horrors of American racism, even though the term itself was not coined until 1902:

First, this hellish gang [white Americans] hunts down free, harmless people like wild animals, then drags them from Africa to America, where they're treated like cattle and sold. Then, this gang engages in systematic inbreeding and rape of the females; and wastes away, so to speak, their own children. Now that slavery has been abolished, [this hellish gang] vents its anger about this circumstance by whipping to death, hanging, burning alive, castrating, torturing, and tyrannizing in the most unbelievable ways on the flimsiest of pretexts, black, brown, and yellow people, many of whom are, as I said, their own offspring. This is not done by individual monsters but by entire gangs and with the consent of "public opinion."[87]

10   I'm Far from Old, I'm Just Gray

AS JOHN MOST RETURNED TO NEW YORK from Buffalo, the toll of his years of activism and the rigors of life—stress, imprisonment, and extensive rail travel—had visibly aged him. Now in his early fifties, he was no longer the lean, energetic firebrand of his youth who rarely fell ill. He had gained weight, filling out his familiar frock coat, and his face showed the signs of age with wrinkles, while his hair and beard had turned white. Rheumatism had begun to affect his gait, and he showed signs of fatigue and increased susceptibility to infectious diseases.[1] Similarly, the German anarchist movement in New York had aged and slowed, struggling to maintain its influence in a changing and increasingly diverse radical landscape. In the 1890s, there had been forty-three German anarchist groups in the greater New York area; by the next decade, only fifteen remained, a 65 percent decline.[2] Many senior members of the movement had retreated to more comfortable lives or limited their involvement to recreational and commemorative events. One editorial described German radicals as grumpy old beer drinkers: "So it has come about that the old-time German Anarchists, one after the other, have dropped out of the game in New York City."[3]

The transition from Most to Emma Goldman marked a significant shift within American anarchism, reflecting broader changes within the movement. As immigrant communities diversified and the older generation of German, French, and Czech anarchists waned, a new generation of anarchists speaking Italian, Spanish, Yiddish, and English emerged. "Well, fortunately, not much is left of a German movement," wrote Goldman in 1898. Alluding to a sharp generational divide, she explained that the Old only belong to singing societies and lodges; they hide away in their beer shops, where they inveigh against the immorality and disobedience of the youth. The Young, who have emancipated themselves from the anarchist-communist-autonomist dogmas and petty club mentality went their own way and are spreading the ideas of freedom independently.[4]

The end of the decade saw a resurgence of anarchist activity in the United States, with influential figures like Peter Kropotkin, Pietro Gori, and Errico Malatesta touring the country. *Freiheit* returned to New York to celebrate its twentieth anniversary in 1899, benefiting from improved finances thanks to Helene Minkin's administrative talents. That same year, *Fraye Arbeter Shtime* reappeared as the voice of a youthful Jewish movement. Most was well aware of the evolving character of American anarchism and radical politics in general, and in many ways, he embraced it. There was a dual sense of accomplishment and frustration: he relished his new status as a battle-hardened veteran, unwilling to retire, but he also bore the scars of those battles. A decline in his physical endurance and oratory prowess had weakened one of his trademark weapons: his passionate, gesticulating speaking style.

Most's decision to embark on another lecture tour in 1899, this time to the West Coast, marked a significant period of strain in his relationship with Minkin. John Jr., who was five at the time, remembered the quarrels between his parents and later believed that his mother was too young for his father.[5] An argument likely erupted over Most's travel plans, leaving Minkin once again to care for the children and celebrate the turn of the new millennium on her own. Most faced the daunting prospect of long-distance rail travel, which had previously taken a toll on his physical and mental health. Train cars were often unheated and poorly ventilated, making for a harsh, loud, and tedious journey, frequently interrupted by breakdowns or accidents. After a harrowing trip across the Rocky Mountains, Most arrived in San Francisco on December 17, 1899. The city's anarchist movement was diverse and cosmopolitan, encompassing German, Italian, French, and American groups. The Italian anarchist Pietro Gori and Goldman had lectured there in 1896 and 1898, respectively.[6] With the help of comrades like Richard Rieger, an agent for *Freiheit*, Most organized lectures in California, Washington, and Oregon.[7] Several hundred people attended his talk at the Metropolitan Temple, where he delivered a somewhat stale lecture in English.[8] "I am the despised and notorious Anarchist who has been driven from France, Germany, England, Switzerland, Austria, and Belgium," he began, "and has been received with hesitation and mistrust in America."[9] He outlined his case for anarchism, covering familiar themes such as the rejection of religion and superstition, criticism of the oppressive education system, and condemnation of capitalist exploitation, which he believed could lead to class war within a decade. He also spoke against imperialism and racism, the new frontiers of capitalist domination, specifically condemning America's actions in the Philippines and British policies in Africa.[10] In October 1899, during a train journey, Most witnessed a group of rowdy army soldiers, bound for the Far East, mistreating a Chinese American passenger. He was deeply disturbed by the potential harm such "rogues" could inflict on a vulnerable population. Most denounced the American occupation of the Philippines as a "barbarian invasion" and predicted that future historians would record the "land and sea robberies committed by the Americans" as "among the most shameful atrocities ever perpetrated" by a state.[11]

Sarah Comstock, a young reporter educated at Stanford and working for the *San Francisco Call*, secured an interview with Most. When she met him, she bluntly described him as quite different from the robust and passionate "Teuton" she had expected, observing instead "short heaviness, distorted face, bleary eyes; a mass of drowsy, grumbling greasiness." Comstock broached the topic of the "woman question," which seemed to touch a personal nerve. Most lamented the influence of his three wives—Clara Hänsch, Lena Fischer, and Minkin—portraying them as obstacles to his work within the movement. "Those women made my life a misery," he confided. "They fought, fought, fought me all the time." However, when Comstock persisted, seeking his insights on women's rights and gender equality, Most acknowledged that true equality could only be realized later: "The woman of the future . . . will no longer be a mere housewife but enter all fields open to man and be his companion in art, science, and labor." Most's impressions of California were a mix of optimism and dismay. He believed the West to be fertile ground for the growth of anarchism and socialism. "People are more ready for new ideas than in the East," he assured Comstock. "They are more radical. They learn and think quickly."[12] However, he also criticized San Francisco for its lack of refinement, citing homelessness, gambling dens, brothels, and gang violence as signs of its troubles.[13] Before leaving the city, Most organized a performance of his cherished play *The Weavers*, aimed at spreading anarchist propaganda and raising funds for his travels.[14] On his fifty-fourth birthday, February 4, 1900, he arrived in Seattle, a city with a population of eighty thousand. Scheduled to speak in a saloon, he postponed his lecture upon seeing only a few dozen attendees, promptly refunding their money.[15] After a brief visit to Portland, he embarked on the challenging journey back east, reaching New York by the end of March.

The onset of the new millennium marked the passing of two significant figures in Most's life: Wilhelm Liebknecht and Justus Schwab. Their deaths closely followed those of three other pillars of the German American radical movement in 1898: Wilhelm Könnecke, Robert Reitzel, and Paul Grottkau, Most's longtime friend from Berlin. Liebknecht, Most's former socialist mentor, died at seventy-four on August 7, 1900, just four months after Most's return from the West Coast. Despite occasional discord, Most greatly valued Liebknecht's influence on his early socialist education. Historian Heiner Becker noted Liebknecht's significant impact on Most, whom he viewed as a "fatherly friend" in every sense. Most's son, John Jr., recalled how his father's eyes welled up with tears for weeks following Liebknecht's demise—a poignant memory, as he had never seen his father cry before.[16] Schwab passed away from tuberculosis at fifty-three on December 18 of the same year, leaving behind his wife, Louise, and four children. Afflicted since the winter of 1895, Schwab spent his final days confined to bed, tended to by Julius Hoffmann, an anarchist physician and close confidant of Most. Schwab's funeral became a significant event for the community. "As the hearse started slowly down Second Avenue, followed by a few carriages," observed a *New York Times* reporter, "nearly 2,000 people, many of them in tears, fell in line behind it." The entire neighborhood was transformed. "The procession," continued the reporter, "passed the little saloon where Schwab had lived and then proceeded slowly to the ferry at the foot of East Houston Street. All along the route, the windows of the tenements were filled with people. The body was taken to Fresh Pond, L.I., for cremation." Even in death, Schwab managed to bring Goldman and Most together, who appeared side by side at his funeral for the first time since their altercation in 1892. Although they did not reconcile, both delivered heartfelt eulogies. Most was visibly shaken and broke down multiple times during his speech, while Goldman "was the only one present who did not give some indication of emotion."[17] Schwab's son, Justus Jr., eventually took his father's place behind the bar of the famous saloon.

* * *

On Friday, September 6, 1901, Leon Czolgosz, a self-proclaimed anarchist, shot President William McKinley with a .32 caliber revolver during a public event at the Pan-American Exposition in Buffalo, New York. Czolgosz was quickly apprehended, while McKinley was rushed to the hospital, where surgeons tried unsuccessfully to extract the bullet. Early reports suggested that the president might survive, and it emerged that the assailant had confessed to being an anarchist. New York reporters scoured known anarchist meeting places for information on Czolgosz, but no one recognized him. "He is likely a crank or perhaps downright crazy," Most told a reporter, adding, "I cannot say too strongly that we deplore this man's act."[18] Across the country, the shooting triggered a wave of violent anti-anarchist hysteria worse than what followed the Haymarket incident. In New York, the offices of *Fraye Arbeter Shtime* were ransacked by a mob, and its editor, Saul Yanovsky, was beaten in a restaurant. Most was alarmed when he realized that the latest edition of *Freiheit*, scheduled for distribution that day, featured a fifty-year-old article on tyrannicide on page two. Editors often recycled older material when there was not time to write a new editorial. The article, titled "Mord contra Mord" (Murder versus murder), authored in 1849 by the German radical Karl Heinzen, argued that tyrannicide had historically been an acceptable, even necessary, form of killing.[19] Attempts to recall the issues failed.

The day after the assassination attempt, the New York police commissioner announced that he had no interest in a police crackdown on anarchists, stating, "On the whole, they are a harmless lot." However, he assured the public that anarchists would be closely monitored.[20] Most knew he would be arrested if he made any forceful speech. In other major cities, police detained and interrogated numerous anarchists in the days that followed. Among them was Goldman, who was arrested in Chicago on September 10 and held in the Cook County jail, the same location where the Haymarket defendants had once been imprisoned. Czolgosz claimed during questioning that he had met Goldman and considered himself her disciple but insisted that he acted alone in the Buffalo attack. Months before the shooting, Czolgosz, using the alias Fred Nieman, had interacted with anarchists and expressing an unusual interest in violence and secret societies, raised suspicion. Anarchist editor Abe Isaak had even published a warning in *Free Society*, suggesting that Czolgosz might be a spy. Goldman disputed this, demanding a retraction.[21] Meanwhile, McKinley's condition showed signs of improvement.

In New York, a police detective picked up a copy of *Freiheit* at a Duane Street newsstand, translated the controversial article, and reported his findings. Consequently, on September 12, Most was arrested at Kohle's beer hall on 69 Gold Street, located on the ground floor of the *Freiheit* editorial office. Informing a friend to notify Minkin, Most finished his drink and willingly accompanied the police. George W. Titus, New York's chief of detectives, informed Most that no specific charge had been filed but that the *Freiheit* article was the basis for his detention. Minkin issued a statement asserting that *Freiheit* would continue and that the offending article was fifty years old and irrelevant to American affairs. While in police custody, Most, visibly distressed, was interviewed by reporter Zona Gale, who would later become a Pulitzer Prize–winning playwright. He immediately inquired about McKinley's condition, confiding that he feared for his own life if the president were to die. Although the article called for the death of despots, Most frantically explained to Gale, "McKinley was no despot and no tyrant. The President of a Republic couldn't be a despot if he wanted to be! I never said he was. I never said he should have been killed." When Gale pressed him on the timing of the publication, which she thought looked suspicious, Most exclaimed, "It looks! It looks! Doesn't everybody know a paper like mine goes to press three weeks before it appears? I put that in my paper before McKinley ever went to Buffalo."[22]

Two days later, on September 14—the same day Most was released on bail—President McKinley's health deteriorated, leading to his death in Buffalo. "Now, of course," Most thought, "the rage-snorting against the anarchists would break out again."[23] When he appeared before the city magistrate two days later, accompanied by Minkin but without legal representation, Most faced charges of publishing an article that disturbed the public peace. He argued that Heinzen's article, originally published in 1849 and reprinted in *Freiheit* in 1885 without issue, was included this time due to time constraints, not as a response to Czolgosz's actions. Most emphasized that *Freiheit* was printed on September 5, the day before the assassination attempt, and distributed on September 6. He accused journalists, particularly from the conservative *New Yorker Staatszeitung*, of exploiting the situation for sensationalism. "They wanted a sensation," he told the magistrate. "They wanted to make the most out of Most."[24] Most's defense was particularly pointed against William Randolph Hearst's newspapers. He noted that Hearst's *New York Journal* had repeatedly slandered and degraded the president. "Why don't you read the *New York Journal*?" he told the police. "Look at the caricatures on the last pages, where your President is portrayed in a way that would make even a bootblack ashamed."[25] Despite Most's defense, the magistrate and district attorney maintained that publishing the article was illegal, regardless of timing or context. Most was once again released on bail pending trial in October. During this period, he was arrested once more at an anarchist gathering in Queens, though the charges were ultimately dropped.[26]

The trial of Johann Most on October 9, 1901, was a somber affair, marked by evident prejudice from the start. Justices of the Court of Special Sessions advised Most to secure legal representation, viewing the publication of the Heinzen article not as a misdemeanor but as a serious offense. Justice Elizur Hinsdale openly lamented the lack of anti-anarchy statutes: "To have him arraigned and dismissed as having committed no offense seemed intolerable."[27] The magistrates ultimately invoked Section 675 of the Penal Code, which stipulated that "any person who willfully and wrongfully commits any act which seriously disturbs or endangers the public peace or openly outrages public decency, for which no other punishment is expressly provided, is guilty of a misdemeanor." Numerous lawyers declined to represent Most until Morris Hillquit, a thirty-two-year-old Jewish socialist, agreed to take the case pro bono. "Do you realize," Most asked him, "that a case like mine may ruin the career of any young lawyer?" Hillquit, determined to defend freedom of speech, argued that the court had no authority to create or punish crimes not clearly defined in statutes.[28] He asserted that publishing the article neither constituted an offense nor violated public decency. However, the justices disagreed, maintaining that the publication of the incendiary article was illegal, regardless of its connection to the president's assassination. "The offense here, in the eyes of the law," Hinsdale ruled, "is precisely the same as if that event had never occurred. The murder of the President only serves to illustrate and illuminate the enormity of the crime of the defendant in teaching his diabolical doctrines."[29] His final remark revealed his personal bias: "It would be well if the laws of this country were such that it could be said truthfully that no Anarchist could breathe the free air of America." The verdict sentenced Most to one year of imprisonment, and he visibly struggled to maintain his composure during the sentencing; "he clutched the railing, and only by an effort saved himself from a collapse."[30] Hillquit, considering this case his first cause célèbre, believed that Most was convicted not merely for the untimely publication of an article but for "his general anarchist propaganda" during a period of national mourning.[31] Hillquit appealed the verdict by requesting a "certificate of reasonable doubt" from the New York Supreme Court.

Following his conviction, Most found himself once again incarcerated on Blackwell's Island, enduring a routine reminiscent of a decade earlier: his beard was shaved, he was clothed in a striped uniform, and he was put to work in the blacksmith's shop. Visits were limited to once a month, with Minkin paying a visit on the first Saturday after his conviction. Despite his relatively good spirits, Most expressed pessimism about his chances of overturning the conviction. Minkin discovered that while she could bring food during visits, newspapers and other literature were prohibited, as all correspondence was subject to censorship. Most was permitted to send only one letter per month.[32] On October 29, the Supreme Court granted a stay of proceedings, and Most was released on bail pending the appeal. Justice Charles Maclean argued that the lower court's judgment did not demonstrate how Most's publication of another person's ideas had harmed any individual or the public peace. He also upheld Most's argument that the constitutional guarantee of press freedom protected the publication. Even though Most's release was a cause for celebration, it brought unexpected challenges for the family. His two sons were shocked and distressed when they saw their father's clean-shaven and altered face for the first time. Adding to their difficulties, their Brooklyn neighborhood had become hostile. Minkin recounted instances of neighbors hurling stones and insults: "There goes the family of the leader of the gang that killed President McKinley!" John Jr. and Lucifer faced bully-ing at school despite being enrolled under the pseudonym "Miller." In 1903, Minkin decided to move the children to a school in the Bronx, prompting the family to relocate to an apartment at 678 St. Ann's Avenue in the Morrisania section.[33] Most moved the *Freiheit* office about a mile north to 3465 Third Avenue, where his friend August Albinger managed a hotel and restaurant.

Czolgosz's act reignited the debate over immigration and naturalization, especially concerning the potential criminalization of anarchism at both the

Figure 19. John Jr. and Lucifer Most in 1907. Courtesy of International Institute of Social History, Amsterdam.

federal and state levels. For Most and Minkin, this development heightened their anxiety, as new legislation could severely impact their lives. On December 3, 1901, in his inaugural speech to Congress, President Theodore Roosevelt equated anarchists with criminals, calling them "the deadly foe of liberty" and asserting that "anarchistic speeches, writings, and meetings are essentially seditious and treasonable." He recommended barring all anarchists from entering the country. Incensed by this misrepresentation, Most compiled a twenty-page pamphlet in English to clarify the true essence of anarchism. Rather than presenting a philosophical treatise, he curated eighteen excerpts from anarchist writings, including his own, beginning with the "long train of abuses" clause from the Declaration of Independence.[34] The pamphlet, titled *Down with the Anarchists!*, was intended to catch the attention of politicians. He announced his plan to take a "new departure" by distributing copies to members of Congress and the president.[35] However, despite Most's efforts, public perception of anarchism remained unchanged. In April 1902, New York passed a criminal anarchy law, one of the first to criminalize political advocacy. The law made it a felony to promote, in writing or speech, the "doctrine that organized government should be overthrown by force or violence, or by the assassination of the executive head or any of the executive officials of government, or by any unlawful means." A year later, Roosevelt signed a new immigration act, barring anyone "who disbelieves in or who is opposed to all organized government, or who is a member of or affiliated with any organization entertaining or teaching such disbelief in or opposition to all organized government." Notably, the act prohibited anarchists from entering the country and allowed for their deportation if they had resided in the United States for three years or less. Fortunately for Most and Minkin, this provision spared them from deportation.[36]

The New York Supreme Court upheld Most's conviction just one week after the governor signed the new criminal anarchy law. The five justices argued that the offending article did not fall under the protection of free speech, asserting that the Constitution did not grant the "right to murder, nor does it give him the right to advise the commission of that crime by others."[37] Hillquit pursued another appeal to the court of appeals, New York's highest court, but it also upheld the conviction.[38] With this final decision, Most and his supporters had exhausted their legal options. Most entrusted the full management of *Freiheit* to Minkin, saying, "Hold *Freiheit* tight in your hands, and under no circumstances hand my 'beloved daughter' . . . over to anyone." On June 20, 1902, Most and Minkin, accompanied by friends, appeared at the courthouse for resentencing. Despite the tense atmosphere and the hostile crowd gathered outside, Most remained defiant and composed, even cracking jokes to ease the tension. Minkin, though distressed, tried not to show it. The judge considered the seventeen days he had already served, but it offered little comfort, as he faced many more months of solitude and hardship. After the sentence was pronounced, Most attempted to make a statement on free speech but was swiftly escorted from the courtroom. As he left, Minkin rose, took his hand, and bid him farewell.[39] Reporters noted that Most broke down in tears as he was led back to his cell.[40]

During Most's imprisonment, Minkin took on the responsibility of raising their two sons and managing *Freiheit*'s finances, successfully restoring the publication to financial stability. To support her efforts, she received ten dollars monthly from an anarchist committee, which also helped her buy food for Most during her monthly visits. Additionally, the funds were used to compensate "Uncle," a contact with prison access who delivered a weekly article from Most.[41] To supplement her income, Minkin took in boarders and effectively collected subscription payments through personal letters and notices in *Freiheit*. However, in mid-December, she fell ill with a lung infection and sought temporary assistance with the accounting tasks.[42] In addition to supporting *Freiheit*'s operations, funds were also raised for the legal defense of other anarchists, including the Austrian Rudolf Grossmann, who faced charges related to the Paterson silk workers' strike. Grossmann, convicted and sentenced to five years of hard labor, ultimately fled the country. Most considered himself fortunate to have been sentenced before the Paterson affair, believing that he would have faced similar consequences had he been involved.[43] Settling into the routine at Blackwell's Island, Most reassured *Freiheit* readers of his good spirits and health.[44] Unlike previous incarcerations, the hardest aspect for Most was not being able to see his children, now aged nine and eight. He did not want them to witness him dressed as a common criminal; instead, he requested a picture of them, which Minkin managed to deliver.[45]

On April 6, 1903, Most, now fifty-seven, was released from prison and reunited with his family on the Fifty-Second Street pier. Overwhelmed with emotion, he tried to hide his tears from Minkin. "It's a strange character trait that men have," she wrote later. "They are ashamed of their human feelings. I turned around to give him an opportunity to rejoice with the children undisturbed." They spent the day in the city and later gathered with comrades in a beer hall that evening.

Most was impressed by Minkin's management of *Freiheit* during his absence, unlike previous times when interim leadership had faltered. While

Figure 20. John Most
in 1903. Courtesy of
International Institute of
Social History, Amsterdam.

prison undoubtedly took a toll on Most's health, Hillquit's portrayal of him as "a broken man, sluggish, cynical, and indifferent" seems too harsh.[46] Most had reported good health from prison and was determined to embark on a new chapter in his life. "Although I still feel very young," he wrote to Minkin six weeks before his release, "I understand that life is running out and that I want to accomplish many things I previously neglected." He was resolved to use his time more effectively by focusing on writing books inspired by Peter Kropotkin and the Dutch anarchist Ferdinand Domela Nieuwenhuis, whose ideas he saw as models for the future.[47] He had also decided to write his memoirs, having read Franz Mehring's partisan history of German social democracy, published in 1897–98, while in prison.[48]

* * *

During imprisonment, Most continued to refine his belief that the United States held the greatest potential for spreading anarchism.[49] Through his comprehensive study of the nation and its people, he concluded that there were "unmistakable signs that . . . the 'United States' is the real land of the future, which also gives special hopes regarding the social revolution."[50] He identified several factors supporting this assessment. First, he positioned the United States at the geographic center of the civilized world, with abundant natural resources and enough territory to accommodate people from around the globe. Contrary to prevailing notions of white supremacy and anti-miscegenation, Most argued that the amalgamation of nationalities in America was advantageous, resulting in a populace of "prime physical quality" and, eventually, intellectual distinction.[51] He praised Americans for their practical, energetic, goal-oriented approach to life, reversing his earlier critique of American pragmatism as overly materialistic. He now believed this can-do attitude would facilitate a swift and decisive overturning of existing social structures when necessary.[52] Most foresaw that capitalism's cycles of boom and bust would culminate in a profound revolution among the masses, leading to a violent conflict between labor and capital. He predicted that as Europeans lagged in societal progress, they would flock to America. Drawing on historical analysis, Most pointed out that the European Left's aspiration for a people's state or republic as a solution to social issues had never been tested in monarchical Europe. Since the republic called the United States "has already experienced the most thorough fiasco imaginable," there was no need for further experimentation to demonstrate that any state is an obstacle to freedom.[53] After a lecture in 1906, Most addressed some younger comrades who expressed pessimism about American workers, arguing that their view was unfair. He insisted that American workers would react when their living standards fell behind those of European workers. "They are used to protesting, to walking out spontaneously, without preparation, to fight in the streets," he said. "They are by no means as backward as we portrayed them."[54]

Most believed that revelations of corruption and monopolistic behavior exposed by progressive journalists could awaken the revolutionary spirit in America. He saw the widespread concern over excessive corporate power as an opportunity for anarchists to engage in social change. In 1902, he pointed to the Roosevelt administration's successful antitrust case against the Northern Securities Company and the resolution of the coal strike through arbitration as evidence of this momentum. "Trustism," he declared, "was the most powerful lever for social revolution." He argued that the tyranny of trusts, their stifling of competition, and their manipulation of prices and wages had the potential to radicalize even the most "pigheaded conservative." In a brief essay, Most drew parallels between trustism and state socialism, highlighting how both sought to control labor and regulate production and distribution, albeit in different ways. Trusts championed absolute freedom for themselves while imposing constraints on others.[55]

As Most began to wind down his strenuous activities, Minkin, now in her prime at thirty, sought to establish her own career and independence. Their relationship was marked by an age difference, jealousy, and clashes over gender roles, leading to occasional quarrels. Minkin recalled that the years following his release from prison proved challenging. She encouraged him to write his memoirs, which he did, with the first part published in May 1903.[56] However, his declining health led him to withdraw from social gatherings, prioritizing his time and energy for matters he deemed important. One of the happiest and proudest events for both Most and Minkin was the celebration of the twenty-fifth anniversary of *Freiheit* in January 1904. Still, being at different stages in their lives created tension in the household. While the children were in school, Minkin worked alongside Most at the *Freiheit* office but also pursued courses in obstetrical nursing and massage therapy, eventually becoming a certified midwife and setting up her own home practice.[57] Most's attitudes toward women and family life varied; he sometimes expressed cynicism and jealousy. "Yes," Minkin wrote, "a doubt would sneak into Most's heart as to whether I was really faithful and devoted to him."[58] She accused some comrades of poisoning his mind, causing Most to monitor whom she spoke with at meetings where he was the speaker.[59] Their relationship hit a breaking point in the summer of 1904 when Most's jealousy flared up after Minkin attended a meeting where her anarchist friends Abe and Mary Isaak spoke and then joined others for a drink. This led to a heated argument, resulting in Minkin and the children temporarily renting a different apartment. Most's jealousy was exacerbated by his resentment toward younger comrades, like Abe Isaak, whom he associated with advocating for free love. Individualist anarchists had long demanded that issues of love and sex be dislodged entirely from the state and church in their battle against Victorian morality. In 1903, Most and Isaak engaged in a polemic on the subject, with Most arguing that the practice of free love before the abolition of private property—of which he deemed marriage an example—would destroy healthy relationships. He maintained that free love should not be part of a revolutionary anarchist agenda, while Isaak and others advocated for the inclusion of personal matters such as love and intimacy in anarchist discourse, highlighting that domination also existed in the private sphere.[60] Ultimately, Minkin and Most reconciled, finding humor in their differences. At one time, Minkin playfully stoked Most's suspicions by leaving his hat and a half-smoked cigar on the coffee table to suggest a secret visitor, delighting in Most's reaction upon returning home.

In the fall of 1904, despite suffering from chronic bronchitis, Most embarked on another lecture tour, traveling to cities like Chicago, Milwaukee, and Indianapolis.[61] He was not one to rest on his laurels, a characteristic both friend and foe remembered him for. "At an age when he would've been allowed to spare his overtired physical strength and enjoy a well-deserved rest," wrote a Russian anarchist, "he instead picked up his walking stick to rouse the spirits and wake the world from its slumber."[62] During this tour, Most shifted his focus away from propaganda by the deed and instead discussed the concept of the general strike. His travels eventually took him to St. Louis, where the World's Fair had been ongoing since April. Anarchists organized a convention there to take advantage of reduced train fares, but Most had declined to attend weeks earlier.[63] Instead, he planned to lecture at a friend's house at the end of November, a decision that could potentially invite trouble due to increased police vigilance during the fair.[64] Unbeknownst to Most, President Roosevelt also visited St. Louis for two days. Most's eldest son later claimed that his father was in the crowd when the president railed against anarchism, then shouted, "Shut up! Hot air!"[65] Local anarchists faced heightened surveillance, and the police prevented them from holding a meeting; after all, the previous president had been shot at an exposition. Most was arrested in a saloon on the evening of November 28. Although Roosevelt had left town the previous night, law enforcement was convinced that Most's visit was no coincidence. After pleading with authorities, Most was allowed to sign an agreement to leave town immediately, pledging never to return.[66] Although Most's visit to St. Louis caused some concern, newspapers covered the incident with mockery, reminiscent of their treatment of him when he first arrived in America in 1882. The *New York Times* editorial assured readers that the "smiling old anarchist" wouldn't hurt a fly and that his "mental and moral constitution" consisted of equal parts "fool and humbug."[67]

For all of Most's enthusiasm about the revolutionary potential of the United States, the events of 1905 shifted the focus of the anarchist movement to Russia. Since February 1904, Russia had been engaged in a war with Japan and suffered several defeats. Even though demands to transform Russia from an autocracy into at least a constitutional monarchy had been mounting before 1904, the failing war effort intensified the calls for reform. Initially, Most was skeptical about the revolutionary prospects, believing that the repressive apparatus of the army and police was too powerful.[68] However, developments in the Russian capital would soon change that perspective. In December 1904, thousands of Russians went on strike across hundreds of factories and railroads. The situation escalated on January 22, 1905, when over a hundred peaceful marchers were killed and many more wounded by police in front of the Winter Palace in St. Petersburg. This violence was followed by more strikes, peasant uprisings, and mutinies—what began as calls for reform started to resemble a revolution. Upon hearing the news in New York, anarchists quickly organized lectures and fundraisers. On January 30, Most shared the stage with Emma Goldman to discuss the unfolding events in Russia, both expressing the hope that workers could topple the czar without replacing him with a new government. Most could not resist a quip from his former years: "If an individual throws a bomb he's an Anarchist. If a thousand men throw bombs it's a revolution."[69] At a February gathering to commemorate the recent assassination of Grand Duke Sergius Alexandrovich, then commander of the Moscow military district, Most proclaimed that "the day of the people is coming."[70] His perspective on Russia's defeat in the war against Japan reflected his broader views on global revolutionary movements. He viewed the 1905 peace agreement as a significant "turning point for the world," not only because it marked the modernization of Asia but also because, with half of humanity residing there, the emergence of social-revolutionary movements would have far-reaching implications. Moreover, he believed that the czar's defeat could bolster the ongoing Russian revolution.[71]

Most was also a passive but supportive observer of the founding of the Industrial Workers of the World (IWW) in June 1905, a radical alternative to the American Federation of Labor led by Samuel Gompers. The IWW embraced principles of class struggle, direct action, worker self-management, and the general strike. During the summer of 1905, IWW socialists attempted to organize garment and carpentry workers in New York. Amid the excitement surrounding events in Russia, Most became intrigued and attended a rally at the Palm Garden on Fifty-Eighth Street to seek more information about the new union. For once, he was not on stage but sat quietly in the audience, listening to speeches by IWW president Charles Sherman and secretary William Trautman as they "roasted" Sam Gompers. Even though Most wholeheartedly supported the anti-Gompers message, he allegedly responded to a reporter's inquiry about the event, "Don't ask me. . . . I went to get information, but I got little."[72]

Most's determination to remain active in the movement, despite his physical limitations, was evident in his decision to embark on another lecture tour in the fall of 1905. While he recognized the strain it placed on him physically and acknowledged that he had lost some of his former vigor, he felt compelled to make an appearance as an old fighter. The highlight of this tour was a Haymarket commemorative speech in Chicago alongside Lucy Parsons.[73] He also found solace and purpose in writing his memoirs, which he viewed as a testament to his lifelong dedication to the cause. He announced that ten volumes would be published, each eighty pages long and priced at twenty-five cents.

By January 6, 1906, just before his sixtieth birthday, he completed volume three, covering his experiences in Chemnitz and his unique journey through the German legislature. A fourth volume detailing his years in Berlin was

Figure 21. John Most surrounded by friends in 1903. Top left to right: Marie Isaac, Bessie Shoolman, Rudolph Grossmann. Bottom left to right: "Vertrauensmann," John Most, Adolf Winkler. Courtesy of Acta des Königlichen Polizei-Präsidii zu Berlin, Landesarchiv Berlin.

already typeset.[74] In February 1906, Most embarked on yet another lecture tour, covering New England and the Midwest. Local comrades arranged lodging, booked venues, and printed announcements.[75] Following his New England engagements, he briefly returned to New York, where police disrupted a meeting, leading to Most's detention in a cold cell that left him feverish. Despite Minkin's plea to postpone the tour, Most insisted on proceeding to Philadelphia, where he found himself caught in a rainstorm without spare clothes. Meanwhile, as Minkin resumed her busy routine of managing *Freiheit* and the household, Most communicated from the road that he felt unwell and contemplated canceling the tour, yet he persisted. The Philadelphia meeting, held in honor of his sixtieth birthday, was again disrupted by police. Unbeknownst to him then, it would mark his final public appearance.[76]

Driven by a sense of duty to fulfill his speaking engagements, on March 11, Most boarded a train bound for Chicago, where he was scheduled to deliver a Commune speech on March 14. After a speaking event in Pittsburgh, he returned to the train for his next appointment in Cincinnati. However, the monotonous journey quickly became a nightmare as Most fell seriously ill. Afflicted by headaches, a swollen throat, lightheadedness, and bouts of delirium, he endured a harrowing ordeal. On the morning of March 12, a feverish Most disembarked in Cincinnati and sought refuge at the home of his friend Adolph Emil Krause at 1523 Cutter Street. By the following day, Most's condition had visibly deteriorated, with a flushed face and labored breathing. "I haven't slept for four nights on the trains," he wrote to Minkin, "traveling around sweating profusely; this is what brought me to the point of collapse."[77] Krause summoned Dr. Joseph Meitus, who lived nearby. Upon examination, Meitus diagnosed Most with erysipelas, a potentially serious bacterial skin infection compounded by his chronic bronchitis. Despite administering antitoxin injections, Meitus privately informed Krause that Most's prognosis was dire. On March 15, his condition worsened as he was gripped by a high fever that confined him to bed. In moments of delirium, he murmured to his friends, "Go and get my Helenche!" On the evening of the following day, he lapsed into unconsciousness, briefly regaining awareness the next morning, Saturday, March 17, only to slip back into unconsciousness. Around noon, Johann Joseph Most peacefully passed away, surrounded by comrades.[78]

Meanwhile, Minkin anxiously awaited Most's return in New York, tending to preparations at their apartment. Later that afternoon, she received a telegram from the printer Frederick Heiss, his eyes filled with tears, delivering the devastating news: "Johann passed away 12:00 at noon. Inform Helene." Overcoming the initial shock, a decision was made for Minkin to journey to

Cincinnati to accompany Most's body back to New York, while the children stayed with her sister Rochel. With financial assistance from Heiss, Minkin embarked on the lengthy train journey, traveling through Sunday and collecting newspapers that prominently featured Most's passing. Reflecting on the news, she pondered, "It occurred to me that a great man had died."[79] In Cincinnati, Minkin arranged for Most's body to be transported to New York, where friends and his sons could pay their final respects before cremation. However, even in death, the police intervened, prohibiting the transfer of his body to New York due to concerns that his skin disease might be highly contagious—a rationale Rudolf Rocker dismissed as "flimsy." "We were distraught," recalled Minkin, "that the children [age eleven and ten] wouldn't be able to say goodbye to their father." As Most was laid in a coffin dressed in his familiar black jacket, Minkin affixed a brooch with a picture of his sons to his lapel out of a "desire to still do something for him."[80]

The funeral service took place on Tuesday, March 20, at the Cincinnati Crematory on Dixmyth Avenue, situated in the northern part of the city near Good Samaritan Hospital. The chapel was filled with mourners, both men and women, gathered around a walnut-stained coffin adorned with smilax wreaths. Josephine Krause accompanied a grieving Helene Minkin. All religious rituals were dispensed with; the anarchist Herwegh Choir rendered several songs, including the *Marseillaise*. The first to deliver a eulogy was the editor and poet Martin Drescher, who hailed Most as the "standard-bearer of anarchism, the mighty leader in every battle who thunders through the world, the fearless rebel, ablaze with all the flames of passion." Following Drescher, Frederick Strickland, a socialist from Dayton, Ohio, offered his tribute, succeeded by Julius Zorn, an official of the local brewery workers' union, affirming that "the oppressed proletariat may never have had a more loyal friend and defender of its cause than the deceased."[81] After the cremation, Minkin received Most's ashes.[82] By March 22, she had returned to New York, where August Lott may have shown her a particularly vicious editorial in the *New York Times* calling Most "an enemy of the human race" and "a human mad dog whose rabies was chronic!"[83] Back in the apartment, life without her partner felt lonely and surreal: "No one visited me the entire week. . . . The shadows encircled me, and I sat all by myself. No one came, not my family, not the comrades."[84] These comrades perhaps did not realize that Most's later years cannot be understood without the role of Helene Minkin, a remarkable woman who tended to stay in the background but performed herculean feats for the movement. Most may not always have acknowledged it, but he owed a great deal to Minkin's perseverance and sacrifices. For her, it was never only Most's show but collaborative activism, or as she put it, "our joyous years of struggle."[85] Meanwhile, a Jewish comrade, Benny Moore, ordered five thousand photographs of Most using his own money, hoping these would raise funds for the movement.[86]

Just four days before his passing, while recuperating at the Krauses, John Most penned what would become his final letter to Minkin. Rather than focusing on his own health, he expressed worries about the hurdles he faced in completing his speaking tour. "Fortunately, the illness is external," he wrote, "and I won't become hoarse." This would ensure successful speeches in Chicago, after which he could send Minkin some money. Chicago never materialized. He concluded his letter with,

> I hope that your health is better than mine.
> In the next issue of the paper [*Freiheit*], you'll be able to see how my trip went.
> Give my best to the dear boys.
>
> Yours,
Hans

*   *   *

The anarchists of the city set aside their usual disagreements and united to honor John Most's memory in the city he called home. On March 25, four hundred comrades assembled at the Bronx Casino to establish a fund for the education of John Jr. and Lucifer. An international commemorative gathering convened on April 1 at the majestic Grand Central Palace on Forty-Third Street. The great hall brimmed with people. Red banners draped the walls, while a sizable red-ribboned portrait of Most, flanked by flowers, commanded attention on the stage. The lineup of speakers was formidable: Abe Isaak presided over the event; Emma Goldman, Lucy Parsons, and Harry Kelly spoke in English; Max Baginski and August Lott addressed the crowd in German; Pedro Esteve spoke in Italian; Saul Yanovsky and Hillel Solotaroff expressed their sentiments in Yiddish; and Chaim Zhitlowsky spoke in Russian.[87] Goldman had long since moved past her bitterness toward Most and had expressed remorse over the horsewhipping incident. "Indeed," she wrote to Max Nettlau, "I have often regretted to have attacked the man who was my teacher, and whom I idolized for many years." In recent years, she had tried twice to reconcile with Most but was rebuffed each time.[88] Her tribute to her former mentor that afternoon was brief yet poignant, possibly serving to mend some fences with Most's associates. "Ideas do not die with individuals," she proclaimed, "and John Most's ideas will always live."[89] Following the speeches, photographs and buttons of the old rebel were sold, and contributions were collected for the children's education fund. However, Minkin adamantly declined financial assistance from the comrades for herself and her children. She and Most had discussed the potential sense of obligation their supporters might feel in the event of his passing. "I told him that I will never agree to that," she wrote in *Freiheit*. One of the reasons for her refusal stemmed from the bitterness she harbored toward many of Most's supporters who had criticized him for starting a family in 1893. "Now I feel my strength has grown, and, Comrades, I'm able to support myself and Most's sons," she asserted.[90]

Shortly after the commemorations, the fate of *Freiheit* sparked some disagreement. Minkin had overseen the operation of the paper while Most served as editor, with August Lott as his assistant. In April, she informed Most's associates that he had wished for *Freiheit* to fold in the event of his demise, and she intended to honor that wish. However, the associates had other ideas and pressured her to surrender all *Freiheit* materials, including subscription lists and account books. Eventually, she relented, saying, "I wanted some rest, so I could live calmly and find a way to make a living for me and my children."[91] Before Minkin withdrew from the movement, she penned a remarkable letter in the final issue of *Freiheit* under her stewardship, officially announcing her resignation as publisher. Seizing the opportunity, she spoke candidly about the treatment she endured from (male) comrades during her time with Most. "The comrades were never in agreement with John starting a family," she charged. "They denied him the need to belong to himself and to be a little happy. Base suspicions caused him unspeakable suffering." Now that Most was gone, she felt empowered to set the record straight: having a family gave him comfort and strength, renewing his courage. "If he had not been incited against me," she charged, "if the belief in me and his children had not been poisoned for him, he would not have poured out all the resentment of his tormented soul onto me."[92]

The day following the publication of Minkin's resignation letter, Most's associates convened to establish the Freiheit Publishing Association to continue the newspaper's publication. They likened the gathering to "a meeting of orphans whose father had passed away." While recognizing Most's exceptional talents, the association members saw no reason to shutter a revolutionary newspaper solely because its founder had died. "It is no longer about the individual," they asserted. "It is about the movement as a whole, to feel its pulse." They committed to transparency regarding finances, considering the paper to be "common property" from that point on.[93] By 1908, *Freiheit* began appearing fortnightly under a single editor, Max Baginski, and it endured until August 17, 1910, making it one of the longest running anarchist periodicals.

Relations between Minkin and most German comrades had soured, and the question of how Most would be remembered became a sensitive issue. She presumably possessed much of Most's papers, and the fourth volume of his memoirs had yet to be published. According to her, she was obstructed and ignored at every turn in her efforts to publicize any of Most's writings. The fourth volume was finally released in March 1907, but not thanks to the comrades surrounding *Freiheit*. "Since the existence of the 'Freiheit Publishing Association,' no communication has taken place between them and myself," she wrote in the preface, "and I was thus robbed of any aid that could have allowed the publication of the literary legacy for the Most family."[94] Minkin continued to raise her children while working as a midwife in the Bronx, occasionally assuming the name Miller or Mueller instead of Most as they had done in the past. Lucifer, the youngest son, enlisted to fight in World War I, became a salesman, and by 1930 was married to Nadia Hillman, living in the Bronx.[95] John Jr. attended college, became a dentist, and shared his father's interest in anarchism. He struggled to keep his practice afloat partly because his social activism included caring for the poor, even if they were unable to pay. In the early 1940s, he joined the National Association for the Advancement of Colored People and attended its rallies.[96] In 1932, Minkin published her memoirs in the *Forverts* (*Jewish Daily Forward*), and three years later, she became a U.S. citizen. She died at age eighty in 1954.[97] John Jr. eventually moved with his wife, Rose, a Russian immigrant, to Boston. Their son, Johnny M. Most, born in 1923, would become the celebrated sportscaster for the Boston Celtics, passing away in 1993.[98]

Notes

Introduction

1. Clymer, *America's Culture of Terrorism*, 7–8.
2. Goldman, "Johann Most," 166.
3. Karasek, *Johann Most mit den schiefen Maul*, 6; Szmula, *Johann Most*, 1:11–12.
4. Trautman, *The Voice of Terror*, 19; this assessment is endorsed by the Most scholar Volker Szmula, *Johann Most*, 1:10–11.
5. Welskopp, *Das Banner*, 218.
6. H. Becker, "Johann Most."
7. See Goyens, "Johann Most and Yiddish Anarchism," 21–42.

8. Gage, *The Day Wall Street Exploded*, 69–70.

9. "International Notes," *Freedom* (London) 20, no. 206 (May 1906): 16.

10. Nettlau, "John Most," 19.

11. Avrich, *An American Anarchist*, 95; Goldman, "Johann Most," 166; "Johann Most, der Anarchist, gestorben," *Vorwärts* (Milwaukee), March 25, 1906, 4.

12. Goldman, "Johann Most," 165; Cohen, *The Jewish Anarchist Movement*, 92.

13. Avrich, *An American Anarchist*, 95.

14. Quoted in Rocker, *Johann Most*, 467.

15. *Fraye Arbeter Shtime*, March 25, 1906.

16. Most, "Reisebericht," *Freiheit* (New York), November 18, 1899, 1.

17. Helene Most, "An die Leser der 'Freiheit,'" *Freiheit* (New York), April 21, 1906, 1; Goldman, "Johann Most," 165.

18. [Baginski,] "The Troubles of Socialist Politicians," *Mother Earth* 8, no. 1 (1913): 17.

19. Clymer, *America's Culture of Terrorism*, 21.

20. Gage, "Why Violence Matters," 104.

21. Linse, "'Propaganda by Deed,'" 207.

22. Baker, *Means and Ends*, 202.

23. Nettlau, *Anarchisten und Sozialrevolutionäre*, 166, 317.

24. Gage, "Why Violence Matters," 102–3.

25. Gompers, *Seventy Years*, 177.

26. Hofstadter, "Reflections," 7.

27. "Warning to the Communists," *Chicago Tribune*, November 24, 1875, 4. This feature of Gilded Age American society was also observed by the German economist Waltershausen in 1890 when he wrote that "lynching is quite a common phenomenon. The lynch mob feels itself, by virtue of popular sovereignty, to be judge, prosecutor, and legislator all at once." Waltershausen, *Der moderne Socialismus*, 88.

28. "Albert R. Parsons," *Chicago Tribune*, August 10, 1886, 2.

29. Quoted in Barnard, *Eagle Forgotten*, 81; *Kansas City Pioneer*, July 4, 1878, 4.

30. *New York Times*, July 12 and August 10, 1883.

31. *New York Times* editorials "The Sentence of Most" (June 3, 1886), "The Prosecution of Most" (November 24, 1887), "Free Speech and Sedition" (January 29, 1890).

32. Hunter, *Violence and the Labor Movement*, 74.

33. Clymer, *America's Culture of Terrorism*, 13.

Chapter 1. A Wild Desire for Wander

1. Goldman, "Johann Most," 159; *EW*, October 29, 1889, 5.

2. Fischer, *Industrialisierung*, 62–63, 64; Schönchen, *Geschichte der Stadt Augsburg*, 35, 36; Kollmann and Oldenburg, *Die Wasserwerke von Augsburg*, 7, 124; Zorn, *Augsburg*, 334.

3. *Neueste Sammlung von Verordnungen*, 1, 329; Diözese Augsburg, *Schematismus der Geistlichkeit des Bistums Augsburg: für d. Jahr 1861* (Augsburg, 1861), 20.

4. *Verzeichniss der Hausbesitzer in und um Augsburg*, 74–75.

5. *MM*, 1:10.

6. Fischer, *Industrialisierung*, 62, 69.

7. Joseph Most was born on February 11, 1784; Maria Schleifer was born in Horgaugreut on January 19, 1792. They were married in St. Max Catholic Church in Augsburg on January 16, 1820 but received a civil marriage license on December 13, 1819. Records in St. Maximilian Trauungs-Register 1820, Archiv des Bistums Augsburg.

8. *Städtische Polizei, Familienbögen: Most*, StA.

9. *MM*, 1:9. Joseph was born on November 2, 1820 and baptized at St. Max. His brother Lorenz was born December 20, 1824, and his youngest brother, Johann Carl, on July 13, 1828. *Städtische Polizei, Familienbögen: Most*, StA. Joseph Most's birth record in St. Maximilian Geburts-Register 1820, Archiv des Bistums Augsburg.

10. Viktoria Hinterhuber's birth listed in St. Peter Kirchenbuch, July 12, 1818 (out of wedlock). Her parents' marriage listed in St. Anna Kirchenbuch, September 10, 1822. Both church books at Archiv des Erzbistums München und Freising.

11. *Königlich Baierischer Polizey-Anzeiger von München*, April 7, 1824, 288; *Münchener politische Zeitung*, March 21, 1826, 377.

12. *Verzeichniß derjenigen Schüler und Schülerinnen*, 177.

13. *MM*, 1:9; No homeowners named Hinterhuber are listed in 1844. *Verzeichniss der Hausbesitzer in und um Augsburg*.

14. *MM*, 1:9–10.

15. *Städtische Polizei, Familienbögen: Most*, StA. Katharine Maria was born on April 25, 1847, and died (cause unknown) on February 27, 1848. Viktoria Anna Josepha was born on January 8, 1848, and died a year later.

16. Möller, *Bürgerliche*, 262; Marriage notices in *Der Lechbote. Ein politisches Tagblatt* (Augsburg), October 13, 1848 and *Augsburger Anzeigblatt. Sonntags-Beilage* (Augsburg), October 15, 1848.

17. *MM*, 1:10.

18. *MM*, 1:10.

19. *II. Jahres-Bericht über die Leistungen der städtischen Armenpflege*, 30, StA. See also subsequent reports for 1851–52, 1852–53, and 1853–54, all at StA.

20. "Verzeichniß anderer zur Familie gehörigen Personen," *Städtische Polizei, Familienbögen: Most*. StA.

21. Maximilian was born on July 1, 1850, and died of dental gout on February 4, 1851. Josef Max was born on November 19, 1853, and died on February 21, 1854. Franziska was born in July 1852 and pulled through. *Städtische Polizei, Familienbögen: Most*, StA. See death notice for Max Most in *Der Lechbote: eine Augsburger Morgenzeitung*, Friday, March 7, 1851.

22. *MM*, 1:10; H. Becker, "Johann Most," 6.

23. *MM*, 1:11, 12.

24. Most proudly describes both his young parents as "godless." Most, *Memoiren*, 1:10–11.

25. *Städtische Polizei, Familienbögen: Most*, StA; *Adreßbuch für Augsburg*, 3; *Adreß-buch der Königlichen Kreishauptstadt Augsburg* (1862), 3, 158; Most, *Memoiren*, 1:17.

26. *MM*, 1:12–13.

27. *MM*, 1:13–14.

28. Martin, *Haupt-Bericht*, 75. See also Pettenkofer, *Haupt-Bericht*; Heidenreich, *Vorkehr*. For a recent study, see Mühlauer, *Welch' ein unheimlicher Gast*.

29. Pettenkofer, *Untersuchungen*, 97; *Augsburger Tagblatt*, August 21, 1854, and September 5, 1854.

30. Martin, *Haupt-Bericht*, 75; *Cholera Epidemie 1854 aus den Privat-Papieren des— Comissaer Fiegen*, Magistrat der Stadt Augsburg, Acten, Die Cholera, 1854–1861, Bestand 5, No. 58. See also death list in *Augsburger Tagblatt*, September 18 and 22, 1854.

31. Schmid, *Erinnerungen*, 4:336.

32. *Städtische Polizei, Familienbögen: Most*, StA; *MM*, 1:14. Most mistakenly states that the family deaths due to cholera all occurred in 1856. *Augsburger Tagblatt*, May 25, 1855; death notice in *Augsburger Anzeigeblatt*, May 16, 1855. Most only mentions the death of his mother matter-of-factly and even misremembered the year of her death.

33. She was born on September 7, 1825. See *Städtische Polizei, Familienbögen: Most*, StA.

34. Most claims that his "irrepressible hatred" for his stepmother, whom he called a "female tyrant," gave rise to his hatred of all tyrants. See *MM*, 1:17. On January 2, 1857, Maria Most gave birth to a stepsister Rosa who survived into adulthood. Joseph and Maria had two other children who both died young. *Städtische Polizei, Familienbögen: Most*, StA.

35. Goldman, "Johann Most," 159; Eser, *Verwaltet und verwahrt*, 119.

36. "Georg Joseph Agatz," Einwohnermeldebogen, Stadtarchiv Würzburg. "Agatz, Georg Jos.," Familien-Bogen, StA.

37. [Most, Johann,] *Acht Jahre*, 8; Most, "Von Ort zu Ort," October 2, 1878, 5.

38. Goldman, "Johann Most," 159, 160.

39. *MM*, 1:15.

40. Most, "Von Ort zu Ort," October 2, 1878, 5.

41. *MM*, 1:17.

42. *MM*, 1:18.

43. *MM*, 1:18–19.

44. *MM*, 1:19.

45. Künstner, *Taschen- und Handbuch*, 163–65.

46. Goldman, *Living*, 1:64.

47. *Adreßbuch der Königlichen Kreishauptstadt Augsburg* (1862), 207.

48. *MM*, 1:20, 21, 23.

49. "Herr Most's Autobiography," *Freiheit* (Freedom), May 15, 1881, in Max Nettlau Papers, 2630, IISH.

50. Eschner, *Der Buchbinder*.

51. *MM*, 1:21; Most, "Von Ort zu Ort," October 2, 1878, 5.

52. *MM*, 1:23; Goldman, "Johann Most," 161.

53. H. Becker, "Johann Most," 8.

54. *MM*, 1:24–25.

55. The only information about his journeyman years comes from two autobiographical accounts: "From Place to Place," written in 1878, ten years after the facts, and a second account from 1903. These accounts contain several noteworthy differences. The 1878 account seems more reliable and less subject to the author's revisions.

56. Quoted in Craig, *The Germans*, 24.

57. *MM*, 1:25.

58. *MM*, 1:29; Wadauer, *Die Tour der Gesellen*, 35–36.

59. Wadauer, *Die Tour der Gesellen*, 194–5; *MM*, 1:34–35.

60. Most, "Von Ort zu Ort," October 3, 1878, 2 and October 4, 1878, 5. On Ewald, see *Staats- und Adreß-Handbuch der freien Stadt Frankfurt 1852*, 2:75; On Ledermann, see *Adreßbuch der Kaufleute* (1860), 28; Grebing, *The History of the German Labour Movement*, 34.

61. Quoted in John, *"Im Geruch eines Bombenwerfer,"* 95–96; *AZ*, May 22, 1863; Most, *Memoiren*, 1:32–33; Birker, *Die deutschen Arbeiterbildungsvereine*, 119.

62. Lassalle, *Arbeiterlesebuch. Rede Lassalle's*. See also Lassalle, *Ferdinand Lassalle's Reden und Schriften*, 2:3–50.

63. Birker, *Die deutschen Arbeiterbildungsvereine*, 56–87; Grebing, *The History of the German Labour Movement*, 42, 37.

64. Most, "Von Ort zu Ort," October 4, 5, 6, and 9, 1878. His 1903 account mentions a brief visit to Rome, which is almost certainly false; his 1886 account says, "Northern Italy." See [Most,] *Acht Jahre*, 11.

65. *MM*, 1:39, 43, 45; Most, "Von Ort zu Ort," October 9, 10, 11, 12, 13, 1878.

66. *MM*, 1:46–47.

67. Records list August Kloß as a bookbinder and distributor of a local weekly. See *Archiv für Landeskunde in den Grossherzogthümern Mecklenburg*, 194; *Adreßbuch über und für den Gewerbe- und Handelsstand*, 155.

68. Most, "Von Ort zu Ort," October 15, 1878, 2.

69. *MM*, 1:48.

70. *AZ*, July 22, 1866.

71. *MM*, 1:48–49.

72. *Augsburger Tagblatt*, April 19, 1863.

73. Adolf Geck's introduction to Auer, *Nach zehn Jahren*, vi.

74. Quoted in H. Becker, "Johann Most," 10. Most and Auer have identical birth and death years.

75. H. Becker, "Johann Most," 10; Bernstein, *Ignaz Auer*, 9.

76. Baedeker, *Switzerland*, 170.

77. Most, "Von Ort zu Ort," October 18, 1878, 2.

Chapter 2. Lost in a World of Ideals

1. Reichard, *Crippled from Birth*, 176.
2. Guillaume, *L'internationale*, 1:2, 124.
3. Most, "Von Ort zu Ort," October 18, 1878, 2.
4. *MM*, 1:52.
5. *MM*, 1:51.
6. *MM*, 1:52.
7. Harreck-Haase, *Der Agitator*, 1:208–9.
8. The anarchist historian Max Nettlau noted that if Most had lingered in Locle for a few more months, he likely would have heard Mikhail Bakunin give a lecture there in February 1869 and may have become a propagandist for anarchism. See Nettlau, "John Most"; Enckell, "Bakunin and the Jura Federation."
9. Langhard, *Die anarchistische Bewegung*, 217.
10. Guillaume, *L'internationale*, 1:253; *Zürcherische Freitagszeitung* (Zurich), November 12, 1869.
11. Bernstein, *My Years of Exile*, 98.
12. According to a Zurich paper, Most made a mark as a mime during a theatrical performance; "he played well, as befits the son of an actor." Quoted in Attenhofer, *"Der rothe Teufel,"* 98.
13. Greulich, *Das grüne Hüsli*, 36–37.
14. *MM*, 1:56; Most, "Von Ort zu Ort," October 22, 1878, 2.
15. *MM*, 1:57; Harreck-Haase, 1:217–18.
16. *Arbeiterbildungs-Verein Eintracht: Protokolle Vereinssitzungen 1866–1870*, Schweizerisches Sozialarchiv.
17. Künzle and Bänninger, *Geschichte des Konsumvereins Zürich*.
18. *Arbeiterbildungs-Verein Eintracht: Protokolle Vereinssitzungen 1866–1870*, Schweizerisches Sozialarchiv; *Der Vorbote. Politische und sozial-ökonomische Monatsschrift* 3, 9 (September 1868): 140.
19. Most, "Von Ort zu Ort," October 22, 1878, 2.
20. H. Becker, "Johann Most," 13.
21. His 1903 account also features a return to Augsburg in 1868 to report for military service (he was declared unfit). This episode likely occurred in 1867 when Most turned twenty-one, not 1868. Most, "Von Ort zu Ort," October 22, 1878, 2; *MM*, 1:57.
22. Most, "Von Ort zu Ort," October 23, 1878, 5.
23. *MM*, 2:61. He devoted the entire second volume to the Austrian years.
24. Rocker, *Johann Most*, 30.
25. Taylor, *The Habsburg Monarchy*, 138–39.
26. R. Meyer, *Der Emancipationskampf*, 42–44; Barea, *Vienna*, 251.
27. Umlauft, *Die Oesterreichisch-Ungarische Monarchie*, 589.
28. Quoted in Macartney, *The Habsburg Empire*, 630n2.
29. Deutsch, *Die Geschichte*, 32–33.

30. R. Meyer, *Der Emancipationskampf*, 2:42–43. Most, "Zur Geschichte der Arbeiterbewegung in Oesterreich," 147.

31. Steiner, *Die Arbeiterbewegung Österreichs*, 6.

32. Most, "Zur Geschichte der Arbeiterbewegung," 146.

33. Quoted in Deutsch, *Die Geschichte*, 34–35.

34. Quoted in R. Meyer, *Der Emancipationskampf*, 2:44–45.

35. Quoted in R. Meyer, *Der Emancipationskampf*, 2:45.

36. Quoted in Macartney, *The Habsburg Empire*, 631; Goldstein, *Political Repression*, 4.

37. *Morgen-Post* (Vienna), January 28, 1869. According to its first annual report, this socialist association staged eighteen rallies and sixty-seven committee meetings during its first year.

38. [Most,] *Acht Jahre*, 13.

39. [Most,] *Acht Jahre*, 18; H. Scheu, *Der Hochverratsprozeß*, 243.

40. Deutsch, *Die Geschichte*, 38, 54; H. Becker, "Johann Most," 17.

41. H. Becker, "Johann Most," 14; *MM*, 2:62, 63.

42. [Most,] *Acht Jahre*, 13.

43. *MM*, 1:58–59.

44. H. Becker, "Johann Most," 45n131.

45. Steiner, *Die Arbeiterbewegung Österreichs*, 13.

46. Quoted in Steiner, *Die Arbeiterbewegung Österreichs*, 16.

47. Steiner, *Die Arbeiterbewegung Österreichs*, 17.

48. *Morgen-Post* (Vienna), April 5, 1869. This is the first time his name appears in a newspaper in the context of his political career.

49. *Neues Wiener Tagblatt* (Vienna), April 6, 1869.

50. See, for example, *Neue Zeit: Organ der sozialistischen Partei Steiermarks* (Graz), December 8, 1945, and December 5, 1947.

51. *MM*, 1:59.

52. *MM*, 2:21; Brügel, *Geschichte*, 1:204.

53. *Morgen-Post* (Vienna), May 31, 1869.

54. *Volkswille* (Vienna), June 6, 1869, quoted in H. Becker, "Johann Most," 15–16; *MM*, 1:59–60.

55. *Morgen-Post* (Vienna), May 31, 1869; *Neues Fremden-Blatt* (Vienna), June 1, 1869.

56. H. Becker, "Johann Most," 16–17. Charges listed in an official letter from Landesgericht in Vienna to Bezirksgericht Chemnitz, September 5, 1871. Königliches Bezirksgericht Chemnitz, 1871–72, Sächsisches Staatsarchiv Chemnitz, folder 33071–36, 30ab.

57. A. Scheu, *Umsturzkieme*, quoted in H. Becker, "Johann Most," 20–21.

58. Mehring, *Die deutsche Socialdemokratie*, 110.

59. Steiner, *Die Arbeiterbewegung Österreichs*, 19.

60. H. Scheu, *Der Hochverratsprozeß*, 333–34; H. Becker, "Johann Most," 17; Steiner, *Die Arbeiterbewegung Österreichs*, 18.

61. *MM*, 2:64.

62. "Minister und Arbeiter. Der Wiener Arbeiterprozess von 1870," *Neues Wiener Journal*, April 1, 1906.

63. *Morgen-Post* (Vienna), December 2 and 3, 1869.

64. *Morgen-Post* (Vienna), December 3, 1869.

65. *Morgen-Post* (Vienna), December 3, 1869.

66. Quoted in Steiner, *Die Arbeiterbewegung Österreichs*, 21.

67. *Arbeiter-Zeitung* (Vienna), December 13, 1919.

68. H. Scheu, *Der Hochverratsprozeß*, 68.

69. *NFP*, December 13, 1869.

70. Quoted in Steiner, *Die Arbeiterbewegung Österreichs*, 22.

71. *MM*, 1:66.

72. Quoted in *MM*, 1:67.

73. H. Scheu, *Der Hochverratsprozeß*, 241; *MM*, 2:28.

74. *Die Presse* (Brünn), January 8, 1870; *Hans-Jörgel* (Gumpoldskirchen), January 8, 1870; *Morgen-Post* (Vienna), January 10, 1870.

75. *MM*, 2:63.

76. *Augsburger Postzeitung*, July 16, 1870, 5.

77. *Augsburger Tagblatt*, January 12, 1870.

78. For the entire letter, see H. Scheu, *Der Hochverratsprozeß*, 241.

79. Bebel, *Aus meinem Leben*, 2:226–27.

80. Quoted in H. Scheu, *Der Hochverratsprozeß*, 263.

81. One issue was titled "Crime Gazette. Organ for Treasonous Interests," expedited "At the Courtyard under the Stone." Brügel, *Geschichte*, 1:204–5.

82. *MM*, 1:70–71.

83. *Morgen-Post* (Vienna), July 4, 1870.

84. Brügel, *Geschichte*, 1:204

85. *Augsburger Anzeigblatt*, July 10, 1870.

86. Steiner, *Die Arbeiterbewegung Österreichs*, 53.

87. Steiner, *Die Arbeiterbewegung Österreichs*, 53–54.

88. H. Scheu, *Erinnerungen*, 33.

89. See [Most,] *Acht Jahre*, 25; also quoted in Kühn, *Johann Most*, 63.

90. H. Scheu, *Der Hochverratsprozeß*, 65–67, 71.

91. H. Scheu, *Der Hochverratsprozeß*, 341, 386–87, 422, 424–25; *NFP*, July 16, 1870, 8; May, *The Hapsburg Monarchy*, 94–95.

92. *Allgemeine Arbeiter-Zeitung* (Budapest), July 17, 1870, quoted in H. Becker, "Johann Most," 18.

93. H. Scheu, *Der Hochverratsprozeß*, 439.

94. H. Scheu, *Der Hochverratsprozeß*, 433, 440.

95. *MM*, 2:64.

96. *MM*, 2:64.

97. *Neues Fremden-Blatt* (Vienna), September 24, 1870.

98. Kautsky, *Erinnerungen*, 184.

99. *Pfälzer Zeitung* (Speyer), July 23, 1870.

100. Steiner, *Die Arbeiterbewegung Österreichs*, 30. Nearly all original court records in Vienna were destroyed by fire in the 1920s.

101. *MM*, 2:5, 51.

102. *MM*, 2:55, 57, 63, 68. This story cannot be corroborated; no press reports have been found.

103. Taylor, *The Habsburg Monarchy*, 145.

104. *Morgen-Post* (Vienna), February 8, 1871; *NFP Abendblatt*, February 8, 1871; *NFP*, February 9, 1871.

105. *NFP*, February 11, 1871.

106. *MM*, 2:59.

107. *Morgen-Post* (Vienna), February 28, 1871.

108. H. Scheu, *Erinnerungen*, 105.

109. *NFP Abendblatt*, February 28, 1871; *MM*, 2:60.

110. Quoted in H. Becker, "Johann Most," 19.

111. *Volkswille* (Vienna), March 18 and 25, 1871; *Grazer Volksblatt* (Graz), March 16, 1871.

112. *Volkswille* (Vienna), April 1, 1871.

113. Karl von Thaler, "Wiener Briefe," *[Beilage zur] AZ*, April 14, 1871. His writings also appeared in the *AZ*, Germany's largest newspaper. See Wurzbach, *Biographisches Lexikon*, 138–40.

114. *NFP Abendblatt*, May 3, 1871; *Neues Fremden-Blatt* (Vienna), May 10, 1871. In his memoirs, Most tells about his encounter with the police officer. See *MM*, 2:60–61.

115. *MM*, 2:61.

116. *Neues Fremden-Blatt. Abendblatt* (Vienna), May 12, 1871.

Chapter 3. A Smithy's Hammer

1. Lidtke, *The Outlawed Party*, 59.

2. Szmula, *Johann Most*, 1:28.

3. Most, *Die Lösung*, 4–5; Szmula, *Johann Most*, 3:13, 4:18.

4. Quoted in Braunthal. *History of the International*, 1:144. Bonnell, "Between Internationalism."

5. Schaller, *Einmal kommt die Zeit*, 226–27.

6. *Augsburger Abendzeitung*, June 7, 1871; *AZ*, June 8, 1871; *Regensburger Morgenblatt*, July 19, 1871. Most employed the "traitor" epithet as late as 1873 (*Volksstaat* [Leipzig], December 3, 1873).

7. *Volksstaat* (Leipzig), June 3, 1871.

8. *Augsburger Anzeigeblatt*, June 4, 1871. One newspaper characterized the Most family as the "most beautiful personification of the interrelationship between ultramontanism and communism." *Augsburger Anzeigeblatt*, June 15, 1871.

9. *Volksstaat* (Leipzig), May 31, 1871.

10. Most to Minkin, February 21, 1903, in *Freiheit* (New York), February 28, 1903, 2.

11. Szmula, *Johann Most*, 4:7.

12. Speech delivered on May 25, 1871. See Bebel, *Aus meinem Leben*, 2:223; Lidtke, *The Outlawed Party*, 41–42.

13. Heilmann, *Geschichte der Arbeiterbewegung*, 51–52.

14. See Luksch, "Der Beitrag der 'Chemnitzer Freie Presse'"; Held, *Die deutsche Arbeiterpresse*.

15. Hofmann, "Die Anfänge sozialistischer Presse," 37; Strauss, "Die Sozialdemokratische Arbeiterpartei in Chemnitz"; Strauss, "Die 'Chemnitzer Freie Presse.'"

16. *MM*, 3:6; Welskopp, *Das Banner der Brüderlichkeit*, 150.

17. Dominick, *Wilhelm Liebknecht*.

18. [Most,] *Acht Jahre*, 33.

19. *MM*, 3:7. Most reproduces the conversation in his memoirs in a slightly different version.

20. *MM*, 3:7; Schröder, "Wilhelm Liebknecht," 70–71.

21. See, for instance, Lidtke, "August Bebel."

22. *Volksstaat* (Leipzig), April 29, 1871 puts the attendance at 18,000. Quoted in Stöbe, *Der große Streik*, 15.

23. Quoted in Heilmann, *Geschichte der Arbeiterbewegung*, 65.

24. *MM*, 3:8, 12; H. Becker, "Johann Most," 71; Bebel, Mehring, and Vahlteich, *Die Gründung*, 59; Bebel, *Aus meinem Leben*, 1:133.

25. Schröder, "Wilhelm Liebknecht," 71; *AZ*, December 16, 1871.

26. *MM*, 3:9. Subscriptions were low (two hundred according to Most), and due to insufficient funds to purchase a hand press, the editorial committee was forced to contract out the printing to C. A. Hager, who was unconnected to the party. In April 1871, Hager unexpectedly pulled the plug, and a fundraising campaign had to be launched while the ink remained dry. Otto Freytag, a sympathetic Leipzig lawyer, loaned five hundred thaler, and together with additional funds from activists, the committee purchased its own hand press that operated inside a horse's stable. Eventually, they rented a space in Zschopauerstrasse 2 just south of the center. *MM*, 3:10; Schlimper, "Vom Volksagitator zum Redakteur," 141–42; Heilmann, *Geschichte der Arbeiterbewegung*, 62.

27. Heilmann, *Geschichte der Arbeiterbewegung*, 65; Schlimper, "Vom Volksagitator zum Redakteur," 143. Beginning in 1871, a new national currency, the reichsmark, was introduced. The exchange rate was set at three mark for every thaler and two mark for every gulden (still in use in southern Germany and Austria). The thaler remained in circulation for years, especially in Saxony, and many accounts were recorded in thaler but perhaps paid in mark.

28. In 1877, of the forty-four socialist editors, only twelve were academically trained. Mehring, *Geschichte der deutschen Sozialdemokratie. Vierter Band*, 111.

29. No copies of the *Chemnitzer Freie Presse* from 1871 are extant except one reprint of a title page. See Schlimper, "Vom Volksagitator zum Redakteur," 142n22. The

August 23 issue is one of the few surviving from 1871. It is included as evidence in a case against Most. See Sächsisches Staatsarchiv, Chemnitz.

30. Schlimper, "Vom Volksagitator zum Redakteur," 140–41.

31. Mengers, *Aus den letzten Tagen der Zunft*, 59.

32. Since September 1870, the neighboring textile town of Crimmitschau, with only 17,000 residents, boasted the radical-democratic *Crimmitschauer Bürger- und Bauernfreund* with a circulation of about six hundred. Schlimper, "Vom Volksagitator zum Redakteur," 143.

33. *Adreßbuch der Fabrik- und Handelstadt Chemnitz für das Jahr 1872*, 114, 309; H. Becker, "Johann Most," 21n72.

34. Held, *Die deutsche Arbeiterpresse*, 67.

35. Heilmann, *Geschichte der Arbeiterbewegung*, 63.

36. *MM*, 3:11; Schlimper, "Vom Volksagitator zum Redakteur," 143; "Ein ernstes Wort in ernster Zeit," *Chemnitzer Freie Press*, February 6, 1872. Smithy's hammer reference is quoted in Hofmann, "Die Anfänge sozialistischer Presse," 40.

37. H. Becker, "Johann Most," 22n73.

38. H. Becker, "Johann Most," 22.

39. Goodman, *Speaking and Language*, 202. Thanks to Naama Cohen for finding this reference.

40. Szmula, *Johann Most*, 4:45–46; Most, "Briefe an einen Philanthropen," in Szmula, *Johann Most*, 2:80; Most, "Protestantische Finsterlinge," *Chemnitzer Freie Presse*, November 1, 1875, reprinted in Szmula, *Johann Most*, 2:132.

41. See Goldstein, *Political Repression*, 38–39.

42. *MM*, 3:13; H. Becker, "Johann Most," 23n78. Several such cases are stored at Sächsisches Staatsarchiv Chemnitz.

43. Sächsisches Staatsarchiv Chemnitz, document 49a.

44. Most, "Briefe an einen Philanthropen," in Szmula, *Johann Most*, 2:99. Most comes close to adopting Jean-Jacques Rousseau's concept of the "general will," which would contradict Most's apparent embrace of the liberal concept of majoritarianism.

45. Most, *Der Kleinbürger*, 45.

46. *Protokoll über den zweiten Congreß*, 1–4. Most was also elected as one of four secretaries.

47. *Protokoll über den zweiten Congreß*, 132–33.

48. *MM*, 3:12; *Protokoll über den zweiten Congreß*, 61.

49. *Chemnitzer Freie Presse*, August 23, 1871.

50. Most, "Die politische Stellung der Partei," in Szmula, *Johann Most*, 1:45–46.

51. Szmula, *Johann Most*, 4:32; Most, "Briefe an einen Philanthropen," in Szmula, *Johann Most*, 2:103.

52. Most, "Ein Mahnruf an die Landwirtschaftliche Bevölkerung," in Szmula, *Johann Most*, 1:62, 64.

53. *Die Verhandlungen der Berliner Conferenz*, 23.

54. *MM*, 3:27. He does not mention her name in his memoirs.

55. *MM*, 3:27; Heilmann, *Geschichte der Arbeiterbewegung*, 84. Heilman does not provide any evidence.

56. *MM*, 3:27.

57. *MM*, 1:56.

58. *MM*, 2:62–63.

59. Stöbe, *Der große Streik*, 5.

60. Stöbe, *Der große Streik*, 6.

61. Quoted in Stöbe, *Der große Streik*, 14.

62. *Protokoll über den zweiten Congreß*, 25–26.

63. Heilmann, *Geschichte der Arbeiterbewegung*, 66.

64. Most, "Betrachtungen," in Szmula, *Johann Most*, 1:79.

65. Heilmann, *Geschichte der Arbeiterbewegung*, 68; Stöbe, *Der große Streik*, 19, 22, 28–31; *MM*, 3:9; John, "Im Geruch eines Bombenwerfer," 19–20.

66. Quoted in Stöbe, *Der große Streik*, 32–33.

67. Stöbe, *Der große Streik*, 35, 40, 42.

68. *AZ*, November 1 and 17, 1871, where Most is labeled the "lead instigator." For the legal actions against Most, see H. Becker, "Johann Most," 23n78.

69. Heilmann, *Geschichte der Arbeiterbewegung*, 70–71.

70. Mehring, *Geschichte der deutschen Sozialdemokratie*, 2:322.

71. *Volksstaat*, November 18, 1871, quoted in H. Becker, "Johann Most," 22. *Volksstaat* stated, "We can prove . . . with Most's letters that he did not want the strike." Quoted in H. Becker, "Johann Most," 22n75.

72. H. Becker, "Johann Most," 23n78; Heilmann, *Geschichte der Arbeiterbewegung*, 71.

73. Heilmann, *Geschichte der Arbeiterbewegung*, 71, 75.

74. Schlimper, "Vom Volksagitator zum Redakteur," 147–48.

75. Hofmann, "Die Anfänge sozialistischer Presse," 42; Schlimper, "Vom Volksagitator zum Redakteur," 147.

76. *Sechs Proletarier-Lieder, gewidmet den Arbeitern Österreichs* (Six proletarian songs, dedicated to the workers of Austria).

77. *Neuestes Proletarier-Liederbuch von verschiedenen Arbeiterdichtern* (Latest proletarian songbook by various worker-poets). Hofmann, "Die Anfänge sozialistischer Presse," 42.

78. On labor songs in Germany, see Lammel, *Arbeitermusikkultur*; on works by Inge Lammel, see Körner, *Das Lied von der anderen Welt*; Meyer, *Die Herausbildung*; Bowan, "Friendship."

79. Hofmann, "Die Anfänge sozialistischer Presse," 42.

80. Cohn, *Underground Passages*, 100.

81. Hinze, *Johann Most und sein Liederbuch*, 7; Rocker, *Johann Most*, 17.

82. *MM*, 3:14.

83. His lecture of April 22, 1872 in Glauchau is reprinted in John, "Im Geruch eines Bombenwerfer," 39–110.

84. John, *"Im Geruch eines Bombenwerfer,"* 71, 73, 97, 102.

85. Most, "Abenteur im Rothem Thurm," *Der Nußknacker,* September 1, 1872, in Stadtarchiv Chemnitz; Schaller, *Einmal kommt die Zeit,* 231; *MM,* 3:14.

86. Heilmann, *Geschichte der Arbeiterbewegung,* 88–89.

87. *MM,* 3:27.

88. Heilmann, *Geschichte der Arbeiterbewegung,* 85, 86.

89. Heilmann, *Geschichte der Arbeiterbewegung,* 85–86.

90. Most, "Abenteur im Rothem Thurm," *Der Nußknacker,* September 1, 1872, in "Fascikel des Raths der Stadt Chemnitz," Stadtarchiv Chemnitz; *MM,* 3:15–16.

91. *Chemnitzer Freie Presse,* August 25, 1872, Beilage *Der Nußknacker,* quoted in Hofmann, "Die Anfänge sozialistischer Presse," 43; *MM,* 3:16.

92. Schaller, *Einmal kommt die Zeit,* 231.

93. *Chemnitzer Freie Presse,* September 1, 1872; Heilmann, *Geschichte der Arbeiterbewegung,* 82; *MM,* 3:17. On the German socialists' opposition to the Sedan festivities, see Lausch, *Wider den "Hurra-Patriotismus."*

94. *Chemnitzer Freie Presse,* September 1, 1872.

95. *MM,* 3:16.

96. *Chemnitzer Freie Presse,* September 4, 1872; Heilmann, *Geschichte der Arbeiterbewegung,* 81.

97. *Volksstaat* (Leipzig), September 21, 1872.

98. *Protocoll über den dritte Congreß,* 55, 5.

99. *Protocoll über den dritte Congreß,* 8; Most, "Über die Grundsätze der Sozialdemokratie," in Szmula, *Johann Most,* 1:48–52.

100. Szmula, *Johann Most,* 4:11.

101. *Protocoll über den dritte Congreß,* 9–10.

102. *Protocoll über den dritte Congreß,* 10. Most likely intended a pun: "I believe I'm *quite moderate*" (*recht mäßig*) can also mean "lawful" (*rechtmäßig,* in one word).

103. *Protocoll über den dritte Congreß,* 33.

104. The Sonvillier Circular (1871), quoted in Graham, *Anarchism,* 1:98; For an excellent narrative of the First International and the anarchists, see Graham, *We Do Not Fear Anarchy.*

105. *MM,* 3:20; *Volksstaat,* September 25, 1872; *Fränkischer Anzeiger* (Rothenburg), September 25, 1872.

106. *Chemnitzer Tageblatt und Anzeiger,* September 25, 1872; *MM,* 3:20.

107. *MM,* 3:20; Most, "Erklärung," *Der Volksstaat,* October 2, 1872.

108. *MM,* 3:20. Charges are listed in Stadtarchiv Chemnitz.

109. *MM,* 3:20; *Chemnitzer Tageblatt und Anzeiger,* December 4, 1872; *Volksstaat,* December 7, 1872.

110. *Volksstaat,* October 19, 1872.

111. H. Becker, "Johann Most," 26, 73.

112. *MM,* 3:24–25; *Volksstaat,* October 12, 1873; Most to Bebel, April 21, 1873, reprinted in Bebel, *Aus meinem Leben,* 269–70.

113. Rocker, *Johann Most*, 434.

114. Hecker, "Die Popularisierung des 'Kapitals' durch Johann Most," 118; Sperber, *Karl Marx*, 421.

115. Dlubek and Skambraks, *"Das Kapital" von Karl Marx*, 71.

116. Dlubek and Skambraks, *"Das Kapital" von Karl Marx*, 90–91. Liebknecht laughed at the notion that Most had produced a summary of Marx's great book; Bebel was more encouraging. *MM*, 3:26.

117. Dlubek and Skambraks, *"Das Kapital" von Karl Marx*, 93.

118. Hecker, "Die Popularisierung des "Kapitals" durch Johann Most," 118–19; Sperber, *Karl Marx*, 458.

Chapter 4. Awaken the Mind of the People

1. *MM*, 3:27.

2. Kläger, "Mainz auf dem Weg zur Großstadt," 433, 435–36, 444–46.

3. Johann Most to Wilhelm Liebknecht (Hubertusburg), November 15, 1873, quoted in Schröder, "Wilhelm Liebknecht," 73.

4. Most to Bebel, April 21, 1873, reprinted in Bebel, *Aus meinem Leben*, 2:270.

5. *Volksstaat*, May 5, 1873, quoted in Schröder, "Wilhelm Liebknecht," 73. Most was also on the ballot in six other districts, including Augsburg, where he campaigned briefly.

6. *Städtische Polizei, Familienbögen: Most*. Stadtarchiv Augsburg.

7. Most, "Offene Briefe an meine Wähler," *Chemnitzer Freie Press*, July 18, 19, and 21, 1874, reprinted in Szmula, *Johann Most*, 2:63–71; *Stenographische Berichte*, 2nd Legislative Period, 1st Session, 40th Meeting (April 24, 1874); *MM*, 3:29–55.

8. Most, "An die Sozialdemokratischen Wähler von Chemnitz und Umbegung," *Chemnitzer Freie Press*, January 18, 1874.

9. Most, "Offene Briefe an meine Wähler," reprinted in Szmula, *Johann Most*, 2:64–65, 68.

10. Lidtke, *The Outlawed Party*, 53.

11. Holborn, *A History of Modern Germany*, 253.

12. *MM*, 3:44.

13. Hennock, "Vaccination Policy," 49–71; Huerkamp, "The History of Smallpox Vaccination," 617–35.

14. Most, "Offene Briefe an meine Wähler," 2:70; *MM*, 3:42; Huerkamp, "The History of Smallpox Vaccination," 627; *Stenographische Berichte*, 2nd Legislative Period, 1st Session, 13th Meeting (March 6, 1874).

15. Rolleston, "The Smallpox Pandemic," 187.

16. "Stadtgericht," *Berliner Gerichts-Zeitung*, May 19 and 21, 1874; Ingo Materna, "Johann Most," 106–7.

17. Bebel, *Aus meinem Leben*, 2:311.

18. Most, *Die Pariser Commune*, 5–7; *Volksstaat*, October 13, 1874; *Berliner Gerichts-Zeitung*, May 19, 1874, 2.

19. *Stenographische Berichte*, 1st Legislative Period, 1st Session, 28th Meeting (May 2, 1871).

20. *Stenographische Berichte*, 2nd Legislative Period, 1st Session, 21st Meeting (March 21, 1874), and 27th Meeting (April 9, 1874); Kreishauptmannschaft Leipzig, Nr. 248–114–6, Staatsarchiv Leipzig; H. Becker, "Johann Most," 29; *AZ*, July 6, 1874;

21. *Volksstaat*, September 6, 1874; *MM*, 4:52; *Freiheit* (London), February 21, 1880, clipping in Landesarchiv Berlin, Acta 11724.

22. Most to Bebel, September 27, 1875, quoted in Welskopp, *Das Banner*, 713.

23. *MM*, 4:76; Most, *Die Bastille*, 41. Visitations were restricted to one every fourteen days.

24. Lindau, "Vom Plötzensee," 219.

25. "Funfzehnter Bericht der Kommission für Petitionen," in *Sammlung sämmtlicher Drucksachen des Deutschen Reichstags*, 2nd Legislative Period, 2nd Session (1874); Most, *Die Bastille*, 75; Most, "Die Behandlung politischer Gefangenen in Preußen," *Der Volksstaat*, December 1, 1874, reprinted in Szmula, *Johann Most*, 2:72.

26. *AZ*, June 21, 1876; Polizeimeldeamt, "Klara F. Most (Hänsch)," Stadtarchiv Chemnitz; *MM*, 4:92; *Neue Social-Demokrat*, June 21, 1876, quoted in H. Becker, "Johann Most," 29.

27. H. Becker, "Johann Most," 30.

28. Landesarchiv Berlin, Acta Nr. 11724; Lidtke, *The Outlawed Party*, 55.

29. H. Becker, "Johann Most," 270–71. Most wrote ninety-seven articles in 1877 alone.

30. H. Becker, "Johann Most," 30.

31. Kautsky, "Johann Most," 547.

32. *Berliner Adreßbuch* for 1875–78, accessible at the Zentral- und Landesbibliothek Berlin: https://digital.zlb.de/viewer/; Large, *Berlin*, 8–35.

33. *Berliner Tageblatt*, October 17, 1876, clipping in Landesarchiv Berlin, Acta Nr. 11724.

34. Fishman, *East End Jewish Radicals*, 126; Sapir, "Liberman," 25–88; Bloom, "Aaron Liebermann," 139–46.

35. Most, "Materialistische Gedanken," in Szmula, *Johann Most*, 4:162.

36. Emden, *Friedrich Nietzsche*, 248.

37. Most, "Materialistische Gedanken," 162, 163–64.

38. Szmula, *Johann Most*, 4:15.

39. Most, *Der Kleinbürger*, 41.

40. Most, *Der Kleinbürger*, 45.

41. Quoted in Lidtke, *The Outlawed Party*, 31, 39–66. See also Bebel, *Unsere Ziele*.

42. Most, "Briefe an einen Philanthropen," in Szmula, *Johann Most*, 2:117; italics in original.

43. Most, *Der Kleinbürger*, 35.

44. Most, *Der Kleinbürger*, 5.

45. Most, "Reform oder Revolution," in Szmula, *Johann Most*, 2:31, 37, 40; Most, *Die Pariser Commune*, 10.

46. Most, "Gewalt und Gesetz," in Szmula, *Johann Most*, 1:113–14.

47. Adamiak, "Marx, Engels, Dühring," 106; Dowe and Tenfelde. "Zur Rezeption Eugen Dührings," 25–58; Welskopp. *Das Banner*, 714; Bernstein, *Sozialdemokratische Lehrjahre*, 52–55.

48. Adamiak, "Marx, Engels, Dühring," 104.

49. Most, *Die Lösung*, 23.

50. Most to Liebknecht, February 21, 1876, quoted in Schröder, "Wilhelm Liebknecht," 77–78. Most pitched his articles to *Volksstaat*, not *Vorwärts* as Rocker and then Szmula and Adamiak wrote in Rocker, *Johann Most*, 54, Adamiak, "Marx, Engels, Dühring," 106, and Szmula, *Johann Most*, 1:21. The first issue of the newspaper *Vorwärts* appeared on October 1, 1876.

51. Most to Liebknecht, July 20, 1876, in Liebknecht, *Briefwechsel mit deutschen Sozialdemokraten*, 1:688–69; italics in original.

52. Rocker, *Johann Most*, 55; Most, "Ein Philosoph," *Berliner Freie Presse*, September 10–October 21, 1876, reprinted in Szmula, *Johann Most*, 3:120–68.

53. Welskopp, *Das Banner*, 715.

54. Welskopp, *Das Banner*, 715; Dühring, *Sache, Leben und Feinde*, 192.

55. Sperber, *Karl Marx*, 177–85; Marx to Wilhelm Bracke, April 11, 1877, quoted in Szmula, *Johann Most*, 1:36n61.

56. Marx to Friedrich Sorge, October 19, 1877, quoted in Szmula, *Johann Most*, 1:36n61; italics in original.

57. Bernstein, *Sozialdemokratische Lehrjahre*, 55–58.

58. Hart, *Gesammelte Werke*, 3:36.

59. Adolph Hoffmann, "Sozialistenschnitzer von Berlin. Jugenderinnerungen," *Salzburger Wacht*, January 12, 1926, 3.

60. Quoted in Most, *August Reinsdorf*, 9; Nettlau, *Anarchisten und Sozialrevolutionäre*, 132–33; Most, *August Reinsdorf*, 16. The friendship between Most and Reinsdorf allegedly dates back to 1867 when they met as traveling journeymen, possibly in the textile town of Lörrach in Baden, close to the French and Swiss border. In the early spring of 1867, Most traveled from Stuttgart to Switzerland. See Most, *August Reinsdorf*, 9, 16.

61. Most, *August Reinsdorf*, 17.

62. According to Nettlau, the party press and leadership were busy "building a Chinese wall around the German social democrats." Nettlau, *Anarchisten und Sozialrevolutionäre*, 129. Liebknecht and others spread the word that Reinsdorf was suspicious (a potential police spy) and should be avoided. Nettlau, *Anarchisten und Sozialrevolutionäre*, 133n119; Most, *August Reinsdorf*, 16.

63. See Carlson, *Anarchism in Germany I*, chap. 3; Wagner, *Missionare der Gewalt*, 77–83; Nettlau, *Anarchisten und Sozialrevolutionäre*, chap. 7; Avrich, *Anarchist Portraits*, 240–44; Mühlnikel, "*Fürst, sind Sie unverletzt?*" 41–42.

64. Blos, *Denkwürdigkeiten*, 1:231; Rocker, *Johann Most*, 56–57. More recently, the late Thomas Welskopp wrote that Most's unique qualities as an emotional, passion-

ate rabble-rouser "prepared the way for his anarchism because his language lived on verbal radicalism." Welskopp, *Das Banner*, 405.

65. [Schneidt,] *Die Hintermänner*, 26; Nettlau, *Anarchisten und Sozialrevolutionäre*, 149.

66. Szmula, *Johann Most*, 4:10, 63.

67. Most, *Der Kleinbürger*, 43, quoted in Szmula, *Johann Most*, 4:6–7.

68. Most, *Die Pariser Commune*, 11, 29–30.

69. Most, *Die Lösung*, 16; see also Szmula, *Johann Most*, 4:7–8.

70. Most, "Offene Briefe an meine Wähler," reprinted in Szmula, *Johann Most*, 2:65; Most, "Die Behandlung politischer Gefangenen in Preußen," reprinted in Szmula, *Johann Most*, 2:72; Most, *Die socialen Bewegungen*, 106; *Intelligenzblatt für die Stadt Bern*, March 21, 1877.

71. Harreck-Haase, 1:210; *MM*, 1:57; H. Becker, "Johann Most," 32n100. In his memoirs, Most reinterprets (or distorts) his 1876 Reichstag speech as revolutionary and uncompromising, going against his own party. Official transcripts prove this is false. *MM*, 3:59–60.

72. *Stenographische Berichte*, 3rd Legislative Period, 2nd Session, 42nd Meeting (May 7, 1878).

73. Bernstein, *Die Geschichte*, 1:327.

74. *MM*, 3:68; *Vorwärts* (Leipzig), July 1, 1877.

75. Bernstein, *Die Geschichte*, 1:339; Landesarchiv Berlin, Acta 14932; Most, *Die socialen Bewegungen*, 21; Large, *Berlin*, 80. Most was not the first socialist to engage with the politically active Mommsen; in October 1876, a socialist named Mr. Fähse denounced the historian's call for a fourth Bismarck war. *Vorwärts* (Leipzig), October 22, 1876.

76. Mehring, *Geschichte der deutschen Sozialdemokratie*, 2:381; Bernstein, *Die Geschichte*, 1:339. The affair did move Leopold von Ranke, the other towering German historian, to read Most's writings on ancient Rome. Wiedemann, "Sechzehn Jahre in der Werkstatt," 232n1.

77. *Vorwärts* (Leipzig), November 16, 1877.

78. *Vorwärts* (Leipzig), March 15, 1878; Bernstein, *Die Geschichte*, 1:353–56; Bebel, *Aus meinem Leben*, 2:398–99.

79. *Berliner National-Zeitung*, quoted in *Vorwärts* (Leipzig), March 15 and 17, 1878.

80. Bernstein, *Die Geschichte*, 1:325, 359.

81. Quoted in Lidtke, *The Outlawed Party*, 67.

82. They are listed as "dissident" on their daughter Melita's birth certificate, May 9, 1878, at Landesarchive Berlin, Geburtenregister.

83. *AZ*, January 7, 1878.

84. Oertzen, *Adolf Stoecker*, 1:144.

85. "Das erste Debüt der Kanzelsocialisten," *AZ*, January 11, 1878.

86. Prüfer, "Johann Most," 131–32; *AZ*, January 26 and 31, 1878; *Vorwärts* (Leipzig), February 10, 1878.

87. *Vorwärts* (Leipzig), February 15, 1878. For Most's writings on Darwinism, see "Der Mensch," in Szmula, *Johann Most*, 1:44; "Ein Philosoph," in Szmula, *Johann Most*, 3:131–33.

88. Bernstein, *Die Geschichte*, 1:353.

89. *AZ*, February 9 and May 2, 1878; Hölscher, *Weltgericht oder Revolution*, quoted in Prüfer, "Johann Most," 133–34.

90. Prüfer, "Johann Most," 130, 134–35.

91. Quoted in Rocker, *Johann Most*, 399.

92. *AZ*, May 2, 1878; H. Becker, "Johann Most," 34n102; *Vorwärts* (Leipzig), February 3 and 6, 1878; *AZ*, May 25, 1878.

93. She did know Wilhelm Liebknecht through Most: see Most to Liebknecht, July 20, 1876, in Liebknecht, *Briefwechsel mit deutschen Sozialdemokraten*, 1:689. The historian Ernst Heilmann asserted (without evidence) that Clara Most had "relations" with other party leaders during Most's prison terms. Heiner Becker stated that similar rumors circulated in 1877–88 when two colleagues, Ignaz Auer and Richard Fischer, boarded with the Mosts in Berlin, though city directories do not list them. See Heilmann, *Geschichte der Arbeiterbewegung*, 84; H. Becker, "Johann Most," 27n89, 10n24.

94. "Klara F. Most (Hänsch)," Polizeimeldeamt, Stadtarchiv Chemnitz; Landesarchiv Berlin, Acta Nr. 11724.

95. Most, "Die 'Freiheit,'" *Freiheit* (New York), June 20, 1896. The historian Heiner Becker claims that in Berlin, Most had a relationship with a governess named Clara Ringius, who was active in the socialist movement. H. Becker, "Johann Most," 27n89. The 1878 Berlin directory lists a widow named "A. Ringius." See *Berliner Adreß-Buch für das Jahr 1878*, 741.

96. *MM*, 3:28.

97. Lidtke, *The Alternative Culture*, 37.

98. Most, "Noch einmal an die Frauen," *Chemnitzer Freie Presse*, September 30, 1871. This issue is included in Most's legal file at the Sächsisches Staatsarchiv Chemnitz.

99. Most, "Briefe an einen Philanthropen," in Szmula, *Johann Most*, 2:121–22; italics in original.

100. Most, "Der Sozialismus und die häuslichen Arbeiten," in Szmula, *Johann Most*, 1:91, 92.

101. Most, "Briefe an einen Philanthropen," in Szmula, *Johann Most*, 2:125.

102. Mühlnikel, *"Fürst, sind Sie unverletzt?"* 38; *AZ*, May 14, 1878; *MM*, 3:75; Auer, *Nach zehn Jahren*, 37.

103. *Vorwärts* (Leipzig), May 12, 1878.

104. Historian Andrew Carlson believes that Hödel and Werner planned the deed in Leipzig, but a recent study questions the suggestion of an anarchist conspiracy. See Gabriel, *Assassins & Conspirators*; Carlson, "Anarchism," 178; Mühlnikel, *"Fürst, sind Sie unverletzt?"* 41–48.

105. Lidtke, *The Outlawed Party*, 70–73.

106. H. Becker, "Johann Most," 34; Rocker, *Johann Most,* 59; *AZ,* May 30, 1878; *Vorwärts* (Leipzig), May 31, 1878.

107. Mühlnikel, *"Fürst, sind Sie unverletzt?"* 51–67.

108. [Most,] *Acht Jahre,* 55.

109. *Vorwärts* (Leipzig), October 20, 1878.

110. *Vorwärts* (Leipzig), June 7, 1878; *AZ,* June 5 and July 12, 1878; Lidtke, *The Outlawed Party,* 73; on his expulsion, see "Most, Johann Josef," Rat der Stadt Chemnitz, Polizeimeldeamt, Abteilung A/Punkt, L-M (ca. 1864–1876), Stadtarchiv Chemnitz; Mühlnikel, *"Fürst, sind Sie unverletzt?"* 49. On August 16, Hödel was beheaded in Moabit prison, and on September 10, Nobiling died unexpectedly in prison of meningitis.

111. For the entire text, see appendix C in Lidtke, *The Outlawed Party,* 339–45.

112. Liebknecht to Engels, October 20, 1878, in Liebknecht, *Briefwechsel mit Karl Marx,* 257, quoted in Harreck-Haase, *Der Agitator,* 2:35.

113. Lidtke, *The Outlawed Party,* 78–82.

114. *Berliner Tageblatt,* November 24, 1878, clipping in Landesarchiv Berlin, Acta 11724.

115. Landesarchiv Berlin, Acta 11724.

116. Rocker, *Johann Most,* 62; H. Becker, "Johann Most," 35; Materna, "Johann Most," 110.

117. [Most,] *Acht Jahre,* 57; Polizeimeldeamt, "Klara F. Most (Hänsch)," Stadtarchiv Chemnitz. Police reports suggest that Most may have traveled to Augsburg to visit his father before heading to Hamburg. Landesarchiv Berlin, Acta 11729.

118. Rocker, *Johann Most,* 63; "An Unsere Parteigenossen!" (June 1880), pamphlet signed by I. Auer, A. Bebel, W. Liebknecht, F. W. Fritzsche, W. Hasenclever, M. Kayser, J. Vahlteich, and Ph. Wiemer, inserted in *Sozialdemokrat,* May 30, 1880.

119. Quoted in H. Becker, "Johann Most," 46.

120. Quoted in H. Becker, "Johann Most," 46. In 1886, Most remembered that in Hamburg, his comrades gave him "dirty looks," telling him that "he would ruin everyone if he didn't go away. They'll declare a state of siege in Hamburg because of him." [Most,] *Acht Jahre,* 57.

Chapter 5. Exile in London

1. Most, "Die 'Freiheit,'" *Freiheit* (New York), June 20, 1896.

2. Quoted in Auer, *Nach zehn Jahren,* 98–99.

3. For more on Ehrhart (1853–1908), see b. h., "Franz Josef Ehrhart," in *Der Wahre Jacob* Nr. 575, August 4, 1908, 5890; Schneider, *'Die Presse ist das Herzblut unserer Bewegung.'* Ehrhart offered Most the editorship of the *Süddeutsche Volksstimme* back in 1873. Harreck-Haase, *Der Agitator,* 2:13; see two letters between Most and Ehrhart from 1872 to 1873 in Kleine Korrespondenz (from SPD Archives) Archives, 1844–1931, IISH.

4. Ehrhart, "Aus meiner Londoner Zeit," 58–62. For more on the CABV, see Lattek, *Revolutionary Refugees*; Brandenburg, "Zur Geschichte des Londoner Arbeiterbil-dungsvereins," 71; Ashton, *Little Germany.*

5. Ehrhart, "Johann Most (†)," quoted in H. Becker, "Johann Most," 36.

6. Most credited CABV members for the *Freiheit* initiative in 1886 but later presented himself as the sole founder when he declared that "on December 26, 1878, at ten in the evening . . . I decided on a literary thunderbolt. I founded *Freiheit.*" [Most,] *Acht Jahre*, 57; Most, "Die 'Freiheit,'" *Freiheit* (New York), June 20, 1896. He initially signed a monthly contract that could be terminated within a week since he was awaiting news regarding a possible American lecture tour, but this did not materialize. H. Becker, "Johann Most," 38.

7. *Freiheit* (London), January 4, 1879; Ehrhart, "Aus meiner Londoner Zeit," 61; H. Becker, "Johann Most," 37n113, 38; Nettlau, *Anarchisten und Sozialrevolutionäre*, 150. The *Freiheit* circle consisted of John Neve, the Swiss tailor Georg C. Uhly, Franz J. Ehrhart, A. Benek, F. Aumann, W. Hoffmann, watchmaker Louis Weber, the Bavarian cabinetmaker Johann Sebastian Trunk, Wilhelm Merten, Paul and Moritz Schultze, cabinetmaker Hermann Stenzleit, and others.

8. Most, "'FREIHEITs'-Reminiszenzen," *Freiheit*, January 7, 1899, printed in Most, *Marxereien*, 29–30. For more on Neve, see Becker, "Johann Neve"; Nettlau [M. N.], "Johann Neve"; Gotthardt, "Johann Christoph Neve."

9. *Freiheit* (London), January 4, 1879.

10. A. Scheu, "Erlebnisse eines Kämpfers"; London Metropolitan Archives, *London City Directories*, 1879 and 1881.

11. *Berliner Börsen-Courier*, January 10, 1879, clipping in Landesarchiv Berlin, Acta 11724, 94; Polizeimeldeamt, "Klara F. Most (Hänsch)," Stadtarchiv Chemnitz. Police reports from January 1879 indicate that Most "is now in London with his wife." Landesarchiv Berlin, Acta 11724, 1 and 13031, 11–12.

12. *Freiheit* [Freie Presse] (London), July 5, 1879, 4. An English reporter described his oratory: "His habit of raising high his right eye-brow occasionally when speaking is the only peculiarity he has in addressing an assembly. . . . The voice is not strong, perhaps rather thin—at least he speaks in a high key—but he seems to exercise an influence over his hearers, which his style, though often impassionate, would not account for." See "London Letter," *Sheffield Daily Telegraph*, March 25, 1879, 2.

13. Johann Most to Karl Marx, January 19, 1879 (IISH), cited in Harreck-Haase, *Der Agitator*, 2:25.

14. H. Becker, "Johann Most," 45n130; Landesarchiv Berlin, Acta 11724, fol. 130.

15. Fricke, *Dokumente*, 1:27.

16. Historian John Quail wrote that bundles of *Freiheit* were hidden in mattresses and loaded onto ships in Hull bound for Hamburg, but his source, Frank Kitz's recollections, does not mention this. See Quail, *The Slow Burning Fuse*, 30; Kitz, "Recollections and Reflections."

17. For a detailed study of the smuggling during the Anti-Socialist Law in Hamburg, see Jensen, *Presse und politische Polizei*, 61–72. At one point, the spy Oskar Neumann, who had infiltrated the *Freiheit* editorial office, relayed information to the Hamburg police, who conducted a house search where they found 663 issues of *Freiheit*, letters, and subscription information. This led to the arrest of forty-five people in the Hamburg area, with some reports of mistreatment.

18. Fricke, *Dokumente*, 1:37.

19. Jensen, *Presse und politische Polizei*, 63; H. Becker, "Johann Most," 37n114. This report is filed in Landesarchiv Berlin, Acta 11724, fol. 109–10.

20. Bebel, *Aus meinem Leben*, 3:44; Mehring, *Geschichte der deutschen Sozialdemokratie*, 6:161.

21. Harreck-Haase, *Der Agitator*, 2:29–30.

22. Engels to Becker, January 30, 1879, in *Karl Marx, Friedrich Engels Werke*, 34:368; Engels to Liebknecht, March 1, 1879, in Liebknecht, *Briefwechsel mit Karl Marx*, 264, both letters quoted in Harreck-Haase, *Der Agitator*, 2:30.

23. H. Becker, "Johann Most," 41; Harreck-Haase, *Der Agitator*, 2:33. When the Chemnitz police searched Julius Vahlteich's house in early 1880, they found the entire first quarter of *Freiheit*. See Carlson, *Anarchism in Germany*, 244n59.

24. *Stenographische Berichte*, 4th Legislative Period, 2nd Session, 21st Meeting (March 17, 1879), 441, 443. Liebknecht went on to say that "the Anti-Socialist Law cannot destroy our party," and anyone who believes "that we will give up our principles and stop being social-democrats" is profoundly mistaken.

25. *Freiheit* [Der Argus] (London), April 26, 1879.

26. *Freiheit* [Thatsachen] (London), May 3, 1879 and *Freiheit* (London), July 19, 1879.

27. Liebknecht to Johann Voss, May 10, 1879; *Freiheit*, June 7, 1879, both quoted in Schröder, "Wilhelm Liebknecht," 86.

28. Most to Vollmar, August 20, 1879 (IISH), quoted in H. Becker, "Johann Most," 41.

29. H. Becker, "Johann Most," 42; Harreck-Haase, *Der Agitator*, 2:42.

30. H. Becker, "Johann Most," 42–44; A. Scheu, Andreas *Scheu Papers*, IISH.

31. Waldeck, "Die russischen Nihilisten"; H. Becker, "Johann Most," 44–45; Sapir, "Liberman," 50.

32. Alston, "News of the Struggle," 157. On Russian revolutionary terrorism, see Venturi, *Roots of Revolution*; Borcke, "Violence and Terror"; Anemone, *Just Assassins*.

33. Most, "Schliesst die Phalanx," *Freiheit* [Die Solidaritaet] (London), September 18, 1879, 1.

34. Most, "Die Sociale Revolution," *Freiheit* [Die Revolutionaer] (London), October 4, 1879, 1.

35. Most, "Die Sociale Revolution"; Most, "Der Terrorismus," *Freiheit* [Der Gerechtigkeit] (London), October 11, 1879, 1.

36. Quoted in Eade, *Placing London*, 55.

37. H. Becker, "Johann Most," 45n130; London Metropolitan Archives, *London City Directories*, 1882, 237; *La première internationale*, 4:638n335. A. Scheu, *Umsturzkeime*, 1:153. On November 7, 1880, the last ship carrying amnestied Communards, Louise Michel among them, disembarked in London, having sailed from the penal colony at New Caledonia. Victor Dave welcomed them upon their arrival at Victoria Station. See "Louise Michel," *Freiheit* (London), November 13, 1880; Butterworth, *The World That Never Was*, 162.

38. On Vaillant, see Candar and Duclert, *Édouard Vaillant*; Dommanget, *Édouard Vaillant*; Howorth, *Edouard Vaillant*; Howorth, "The Myth of Blanquism"; Vaillant to Most, December 17, 1879, in Kleine Korrespondenz (from SPD Archives) Archives, 1844–1931, IISH.

39. *Freiheit* (London), July 19, 1879. German spies in London knew about the trip only weeks after Most's return to London. Agent's report, July 25, 1879 (London) in Landesarchiv Berlin, Acta 11724, 194.

40. *Journal de Bruxelles*, August 12 and 14, 1879; *L'écho du parlement* (Brussels), August 12, 1879.

41. Bebel, *Aus meinem Leben*, 3:52; Most, *"Taktik" contra "Freiheit,"* 39.

42. *Der Sozialdemokrat* (Zurich), January 11, 1880, 3.

43. See Waddington, "Sleazy Digs"; *Het Nieuws van den Dag* (Amsterdam), June 18, 1880, 3.

44. Tcherikower, *The Early Jewish Labor Movement*, 1, 183; *Freiheit* (London), March 13, 1880; Fishman, *East End Jewish Radicals*, 129n44; Rocker, *The London Years*, 50–56. In London, there was more contact between Jews and followers of Most than between Jews and followers of Marx and Engels.

45. Devreese, "Militanten rond de Eerste Internationale," 513.

46. Musto, *Another Marx*, 226; Nettlau, "La muerte."

47. Nettlau, "La muerte."

48. H. Becker, "Johann Most," 87. The printer Henry James Bale testified that 1,200 copies were printed during 1880, but with special issues, 500 extra copies were printed. See *Old Bailey Proceedings Online*, May 23, 1881, "Trial of Johann Most."

49. Most, "Offener Brief an die Wähler des V. Berliner Reichstagswahlkreises," *Freiheit* (London), May 5, 1880.

50. *Freiheit* (London), February 28, 1880.

51. *Freiheit* (London), March 13 and 27, May 1, 1880.

52. Quoted in Carlson, *Anarchism in Germany*, 191.

53. [Schneidt,] *Die Hintermänner*, 66.

54. *Der Sozialdemokrat* (Zurich), May 16, 1880, 2.

55. Julius Motteler, "Werther Genosse 1880," with added notes "Vom vereitelten Congress zu Rorschach 1880 und H. Most Citation nach Zuerich," in Julius Motteler Papers #262, IISH, and also quoted in Harreck-Haase, *Der Agitator*, 2:56–57.

56. Most, *August Reinsdorf*, 25; Most, "Die 'Freiheit,'" *Freiheit* (New York), July 4, 1896; Rocker, *Johann Most*, 76; Lidtke, *The Outlawed Party*, 118n24.

57. "Correspondenzen," *Freiheit* (London), May 29, 1880, 3; Rocker, *Johann Most*, 76.

58. Langhard, *Die anarchistische Bewegung*, 218; *Freiheit* (London), May 29, 1880, 3; Harreck-Haase, *Der Agitator*, 2:56–57.

59. Most, "Die 'Freiheit,'" *Freiheit* (New York), July 4, 1896.

60. Motteler, "Werther Genosse 1880," quoted in Harreck-Haase, *Der Agitator*, 2:59–60; Most, "Die 'Freiheit,'" *Freiheit* (New York), July 4, 1896; *Der Sozialdemokrat* (Zurich), June 27, 1880, 2–3; *Freiheit* (London), May 29, 1880, 3.

61. Harreck-Haase, *Der Agitator*, 2:60.

62. Most, *"Taktik" contra "Freiheit,"* 43–46; "Mittheilung," *Der Sozialdemokrat* (Zurich), May 30, 1880, 1.

63. Most, "'Waffenstillstand,'" *Freiheit* (London), June 5, 1880, 1; *Sozialdemokrat* (Zurich), June 13, 1880, 3.

64. Fricke, *Dokumente*, 1:59.

65. Walther [Georg von Vollmar], "Werther Genosse," July 1880, in Julius Motteler Papers #263, IISH, quoted in Lidtke, *The Outlawed Party*, 118–19.

66. Harreck-Haase, *Der Agitator*, 2:63–65; Goodrich, "On the Road"; Bers, *Wilhelm Hasselmann*, 52.

67. Most, *"Taktik" contra "Freiheit"*; Police report of September 21, 1880 (London) in Landesarchiv Berlin, Acta 11725, 88. The full expulsion resolution is quoted in Harreck-Haase, *Der Agitator*, 2:65–66.

68. Trautmann, *The Voice of Terror*, 19.

69. Mehring, *Geschichte der deutschen Sozialdemokratie*, 2:413.

70. Lidtke, *The Outlawed Party*, 120.

71. H. Becker, "Johann Most," 45.

72. In December 1880, cabinetmaker Wentker suggested that Most was working with a police spy, for which he was roundly condemned by the press commission and by John Neve. See Wentker, "'Denunziation' und 'Attentat,'" *Sozialdemokrat* (Zurich), December 12, 1880, 4 and *Freiheit* (London), December 18, 1880, 4. In 1881, William and Clara Wentker lived at 65 Latymer Road in the Hammersmith district of London. Clara died in December 1882. See England and Wales, Civil Registration Death Index, 1837–1915 (Ancestry.com); 1881 England Census (Ancestry.com).

73. *Old Bailey Proceedings Online*, May 23, 1881, "Trial of Johann Most"; London Metropolitan Archives, *London City Directories*, 1880, 350.

74. H. Becker, "Johann Most," 27n89. Becker provides no sources. England and Wales Census, 1911.

75. Szmula, *Johann Most*, 4:60.

76. In December 1880, Most wrote, "Our ideal is not the improved liberal state but a free society where there is no such thing as governing." Most, "Durch Terrorismus zur Freiheit," *Freiheit* (London), December 11, 1880, 1.

77. Rocker, *Johann Most*, 11.

78. Szmula, *Johann Most*, 4:61.

79. Dave's conversations with Max Nettlau in Nettlau, *Anarchisten und Sozialrevolutionäre*, 157. Whereas Most clung to the idea that the proletariat must conquer

political power, Dave argued for abstaining from politics and rejecting a socialist people's state. Rocker, *Johann Most*, 93.

80. "Bacunin's Revolutions-Grundsätze," *Freiheit* (London), September 18, 1880, 1–2; "Einiges über Anarchismus," *Freiheit* (London), September 25, 1880, 1–2; "Zur Organisation und Taktik der Anarchisten," *Freiheit* (London), September 25, 1880, 2; "Zur Organisationsfrage," *Freiheit* (London), October 8, 1880, 1. Brussels readers responded, "We have not become anarchists, though we consider them honest social revolutionaries." Quoted in Nettlau, *Anarchisten und Sozialrevolutionäre*, 158.

81. Nettlau, *Anarchisten und Sozialrevolutionäre*, 166.

82. Malatesta and Cafiero quoted in Linse, "'Propaganda by Deed' and 'Direct Action,'" 202; Carlson, *Anarchism in Germany*, chap. 8.

83. Nettlau, *Anarchisten und Sozialrevolutionäre*, 163; Rocker, *Johann Most*, 87, 92–93. During his trial, Dave characterized Most's oft-quoted pamphlet *"Taktik"* v. *"Freiheit"* as "thoroughly Jacobin tempered by Blanquist ideas." Quoted in Rocker, *Johann Most*, 92–93.

84. Most, "Weshalb wir uns Socialrevolutionäre nennen," *Freiheit* (London), November 27, 1880, 1.

85. Jensen, *Presse und politische Polizei*, 68.

86. See Eisenhauer obituary in *Freiheit* (London), February 25, 1882, 1. For a detailed study of underground *Freiheit* groups in the Frankfurt area, see Eichler, *Sozialistische Arbeiterbewegung*, 61–75.

87. Carlson, *Anarchism in Germany*, 217; Jensen, *Presse und politische Polizei*, 69; Ernst, *Polizeispitzeleien und Ausnahmegesetz*, 22.

88. *Freiheit* (London), October 16, 1880, 4. According to Ehrhart, it was Most's wife, Clara, who first raised suspicions against Neumann. Ehrhart, "Aus meiner Londoner Zeit," 62.

89. See Carlson, *Anarchism in Germany*, 205–47; Harreck-Haase, *Der Agitator*, 2:75–76. *AZ*, December 31, 1880, January 5, 1881, October 10, 15, and 22, 1881; *Times of London*, February 12, 1881; *Pall Mall Gazette* (London), February 11, 1881; *Freiheit* (London), December 11 and 18, 1880.

90. *AZ*, March 15, 1881, 2.

91. *Times of London*, March 14, 1881, 9.

92. Kelly, *British Humanitarian Activity*, 135; Hughes, "British Opinion," abstract.

93. *NYT*, March 15 and 16, 1881; *New York Standard*, March 15 and 16, 1881; *Newcastle Courant*, March 25, 1881; Harreck-Haase, *Der Agitator*, 2:79.

94. "Endlich!" *Freiheit* (London), March 19, 1881, 1. The translation is the version read in Parliament. See *Hansard* HC Deb 31 March 1881 vol 260 cc344–7, https://www.parliament.uk/.

95. Porter, "The Freiheit Prosecutions," 841n50.

96. *Old Bailey Proceedings Online*, May 23, 1881, "Trial of Johann Most"; *Times of London*, April 8, 1881; Porter, "The Freiheit Prosecutions," 850.

97. Section 4 reads, "All Persons who shall conspire, confederate, and agree to murder any Person, whether he be a Subject of Her Majesty or not, and whether he

be within the Queen's Dominions or not, and whosoever shall solicit, encourage, persuade, or endeavour to persuade, or shall propose to any Person, to murder any other Person, whether he be a Subject of Her Majesty or not, and whether he be within the Queen's Dominions or not, shall be guilty of a Misdemeanor, and being convicted thereof shall be liable, at the Discretion of the Court, to be kept in Penal Servitude for any Term not more than Ten and not less than Three Years,—or to be imprisoned for any Term not exceeding Two Years, with or without Hard Labour." See https://www.legislation.gov.uk/ukpga/Vict/24-25/100/section/4/enacted.

98. *Hansard* HC Deb 11 November 1882 vol 274 c1634, https://www.parliament .uk/.

99. Quoted in Porter, "The Freiheit Prosecutions," 849–50.

100. *Wiener Allgemeine Zeitung*, May 1, 1881, 5.

101. *London Daily News*, May 4, 1881, 5; *London Evening Standard*, May 6, 1881, 2.

102. "The Prosecution of the 'Freiheit,'" *Dublin Daily Express*, April 6, 1881, 4.

103. Harreck-Haase, *Der Agitator*, 2:86–87.

104. Quoted in Porter, "The Freiheit Prosecutions," 836n17.

105. *Times of London*, May 26, 1881. The French anarchist Gustave Brocher, who knew Most and was in London then, has pointed out that curiously, Most's Cleveland Hall speech on March 18 was never mentioned during his trial. Brocher, who also spoke that day, believed speeches to be more "dangerous" than an article in an obscure paper. See Rocker, *Johann Most*, 459.

106. *Times of London*, May 26, 1881.

107. For more details about the proceedings, see *Reports of All the Cases Decided by All the Superior Courts Relating to Magistrates, Municipal, and Parochial Law* (Law times office, 1882), 12:467–72; *Times of London*, June 20, 1881.

108. *Pall Mall Gazette* (London), June 29, 1881, 8; *Reynolds's Newspaper* (London), July 3, 1881, 2.

109. *Reynolds's Newspaper* (London), July 3, 1881, 5.

110. Porter, "The Freiheit Prosecutions," 835.

111. In public, the government regarded the *Freiheit* incident as a "domestic crime" and a "flagrant breach of our public morals." See *Hansard* HC Deb 31 March 1881 vol 260 cc344–7, https://www.parliament.uk/. Friedrich Engels alluded to such collusion when he wrote to Bebel that "the Russian embassy and [Prime Minister] Gladstone certainly don't need any help turning silly Hans into a great man." Quoted in Harreck-Haase, *Der Agitator*, 2:92.

112. Quoted in Porter, "The Freiheit Prosecutions," 838.

113. In December 1907, a German monthly magazine published letters by the German ambassador in London, Count Münster, showing that he pushed for the arrest and jailing of Most. The Milwaukee socialist *Vorwärts* (November 17, 1907) reported on it. Oncken, "Aus den Briefen Rudolf von Bennigsen," 19.

114. Porter, "The Freiheit Prosecutions," 846.

115. Porter, "The Freiheit Prosecutions," 844–45.

116. Quoted in Porter, "The Freiheit Prosecutions," 846.

117. Porter, "The Freiheit Prosecutions," 851. In April 1881, Lord Randolph Churchill (father of Winston), a Conservative MP, alleged that two members of the government—Undersecretary of State for Foreign Affairs Charles Dilke and Civil Lord of the Admiralty Thomas Brassey—made financial contributions to *Freiheit*. Both officials denied the charge, but research shows that Brassey and Dilke likely made contributions to aid socialists, which ended up in the *Freiheit* account books. Porter, "The Freiheit Prosecutions," 841n49. Churchill's source was the Marxist Maltman Barry.

118. 1881 England Census, Enumeration Book, Her Majesty's Prison, Clerkenwell, London, 12.

119. [Most,] *Acht Jahre*, 65; *Pall Mall Gazette* (London), August 25, 1881, 8.

120. *Pall Mall Gazette* (London), August 25, 1881, 8. Most did complain about the condition to Harcourt, who made some effort to address them. Porter, "The Freiheit Prosecutions," 854n125.

121. *London Evening Standard*, April 19, 1881, 6; *Pall Mall Gazette* (London), August 25, 1881, 8.

122. *AZ*, April 28, 1881, 6.

123. Cohen, *The Jewish Anarchist Movement*, 146–47.

124. Fricke and Knaack, *Dokumente*, 1:119.

125. Peukert, *Erinnerungen*, 49, 62; Harreck-Haase, *Der Agitator*, 2:93–94.

126. [Most,] *Acht Jahre*, 67–68; Rocker, *Johann Most*, 123.

127. To ensure the attendants' safety, all delegates were designated by numbers and referred to as such in the radical press. For a list of names *and* numbers, see Nettlau, *Anarchisten und Sozialrevolutionäre*, chap. 10.

128. A German police report stated that the idea for an international congress stemmed from Most. Fricke and Knaack, *Dokumente*, 1:98. Bantman, "Internationalism without an International," 963–66.

129. Goyens, *Beer and Revolution*, 80–85; *Freiheit* (London), November 19, 1881.

130. Carlson, *Anarchism in Germany*, 221–29; Wagner, *Missionare der Gewalt*, 80; *AZ*, October 11–26, 1881.

131. Carlson, *Anarchism in Germany*, 229.

132. Carlson, *Anarchism in Germany*, 230–31; Porter, "The Freiheit Prosecutions," 851–52; *Old Bailey Proceedings Online*, June 1882, "Trial of Frederick Schwelm," and July 1882, "Trial of William Mertens."

133. Eduard Joos, "Wilhelm Bührer: Schriftsetzer, Buchdrucker, Anarchist," Stadtarchiv Schaffhausen, https://www.yumpu.com/de/document/read/6440629/buhrer-wilhelm-stadtarchiv-schaffhausen; Langhard, *Die anarchistische Bewegung*, 220–24.

134. *Freiheit*, October 21, 1882.

135. Agent's report, November 8, 1882 (London) in Landesarchiv Berlin, Acta 11726, 74.

136. Quoted in Langhard. *Die anarchistische Bewegung*, 221–22. Carlson has suggested that Stellmacher offered his service as a spy after his dismissal by Most. See Carlson, *Anarchism in Germany*, 264–65.

137. *Hansard* HC Deb 11 November 1882 vol 274 c1634.

138. Agent's report of November 29, 1882 (London) in Landesarchiv Berlin, Acta 11726, 80–81; Fricke and Knaack, *Dokumente*, 1:169; [Schneidt,] *Die Hintermänner*, 99–100.

139. *CT*, December 25, 1882.

140. FamilySearch: Passenger Lists of Vessels Arriving at New York, New York, 1820–1897 (National Archives Microfilm Publication M237, roll 460); Records of the U.S. Customs Service, Record Group 36; "Notizen," *Der deutsche Correspondent* (Baltimore), December 20, 1882, 3.

141. She was buried in Camden, London, on December 9. See UK, Burial and Cremation Index, 1576–2014 (Ancestry.com). Months earlier, on July 2, Most's father had passed away in Augsburg, but it is unknown how, or even if, he received this news. *Städtische Polizei, Familienbögen: Most.* Stadtarchiv Augsburg.

Chapter 6. Sturm und Drang

1. "The Bark Ella's Signals," *NYS*, December 19, 1882; *DC*, December 19, 1882; "Waiting for Herr Most," *NYS*, December 18, 1882, 1.

2. "A Bearer of the Red Flag," *NYS*, December 19, 1882, 1; "Arrival of Herr Most," *NYT*, December 19, 1882, 8; "Arrival of John Most," *Evening Post* (New York), December 18, 1882, 1.

3. For more on Mégy and Drury, see Cordillot, *La sociale en Amérique*, 167–70, 304–7.

4. *Freiheit* (London), January 3 and February 28, 1880, 4. By December 1882, *Freiheit* counted seven subscription agents in the United States (other than Schwab): in Chicago, Cleveland, Milwaukee, Philadelphia, Jersey City and Union Hill, New Jersey, and Baltimore. *Freiheit* (New York), December 9, 1882, 1.

5. "Arrival of Herr Most," *NYT*, December 19, 1882, 8; "A Bearer of the Red Flag," *NYS*, December 19, 1882, 1; "Most in New-York," *DC*, December 19 and 20, 1882.

6. *Freiheit* (New York), December 23, 1882.

7. *Freiheit* (New York), December 9, 1882, quoted in Nettlau, *Anarchisten und Sozialrevolutionäre*, 377.

8. Most, *Die freie Gesellschaft*, 54.

9. Most, *Die freie Gesellschaft*, 33.

10. Kropotkin's idea goes back to the ancient phrase "From each according to his ability, to each according to his needs," which Most once referred derisively as "a Saint Simonian slogan" in a letter to his rival Josef Peukert. Peukert, *Erinnerungen*, 150.

11. Avrich, *The Haymarket Tragedy*, 48; See receipts in *Freiheit [Festzeitung]* (London), June 7, 1879, 4.

12. Schmidt, *Der rothe Doktor von Chicago*.

13. *Freiheit* (New York), December 30, 1882; Harreck-Haase, *Der Agitator*, 2:117.

14. *Freiheit* (New York), December 30 and January 6, 1883; "Die Revolution und der Aufbau einer neue Gesellschaft," *Freiheit* (New York), January 13 and 20, 1883; [Most,] "Die Arbeiterbewegung in Amerika," *Freiheit*, December 13, 1884.

15. According to one report, Most planned to return to England with Hartmann. "Nihilists in Conference," *NYS*, February 9, 1883, 1; "A Flaming Radical," *Philadelphia Inquirer*, February, 5, 1883, 8.

16. For selected travel coverage, see "Most in Milwaukee," *DC*, January 6, 1883, 1; "Herr Most," *Daily Wabash Express* (Terre Haute, IN), January 10, 1883, 1; "Most in Baltimore," *DC*, February 12 and 15, 1883; "Herr Most in Baltimore," *Baltimore Sun*, February 12, 1883, 3; "Herr Most in the City," *Washington Post*, February 14, 1883, 2; *Freiheit* (New York), December 23 and 30, 1882, and January 6 and 20 and February 3 and 17, 1883; "The German Socialist," *Evening Star* (Washington, DC), February 14, 1883, 3.

17. *Freiheit* (New York), January 20, 1883; "Herr Most in the City," *Washington Post*, February 14, 1883, 2.

18. "Herr Most's Great Scheme," *Wheeling Register*, April 10, 1883, 1.

19. "Shouting for the Commune," *NYT*, March 19, 1883, 8; *DC*, March 20, 1883, 1.

20. "Herr Most's Views," *Washington Post*, April 18, 1883, 1.

21. For selected travel coverage, see *DC*, April 9, 1883, 2; "Herr Most's Discourse," *Baltimore Sun*, April 10, 1883, 4; "The Socialist Leader," *Daily Cairo Bulletin* (Cairo, IL), May 6, 1883, 1; "Most in St. Louis," *DC*, May 10, 1883, 2; "A Trusted Traitor," *Daily Alta California* (San Francisco), May 12, 1883, 1; "Herr Most," *Omaha Daily Bee*, May 21, 1883, 8; *DC*, May 25, 1883, 3; "Herr Most, the Socialist," *Wheeling Register*, May 31, 1883, 1.

22. *DC*, April 26, 1883, 1; "Most in St. Louis," *Freiheit* (New York), May 19, 1883, 2–3; Harreck-Haase, *Der Agitator*, 2:123.

23. *Freiheit* (New York), August 11, 1883. Twenty-six locations were represented at the Pittsburgh congress, which opened on October 14, 1883. For more on the Pittsburgh congress, see Goyens, *Beer and Revolution*, 102–9.

24. *The Alarm* (Chicago), April 4, 1885; *Life of Albert R. Parsons*, 108, quoted in Avrich, *The Haymarket Tragedy*, 73; Zimmer, "Haymarket."

25. Quoted in Goyens, *Beer and Revolution*, 106–7; the German text in Rocker, *Johann Most*, 146–9; English version in Ely, *The Labor Movement*, 358–63 and Fried, *Socialism*, 208–12.

26. Creagh, *L'anarchisme aux États-Unis*, 1:652.

27. Quoted in Waltershausen, *Der moderne Socialismus*, 236.

28. Fricke, *Dokumente*, 1:239.

29. "Arrival of Herr Most," *NYT*, December 19, 1882, 8.

30. "Herr Most, the Socialist," *Frank Leslie's Illustrated Newspaper*, January 6, 1883, 332.

31. Most to Dave, New York, August 10, 1884, in Nettlau, "Most," 13 and Most to Dave, New York, January 13, 1885, in Nettlau, "Most," 41.

32. Most, *Zwischen Galgen und Zuchthaus*, 1.

33. Kautsky, "Johann Most," 555.

34. *DC*, December 20, 1882, 3.

35. Fricke, *Dokumente*, 1:197; [Most,] *Acht Jahre*, 70–71. Also, *Freiheit* did not accept business advertisements to raise revenues, unlike when it appeared in London. See letterbox response: "Business advertisements do not appear in *Freiheit*" (February 24, 1883, 4).

36. Rocker, *Johann Most*, 143; Nettlau, "Most," 11, IISH.

37. *Freiheit* (New York), December 9, 1882, 1 and December 1, 1883, 4.

38. Most to Dave, New York, September 24, 1885, in Nettlau, "Most und Neve," 57, Nettlau Archives, IISH; U.S. Department of Labor, *History of Wages*, 350.

39. Fricke, *Dokumente*, 1:196.

40. Most to Dave, New York, March 21, 1886, in Nettlau, "Most und Neve," 62, Nettlau Archives, IISH.

41. Starting in July 1883, the acknowledgment "Published by the Communist Workers' Educational Association London," printed at the bottom of the last page disappeared.

42. Rocker, *Johann Most*, 144.

43. Peukert to Dave, September 20, 1880, in Nettlau, "Most und Neve," 7–8, Nettlau Archives, IISH; Peukert, *Erinnerungen*, 112.

44. Most to Dave, New York, September 6, 1884, in Nettlau, "Most und Neve," 14, Nettlau Archives, IISH. Peukert flatly denied these allegations. Peukert, *Erinnerungen*, 144.

45. Nettlau, "Most und Neve," 5, Nettlau Archives, IISH. In 1884, he tried to undermine a New Jersey paper out of Hudson County by accusing its editor of sowing discord and defrauding workers, and a year later, he considered taking over a new paper in Connecticut. The next year, Hasselmann launched *Amerikanische Arbeiterzeitung* expressly to compete with *Freiheit* and to showcase that a paper can function without a controlling editor. The paper lasted for six months. Goyens, *Beer and Revolution*, 117–18.

46. Carlson, *Anarchism in Germany*, 321–37.

47. The current Belgian-German border lies farther east because Belgium was awarded the Eupen-Malmédy cantons after World War I.

48. Most to Dave, New York, August 10, 1884, in Nettlau, *Most und Neve*, IISH. On anarchist terrorism, see Jensen, *The Battle against Anarchist Terrorism*; Carlson, "Anarchism and Individual Terror"; Carlson, *Anarchism in Germany*.

49. Most, "Die Revolution und der Aufbau einer neuen Gesellschaft," *Freiheit* (New York), January 13 and 20, 1883; Most, *Die Eigenthumsbestie* (1883), translated as *The Beast of Property* (1890); Most, *Die Gottes-Pest und Religions-Seuche* (1883), translated as *The Deistic Pestilence and Religious Plague of Man* (1883) and *The God Pestilence* (1887); Most, *Die freie Gesellschaft* (1884), translated as *The Free Society* (1891); *Diskussion über das Thema "Anarchismus oder Communismus"* (1884); Most, *August Reinsdorf* (1885); Most, *Revolutionäre Kriegswissenschaft* (1885), translated as *Military Science for Revolutionaries* (1978) and *Science of Revolutionary Warfare* (1978).

50. Whelehan, "'Cheap as Soap,'" 108, 115–16.

51. Most, *Die Eigenthumsbestie*, 1.

52. Most, *Die freie Gesellschaft*, 62.

53. Most, "Die Revolution und der Aufbau einer neuen Gesellschaft." On urban warfare, see "Revolutionäre Kriegskunst," *Freiheit* (New York), December 29, 1883; "Neue Kriegstaktik der Revolution," *Freiheit* (New York), March 8, 1884; "Theorie und Praxis der revolutionären Kriegswissenschaft," *Freiheit* (New York), January 17, 1885.

54. "Dynamit," *Freiheit* (New York), May 5, 1883.

55. "Zur Propaganda der That," *Freiheit* (New York), January 12, 1884.

56. Most, *Die freie Gesellschaft*, 65. On the twelfth anniversary of the Commune, Most again published Nechaev's *Catechism*, which spelled out the duties and responsibilities of the ruthless and selfless revolutionary. "Revolutionäre Grundsätze," *Freiheit* (New York), March 18, 1883.

57. Most, *Die freie Gesellschaft*, 71.

58. In December 1882, the executive committee of the Association of the Pioneers of Revolution (Verein der Pioniere der Revolution) announced that if peaceful means to fight capitalist exploitation failed, they would switch to physical means. Fricke, *Dokumente*, 1:185–86.

59. *The Alarm* (Chicago), October 11, 1884; Avrich, *The Haymarket Tragedy*, 67.

60. In October 1884, a Fund for Action and Propaganda was set up to " support the active fighters of the social revolution using every sort of warfare to emancipate the proletariat." *Freiheit* (New York), October 18, 1884, 4.

61. Most, *August Reinsdorf*, 4–5.

62. Quoted in Wagner, *Missionare der Gewalt*, 81.

63. The historian Andrew Carlson has shown that the government did know of the plot and chose not to release any information until April 1884, just in time to convince lawmakers to renew the Anti-Socialist Law and pass a restrictive explosives law. Carlson, *Anarchism in Germany*, 291.

64. Records of the event and subsequent police investigation are at the Hessisches Hauptstaatsarchiv (Wiesbaden). Abt. 405: Preusisches Regierungspräsidium Wiesbaden. Nr. 355: Dynamitattentat (1883–87); Explosion im Polizeidienstgebäude zu Frankfurt (mit Voruntersuchungen gegen Anarchisten), 106 pp. Thanks to Dr. Rouven Pons of the Staatsarchiv for providing this information. Langhard, *Die anarchistische Bewegung*; Müller, *Bericht*.

65. Evidence from city and police records and anarchists point to Joseph Richetzky, a Bohemian tailor who had become an emissary of the London clubs. The anarchist Wilhelm Gebhardt identified Richetzky as the perpetrator in 1890 as part of his statements regarding his activities. Victor Dave also mentions Richetzky as the bomber in a conversation with Max Nettlau. Richetzky adopted the alias Jäger and by the fall of 1884 had arrived in New York. Most then wrote to Dave that "Jäger has straightaway told me a lot, though not yet the right things, although he expressed the desire to

speak with me alone soon, which I take to mean that he'll open up completely." Most to Dave, November 15, 1884, in Nettlau, *Most und Neve*, IISH; Eichler, *Sozialistische Arbeiterbewegung*, 107n122, 107n109, 107n142, 107n110, 107n144; *Freiheit* (New York), October 31, 1883, quoted in Langhard, *Die anarchistische Bewegung*, 280.

66. Müller. *Bericht*, 58.

67. Quoted in Eichler, *Sozialistische Arbeiterbewegung*, 108.

68. *Freiheit* (New York), March 1, 1884.

69. *Freiheit* (New York), December 27, 1884, quoted in Langhard, *Die anarchistische Bewegung*, 259n2. Most later proudly, but erroneously, designated Reinsdorf as the Niederwalt perpetrator. Most, *August Reinsdorf*, 2:58.

70. H. Becker. "Johann Most," 52–53n155, 53n156; *Freiheit* (New York), January 24, 1885.

71. *Freiheit* (New York), December 27, 1884, 4.

72. Steiner, *Die Arbeiterbewegung Österreichs*, 224.

73. After Most dismissed Stellmacher, the latter offered to work as a police spy but was apparently rejected, which may have increased his hatred for the established order. For a detailed account, see Carlson, *Anarchism in Germany*, chap. 8.

74. "Internationale Arbeiter-Assoziation. Zur Propaganda der That," *Freiheit* (New York), February 16, 1884; "Sympathizing with Murder," *NYT*, February 11, 1884, 2. In April 1884, the communist anarchist paper *Le révolté* (Geneva) also praised Stellmacher for his deeds. Langhard, *Die anarchistische Bewegung*, 107.

75. "Socialists in a Cell," *NYT*, August 9, 1884, 1; "Idealizing a Murder," *NYT*, August 12, 1884, 3.

76. Fricke, *Dokumente*, 1:263; "Die Hinrichtung des Mörders Stellmacher in Wien," *DC*, August 13, 1884, 3. A comprehensive account of the affair that included the murder of the Eisert children was not available to American readers until September 1884 when the *New York Evening Post* published "A Disciple of Most" (September 1, 1884), a detailed and mostly accurate article that also appeared in *The Nation* a few days later (September 4, 1884, 194).

77. "Bachmann and the International," *Liberty* (Boston), May 1, 1886, 8. The anarchist editor Robert Reitzel later pointed out that the first edition of Most's popular 1883 pamphlet *Die Eigenthumsbestie* (The beast of property) included the line, "Take private property, kill innocents if necessary, but take it by all means!" Interestingly, Most removed this line from the 1887 edition. "Heraus mit der Farbe!" *Der arme Teufel* (Detroit), April 10, 1886.

78. The Wirths operated a card publishing company with a storefront on Bond Street in Manhattan. They lived in Jersey City from 1876, when Maurice immigrated, until 1882, when they moved to Manhattan. Moritz Schultze, who was temporary editor of *Freiheit*, informed Dave that Most had for years lodged with the Wirths family in New York and is very respected and loved by them. Most used their addresses as cover. In June 1886, it was 204 Eleventh Street in Brooklyn (confirmed by city directory). In August 1886, Most's new cover address was "A. Wirths [Arabella or Bella],

Hill Cottage, Point Pleasant, Ocean County, NJ." Schultze to Dave, Hoboken, June 24, 1886, etc., in Victor Dave Paper, #108; Nettlau, "Most und Neve," Max Nettlau Papers, #1857, 66, IISH; *Lain's Brooklyn Directory for the Year Ending May 1st, 1887*, 1249. On the Wirths, see *Gopsill's Jersey City and Hoboken Directory, 1883–1884*, 484; *Trow's New York City Directory*, 1884, 1819; U.S. Census, 1880; "United States Passport Applications, 1795–1925" (FamilySearch).

79. Most to Dave, New York, September 19, 1884, in Nettlau, *Most und Neve*, IISH. The facility may have been the newly built American Forcite Powder Manufacturing Company (or Forcite Powder Works) on the shores of Lake Hopatcong, a two-hour train ride west from Jersey City. The company produced the first gelatin dynamite (forcite), mixed by hand, in the United States. Another candidate is the older Atlantic Dynamite Company located in Kenvil, New Jersey, not far from Lake Hopatcong. Eissler, *A Handbook on Modern Explosives*, 73–74.

80. "Theorie und Praxis der revolutionären Kriegswissenschaft" (January 17, 1885), "Spreng-Übungen" (February 21, 1885), "Einfache Chemie" (March 10, 1885), "Schiess-baumwolle und Nitrogelatin" (March 21, 1885), "Knallquecksilber" (March 28, 1885), "Weitere chemische Winke" (June 27, 1885).

81. Most to Dave, New York, October 2, 1884, in Nettlau, *Most und Neve*, IISH.

82. Most to Dave, New York, November 19, 1884, in Nettlau, *Most und Neve*, IISH.

83. *Freiheit* (New York), September 20, 1884, 4; Messer-Kruse, *The Trial*, 96; Messer-Kruse, *The Haymarket Conspiracy*, 119; Spies, "Autobiography," 71; Nuhn, *August Spies*, 188. On October 18, 1884, Group New York held an "extra-ordinary business meeting" to discuss "urgent and extremely important matters," which required the presence of "all comrades without fail." Whether this closed meeting had anything to do with shipping explosives is not known. *Freiheit* (New York), October 18, 1884, 4.

84. The translated subtitle is, *A Handbook of Instruction concerning the Use and Manufacture of Nitroglycerin, Dynamite, Guncotton, Fulminating Mercury, Bombs, Arson, Poisons.* Eugene Seeger translated it into English. *Chicago Tribune*, March 24, 1886. Testimony of Eugene Seeger, July 20, 1886, Haymarket Affair Digital Collection (HADC), https://www.chicagohistoryresources.org/hadc/transcript/volumei/451-500/I500-505.htm.

85. Most, *Revolutionäre Kriegswissenschaft*, 4, 46.

86. "Anarchisten-'Kriegswissenschaft,'" *Illinois Staats-Zeitung* (Chicago), August 2, 1886, 4; "A Nest of Nihilists," *Daily Alta California* (San Francisco), December 16, 1885; "The Dynamite Plot," *Daily Press* (Santa Barbara, CA), December 17, 1885; "A Gang of Dynamiters," *NYT*, December 17, 1885; Messer-Kruse, *The Haymarket Conspiracy*, 115–16.

87. An 1884 German police report sent to Berlin warned, "Particularly dangerous for the old world are the social-revolutionary clubs in New York where members of all countries come together and who are not afraid to use any criminal means to bring about the overthrow of state and society." Fricke, *Dokumente*, 1:239.

88. Quoted in Messer-Kruse, *The Haymarket Conspiracy*, 131.

89. "Six Men and Women Burned," *NYS*, June 3, 1885, 1; "A Chapter on Anarchism," *NYS*, May 3, 1886, 1.

90. For example, Joseph Kaiser was identified by Most as a member of an anarchist rifle club. Kaiser also made financial contributions to *Freiheit* in 1886 and spoke at an anarchist meeting in Irving Hall criticizing the verdict in the Haymarket trial. John Charles Panzenbeck, an engineer, also made financial contributions to *Freiheit* in 1884 and 1886 and contributed to an 1884 Fund for Action and Propaganda. Most praised Panzenbeck as a trustworthy man. In December 1884, he was elected to the Control Committee of *Freiheit*. Hermann Wabnitz was an exile from Germany who joined the New York Group I. Otto Nicolai was the agent for *Freiheit* in Jersey City Heights in 1884. Fritz Schärr was one of the original social revolutionaries in New York who signed the 1882 letter inviting Most to the United States. In 1883, he acted as secretary of New York Group I. Most to Dave, New York, December 4, 1884 and April 28, 1885, in Nettlau, *Most und Neve*, IISH; *Freiheit* (New York), October 21, 1882; April 14, 1883; March 15, 1884; October 18 and 25, 1884; December 20, 1884; July 31, 1886; August 28, 1886; October 9, 1886; Goyens, *Beer and Revolution*, 73.

91. "Bachmann and the International," *Liberty* (Boston), May 1, 1886, 8.

92. "Dynamit," *Der arme Teufel* (Detroit), February 7, 1885, 5. Reitzel disapproved of Most's rhetoric, but he respected Most's energy and sincerity: "I have never been able to get a taste for Most's tirades and I emphasized at the time that no educated elements could be won over to our cause in this way." "Die Socialisten im deutschen Reichstag," *Der arme Teufel* (Detroit), March 7, 1885, 3.

93. "All Ready to Lynch Him," *NYT*, November 24, 1885, 1; "Kohout an Anarchist," *NYTs*, November 30, 1885, 5; "City and Suburban News," *NYT*, December 1, 1885, 8; "The Kohout Murder Trial," *NYS*, January 28, 1886, 3; Messer-Kruse, *The Haymarket Conspiracy*, 133–35.

94. "Aus der Zeitungswelt," *Der arme Teufel* (Detroit), January 9, 1886.

95. "The Beast of Communism," *Liberty* (Boston), March 27, 1886, 1. In the wake of Tucker's article, the Chicago revolutionary anarchist Dyer D. Lum, an editorial writer for the radical journal *The Alarm*, also spoke out. However, his article was refused by his own journal; it appeared in *Liberty* instead. Lum defended Schwab's decision to break with Most and *Freiheit*, and he admitted that his own sources corroborated the charges leveled by Tucker: "Unfortunately, men in whom I have the greatest confidence, and in whose word I have unbounded trust, have reason to believe that the charge is true." "The Beast of Communism," *Liberty* (Boston), May 1, 1886, 5. Reitzel also saw no reason to doubt the veracity of the arson frauds; the question was whether these actions were sponsored by the party. "Heraus mit der Farbe!" *Der arme Teufel* (Detroit), April 10, 1886.

96. "Plotting Against New-York," *NYTR*, April 1, 1886, 1; "A Chapter on Anarchism," *NYS*, May 3, 1886, 1.

97. Willmund had made a financial contribution to *Freiheit* (October 25, 1884). "Dagger, Pepper, and Gun," *NYS*, March 10, 1886; "Ein deutscher Anarchist zu 3½ Jahre Zuchthaus verurtheilt," *DC*, April 28, 1886.

98. Quoted in Rocker, *Johann Most*, 301.

99. *Diskussion über das Thema: "Anarchismus oder Communismus?"* (1884). Waltershausen, *Der moderne Socialismus*, 178.

100. Letter quoted in Peukert, *Erinnerungen*, 150.

101. "Sozialisten und Anarchisten," *DC*, February 4, 1885, 4.

102. "Driven Out with Clubs," *NYS*, February 3, 1885, 3; "Sozialisten und Anarchisten," *DC*, February 4, 1885, 4.

103. "Sozialisten und Anarchisten," *DC*, February 4, 1885, 4. Two weeks later, at a meeting in Baltimore, Most delivered a glowing eulogy for August Reinsdorf, who had been executed in Germany. An SLP member attacked Most and the anarchists for their violent, ineffective politics. The exchange got heated and personal, but the meeting did not descend into a brawl. "Revolutionists at Odds," *Baltimore Sun*, February 23, 1885, 1.

Chapter 7. Facing America

1. H. Becker, "Johann Most," 51; Most to Dave, New York, September 24, 1885, in Nettlau, "Most und Neve," 57 and Most to Dave, New York, March 21, 1886, in Nettlau, "Most und Neve," 62, Nettlau Archives, IISH.

2. "An Anarchist's Sanctum," *NYS*, December 5, 1885, 6.

3. Goldman, *Living My Life*, 1:29. Louis Schürer and Herman Fajen's restaurant occupied the ground floor. *Trow's New York City Directory*, 1882–88.

4. "New Yorker Angelegenheiten," *Amerikanische Arbeiter-Zeitung* (New York), May 15, 1886.

5. [Most,] *Acht Jahre*, 73–74.

6. Most to Dave, New York, December 10, 1885 and March 21, 1886, in Nettlau, "Most und Neve," Nettlau Archives, IISH. Roth eventually married the Scottish trade unionist John Lincoln Mahon in 1888. Most, "Die 'Freiheit,'" *Freiheit* (New York), June 20, 1896, 1.

7. Most, "Die 'Freiheit,'" *Freiheit* (New York), August 1, 1896; "Grundsätze," *Freiheit* (London and New York), November 7, 1885, 1.

8. "Revolutionäre Kriegskunst," *Freiheit* (London and New York), January 9, 1886, 1; "An die Gewehre," *Freiheit* (London), July 8, 1882, 1–2; "Revolutionäre Kriegskunst," *Freiheit* (New York), December 29, 1883, 2.

9. Advertisement in *Frank Leslie's Illustrated Newspaper*, April 7, 1877, quoted in Green, *Death in the Haymarket*, 70.

10. "Protection against Tramps," *CT*, July 12, 1877, 8.

11. Quoted in Avrich, *The Haymarket Tragedy*, 28.

12. Green, *Death in the Haymarket*, 78–79, 80.

13. Green, *Death in the Haymarket*, 80.

14. After a speech by Most in the mill town of Webster, Massachusetts, one weaver remembered that several militants purchased rifles, founded a rifle club, and began practicing every Sunday morning in the woods. Dreisel, *Gesammelte Schriften*, 183.

15. "Zur Bewaffnungsfrage," *Freiheit* (New York), May 2, 1885, 1.

16. "Eight Hours' Work a Day," *NYS*, November 14, 1885, 3.

17. "Eight Hours," *The Alarm* (Chicago), September 5, 1885, 4.

18. Most, "Die 'Freiheit,'" *Freiheit* (New York), August 1, 1896.

19. "Life in the Metropolis," *NYS*, July 26, 1889, 1.

20. Most to Dave (New York), [April 29, 1886] in Nettlau, "Most und Neve," 64, Nettlau Archives, IISH.

21. "A Mild Mannered Crowd," *NYT*, May 2, 1886, 2.

22. "1,000 Men to Go Out," *CT*, May 1, 1886, 2.

23. Nelson, "*Arbeiterpresse und Arbeiterbewegung*," 87; "People's Exhibits," Haymarket Affair Digital Collection, https://www.chicagohistoryresources.org/hadc/transcript/trialtoc.htm#EXHIBITS.

24. For more information, see Green, *Death in the Haymarket*; Nelson, *Beyond the Martyrs*; Avrich, *The Haymarket Tragedy*; Schneirov, *Labor and Urban Politics*.

25. Wish, "Governor Altgeld Pardons the Anarchists," 426.

26. Nuhn, *August Spies*, 84; Barnard, *Eagle Forgotten*, 107–8.

27. "Rioting and Bloodshed in the Streets of Chicago," *NYT*, May 5, 1886, 1; "Restricting Immigration," *NYT*, May 9, 1886, 8.

28. Donner, *Protectors of Privilege*, 21–22.

29. "Most's Breech-Loaders," *NYT*, May 8, 1886, 4.

30. Most, "Eine schurkische Gemeinheit," *Freiheit* (New York), May 22, 1886; *Evening Telegram* (New York), May 3, 1886; "Most in Police Hands," *NYT*, May 12, 1886, 2; "Most Verhaftet," *DC*, May 12, 1886, 1. Most sent out a correction to several newspapers stating that the police broke into three other apartments until they found Most "standing up in the middle of the room." "New Yorker Angelegenheiten," *Amerikanische Arbeiter-Zeitung* (New York), May 15, 1886.

31. McLean, *The Rise and Fall*, 182. The press briefly speculated that Lena Fischer was the sister of Adolph, one of the Haymarket defendants (she is not) and that both Fischer and Most traveled to Chicago, which is unlikely and unsubstantiated. "Not Fischer's Sister," *St. Paul Daily Globe* (St. Paul, MN), May 15, 1886, 4.

32. *Grazer Tagblatt*, June 29, 1893, 8.

33. The city directory lists a tailor, Christian Broun. *DC*, May 13, 1886, 3; "Most's Incendiary Talk," *NYS*, May 28, 1; *Trow's New York City Directory for the Year Ending May 1, 1887* (New York, 1887), 227.

34. *Freiheit* (New York), May 22, 1886.

35. "Getting a Jury to Try Most," *NYT*, May 27, 1886, 8; "Evidence against Most," *NYT*, May 28, 1886, 3; "It Was Inciting to Riot," *NYT*, May 29, 1886, 8.

36. "Most Is on the Island," *NYT*, June 3, 1886, 8.

37. "The Conviction of Most," *NYT*, May 29, 1886, 4.

38. [Most,] *Acht Jahre*, 76.

39. *Annual Report of the State Board of Charities* (1887), 223.

40. [Most,] *Die Hoelle*, 16.

41. [Most,] *Die Hoelle*, 3.

42. Doutney, *Thomas N. Doutney*, 317; [Most,] *Acht Jahre*, 76–80; [Most,] *Die Hoelle*, 1–2.

43. [Most,] *Die Hoelle*, 4.

44. "Ein Brief von unserem Genossen John Most," *Freiheit*, August 14, 1886.

45. *Freiheit*, August 28, 1886, quoted in Avrich, *The Haymarket Tragedy*, 310–11.

46. "Der Grundcharakter des amerikanischen Volkes," *Freiheit* (New York), February 26, 1887, 1.

47. "Eine Spottfigur," *Freiheit*, September 27, 1886.

48. *Freiheit*, November 27, 1886.

49. Rocker, *Johann Most*, 316–17.

50. "Most's Term Nearly Over," *NYS*, March 30, 1887, 7.

51. [Most,] *Die Hoelle*, 16.

52. "Most Kissed by His Crowd," *NYTR*, April 2, 1887, 8; "John Most Loose Again," *NYS*, April 2, 1887, 3.

53. Since 1885, Most adopted "John Mueller" as his new professional name and was so listed in the city directories of 1887 and 1888. "Most Can't Have a Vote," *NYS*, September 13, 1887, 3.

54. Anyone wanting to visit the office at 167 William Street was greeted by a sign on the door: "To the capitalist press gang and the beasts of law and order: those who seek will find 'Freiheit.'" *DC*, June 11, 1886, 1; "The *Freiheit* Moves Back from Jersey," *NYS*, November 12, 1886, 1.

55. Fricke, *Dokumente*, 1:347.

56. *Freiheit* (New York), April 16, 1887; "Anarchists Disheartened," *Philadelphia Inquirer*, April 21, 1887, 8.

57. Most, *An das Proletariat*, quoted in Rocker, *Johann Most*, 304–5. As far as we know, this pamphlet was never translated into English.

58. *Freiheit* (New York), April 16, 1887.

59. *Freiheit* (New York), June 4, 1887.

60. Harreck-Haase, *Der Agitator*, 2:178; H. Becker, "Johann Most," 54n161; "Summary of the Week's News," *The Nation*, June 3, 1886, 460. According to Most, the *New-Yorker Staats-Zeitung* suggested that the governor of New York pardon Most and extradite him to Illinois. Most, "'Freiheits'-Reminiszenzen" (1899), in H. Becker, *John Most: Marxereien*, 34–35.

61. Rocker, *Johann Most*, 328–9.

62. Green, *Death in the Haymarket*, 247.

63. "Our Naturalization Laws," *NYT*, June 16, 1887, 4; "Foreign Socialists," *NYT*, September 10, 1887, 4.

64. "In and about the City," *NYT*, September 13, 1887, 8; "Most Can't Have a Vote," *NYS*, September 13, 1887, 3.

65. Daniels, "In Memoriam," 12.

66. Most, "Nun danket alle Gott!" *Freiheit* (New York), November 21, 1885, quoted in H. Becker, *John Most: Marxereien*, 51.

67. "Convict Most Shrieks," *Philadelphia Times*, April 18, 1887, 1; "Anarchist Most in Philadelphia," *New York Sun*, April 18, 1887, 1. Most made a similar argument to the same crowd of Philadelphia anarchists four years earlier when he said, "The condition of the working classes in America is much worse than among the same people in the revolutionary States of Europe" and "America is in its ignorance of journalism fully ten years behind Europe, and I am only surprised that you are not aware of the fact." "The Audacious Mr. Most," *Philadelphia Times*, February 3, 1883, 4.

68. "Der Grundcharakter des amerikanischen Volkes," *Freiheit*, February 26, 1887. Anarchist historian Max Nettlau once described Most as "a German idealist of the old days." Nettlau, "John Most," *Freedom* (London) 20, no. 207 (1906): 18.

69. Most, *Zwischen Galgen*, 1.

70. Goldman, *Living My Life*, 1:217.

71. See announcements for 1887 fundraisers in *Freiheit*, April 2, 23, May 21, June 4, 11, 25, August 6, 20, September 17, 24, October 1, 29.

72. "More than 7 Gallowses," *NYS*, September 20, 1887, 1.

73. "The Local Anarchists Aroused," *NYS*, November 3, 1887, 2; *DC*, November 4, 1887, 3. The location was Henry Stender's eating house at 179 William Street.

74. "Didn't Hear Most Threaten," *NYW*, November 28, 1.

75. Most, *Zwischen Galgen*, 2–7.

76. "Most Says Anarchy Lives," *NYS*, November 13, 1887, 2.

77. "A Mock Funeral Prevented," *NYTR*, November 13, 1887, 2.

78. Quoted in "The Anarchists," *Evening Post* (New York), November 14, 1887, 1.

79. "No Notes of Most's Speech," *NYS*, November 24, 1887, 1. See excerpts from his speech in *NYS*, November 13, 1887, that differed from the *World* version.

80. "The Anarchists," *Evening Post* (New York), November 14 and 15, 1887, 1; "No Room for Anarchists," *NYT*, November 15, 1887, 1. According to Most, police captain John McCullagh simply enlisted two German American detectives (John Sachs and Louis Roth) who "verified" that the *NYW* account was accurate. Most, *Zwischen Galgen*, 7.

81. "Most's Prozeß," *Freiheit* (New York), December 3, 1887, 1; "Most's Case Finished," *NYW*, November 29, 1887 (6 o'clock extra edition), 1; "No Notes of Most's Speech," *NYS*, November 24, 1887, 1; "Didn't Hear Most Threaten," *NYW*, November 28, 1887 (last edition), 1. "Most Convicted," *NYT*, November 30, 1887, 1; "Most Must Serve a Year," *NYT*, December 9, 1887, 1. "*People v. Most*," in *New York Criminal Reports*, 376–93. Most later claimed that the judge told a split jury that they had come to an agreement before 11:00 p.m. or they would have to remain in the court building through the night. Ac-

cording to Most, this pressure prompted five jury members to change their minds in favor of conviction. Comstock, "Why Herr Most Likes California," *San Francisco Call*, December 24, 1899, 3; Murphy, *Scoundrels in Law*, chap. 7.

82. Salisbury, *The Career of a Journalist*, 109–11. In 1908, the muckraking journalist Benjamin Flower, using Salisbury's exposé, specifically decried the practice of fabricating or distorting facts about anarchists to " inflame . . . the public mind" against them. Flower, "American Daily Journalism," 491.

83. "Most Must Serve a Year," *NYT*, December 9, 1887, 1.

84. Most, *Zwischen Galgen*, 15–16. Most claimed that Chicago police captain John Bonfield came to New York in October (he did) to discuss his arrest and extradition with New York inspector Thomas Byrnes. "Herr Most and the Chicago Authorities," *Washington Post*, October 1, 1887, 1.

85. When a Philadelphia paper folded in the fall of 1885, many readers blamed Most and even accused him of using funds raised for the cause to help *Freiheit*, an unfounded charge. "A Row among Anarchists," *NYT*, August 28, 1885, 2; *DC*, September 1, 1885, 3.

86. Most, "Revolutionäre Propaganda," *Freiheit* (New York), June 16, 1888, 1.

87. For more details, see Carlson, *Anarchism in Germany*, chap. 10; Rocker, *Johann Most*, chaps. 13, 14, 15; Peukert, *Erinnerungen*, 185–86.

88. Carlson, *Anarchism in Germany*, 369. When Neve died in an insane asylum in December 1896, Most was devastated. "Tears ran down his cheeks," remembered August Lott. "For days he wasn't the same companion." Lott, "John Most," *Internationale Arbeiter-Chronik* (New York), March 30, 1914, 2.

89. Carlson, *Anarchism in Germany*, 377.

90. Rocker, *Johann Most*, 282–83.

Chapter 8. Land of the Future

1. Rocker, *Johann Most*, 327.

2. "Amerikania," *Freiheit* (New York), October 19, 1889. In October 1888, a Socialist Party newspaper declared the IWPA dead as an organization and only persisting in the person of Most: "As soon as you leave the tragi-comic stage, the last of the Mohicans of your style will have died." Quoted in Waltershausen, *Der moderne Socialismus*, 366.

3. Most, *Zwischen Galgen*, 13–14. The autonomists publicly denounced Most's switch to "propaganda of talk" as cowardly and a betrayal. "Maybe They'll Kill Most," *NYS*, January 14, 1889, 1.

4. Most, "Bewaffnung u. Aufklärung," *Freiheit* (New York), February 4, 1888, 1.

5. [Most,] *Der kommunistische Anarchismus*, 2; [Most,] "Die Stellung der Anarchisten gegenüber anderen Arbeiterparteien," *Freiheit*, November 30, 1889.

6. Most, "Bewaffnung u. Aufklärung," *Freiheit* (New York), February 4, 1888, 1.

7. Most, "Revolutionäre Propaganda," *Freiheit* (New York), June 16, 1888, 1; emphases in original.

8. Most, *Zwischen Galgen*, 14–15.

9. Most, "Revolutionäre Propaganda," *Freiheit* (New York), June 16, 1888, 1.

10. [Most,] "An die Ungeduldigen," *Freiheit*, September 29, 1888.

11. [Most,] *Der Narrenthurm*, 7, 13–14. Bakunin and Most's arguments about theology are also reflected in George Orwell's statement, "A totalitarian state is in effect a theocracy, and its ruling caste, in order to keep its position, has to be thought of as infallible" (from his 1946 essay "The Prevention of Literature").

12. Ishill, *Elisée Reclus*, 125.

13. [Most,] *Die freie Gesellschaft* (1887). An English translation appeared in 1891 as *The Free Society*.

14. [Most,] *Der Narrenthurm*, 15. Rudolf Rocker's sentiment, "I am an Anarchist not because I believe Anarchism is the final goal, but because there is no such thing as a final goal," echoes this idea (Rocker, *The London Years*, 111).

15. "From the World of Labor," *EW*, April 23, 1890, 2; John Most, "Why I Am a Communist," *Twentieth Century*, May 22, 1890, 4–6.

16. Sveida, *Castle Garden*, 124–34, 134–37; Cannato, *American Passage*.

17. "Listening to John Most," *NYTR*, August 10, 1888, 4; "Herr Most on Exhibition," *NYS*, August 10, 1888, 1.

18. U.S. Congress, *Report of the Select Committee*, 5, 246–54, 509, 673.

19. Fricke, *Dokumente*, 1:377; "Life in the Metropolis," *NYS*, July 26, 1889, 1.

20. Most showed the delegates that going from four to eight pages would increase production costs by 57 percent. "Der Parteitag," *Freiheit* (New York), July 20, 1889. "Wore Red and Celebrated," *NYS*, July 14, 1889, 1; on Brecht's hall, see *The Record and Guide* 35 (1887): 614.

21. The impetuous Richard Braunschweig, who was kicked out of the conference, formed the Independent Revolutionists of New York with sixty others and cut off all support for *Freiheit*. "Anarchs Boycott Most," *NYS*, July 22, 1889, 1; Harreck-Haase, *Der Agitator*, 2:211.

22. [Most,] *Der kommunistische Anarchismus*, 8–9. This pamphlet was later translated and shortened as *The Social Monster*.

23. Kopeloff believed that the radical movement was the "fountain of Jewish labor" and that Most had "infused strength" into this movement. Quoted in Epstein, *Jewish Labor*, 196.

24. Nadel, "The German Immigrant Left"; Keil, *German Workers' Culture*.

25. Zimmer, *Immigrants against the State*, 20; Maffi, *Gateway to the Promised Land*.

26. Khaykin, *Yidishe bleter in Amerike* (New York, 1946), quoted in Ribak, *Gentile New York*, 70; Bartal, "The Image of Germany," 3–17.

27. Quoted in Michels, *A Fire*, 46; Ribak, *Gentile New York*, 23.

28. Quoted in Tcherikower, *The Early Jewish Labor Movement*, 221; Kopeloff, *Amol in Amerike*.

29. Yecheved, *Transplanted People*, 191; Cohen, *The Jewish Anarchist Movement*, 48–49.

30. Avrich and Avrich, *Sasha and Emma*, 29; *Freiheit* (New York), December 11, 1886 and April 2, 1887; *Freiheit* (New York), February 5, 1889.

31. *Freiheit* (New York), December 28, 1889.

32. *Freiheit* (New York), December 11, 1886 and April 2, 1887; *Freiheit* (New York), February 5, 1889.

33. *Freiheit* (New York), February 1, 1890.

34. *Freiheit* (New York), August 1, 1891.

35. "Anarchists in Council," *NYS*, December 27, 1894, 7; Epstein, *Jewish Labor*, 203–7; *Freiheit* (New York), December 28, 1889; "Many Hebrew Anarchists," *NYS*, December 27, 1889; "Topics in New York," *Baltimore Sun*, December 28, 1889; Waltershausen, *Der moderne Socialismus*, 364; Goldman, *Living My Life*, 1:34.

36. Most, *Die Gottespest*, 3, 7; "Die 'Freiheit,'" *Freiheit* (New York), August 1, 1896.

37. The announcement in *Freiheit* promised a "keynote speech, singing, music, dancing, raffle. Everyone welcome!" *Freiheit* (New York), October 5, 1889.

38. Tcherikower, *The Early Jewish Labor Movement*, 246, 249; Cohen, *The Jewish Anarchist Movement*, 81.

39. "To Restrain the Anarchists. The Hebrew Rabbis Petition Police Commissioner Hayden," *BDE*, September 19, 1890, 6; "Most to Speak. The Anarchist Is Coming to Brooklyn," *BDE*, September 22, 1890, 6.

40. "Still on Guard. Police Keep Watch at the Labor Lyceum," *BDE*, September 24, 1890, 6.

41. Zimmer, *Immigrants against the State*, 26.

42. *NYS*, November 11, 1890, 6.

43. Minkin, *Storm in My Heart*, 25–26, 30, 67–68.

44. Avrich and Avrich, *Sasha and Emma*, 26; Berkman, *Prison Memoirs*, 79. Berkman had read about Most in a library in Russia. The fact that *most* means "bridge" in Russian was a sign for Berkman that the great orator was to be a great mentor—the "hero of my first years in America." Berkman, *Prison Memoirs*, 79.

45. "Preaching Red Anarchy," *NYS*, November 11, 1888, 2.

46. "They Mourn Their Dead," *NYT*, November 11, 1888, 5.

47. Goldman, *Living My Life*, 1:6, 9–10, 29, 65.

48. Goldman, *Living My Life*, 1:34–35, 40.

49. Quoted in Avrich and Avrich, *Sasha and Emma*, 40.

50. "John Most Arrested," *NYS*, January 25, 1890, 1; "Most Out on Bail," *Evening Post* (New York), January 28, 1890, 10.

51. *DC*, December 29, 1890, 4.

52. Rocker, *Johann Most*, 336; *DC*, October 17, 1890, 1.

53. See, for example, Lidtke, *The Outlawed Party*, 305–19.

54. Quoted in Avrich and Avrich, *Sasha and Emma*, 40.

55. Avrich, *Anarchist Voices*, 19.

56. Falk, Pateman, and Moran, *Emma Goldman*, 1:493–94.

57. "Kicked by Anarchists," *NYS*, June 19, 1890, 1.

58. *Der Anarchist* (New York), April 30 and June 18, 1892.

59. Goldman, *Living My Life*, 1:75; *Fraye Arbeter Shtime* (New York), January 1, 1891, 5. Thanks to Kenyon Zimmer for this reference.

60. Minkin, *Storm in My Heart*, 31, 34, 46, 52–53.

61. Minkin mentioned that Most had a housekeeper, and she may have believed it was Lena Fischer. "Most Talks Red Pepper," *NYS*, April 5, 1887, 1; "Two Pertinent Questions," *BDE*, May 16, 1887, 1; "Most's Understudy in Jail," *NYS*, September 21, 1891, 1; "An Anarchist Wife," *Pittsburg Dispatch*, September 21, 1891, 6; *Abendblatt der Illinois Staats-Zeitung* (Chicago), June 29, 1893, 2; Minkin, *Storm in My Heart*, 52.

62. *The People v. John Most*, June 16, 1891, in *The New York State Reporter* (New York: W. C. Little, 1891), 38:829–34.

63. "Jail for Herr Most," *EW*, June 16, 1891, 3; "John Most Properly Convicted," *NYS*, June 17, 1891, 3; "Most to Don the Stripes," *EW*, June 19, 1891, 1; Minkin, *Storm in My Heart*, 46, 50, 52. Emma Goldman was sometimes referred to as "Mrs. Most" in the press.

64. Goldman, *Living My Life*, 1:80.

65. "Die Massen-Protestversammlung," *Freiheit* (New York), June 27, 1891.

66. *Jersey City News*, November 2, 1891, 2.

67. "Most's Understudy in Jail," *NYS*, September 21, 1891, 1; "Die Massen-Protestversammlung," *Freiheit* (New York), June 27, 1891.

68. Avrich and Avrich, *Sasha and Emma*, 43–44. Goldman wrote to Most in prison, but he never replied. Goldman, *Living My Life*, 89.

69. Rocker, *Johann Most*, 337; *Freiheit* (New York), August 22, 1891.

70. "Most's Understudy in Jail," *NYS*, September 21, 1891, 1; "An Anarchist Wife," *Pittsburgh Dispatch*, September 21, 1891, 6.

71. "No Writ for Most," *EW*, July 31, 1891, 4.

72. Most, "Die anarchistischen Kommunisten an das Proletariat," *Freiheit* (New York), February 6, 1892.

73. Most, "Herzensergüße," *Freiheit* (New York), April 23, 1892. In her memoirs, Minkin suggested that Berkman was jealous of Most. Minkin, *Storm in My Heart*, 70.

74. Minkin, *Storm in My Heart*, 51–52, 65.

75. Rocker, *Johann Most*, 355; Most, "Selbstkritik," *Freiheit* (New York), June 4, 1892; Merlino, "Zur Verständigung," *Freiheit* (New York), June 4, 1892; Merlino, *Nécessité et bases*, 8, 9; Cohen, *The Jewish Anarchist Movement*, 543–44.

76. Minkin, *Storm in My Heart*, 70.

77. Harreck-Haase, *Der Agitator*, 2:245.

78. "Most Did Not Speak," *Pittsburgh Dispatch*, July 4, 1892; *Freiheit*, June 11 and 18, 1892.

79. *Freiheit* reported 16 dead and 147 wounded (mostly Pinkertons). "Wie man's macht," *Freiheit*, July 16, 1892, 1.

80. Avrich and Avrich, *Sasha and Emma*, 61–62; "No Plot Says Most," *EW*, July 26, 1892, 1.

81. Avrich and Avrich, *Sasha and Emma*, 56.

82. Avrich and Avrich, *Sasha and Emma*, 58.

83. Goldman, *Living My Life*, 1:88.

84. Goldman, *Living My Life*, 1:89.

85. Most believed Berkman was organizing an autonomist group and warned Nold and Bauer of Berkman's loyalties to Peukert, which made him "dangerous and suspicious." Avrich and Avrich, *Sasha and Emma*, 62; "No Plot Says Most," *EW*, July 26, 1892, 1.

86. "Aufgepaßt," *Freiheit*, July 16, 1892, 1; "Wie man's macht," *Freiheit*, July 16, 1892, 1.

87. Most, "Friktionen," *Freiheit* (New York), July 30, 1892, 1.

88. Goldman, *Living My Life*, 1:97.

89. As it happened, his close friend and supporter Ida Hoffmann passed away on July 26, which added to his emotional state.

90. "Most's Last Pittsburgh Visit," *EW*, July 27, 1892, 2. Rocker credits Berkman for resisting all threats and temptations by the Pittsburgh police to implicate more anarchists. Rocker, *Johann Most*, 347.

91. "No Plot Says Most," *EW*, July 26, 1892, 1.

92. Rocker, *Johann Most*, 354.

93. "Eingesandt," *Der Anarchist* (New York), July 30, 1892.

94. Berkman, *Prison Memoirs*, 84, 101; Goldman, *Living My Life*, 1:99, 105.

95. Rocker, *Johann Most*, 347.

96. Quoted in Rocker, *Johann Most*, 356–57.

97. "Die 'Freiheit,'" *Freiheit* (New York), September 19, 1896.

98. Most, "Attentats-Reflexionen," *Freiheit* (New York), August 27, 1892, 1.

99. Quoted in Avrich and Avrich, *Sasha and Emma*, 90.

100. Most, "Zur Propaganda der That," *Freiheit* (New York), September 17, 1892, 1.

101. Minkin was also present and stated that Goldman was accompanied by two bodyguards with iron rods under their coats. Minkin, *Storm in My Heart*, 72.

102. Avrich and Avrich, *Sasha and Emma*, 90; *Freiheit* (New York), December 24, 1892; Goldman, "Warum ich Most durchpeitschte," *Der Anarchist* (New York), December 31, 1892.

103. Rocker, *Johann Most*, 357.

104. Quoted in Rocker, *Johann Most*, 356.

105. Most, "Präsente," *Freiheit* (New York), December 24, 1892, quoted in H. Becker, *John Most: Marxereien*, 116–17.

Chapter 9. Hard Times

1. Minkin, *Storm in My Heart*, 73–77.

2. Quoted in Minkin, *Storm in My Heart*, 78.

3. Minkin, *Storm in My Heart*, 78.

4. One indication that Lizzie and Lena are the same person is that one newspaper listed Lizzie's maiden name as "Georgen," similar to "Georges," the alias Lena Fischer used in 1886. "Herr Most Has Come Back," *NYS*, October 21, 1893, 4; "Most's Wife Has Small-Pox," *NYS*, October 16, 1893, 1.

5. It seems likely that Fischer and Most separated a few years earlier but now briefly shared the same house again. An article in an Austrian newspaper from June 1893 stated, "The former typesetter Richard Fischer has been the Social Democratic Party secretary for two years with a salary of 3,000 marks. Until the Socialist Law was passed, Fischer worked in the Berlin cooperative printing works. At that time, he was a housemate of the anarchist Johann Most and was close friends with the unequal couple (who later separated in America because Mrs. Most put the theories of 'free love' preached by her husband all too clearly into practice)." "Der neugewählten Reichstagsabgeordneten der Stadt Berlin," *Grazer Tagblatt*, June 29, 1893, 8.

6. FamilySearch, "New York, U.S. District Court Naturalization Records, 1824–1991," Helene Most, 1932. In the 1930s, Minkin remembered the date as July 15, 1893, but on a different copy, she wrote "May 1893." Since these official documents contain other errors, they may have married in 1894.

7. "John Most in Brooklyn," *BDE*, December 18, 1893, 1; Minkin, *Storm in My Heart*, 89.

8. Minkin, *Storm in My Heart*, 91–92.

9. "What Anarchists Say," *EW*, June 25, 1894, 1.

10. *Trow's New York City Directory for the Year Ending July 1, 1894*, 771; *Trow's New York City Directory for the Year Ending July 1, 1895*, 998; "Most and His 'Freiheit' Move," *NYS*, April 8, 1894, 1; Minkin, *Storm in My Heart*, 92.

11. John Jr. was not circumcised at birth, but at age three and a half, he suffered an infection and had to undergo the procedure. Interview with John Most Jr. in Avrich, *Anarchist Voices*, 19.

12. Guglielmo, *Living the Revolution*, 151; Cornell, *Unruly Equality*, 25.

13. Minkin, *Storm in My Heart*, 90–91.

14. Goldman, *Living My Life*, 1:151; Goldman to Berkman, St. Tropez (France), February 20, 1929, in Goldman and Berkman, *Nowhere at Home*, 145.

15. Burrows and Wallace, *Gotham*, 1186.

16. Minkin, *Storm in My Heart*, 93.

17. See ads starting in *Freiheit*, May 26, 1894.

18. Interview with John Most Jr. in Avrich, *Anarchist Voices*, 19.

19. Minkin, *Storm in My Heart*, 96, 109.

20. Minkin, *Storm in My Heart*, 110–11.

21. Quoted in Avrich and Avrich, *Sasha and Emma*, 113.

22. [Most,] "Die Arbeitslosen," *Freiheit* (New York), August 26, 1893, 1.

23. Burrows, "The Need of National Legislation against Anarchism," 733–38.

24. Minkin, *Storm in My Heart*, 95–96.

25. "A Socialistic People," *Richmond County Advance* (West New Brighton, NY), May 4, 1895, 2.

26. A large meeting at the Hebrew Institute caused some commotion. Most was billed to speak, but a rumor circulated that Emma Goldman planned to confront Most a second time, which caused the organizers to alert the police. Goldman did not show, and Most delivered a lecture on the Panama Canal scandal that had just rocked the French Republic to its core. *EW*, January 14, 1893; "No Disorderly Anarchists Wanted," *NYS*, January 22, 1893, 9; "Most Was Mild," *NYT*, January 23, 1893, 5.

27. "Anarchists in Cooper Union," *NYS*, January 6, 1899, 4; R. Jensen, *The Battle*, 131–84.

28. "Altgeld and the Anarchists," *NYT*, June 28, 1893, 4; "Altgeld's Infamy," *Washington Post*, June 30, 1893, 4. Altgeld pardoned or commuted the sentences of dozens of people convicted of violent crimes.

29. "Most Will Hold a Meeting," *EW*, June 28, 1893, 2.

30. "Anarchists Will Shout," *NYTR*, July 7, 1893, 2; "Bomben," *Freiheit* (New York), July 8, 1893.

31. "Most's Red Beer Checks," *NYT*, July 5, 1896, 8.

32. "John Most for Gold," *NYT*, July 20, 1896, 2; "A Small Gathering," *NYT*, July 23, 1896, 2; Most, "Silberwirren," *Freiheit* (New York), August 12, 1893, 1.

33. *Solidarity*, July 9, 1892 and February 9, 1893; *The Rebel*, November 20, 1895.

34. *Freiheit* (New York), February 3, 1894.

35. "Herr John Most, Actor," *NYT*, March 21, 1896.

36. Blankenagel, "Early Reception," 335. German anarchist and native Silesian Max Baginski, who later immigrated to New York, provided Hauptmann with real-life material about the region's dire conditions.

37. Clark, *The Continental Drama*, 91.

38. *Freiheit* (New York), September 22, 1894; "Herr Most for the Star," *EW*, September 6, 1894, 3. Most received permission from Hauptmann to perform the play.

39. Blankenagel, "Early Reception," 336–37

40. Cohn, *Underground Passages*, 62.

41. Quoted in Rocker, *Johann Most*, 382.

42. Quoted in "Die 'Weber'-Aufführung in New York und die Presse," *Freiheit* (New York), October 20, 1894.

43. "Anarchists on the Stage," *BDE*, October 17, 1894, 6; quoted in "Die 'Weber'-Aufführung in New York und die Presse," *Freiheit* (New York), October 20, 1894.

44. Blankenagel, "Early Reception," 338–39; *Liberty*, November 17, 1894; "Herr Most Took to His Heels," *NYT*, October 29, 1894, 5.

45. "Herr Most as an Actor," *NYS*, December 3, 1894, 1.

46. Circulation dropped to between four thousand and five thousand copies. Harreck-Haase, *Der Agitator*, 2:257.

47. See expense reports in *Freiheit* (New York), January 11, 1890, January 6, 1894, and March 2, 1895.

48. "Abrechnung," *Freiheit* (New York), May 25, 1895. One of the expenses included an "allowance for beer during rehearsals."

49. *Freiheit* (New York), June 15, 1895.

50. Ferguson, *Letterpress Revolution*, 53.

51. Rocker, *Johann Most*, 387.

52. Minkin, *Storm in My Heart*, 109.

53. *Buffalo City Directories*, 1897, 1898.

54. Rocker, *Johann Most*, 387; Minkin, *Storm in My Heart*, 98–99.

55. Minkin, *Storm in My Heart*, 99; *Buffalo City Directories*, 1898, 936.

56. Minkin, *Storm in My Heart*, 99; Rocker, *Johann Most*, 388.

57. Most, "An die Leser," *Freiheit* (New York), August 6, 1898. His friend Krämer had already left: Most, "Beitrage zur Geschichte der 'Freiheit,'" *Freiheit* (New York), August 13, 1898.

58. Rocker, *Johann Most*, 388–89.

59. Avrich, "Kropotkin in America," 7.

60. Minkin, *Storm in My Heart*, 102–3.

61. Most, "Beitrage zur Geschichte der 'Freiheit,'" *Freiheit* (New York), August 13, 1898.

62. Most, "'Freiheit's'-Reminiszenzen," 37.

63. Quoted in Rocker, *Johann Most*, 389.

64. Rocker, *Johann Most*, 394.

65. [Most,] "Krisen," *Freiheit* (New York), September 9, 1893, 1.

66. [Most,] "Amerikanische Ideen," *Freiheit* (New York), August 20, 1898.

67. Most, "Eseleien," *Freiheit* (New York), September 19, 1885, quoted in H. Becker, *John Most: Marxereien*, 46. Pride and confidence in the American system were especially strong in the mainstream immigrant press. A German-language paper from Baltimore, perhaps irritated by the naivete of one of their own, was convinced that America would ignore Most's rhetoric, and "once he is better informed about the local conditions, his revolutionary ideas will appear to him just as monstrous as they are now to those who have settled into the free institutions." *DC*, December 27, 1882, 2. One editorial wished Most "had left this fair land and returned to Europe, where the people have good reason to complain, but it seems that he is still inflicting his presence upon the United States." "Most and Boyd," *Buffalo Evening News*, March 13, 1883, 2.

68. Thanksgiving was to Most a pretentious farce in which the rich give pious thanks while the working classes live in misery, and the ritual of gift-giving at Christmas was a "simple-minded sport." Most, "Nun danket alle Gott!" *Freiheit* (New York), November 21, 1885; Most, "Präsente," *Freiheit* (New York), December 24, 1892, quoted in H. Becker, *John Most: Marxereien*, 113, 116.

69. Most deemed the framers of the French Constitution of 1793 more courageous and more creative than the American framers. [Most,] "Das Wesen der amerikanischen Constitution," *Freiheit*, February 19, 1898.

70. Most, "Zur Columbus-Posse," *Freiheit*, October 8, 1892, quoted in H. Becker, *John Most: Marxereien*, 102, 105; "Herr Most on Liberty," *NYT*, May 18, 1901, 9. President Benjamin Harrison created Columbus Day partly to mend fences with Italy and Italian Americans in the wake of the lynching of eleven Italian immigrants in New Orleans in March 1891. This incident sparked a diplomatic rift.

71. [Most,] "Der Parlamentarismus," *Freiheit* (New York), September 8, 1894, quoted in H. Becker, *John Most: Marxereien*, 143.

72. [Most,] "Der Parlamentarismus," 144–45.

73. Hoerder, "German Immigrant Workers' Views," 25; Hoerder, "The German-American Labor Press," 189–90.

74. [Most,] "Katzenjammer," *Freiheit* (New York), November 24, 1894, quoted in H. Becker, *John Most: Marxereien*, 148. The findings of the Lexow Committee contributed to the defeat of Tammany Hall and the election of the reform administration of William Strong.

75. [Most,] "Katzenjammer," 150. *Katzenjammer* means a hangover or the postelection blues for the Democrats. In 1899, Most explained to readers that "'Democracy' means rule by the people and is nonsensical because if the people *rule*, then, in fact, *nobody* rules since nobody *exists* outside or underneath them." *Freiheit* (New York), January 28, 1899, 4.

76. [Most,] "Der Parlamentarismus," 143; [Most,] "Stimmvieh auf der Weide," *Freiheit* (Chicago and New York), September 22, 1888.

77. [Most,] "Agitationswinke," *Freiheit* (New York), June 10, 1899, quoted in H. Becker, *Johann Most. Anarchismus in einer Nußschale*, 19; [Most,] "Nieder mit dem Stimmkasten!" 87.

78. Quoted in Dray, *There Is Power*, 193.

79. Quoted in Dray, *There Is Power*, 194, 200; Goyens, *Beer and Revolution*, 44.

80. Rocker, *Johann Most*, 392.

81. Most, *Unsere Stellung*, 4.

82. Most, *Unsere Stellung*, 5–6.

83. Rocker, *Johann Most*, 394.

84. Rocker, *Johann Most*, 395.

85. "Spain Tortures Her Prisoners," *Buffalo Courier*, August 16, 1897, 3. The pamphlet was *Die Justizgreuel von Barcelona. Dokumentarisch belegter Bericht über die Anwendung der Tortur im heutigen Spanien* (Berlin: Verlag von Wilhelm Spohr, 1897).

86. "Der Krieg," *Freiheit* (Buffalo), May 7, 1898; "Zur Situation," *Freiheit* (Buffalo), May 14, 1898.

87. *Freiheit* (New York), September 23, 1899.

Chapter 10. I'm Far from Old, I'm Just Gray

1. Minkin, *Storm in My Heart*, 117; H. Becker, "Johann Most," 61.

2. Goyens, *Beer and Revolution*, 184.

3. *NYT*, March 8, 1908.

4. *Sturmvogel* (New York), February 15, 1898.

5. Interview with John Most Jr. in Avrich, *Anarchist Voices*, 19.

6. Zimmer, *Immigrants against the State*, 88–93.

7. "Most Returns to New York," *Evening Times* (Washington, DC), March 26, 1900, 4.

8. Comstock, "Why Herr Most Likes California," *San Francisco Call*, December 24, 1899, 3.

9. Quoted in "Comrade Most's Propaganda," *Free Society* (San Francisco), December 31, 1899, 2–3.

10. "Herr Most Predicted War," *San Francisco Call*, December 21, 1899, 8.

11. Most, "Reisebericht," *Freiheit* (New York), October 21, 1899, 1.

12. Comstock, "Why Herr Most Likes California," *San Francisco Call*, December 24, 1899.

13. "Comrade Most in San Jose," *Free Society* (San Francisco), January 7, 1900, 2–3.

14. "Socialists as Actors," *San Francisco Call*, January 24, 1900, 9.

15. "Herr Most Nearly Mobbed," *Seattle Post-Intelligencer*, February 5, 1900, 10; "Bloodshed Der Only Vay," *Seattle Post-Intelligencer*, February 6, 1900, 12.

16. H. Becker, "Johann Most," 41n119.

17. "Justus Schwab Mourned," *NYT*, December 21, 1900, 7; *NYS*, December 26, 1900, 7.

18. "Anarchists Don't Know Him," *NYT*, September 7, 1901, 5; "The Anarchists Here under Close Watch," *NYT*, September 8, 1901, 4.

19. "Mord contra Mord," *Freiheit* (New York), September 7, 1901, 2; Wittke, *Against the Current*, 73–75; Avrich, *An American Anarchist*, 133–34.

20. "The Anarchists Here under Close Watch," *NYT*, September 8, 1901, 4.

21. Avrich and Avrich, *Sasha and Emma*, chap. 12.

22. Gale, "Most Fumes in His Defense," *EW*, September 13, 1901, 3. Using language threatening to the president was, of course, not limited to anarchists. In October 1904, the racist Alabama congressman Tom Heflin lamented the fact that President Theodore Roosevelt had invited the Black educator Booker Washington to the White House in 1901. "There they sat, Roosevelt and Booker," he told an audience in Tuskegee, "and if some Czolgosz or one of his kind had thrown a bomb under table no great harm would have been done to the country." Heflin was criticized for his remarks, but he suffered no legal repercussions. Four years later, he shot and wounded a Black streetcar rider in Washington, DC. The charges were dismissed, and Heflin considered the incident a major career accomplishment. "The New Humorist," *NYS*, October 11, 1904, 6; "Heflin Held for Trial," *Washington Post*, May 12, 1908.

23. *Freiheit* (New York), September 21, 1901, 1.

24. "Anarchist Most Acts as His Own Lawyer in Court," *EW*, September 16, 1901, 10.

25. Quoted in "Yellow Press Receives Sharp Rebuke," *San Francisco Call*, September 21, 1901, 6.

26. "Johann Most's Bond Reduced," *NYT*, September 17, 1901, 14.

27. Hinsdale, *Autobiography*, 57.

28. Hillquit, *Loose Leaves*, 126.

29. Harreck-Haase, *Der Agitator*, 2:339–40.

30. "Most Given a Year in the Penitentiary," *BDE*, October 14, 1901, 1.

31. Hillquit, *Loose Leaves*, 127.

32. "Der erste Besuch," *Freiheit* (New York), October 26, 1901.

33. Minkin, *Storm in My Heart*, 112–13; Interview with John Most Jr. in Avrich, *Anarchist Voices*, 18. An editor named "John Mueller" (he often used this alias) is listed at this address in *Trow's General Directory of the Boroughs of Manhattan and Bronx, Year Ending July 1903*, 995.

34. *Down with the Anarchists!* (New York: John Most, [1901]). It included excerpts from Errico Malatesta, Carlo Cafiero, Peter Kropotkin, Élisée Reclus, Albert Parsons, August Spies, Michael Schwab, Saverio Merlino, Emil Steinle, Jean Grave, and Most himself.

35. "Most to 'Enlighten' Congress," *NYT*, December 25, 1901, 12; "Most Writes to Roosevelt," *NYS*, December 25, 1901, 7. Most serialized a translation of this pamphlet in *Freiheit* in June 1905 ("Nieder mit den Anarchisten!").

36. Hester, "'Protection, Not Punishment,'" 14.

37. *People v. Most*, 71 App. Div. 160, 75 N.Y.S. 591 (N.Y. App. Div. 1902), https://casetext.com/case/people-v-most-3.

38. "*People v. Most*," in *Reports of Cases Decided*, 423–32.

39. Minkin, *Storm in My Heart*, 113.

40. "Anarchist Most in Tears," *Evening Post* (New York), June 20, 1902, 1; "Most Sentenced to One Year," *NYTR*, June 21, 1902, 3.

41. He used the penname "Ahasverus" because it traditionally signified the Eternal or Wandering Jew, a legend of a man who taunted Jesus and was condemned to wander the earth until the Second Coming. Or as Most put it, "A person who cannot die, in other words, cannot be killed." *Freiheit* (New York), April 11, 1903.

42. Minkin, *Storm in My Heart*, 114; "General-Abrechnung," *Freiheit* (New York), December 13, 1902.

43. Most, "Neues von Blackwell's Island," *Freiheit* (New York), January 13, 1903, 6.

44. Most, "Eine Stimme von der schwarzen Insel," *Freiheit* (New York), July 19, 1902, 1.

45. Minkin, *Storm in My Heart*, 115, 117.

46. Hillquit, *Loose Leaves*, 128.

47. Most to Minkin, February 21, 1903, in *Freiheit* (New York), February 28, 1903, 2; italics in original.

48. Quoted in H. Becker, "Johann Most: eine kleine Bibliography," 293.

49. Most, "Das Land der Zukunft," *Freiheit* (New York), December 13, 1902, quoted in H. Becker, *Johann Most: Anarchismus in einer Nußschale*.

50. Most, "Das Land der Zukunft," 124.

51. Most, "Das Land der Zukunft," 124. Most once described New York City as "Kosmopolitania." [Most,] "Von Krähwinkel nach Babylon," *Freiheit* (New York), May 30, 1903, quoted in H. Becker, *John Most: Marxereien*, 170.

52. Most, "Das Land der Zukunft," 124.

53. Most, "Unsere Widersacher," *Freiheit* (New York), October 28, 1905, quoted in H. Becker, *Johann Most: Anarchismus in einer Nußschale*, 226–27.

54. Cohen, *The Jewish Anarchist Movement*, 214.

55. Most, "Trust-Streiflichter," *Freiheit* (New York), December 20, 1902, quoted in H. Becker, *Johann Most: Anarchismus in einer Nußschale*, 127–28, 130.

56. Most, "Meine Memoiren," *Freiheit* (New York), May 9, 1903; Minkin, *Storm in My Heart*, 118.

57. Minkin, *Storm in My Heart*, 119–20.

58. Minkin, *Storm in My Heart*, 104–5.

59. In a 1979 interview, John Jr. claimed that his mother had an affair with the anarchist and assistant editor August Lott while Most was alive. Interview with John Most Jr. in Avrich, *Anarchist Voices*, 19.

60. Isaak, "Freie Liebe," *Freiheit* (New York), October 3, 1903.

61. "Most's Life Near End," *Washington Post*, March 17, 1906, 1.

62. "Johann Most," *Freiheit* (New York), March 24, 1906, 1.

63. *Freiheit* (New York), October 15, 1904; "Johann Joseph Most," *Indiana Tribüne* (Indianapolis), November 19, 1904, 1; "Chicago to Watch Herr Most," *NYS*, October 30, 1904, 1.

64. Carl Nold, "Die Anarchisten-Convention in St. Louis," *Freiheit* (New York), September 25, 1904.

65. Interview with John Most Jr. in Avrich, *Anarchist Voices*, 13.

66. "John Most under Arrest," *St. Louis Republic*, November 29 and 30, 1904, 3.

67. "Most," *NYT*, December 24, 1904, 6.

68. "Anarchists' Big Rally," *NYT*, September 12, 1904, 6.

69. "Anarchists Bury a Hatchet," *NYS*, January 31, 1905. A few weeks later, the two anarchists spoke again, now joined by the Russian revolutionary emissary Chaim Zhitlowski for a mass meeting at Old Homestead Hall on Third Avenue. *Freiheit* (New York), February 5, 1905.

70. "Sergius Not the Last, Herr Most Tells Reds," *NYT*, February 23, 1905, 2.

71. Most, "Eine Weltwende," *Freiheit* (New York), September 2, 1905, 1.

72. "An Anti-Gompers Meeting," *NYT*, September 1, 1905, 3; "Labor Men Denounced," *NYTR*, September 1, 1905, 12.

73. H. Becker, "Johann Most," 61; *Freiheit* (New York), October 7, 1905.

74. H. Becker, "Johann Most: eine kleine Bibliography," 293; *Freiheit* (New York), January 6, 1906. According to Minkin, Most disapproved of his New York comrades' plan for a sixtieth-birthday banquet. Minkin, *Storm in My Heart*, 120.

75. If comrades in small communities could not organize a large event, he would visit smaller, private gatherings and distribute literature. *Freiheit* (New York), January 6, 1906, and February 3, 1906, 1.

76. Joseph Cohen attended the meeting and had to restrain an Italian anarchist about to stab a police officer as they broke up the meeting. Cohen, *The Jewish Anarchist Movement*, 213.

77. Minkin, *Storm in My Heart*, 120–21, 122–23; "Drive Out Anarchists," *NYTR*, March 11, 1906, 1. One New York paper reported that upon his arrival in Cincinnati, Most was carried into an ambulance and driven to the Krause house. "Herr Most, Noted Anarchist, Dying," *EW*, March 16, 1906, 4. Krause was an insurance agent whose full name was Gustav Adolphus Emil Krause.

78. "Most's Life Near End," *Washington Post*, March 17, 1906, 1; "Anarchist Chief, Herr Most, Dead," *EW*, March 17, 1906, 2.

79. Minkin, *Storm in My Heart*, 121–22.

80. Minkin, *Storm in My Heart*, 124; Rocker, *Johann Most*, 428.

81. "Eine Todten-Feier," *Freiheit* (New York), March 31, 1906; J. B. Wilson, "Funeral Ceremonial of the Late John Most," *Blue-Grass Blade* (Lexington, KY), April 1, 1906, 2.

82. Interestingly, the New York comrades were dissatisfied with the amount of ashes Minkin brought with her. More than three years later, the *New York Times* reported that a friend discovered a bottle labeled "Ashes of Herr Johann Most" in the Krause home. Apparently, Krause had retained some of it as a souvenir without informing Minkin. "Kept Herr Most's Ashes," *NYT*, August 22, 1909, 6.

83. "John Most," *NYT*, March 21, 1906, 8.

84. Minkin, *Storm in My Heart*, 125.

85. Minkin, *Storm in My Heart*, 130.

86. Cohen, *The Jewish Anarchist Movement*, 214.

87. "In Memory of Most," *NYS*, March 26, 1906, 2; Rocker, *Johann Most*, 429–30; *Freiheit* (New York), March 24, 1906.

88. Quoted in Avrich and Avrich, *Sasha and Emma*, 188; Goldman, *Living My Life*, 1:379–80.

89. "Meet to Honor Most," *NYTR*, April 2, 1906, 12. Goldman believed that some of Most's supporters, especially Minkin, opposed her speaking at the memorial, but Minkin strongly denied this. Goldman, *Living My Life*, 1:380–81; Minkin, *Storm in My Heart*, 125.

90. Minkin, "An die Leser der 'Freiheit,'" *Freiheit* (New York), April 21, 1906.

91. Minkin, *Storm in My Heart*, 127–28.

92. Minkin, "An die Leser der 'Freiheit,'" *Freiheit* (New York), April 21, 1906, 1.

93. "An die Leser und Freunde der 'Freiheit,'" *Freiheit* (New York), April 28, 1906, 1.

94. Minkin's words were included in the preface to volume four by the anarchist writer Frederick Thaumazo (pseudonym for Frederick Loevius). Thaumazo, "Eine Erklärung als Vorwort," in Most, *Memoiren*, 4:ii–iii. John Most Jr. told Heiner Becker that Most had prepared the remaining six volumes for printing but that none were published or even preserved after his death. Tentative titles (translated): "Berliniana" (vol. 5), "Freiheit" (vol. 6), "Excommunicated and Walled In" (vol. 7), "America in Front and Behind the Scenes" (vol. 8), "The Era of Bombs and Gallows" (vol. 9),

"Recent Reminiscences" (vol. 10). H. Becker, "Johann Most: eine kleine Bibliography," 293.

95. Ancestry.com: World War I Draft Registration Cards, 1917–1918; 1930 U.S. Census. Lucifer J. Most's obituary in *NYT*, August 28, 1949. For more details on Minkin's life after Most, see Goyens, introduction to Minkin, *Storm in My Heart*, 17–19.

96. Carey and Most, *High above Courtside*, 4.

97. There is a "Helen Most" grave at Mount Hebron Cemetery in Flushing, New York, marking her death on February 3, 1954.

98. Ancestry.com: Minkin's Petition of Citizenship, Naturalization Records- Original Documents, 1795–1972; Carey and Most, *High Above Courtside*, 3; "Johnny Most, 69, Radio Voice, That Cheered On Boston Celtics," *NYT*, January 4, 1993.

Bibliography

Archival Material

Archiv des Bistums Augsburg: St. Maximilian Geburts-Register 1820; St. Maximilian Trauungs-Register 1820.

International Institute for Social History, Amsterdam (IISH): Max Nettlau Papers; Pierre Ramus Papers; Johann Philipp Becker Papers; Wilhelm Liebknecht Papers; Georg von Vollmar Papers; Karl Kautsky Papers; Julius Motteler Papers; Kleine Korrespondenz (from SPD Archives) Archives, 1844–1931; Hermann Jung Papers; Photographs.

Labadie Collection. University of Michigan, Ann Arbor, MI: Photographs; *Freiheit* on microfilm.

Landesarchiv Berlin, Acta des Königlichen Polizei-Präsidii zu Berlin (A. Br; Pr. 030): 8577, 8579, 9826, 9892, 11724, 11725, 11726, 11727, 11728, 11729, 13031, 13032, 13034, 14684, 14907, 14908, 14909, 14932, 14933, 14934, 14935; Geburtenregister der Berliner Standesämter (Bestände P Rep. 100 bis P Rep. 840) 1874–99, Nr. 2157.

London Metropolitan Archives, London City Directories, 1879, 1881, 1882.

New York City Department of Records and Information Services, Municipal Archives: Court of General Sessions; Grand Jury Indictments: John Most (04/29/86 Unlawful Assembly folder:2134 box:216 & 11/17/87 Unlawful Assembly folder:2719 box:285) New York Public Library. *Freiheit* on microfilm.

Old Bailey Proceedings Online (www.oldbaileyonline.org, version 6.0, July 2021). May 23, 1881, Trial of Johann Most (t1881052–541); June 1882, Trial of Frederick Schwelm; July 1882, Trial of William Mertens.

Sächsisches Staatsarchiv Chemnitz, Königliches Bezirksgericht Chemnitz, 1871-2: #33071–36, 33071–38.

Sächsisches Staatsarchiv Leipzig, Kreishauptmannschaft Leipzig Nr. 248 (March 1874).

Schweizerisches Sozialarchiv, Zürich: Arbeiterbildungs-Verein Eintracht: Protokolle Vereinssitzungen 1866–70, folder Ar 3.10.4a,

Stadtarchiv Augsburg: Städtische Polizei, Familienbögen; Adreßbücher; Verzeichniß sämmtlicher Hausbesitzer in und um Augsburg (1838–54); Magistrat der Stadt Augsburg. Acten. Die Cholera, 1854–61. Bestand 5, No. 58; Verzeichniß jener Personen welche an der Cholera während der Epidemie des Jahres 1854 in Augsburg gestorben sind. Zusammengestellt von Dr. V. Pettenkofer; Jahres-Bericht über die Leistungen der städtischen Armenpflege in Augsburg (1840–65).

Stadtarchiv Chemnitz: Acten des Raths der Stadt Chemnitz (V. Sect. XIXa Nr. 245); Fascikel des Raths der Stadt Chemnitz, die Vorfälle bei der hiesigen Sedanfeier am 2.ten September 1872 und die Strafantrag gegen Johann Most, C. H. Weck und C. F. C. Dietze betr. V. Sect. XIXa No. 255. Ergangen 1872; Rat der Stadt Chemnitz. Polizeimeldeamt. Abteilung A/Punkt, L-M (ca. 1864–76); Adreßbücher.

Online Databases

Ancestry.com

ANNO-Historische Zeitungen und Zeitschriften (Österreichische Nationalbibliothek): https://anno.onb.ac.at/

BelgicaPress (Royal Library of Belgium): https://www.belgicapress.be/

British Newspaper Archive: https://www.britishnewspaperarchive.co.uk/

Brooklyn Newsstand (Brooklyn Public Library): https://bklyn.newspapers.com/

California Digital Newspaper Collection: https://cdnc.ucr.edu/site/about_us.html

Chronicling America: Historic American Newspapers (Library of Congress): https://chroniclingamerica.loc.gov/

DadA: Datenbank des deutschsprachigen Anarchismus: http://ur.dadaweb.de/

Delpher: https://www.delpher.nl/

digiPress- Das Zeitungsportal der Bayerischen Staatsbibliothek: https://digipress.digitale-sammlungen.de/

Digitale Landesbibliothek Berlin: https://digital.zlb.de/viewer/index/

Digitalisierte Zeitungs- und Zeitschriftenbestände (Friedrich-Ebert-Stiftung): https://www.fes.de/bibliothek/zeitschriften-digitalisierung/

Elephind.com: https://elephind.com/

FamilySearch: https://www.familysearch.org/en/

Gallica (Bibliothèque Nationale de France): https://gallica.bnf.fr/html/und/presse-et-revues/presse-et-revues?mode=desktop

GoogleBooks: https://books.google.com/

HathiTrust Digital Library: https://www.hathitrust.org/

Internet Archive: https://archive.org/

LIDIAP—list of digitized anarchist periodicals: https://lidiap.ficedl.info/

New York State Historic Newspapers: https://nyshistoricnewspapers.org/

Newspapers.com

Proceedings of the Old Bailey, 1674–1913: https://www.oldbaileyonline.org/

ProQuest Historical Newspapers: *New York Times, Washington Post, Baltimore Sun, Wall Street Journal*

Bibliography

Sächsische Landesbibliothek—Staats- und Universitätsbibliothek Dresden (SLUB): https://digital.slub-dresden.de/kollektionen

Statue of Liberty—Ellis Island Foundation, Passenger Search: https://heritage.statue ofliberty.org/passenger

Times Digital Archive, 1785–2014 (Gale): https://go.gale.com/ps/start.do?p=TTDA &u=umd_salisbury&aty=ip

Published Sources

Adamiak, Richard. "Marx, Engels, Dühring." *Journal of the History of Ideas* 35, no. 1 (1974): 98–112.

Adreß- und Geschäftshandbuch der königlichen Haupt- und Residenzstadt Dresden für das Jahr 1861. Dresden, 1861.

Adreß- und Geschäfts-Handbuch der Provinzial-Hauptstadt Mainz. Mainz, 1874.

Adreßbuch der Fabrik- und Handelstadt Chemnitz. Chemnitz, 1871, 1872, 1876.

Adreßbuch der Kaufleute, Fabrikanten und Gewerbeleute der freien Stadt Frankfurt. Nuremberg: Leuchs, 1860.

Adreßbuch der Königlichen Kreishauptstadt Augsburg. nach amtl. Quellen zusammengestellt. Augsburg, 1859, 1862.

Adreßbuch für Augsburg, königl. Regierungs-Bezirks-Hauptstadt von Schwaben und Neuburg. 1855. Augsburg: Kohler, 1855.

Adreßbuch über und für den Gewerbe- und Handelsstand der Großherzogthümer Mecklenburg-Schwerin und Strelitz. Schwerin: A. Schmale, 1862.

Alston, Charlotte. "News of the Struggle: The Russian Political Press in London, 1853–1921." In *The Foreign Political Press in Nineteenth-Century London: Politics from a Distance,* edited by Constance Bantman and Ana Cláudia Suriani da Silva, 155–74. London: Bloomsbury, 2018.

Amts-Blatt der freien Stadt Frankfurt. Jahrgang 1858. Frankfurt: Holzwart, 1858.

Andréas, Bert, and Miklós Molnár, eds. *La première internationale: Recueil de documents publié sous la direction de Jacques Freymond.* Geneva: L'Institut Universitaire de Hautes Études Internationales, 1971.

Anemone, Anthony, ed. *Just Assassins: The Culture of Terrorism in Russia.* Evanston: Northwestern University Press, 2010.

Annual Report of the State Board of Charities for the Year Ending September 30, 1886. Albany, NY: Weed, Parsons, 1887.

Archiv für Landeskunde in den Grossherzogthümern Mecklenburg. Schwerin: Sandmeyer, 1866, vol. 16.

Ashton, Rosemary. *Little Germany: Exile and Asylum in Victorian England.* Oxford: Oxford University Press, 1986.

Attenhofer, Eduard. *"Der rothe Teufel": Mein zehnjähr. Kampf gegen den Umsturz als Redaktor der Schweizerblätter "Limmat" und "Stadtbote."* Zurich: Buchdruckerei Neumünster, 1890.

Auer, Ignaz. *Nach zehn Jahren: Material und glossen zur Geschichte des Sozialistengesetz.* Nuremberg: Fränkische Verlagsanstalt, 1913.

Avrich, Paul. *An American Anarchist: The Life of Voltairine de Cleyre*. Princeton: Princeton University Press, 1978.

Avrich, Paul. *Anarchist Portraits*. Princeton: Princeton University Press, 1988.

Avrich, Paul, ed. *Anarchist Voices: An Oral History of Anarchism in America*. Oakland, CA: AK Press, 2005.

Avrich, Paul. "Kropotkin in America." *International Review of Social History* 25, no. 1 (1980): 1–34.

Avrich, Paul. *The Haymarket Tragedy*. Princeton: Princeton University Press, 1986.

Avrich, Paul, and Karen Avrich. *Sasha and Emma: The Anarchist Odyssey of Alexander Berkman and Emma Goldman*. Cambridge, MA: Belknap, 2012.

Baedeker, Karl. *Switzerland and the Adjacent Portions of Italy, Savoy and the Tyrol. Handbook for Travellers*. Koblenz: K. Baedeker, 1867.

Baker, Zoe. *Means and Ends: The Revolutionary Practice of Anarchism in Europe and the United States*. Chico, CA: AK Press, 2023.

Bantman, Constance. "Internationalism without an International: Cross-Channel Anarchist Networks, 1880–1914." *Revue belge de philologie et d'histoire. Belgisch Tijdschrift voor Philologie en Geschiedenis* 84, no. 4 (2006): 961–81.

Barea, Ilsa. *Vienna*. New York: Knopf, 1966.

Barnard, Harry. *Eagle Forgotten: The Life of John Peter Altgeld*. Indianapolis: Bobbs-Merrill, 1938.

Bartal, Israel. "The Image of Germany and German Jewry in East European Jewish Society during the 19th Century." In *Danzig, between East and West: Aspects of Modern Jewish History*, edited by Isadore Twersky, 1–18. Cambridge, MA: Harvard University Press, 1985.

Bebel, August. *Aus meinem Leben*. 3 vols. Stuttgart: Dietz, 1922.

Bebel, August. *Unsere Ziele. Eine Streitschrift gegen die "Demokratische Korrespondenz."* Zurich, 1886.

Bebel, August, Franz Mehring, and Julius Vahlteich. *Die Gründung der deutschen Sozialdemokratie: eine Festschrift der Leipziger Arbeiter zum 23. Mai 1903*. Leipzig: Leipziger Buchdruckerei Aktiengesellschaft, 1903.

Becker, Bernhard. *Geschichte der Arbeiter-Agitation Ferdinand Lassalle's: nach authentischen Aktenstücken*. Braunschweig: W. Bracke Jr., 1874.

Becker, Heiner, ed. *Johann Most. Anarchismus in einer Nußschale*. Münster: Unrast-Verlag, 2006.

Becker, Heiner, ed. *Johann Most. Die freie Gesellschaft: die "Internationale Bibliothek" und Texte aus der "Freiheit" zum Kommunistischen Anarchismus*. Münster: Unrast-Verlag, 2006.

Becker, Heiner. "Johann Most—ein unterschätzter Sozialdemokrat." *Internationale wissenschaftliche Korrespondenz zur Geschichte der deutschen Arbeiterbewegung* 41, no. 1 (2005): 5–66.

Becker, Heiner. "Johann Most: eine kleine Bibliography." *Internationale wissenschaftliche Korrespondenz zur Geschichte der deutschen Arbeiterbewegung* 41, no. 1 (2005): 255–308.

Becker, Heiner. "Johann Most in Europe." *The Raven. Anarchist Quarterly* 1, no. 4 (1988): 291–321.

Becker, Heiner. "Johann Neve (1844–1896)." *The Raven. Anarchist Quarterly* 1, no. 2 (1987): 99–114.

Becker, Heiner, ed. *John Most: Marxereien, Eseleien & der sanfte Heinrich: Artikel aus der "FREIHEIT."* Wetzlar: Büchse der Pandora, 1985.

Berkman, Alexander. *Prison Memoirs of an Anarchist.* New York: Mother Earth Publishing Association, 1912.

Bernstein, Eduard. *Ignaz Auer. Eine Gedenkschrift.* Berlin: Buchhandlung Vorwärts, 1907.

Bernstein, Eduard. *My Years of Exile: Reminiscences of a Socialist.* New York: Harcourt, Brace and Howe, 1921.

Bernstein, Eduard. *Sozialdemokratische Lehrjahre.* Berlin: der Bücherkreis, 1928.

Bers, Günter. *Wilhelm Hasselmann: 1844–1916: Sozialrevolutionärer Agitator und Abgeordneter des Deutschen Reichstages.* Cologne: Einhorn-Presse, 1973.

Birker, Karl. *Die deutschen Arbeiterbildungsvereine, 1840–1870.* Berlin: Colloquium Verlag, 1973.

Blankenagel, John C. "Early Reception of Hauptmann's *Die Weber* in the United States." *Modern Language Notes* 68 (1953): 335.

Bloom, Cecil. "Aaron Lieberman: The Father of Jewish Socialism." *Jewish Historical Studies* 42 (2009): 139–46.

Blos, Wilhelm. *Denkwürdigkeiten eines Sozialdemokraten.* 2 vols. Munich: Birk, 1914.

Bonnel, Andrew. "Between Internationalism, Nationalism and Particularism: German Social Democrats and the War of 1870–71." *Australian Journal of Politics & History* 38, no. 3 (1992): 375–85.

Borcke, Astrid von. "Violence and Terror in Russian Revolutionary Populism: The Narodnaya Volya, 1879–83." In *Social Protest, Violence and Terror in Nineteenth- and Twentieth-Century Europe*, edited by Wolfgang J. Mommsen and Gerhard Hirschfeld, 48–62. London: Macmillan, 1982.

Bowan, Kate. "Friendship, Cosmopolitan Connections and Late Victorian Socialist Songbook Culture." In *Cheap Print and Popular Song in the Nineteenth Century: A Cultural History of the Songster*, edited by Paul Watt, Derek B. Scott, and Patrick Spedding, 91–111. Cambridge: Cambridge University Press, 2017.

Brandenburg, Alexander. "Zur Geschichte des Londoner Arbeiterbildungsvereins." *Archiv für die Geschichte des Widerstandes und der Arbeit* (AGWA) 1 (1980).

Braunthal, Julius. *History of the International, 1864–1914. Volume 1: 1864–1914.* New York: Praeger, 1967.

Brügel, Ludwig. *Geschichte der österreichischen Sozialdemokratie.* 5 vols. Vienna, 1922–25.

Burrows, Edwin, and Mike Wallace. *Gotham: A History of New York City to 1898.* New York: Oxford University Press, 1999.

Burrows, J. C. "The Need of National Legislation against Anarchism." *North American Review*, December 1901, 733–38.

Butterworth, Alex. *The World That Never Was: A True Story of Dreamers, Schemers, Anarchists, and Secret Agents*. New York: Vintage, 2011.

Campbell, Helen, Thomas Knox, and Thomas Byrnes. *Darkness and Daylight; or, Lights and Shadows of New York Life; a Pictorial Record of Personal Experiences by Day and Night in the Great Metropolis*. Hartford, CT: Hartford Publishing, 1897.

Candar, Gilles, and Vincent Duclert. *Édouard Vaillant: l'invention de la gauche*. Malakoff: Armand Colin, 2018.

Cannato, Vincent J. *American Passage: The History of Ellis Island*. New York: HarperCollins, 2010.

Carey, Mike, and Jamie Most. *High above Courtside: The Lost Memoirs of Johnny Most*. New York: Sports Publishing, 2003.

Carlson, Andrew R. "Anarchism and Individual Terror in the German Empire, 1878–1890." In *Social Protest, Violence and Terror in Nineteenth- and Twentieth-Century Europe*, edited by Wolfgang J. Mommsen and Gerhard Hirschfeld, 175–200. London: Macmillan, 1982.

Carlson, Andrew R. *Anarchism in Germany I: The Early Movement*. Metuchen: Scarecrow, 1972.

Clark, Barrett H. *The Continental Drama of To-Day*. New York: Holt, 1914.

Clutterbuck, Lindsay. "The Progenitors of Terrorism: Russian Revolutionaries or Extreme Irish Republicans?" *Terrorism and Political Violence* 16, no. 1 (2004): 154–81.

Clymer, Jeffory. *America's Culture of Terrorism: Violence, Capitalism, and the Written Word*. Chapel Hill: University of North Carolina Press, 2003.

Cohen, Joseph. *The Jewish Anarchist Movement in America: A Historical Review and Personal Reminiscences*. Edited by Kenyon Zimmer. Translated by Esther Dolgoff. Chico, CA: AK Press, 2024.

Cohn, Jesse. *Underground Passages: Anarchist Resistance Culture, 1848–2011*. Oakland, CA: AK Press, 2014.

Cordillot, Michel. *La sociale en Amérique: Dictionnaire biographique du mouvement social francophone aux États-Unis*. Paris: Les Éditions de l'Atelier, 2002.

Cornell, Andrew. *Unruly Equality: U.S. Anarchism in the Twentieth Century*. Oakland: University of California Press, 2016.

Craig, Gordon A. *The Germans*. New York: New American Library, 1982.

Creagh, Ronald. *L'anarchisme aux États-Unis*. 2 vols. New York: Peter Lang, 1983.

Daniels, Stephen. "In Memoriam of John Most." *Mother Earth* 8, no. 1 (1913): 12.

Der Wiener Hochverratsprozess: Bericht über die Schwurgerichts-verhandlung gegen Andreas Scheu, Heinrich Oberwinder, Johann Most und Genossen. Vienna: Brand, 1911.

Deutsch, Julius. *Die Geschichte der socialistischen Gewerkschaften Oesterreichs bis zur Krise des Jahres 1873*. Vienna: im Selbstverlage des Verfassers, 1907.

Die Verhandlungen der Berliner Conferenz ländlicher Arbeitgeber, herausgegeben im auftrage des geschäftsführenden Ausschusses von den Vorsitzendem Freiherr Theodor von der Goltz. Danzig: A. W. Kafemann, 1872.

Diskussion über das Thema "Anarchismus oder Communismus." Geführt von Paul Grottkau und Johann Most, am 24. Mai 1884 in Chicago. Chicago: das Central-Comite der Chicagoer Gruppen der I.A.A., Office of the "Chicagoer Arbeiter-Zeitung" und der "Vorbote," 1884.

Dlubek, Rolf, and Hannes Skambraks. *"Das Kapital" von Karl Marx in der deutschen Arbeiterbewegung (1867 bis 1878). Abriß und Zeugnis der Wirkungsgeschichte.* Berlin: Dietz, 1967.

Documents of the First International, 1866–1868. The General Council of the First International (1866–1868): Minutes. London: Lawrence and Wishart, 1868.

Dominick, Raymond H. *Wilhelm Liebknecht and the Founding of the German Social Democratic Party.* Chapel Hill: University of North Carolina Press, 1982.

Dommanget, Maurice. *Édouard Vaillant: Un grand socialiste, 1840–1915.* Paris: La Table Ronde, 1956.

Donner, Frank. *Protectors of Privilege: Red Squads and Police Repression in Urban America.* Berkeley: University of California Press, 1990.

Doutney, Thomas N. *Thomas N. Doutney: His Life-Struggle, Fall, and Reformation.* Boston: Rand Avery, 1887.

Dowe, Dieter, and Klaus Tenfelde. "Zur Rezeption Eugen Dührings in der deutschen Arbeiterbewegung in den 1870er Jahren." In *Wissenschaftlicher Sozialismus und Arbeiterbewegung. Begriffsgeschichte und Dühring-Rezeption,* edited by Hans Pelger, Wolfgang Schieder, Dieter Dowe, and Klaus Tenfelde. Trier: Karl Marx Haus, 1980.

Dray, Philip. *There Is Power in a Union: The Epic Story of Labor in America.* New York: Doubleday, 2010.

Dreisel, Hermann O. *Gesammelte Schriften.* Milwaukee: Freidenker, 1905.

Dühring, Eugen. *Sache, Leben und Feinde: als Hauptwerk und Schlüssel zu seinen sämmtlichen Schriften.* Karlsruhe: H. Reuther, 1882.

Eade, John. *Placing London: From Imperial Capital to Global City.* New York: Berghahn, 2000.

Eckert, Georg, ed. *Briefwechsel mit deutschen Sozialdemokraten.* 2 vols. Assen: Van Gorcum, 1973.

Ehrhart, Franz Josef. "Aus meiner Londoner Zeit. Erinnerungen." *Der Neue Welt Kalender für das Jahr 1908,* Jahrgang 32 (Hamburg, 1908), 58–62.

Ehrhart, Franz Josef. "Johann Most (†)." *Pfälzische Post. Organ für die Interessen des Volkes,* Nr. 69 (Ludwigshafen, March 22, 1906), [1].

Eichler, Volker. *Sozialistische Arbeiterbewegung in Frankfurt am Main 1878–1895.* Frankfurt, 1983.

Eissler, Manuel. *A Handbook on Modern Explosives: A Practical Treatise on the Manufacture and Use of Dynamite, Gun-Cotton, Nitro-glycerine, and Other Explosive Compounds, Including Collodion-Cotton.* London: Crosby, Lockwood, 1897.

Ely, Richard T. *The Labor Movement in America.* New York: Thomas Y. Crowell, 1886.

Emden, Christian. *Friedrich Nietzsche and the Politics of History.* Cambridge: Cambridge University Press, 2008.

Enckell, Marianne. "Bakunin and the Jura Federation." In *"Arise Ye Wretched of the Earth": The First International in a Global Perspective*, edited by Fabrice Bensimon, Quentin Deluermoz, and Jeanne Moisand, 355–65. Leiden: Brill, 2018.

Epstein, Melech. *Jewish Labor in U.S.A.: An Industrial, Political, and Cultural History of the Jewish Labor Movement*. New ed. 2 vols. [New York]: Ktav, 1969.

Ernst, Eugen. *Polizeispitzeleien und Ausnahmegesetz 1878–1910. Ein Beitrag zur Geschichte der Bekämpfung der Sozialdemokratie*. Berlin: Buchhandlung Vorwärts, 1911.

Eschner, Max. *Der Buchbinder: ein Lehr- und Lernbuch für Fachschulen, Fortbildungsschulen und zum Selbstunterricht*. Stuttgart: Hobbing & Büchle, 1898.

Eser, Susanne F. *Verwaltet und verwahrt- Armenpolitik und Arme in Augsburg: vom Ende der reichsstädtischen Zeit bis zum ersten Weltkrieg*. Sigmaringen: Thorbecke, 1996.

Evans, Alfred. "Pettenkofer Revisited: The Life and Contributions of Max von Pettenkofer (1818–1901)." *Yale Journal of Biology and Medicine* 46 (1973): 161–76.

Evans, Richard J. *Proletarians and Politics: Socialism, Protest and the Working Class in Germany before the First World War*. New York: St. Martin's, 1990.

Falk, Candace, Barry Pateman, and Jessica Moran, eds. *Emma Goldman: A Documentary History of the American Years*. 2 vols. Urbana: University of Illinois Press, 2003.

Ferguson, Kathy. *Letterpress Revolution: The Politics of Anarchist Print Culture*. Durham, NC: Duke University Press, 2023.

Fischer, Ilse. *Industrialisierung, sozialer Konflikt und politische Willensbildung in der Stadtgemeinde: ein Beitrag zur Sozialgeschichte Augsburgs 1840–1914*. Augsburg: Mühlberger, 1977.

Fishman, William J. *East End Jewish Radicals, 1875–1914*. London: Duckworth, 1975.

Fleming, Marie. *The Geography of Freedom: The Odyssey of Élisée Reclus*. Montreal: Black Rose Books, 1988.

Flower, Benjamin O. "American Daily Journalism in the Making." *The Arena* (Boston) 40, no. 227 (1908): 487–93.

Fricke, Dieter, and Rudolf Knaack. *Dokumente aus geheimen Archiven. Übersichten der Berliner politischen Polizei über die allgemeine Lage der sozialdemokratischen und anarchistischen Bewegung 1878–1913*. Band 1: 1878–1889. Weimar, 1983.

Fried, Albert. *Socialism in America from the Shakers to the Third International: A Documentary History*. New York: Anchor Books, 1970.

Gabriel, Elun. *Assassins & Conspirators: Anarchism, Socialism, and Political Culture in Imperial Germany*. Ithaca: Cornell University Press, 2014.

Gage, Beverly. *The Day Wall Street Exploded: A Story of America in Its First Age of Terror*. New York: Oxford University Press, 2009.

Gage, Beverly. "Why Violence Matters: Radicalism, Politics, and Class War in the Gilded Age and Progressive Era." *Journal for the Study of Radicalism* 1, no. 1 (2007): 99–109.

Goldman, Emma. "Johann Most." *American Mercury* 8 (1926): 158–66.

Goldman, Emma. *Living My Life*. 2 vols. New York: Dover, 1970.

Goldman, Emma, and Alexander Berkman. *Nowhere at Home: Letters from Exile of Emma Goldman and Alexander Berkman*. Edited by Richard and Anna Drinnon. New York: Schocken Books, 1975.

Goldstein, Robert J. *Political Repression in 19th Century Europe*. London: Croom Helm, 1983.

Gompers, Samuel. *Seventy Years of Life and Labor; an Autobiography*. New York: E. P. Dutton, 1925.

Goodman, Paul. *Speaking and Language: Defence of Poetry*. New York: Vintage Books, 1972.

Gopsill's Jersey City, Hoboken, West Hoboken, Union Hill and Weehawken Directory, 1886–7.

Gotthardt, Christian. "Johann Christoph Neve (1844–1896). Teil 1: Sozialrevolutionär aus Uelvesbüll," "Teil 2 Anarchistische Praxis. Aus Neves Briefen an Victor Dave 1885 bis 1887," "Anarchismus und Polizeistaat. Teil 3 und Schluss: die Verhaftung von Johann Christoph Neve in neuer Perspektive." In *Harburger Geschichte und Geschichten in Text und Bild* (January 2015). http://www.harbuch.de/frische-themen -artikel/johann-christoph-neve-1844-1896.html.

Goyens, Tom. *Beer and Revolution: The German Anarchist Movement in New York City, 1880–1914*. Urbana: University of Illinois Press, 2007.

Goyens, Tom. "Johann Most and Yiddish Anarchism, 1876–1906." In *With Freedom in Our Ears: Histories of Jewish Anarchism*, edited by Anna Elena Torres and Kenyon Zimmer, 21–42. Urbana: University of Illinois Press, 2023.

Goyens, Tom. "Road to Notoriety: Johann Most in Austria (1868–1871)." *Journal for the Study of Radicalism* 12, no. 2 (2018): 107–130.

Graham, Robert, ed. *Anarchism: A Documentary History of Libertarian Ideas. Volume 1: From Anarchy to Anarchism (300 CE to 1939)*. Montreal: Black Rose Press, 2004.

Graham, Robert. *We Do Not Fear Anarchy, We Invoke It: The First International and the Origins of the Anarchist Movement*. Oakland, CA: AK Press, 2015.

Grebing, Helga. *The History of the German Labour Movement. A Survey*. London: Oswald Wolff, 1969.

Green, James. *Death in the Haymarket: A Story of Chicago, the First Labor Movement and the Bombing That Divided Gilded Age America*. New York: Anchor Books, 2006.

Greulich, Hermann. *Das grüne Hüsli. Erinnerungen*. Edited by Gertrud Medici-Greulich. Zurich: Genossenschaftsdruckerei, 1942.

Guglielmo, Jennifer. *Living the Revolution: Italian Women's Resistance and Radicalism in New York City, 1880–1945*. Chapel Hill: University of North Carolina Press, 2010.

Guillaume, James. *L'internationale: Documents et souvenirs (1864–1878)*. 4 vols. Paris, 1905–10.

Harreck-Haase, Frank. *Der Agitator- Das Leben des Johann Most*. 2 vols. Chemnitz: Buchverlag Frank Harreck-Haase, 2017, 2019.

Hart, Heinrich. *Gesammelte Werke*. 4 vols. Edited by Julius Hart, unter Mitwirkung von Wilhelm Bölsche [et al.]. Berlin: E. Fleischel, 1907.

Hecker, Rolf. "Die Popularisierung des 'Kapitals' durch Johann Most." In *Internatio- nale wissenschaftliche Korrespondenz zur Geschichte der deutschen Arbeiterbewe- gung* 41, no. 1–2 (2005): 115–25.

Heidenreich, Friedrich Wilhelm. *Vorkehr und Verfahren gegen die Cholera. Nach eigenen Beobachtungen in München und Augsburg.* Ansbach, 1854.

Heilmann, Ernst. *Geschichte der Arbeiterbewegung in Chemnitz und dem Erzgebirge.* Chemnitz: Sozialdemokratischer Verein für den 16. sächsischen Reichstags- wahlkreis, [1911].

Held, Adolf. *Die deutsche Arbeiterpresse der Gegenwart.* Leipzig: Verlag von Duncker & Humblot, 1873.

Hennock, E. P. "Vaccination Policy against Smallpox, 1835–1914: A Comparison of England with Prussia and Imperial Germany." *Social History of Medicine* 11, no. 1 (1998): 49–71.

Hester, Torrie. "'Protection, Not Punishment': Legislative and Judicial Formation of U.S. Deportation Policy, 1882–1904." *Journal of American Ethnic History* 30, no. 1 (2010): 11–36.

Hillquit, Morris. *Loose Leaves from a Busy Life.* New York: Macmillan, 1934.

Hinsdale, Elizur. *Autobiography: With Reports and Documents.* New York: J. J. Little, 1901.

Hinze, Werner. *Johann Most und sein Liederbuch. Warum der Philosoph der Bombe Lieder schrieb und ein Liederbuch herausgab.* Hamburg: Tonsplitter Verlag, 2005.

Hoerder, Dirk. "German Immigrant Workers' Views of 'America' in the 1880s." In *In the Shadow of the Statue of Liberty. Immigrants, Workers and Citizens in the American Republic 1880–1920*, edited by Marianne Debouzy, 17–33. Vincennes: Presses Universitaires Françaises, 1988.

Hoerder, Dirk. "The German-American Labor Press and Its Views of the Political Institutions in the United States." In *The German-American Radical Press: The Shap- ing of a Left Political Culture, 1850–1940*, edited by Elliott Shore, Ken Fones-Wolf, and James P. Danky, 189–90. Urbana: University of Illinois Press, 1992.

Hof- und Staats-Handbuch des Kaiserthumes Österreich für das Jahr 1868. Vienna: G. J. Manz, 1868.

Hofmann, Ernst. "Die Anfänge sozialistischer Presse—und Verlagstätigkeit in Chemnitz. Karl Marx als Mitautor einer in Chemnitz erschienenen Schrift zur Popularisierung seines wissenschaftlichen Hauptwerkes 'Das Kapital.'" In *Region- algeschichtliche Beiträge aus dem Bezirk Karl-Marx-Stadt.* Heft 3. Karl-Marx-Stadt: Rat des Bezirkes, 1981.

Hofstadter, Richard. "Reflections on Violence in the United States." In *American Violence: A Documentary History*, edited by Richard Hofstadter and Michael Wal- lace, 3–43. New York: Knopf, 1970.

Holborn, Hajo. *A History of Modern Germany, 1840–1945.* Princeton: Princeton Uni- versity Press, 1969.

Hölscher, Lucian. *Weltgericht oder Revolution. Protestantische und sozialistische Zu- kunftsvorstellungen im deutschen Kaiserreich.* Stuttgart: Klett-Cotta, 1989.

Howorth, Jolyon. *Edouard Vaillant: La création de l'unité socialiste en France: La politique de l'action totale.* Paris: EDI:Syros, 1982.

Howorth, Jolyon. "The Myth of Blanquism under the Third Republic (1871–1900)." *Journal of Modern History* 48, no. 3 (1976): 37–68.

Huerkamp, Claudia. "The History of Smallpox Vaccination in Germany: A First Step in the Medicalization of the General Public." *Journal of Contemporary History* 20, no. 4 (1985): 617–35.

Hughes, Michael. "British Opinion and Russian Terrorism in the 1880s." *European History Quarterly* 41, no. 2 (2011): 255–77.

Hunter, Robert. *Violence and the Labor Movement.* New York: Macmillan, 1914.

Ishill, Joseph, comp. and ed. *Elisée Reclus and Elie Reclus In Memoriam. Including: Tributes, Appreciations and Essays by Elie Faure, Albert Heim, [a.o.]. Fragments, Letters, and over Sixty Woodcuts by Louis Moreau.* Berkeley Heights, NJ: Oriole Press, 1927.

Jensen, Jürgen. *Presse und politische Polizei: Hamburgs Zeitungen unter d. Sozialistengesetz 1878–1890.* Hannover: Dietz, 1966.

Jensen, Richard. *The Battle against Anarchist Terrorism: An International History, 1878–1934.* Cambridge: Cambridge University Press, 2014.

John, Matthias. *"Im Geruch eines Bombenwerfer": Johann Most (1846–1906) und seine Beziehungen zu Glauchau, einem Zentrum der sächsischen und deutschenArbeiterbewegung.* Berlin: Trafo Verlag, 2007.

Johnson, Steven. *The Ghost Map: The Story of London's Most Terrifying Epidemic and How It Changed Science, Cities, and the Modern World.* London: Riverhead Trade, 2007.

Karasek, Horst. *John Most mit dem schiefen Maul: Restauration an einem entstellten Porträt.* Frankfurt: Verlag Freie Gesellschaft, 1976.

Karl Marx, Friedrich Engels Werke. 44 vols. Berlin: Dietz Verlag, 1956–89.

Kautsky, Karl. *Erinnerungen und Erörterungen.* The Hague: Mouton, 1960.

Kautsky, Karl. "Johann Most." *Die Gesellschaft. Internationale Revue für Sozialismus und Politik* 1, no. 6 (1924): 545–64.

Keil, Hartmut, ed. *German Workers' Culture in the United States, 1850 to 1920.* Washington, DC: Smithsonian Institution Press, 1988.

Kelly, Luke. *British Humanitarian Activity in Russia, 1890–1923.* London: Palgrave Macmillan, 2018.

Kitz, Frank. "Recollections and Reflections." *Freedom* (London), March 1912.

Kläger, Michael. "Mainz auf dem Weg zur Großstadt (1866–1914)." In *Mainz. Die Geschichte der Stadt,* edited by Franz Dumont, Ferdinand Scherf, and Friedrich Schütz. Mainz: Verlag Phillip von Zabern, 1998.

Kollmann, Franz Joseph, and Ferdinand Oldenburg. *Die Wasserwerke von Augsburg: Beschreibung aller hydrotechnischen Anstalten der Stadt, des Lech- und Wertachablasses, der Kanäle, Brunnen etc. mit den wichtigsten baupolizeilichen Bestimmungen: nebst einer Ansicht des Lech-Ablasses und hydrographischen Karte von Augsburg und seinen Umgebungen.* Augsburg: Rieger Verlag, 1850.

Kopeloff, I. *Amol in Amerike: zikhroynes fun dem yidishn lebn in Amerike in di yorn 1883–1904*. Warsaw: Farlag Kh. Bzhoza, 1928.

Körner, Alex. *Das Lied von der anderen Welt: Kulturelle Praxis im französischen und deutschen Arbeitermilieu 1840–1890*. Frankfurt: Campus Verlag, 1997.

Kühn, Dieter, ed. *Johann Most. Ein Sozialist in Deutschland*. Munich: Carl Hanser Verlag, 1974.

Künstner, Karl Theodor von. *Taschen- und Handbuch für Theater-Statistik*. Leipzig: Dürr'sche Buchhandlung, 1857.

Künzle, E., and K. Bänninger. *Geschichte des Konsumvereins Zürich 1851–1926: zum 75-jährigen Vereinsjubiläum*. J. Rüegg, 1926.

Lammel, Inge. *Arbeiterlied- Arbeitergesang. Hundert Jahre Arbeitermusikkultur in Deutschland. Aufsätze und Vorträge aus 40 Jahren. 1959–1998*. Berlin: Hentrich und Hentrich Verlag, 2002.

Lammel, Inge. *Arbeitermusikkultur in Deutschland 1844–1945. Bilder und Dokumente*. Leipzig: Deutscher Verlag für Musik, 1984.

Lammel, Inge, ed. *Hundert Proletarische Balladen 1842–1945*. Berlin: Tribüne, 1985.

Langhard, J. *Die anarchistische Bewegung in der Schweiz von ihren Anfängen bis zur Gegenwart und die internationalen Führer*. Bern: Stämpfli, 1909.

Large, David Clay. *Berlin*. New York: Basic Books, 2000.

Lassalle, Ferdinand. *Arbeiterlesebuch; Rede Lassalle's zu Frankfurt am Main am 17. und 19. Mai 1863, nach dem Stenographischen Bericht*. Frankfurt: in Commission bei Reinhold Baist, 1863.

Lassalle, Ferdinand. *Ferdinand Lassalle's Reden und Schriften. Neue Gesammt-Ausgabe*. Edited by Eduard Bernstein. Berlin: Verlag der Expedition des "Vorwärts" Berliner Volksblatt, 1893.

Lattek, Christine. *Revolutionary Refugees: German Socialism in Britain, 1840–1860*. New York: Routledge, 2006.

Lausch, Karin. *Wider den "Hurra-Patriotismus": die politische Widerstandskultur des sozialdemokratischen Milieus im Kaiserreich von 1870/1 bis 1878 am Beispiel der Sedanfeier*. Munich: Grin Verlag, 2013.

Lehnert, Detlef. *Sozialdemokratie zwischen Protestbewegung und Regierungspartei 1848–1983*. Frankfurt: Suhrkamp, 1983.

Leipziger Hochverrathsprozess: Ausführlicher Bericht über die Verhandlungen des Schwurgerichts zu Leipzig in dem Prozess gegen Liebknecht, Bebel und Hepner wegen Vorbereitung zum Hochverrath vom 11.-26. März 1872. Bearbeitet von den Angeklagten. Leipzig: Genossenschaftsbuchdruckerei, 1874.

Lidtke, Vernon. "August Bebel and German Social Democracy's Relation to the Christian Churches." *Journal of the History of Ideas* 27, no. 2 (1966): 245–64.

Lidtke, Vernon. *The Alternative Culture: Socialist Labor in Imperial Germany*. New York: Oxford University Press, 1985.

Lidtke, Vernon. *The Outlawed Party: Social Democracy in Germany, 1878–1890*. Princeton: Princeton University Press, 1966.

Liebknecht, Wilhelm. *Briefwechsel mit deutschen Sozialdemokraten.* 2 vols. Edited by Georg Eckert. Assen: Van Gorcum, 1973.

Liebknecht, Wilhelm. *Briefwechsel mit Karl Marx und Friedrich Engels.* Edited by Georg Eckert. The Hague: Mouton, 1963.

Lindau, Paul. "Vom Plötzensee." In *Die Gegenwart. Wochenschrift für Literatur, Kunst und öffentliches Leben,* Nr. 14. Berlin, April 3, 1875.

Linse, Ulrich. "'Propaganda by Deed' and 'Direct Action': Two Concepts of Anarchist Violence." In *Social Protest, Violence and Terror in Nineteenth- and Twentieth-Century Europe,* edited by Wolfgang J. Mommsen and Gerhard Hirschfeld, 201–29. London: Macmillan, 1982.

Macartney, C. A. *The Habsburg Empire, 1790–1918.* New York: Macmillan, 1969.

Maffi, Mario. *Gateway to the Promised Land: Ethnic Cultures in New York's Lower East Side.* New York: New York University Press, 1995.

Martin, Aloys, ed. *Haupt-Bericht über die Cholera-Epidemie des Jahres 1854 im Königreiche Bayern.* Munich, 1856.

Materna, Ingo. "'Johann Most und der Berliner Polizeipräsident (1874–1890). Ein Diskussionsbeitrag." *Internationale wissenschaftliche Korrespondenz zur Geschichte der deutschen Arbeiterbewegung* 41, no. 1–2 (2005): 105–14.

May, Arthur J. *The Hapsburg Monarchy, 1867–1914.* New York: Norton, 1968.

McLean, George N. *The Rise and Fall of Anarchy in America. From Its Incipient Stage to the First Bomb Thrown in Chicago. A Comprehensive Account of the Great Conspiracy Culminating in the Haymarket Massacre, May 4th, 1886 . . . the Apprehension, Trail, Conviction and Execution of the Leading Conspirators.* Chicago: R. G. Badoux, 1888.

Mehring, Franz. *Die deutsche Socialdemokratie: ihre Geschichte und ihre Lehre; eine historisch-kritische Darstellung.* Bremen: C. Schünemann, 1878.

Mehring, Franz. *Geschichte der deutschen Sozialdemokratie. Vierter Band: Bis zum Erfurter Programm.* Stuttgart: Dietz, 1913.

Mehring, Franz. *Geschichte der deutschen Sozialdemokratie. Zweiter Theil: Von Lassalles Offenem Antwortschreiben bis zum Erfurter Programm 1863 bis 1891.* Stuttgart: Dietz, 1898.

Meindl, Konrad. *Leben und Wirken des Bischofes Franz Joseph Rudigier von Linz.* Linz: Bischöflichen Priesterseminar, 1891, vol. 1.

Mengers, Christian. *Aus den letzten Tagen der Zunft. Erinnerungen eines alten Handwerkers aus seinen Wanderjahren.* Leipzig, 1910.

Merlino, Francesco Saverio. *Nécessité et bases d'une Entente.* Brussels: Imprimerie Alex. Longfils, 1892.

Messer-Kruse, Timothy. *The Haymarket Conspiracy: Transatlantic Anarchist Networks.* Urbana: University of Illinois Press, 2012.

Messer-Kruse, Timothy. *The Trial of the Haymarket Anarchists: Terrorism and Justice in the Gilded Age.* New York: Palgrave-Macmillan, 2011.

Meyer, Erika. *Die Herausbildung der Arbeiterklasse im Spiegel der zeitgenössischen Lyrik: von Vormärz bis zum Anfang d. siebziger Jahre.* Cologne: Rugenstein Verlag, 1979.

Meyer, R. *Der Emancipationskampf des Vierten Standes*. Berlin: Verlag von August Schindler, 1875, vol. 2.

Michels, Tony. *A Fire in Their Hearts: Yiddish Socialists in New York*. Cambridge, MA: Harvard University Press, 2005.

Minkin, Helene. *Storm in My Heart: Memoirs from the Widow of Johann Most*. Edited by Tom Goyens. Translated by Alisa Braun. Oakland, CA: AK Press, 2015.

Möller, Frank. *Bürgerliche Herrschaft in Augsburg 1790–1880*. Augsburg: Oldenbourg Verlag, 1998.

Most, Johann. *Acht Jahre hinter Schloß und Riegel. Skizzen aus dem Leben Johann Most's*. New York, 1886.

Most, Johann. *An das Proletariat. An- und Absichten eines entlassenen Sträflichs*, Internationale Bibliothek #1. New York: John Müller, April 1887.

Most, Johann. *August Reinsdorf und die Propaganda der That*. New York: Selbstverlag, March 1885.

Most, Johann. *Der Kleinbürger und die Socialdemokratie: ein Mahnwort an die Kleingewerbtreibenden*. Augsburg: Verlag d. Volksbuchh. J. Endres, 1876.

Most, Johann. *Der kommunistische Anarchismus*. New York: John Müller, December 1889; Frankfurt: Verlag Edition AV, 2000.

Most, Johann. *Der Narrenthurm*, Internationale Bibliothek #11. New York: John Müller, February 1888.

Most, Johann. "Der Sozialismus und die häuslichen Arbeiten." In *Johann Most: Dokumente eines sozialdemokratischen Agitators*, edited by Volker Szmula, 1:102–3. Grafenau: Trotzdem Verlag, 1988.

Most, Johann. *Die Bastille am Plötzensee. Blätter aus meinem Gefängniss-Tagebuch*. Braunschweig: W. Bracke, [July] 1876.

Most, Johann. *Die Eigenthumsbestie*. [New York: Internationale Druckerei Freiheit, October 1883.]

Most, Johann. *Die freie Gesellschaft. Eine Abhandlung über Principien und Taktik der kommunistischen Anarchisten*. New York: Selbstverlag, July 1884.

Most, Johann. *Die freie Gesellschaft*, Internationale Bibliothek #5. New York: John Müller, August 1887.

Most, Johann. *Die Gottes-Pest und Religions-Seuche*. [New York, 1883.]

Most, Johann. *Die Gottlosigkeit. Eine kritik der Gottesidee*. [N.p.: (1877).]

Most, Johann. *Die Hoelle von Blackwells Island*. Internationale Bibliothek #2. New York: John Müller, May 1887.

Most, Johann. *Die Lösung der sozialen Frage. Ein Vortrag, gehalten vor Berliner Arbeitern*. Berlin: Allgemeinen Deutschen Associations-Buchdruckerei, 1876.

Most, Johann. *Die Pariser Commune vor den Berliner Gerichten. Eine Studie über deutsch-preußische Rechtszustände*. Braunschweig: W. Bracke Jr., [January] 1875.

Most, Johann. *Die socialen Bewegungen im alten Rom und der Cäsarismus*. Berlin: Druck u. Verlag d. Allgemeinen Deutschen Associations-Buchdruckerei, 1878.

Most, Johann. *Memoiren. Erlebtes, Erforschtes und Erdachtes*. 3 vols. New York: Selbstverlag des Verfassers, 1903; Hannover: Edition Kobaia, 1978.

Most, Johann. *Military Science for Revolutionaries.* Cornville, AZ: Desert Publications, ca. 1978.

Most, Johann. *Revolutionäre Kriegswissenschaft: ein Handbüchlein zur Anleitung betreffend Gebrauches und Herstellung von Nitroglycerin, Dynamit, Schiessbaumwolle, Knallquecksilber, Bomben, Brandsätzen, Giften u.s.w.* [New York: Internationale Zeitungs-Verein, July 1885.]

Most, Johann. *Social Monster: A Paper on Communism and Anarchism.* New York: Bernhard & Schenck, 1890.

Most, Johann. *"Taktik" contra "Freiheit." Ein Wort zum Angriff und zur Abwehr.* [London] Druck der socialdemokratischen Genossenschafts-Buchdr. "Freiheit," October 1880.

Most, Johann. *The Beast of Property: Total Annihilation Proposed as the Only Infallible Remedy: The Curse of the World which Defeats the People's Emancipation.* [2nd ed.] International Working People's Association, Group New Haven, 1890.

Most, Johann. *The Deistic Pestilence and Religious Plague of Man.* [New York?]: Internationale Druckerei des Freidenker, 1883.

Most, Johann. *The Free Society. Tract on Communism and Anarchy.* New York: John Müller, [1891].

Most, Johann. *The God Pestilence.* New York: Freiheit Publishing Association, [1887].

Most, Johann. "Von Ort zu Ort (Handwerkburschen-Skizzen)." *Berliner Freie Presse* 3, no. 229–47 (October 2–23, 1878).

Most, Johann. "Zur Geschichte der Arbeiterbewegung in Oesterreich." *Die neue Gesellschaft* (Zurich) 1 (1877/78): 147.

Most, Johann. *Zwischen Galgen und Zuchthaus,* Internationale Bibliothek #9. New York: John Müller, December 1887.

Most, John, ed. *Down with the Anarchists!* New York: John Most, [1901].

Mühlauer, Elisabeth. *Welch' ein unheimlicher Gast: die Cholera-Epidemie 1854 in München.* Münster: Waxmann, 1996.

Mühlnikel, Marcus. *"Fürst, sind Sie unverletzt?": Attentate im Kaiserreich, 1871–1914.* Paderborn: Ferdinand Schöningh, 2014.

Müller, Eduard. *Bericht über die Untersuchung betreffend die anarchistischen Umtriebe in der Schweiz an den hohen Bundesrath der schweiz. Eidgenossenschaft.* Bern: K. J. Wyss, 1885.

Murphy, Cait. *Scoundrels in Law: The Trials of Howe and Hummel, Lawyers to the Gangsters, Cops, Starlets, and Rakes Who Made the Gilded Age.* New York: Harper, 2011.

Musto, Marcello. *Another Marx: Early Manuscripts to the International.* London: Bloomsbury, 2018.

Nadel, Stan. "The German Immigrant Left in the United States." In *The Immigrant Left in the United States,* edited by Paul Buhle and Dan Georgakas, 45–76. Albany: State University of New York Press, 1996.

Nelson, Bruce C. *"Arbeiterpresse und Arbeiterbewegung*: Chicago's Socialist and Anarchist Press, 1870–1900." In *The German-American Radical Press: The Shaping of a Left Political Culture, 1850–1940*, edited by Elliott Shore, Ken Fones-Wolf, and James Danky, 81–107. Urbana: University of Illinois Press, 1992.

Nelson, Bruce C. *Beyond the Martyrs: A Social History of Chicago's Anarchists, 1870–1900*. New Brunswick, NJ: Rutgers University Press, 1988.

Nettlau, Max. *Anarchisten und Sozialrevolutionäre: die historische Entwicklung des Anarchismus in den Jahren 1880–1886* [Geschichte der Anarchie, vol. 3]. Berlin: Asy-Verlag, 1931.

Nettlau, Max [M. N.]. "Johann Neve." *Freedom*, no. 113 (February 1897).

Nettlau, Max. "John Most." *Freedom* 20, no. 205 (1906): 9–10; no. 206 (1906): 13–14; no. 207 (1906): 18–19.

Nettlau, Max. "La muerte de tres viejos anarquistas. Victor Dave." *La protesta. Suplemento semanal* (Buenos Aires), July 23, 1923.

Neueste Sammlung von Verordnungen und Vorschriften für die königlich bayerische Kreishauptstadt Augsburg: ein unentbehrliches Hand- und Hülfsbuch für jeden Bürger und Einwohner der Stadt. Vol. 1. Augsburg, 1855.

Nomad, Max. *Apostles of Revolution.* Boston: Little, Brown, 1939.

Nuhn, Heinrich. *August Spies: ein hessischer Sozialrevolutionär in Amerika.* Kassel: Verlag Jenior & Pressler, 1992.

Oertzen, Dietrich von. *Adolf Stoecker: Lebensbild und Zeitgeschichte.* 2 vols. Berlin: Verlag der Vaterländischen Verlags- und Kunstanstalt, 1910.

Oncken, Hermann. "Aus den Briefen Rudolf von Bennigsen." *Deutsche Revue* 32, no. 4 (1907): 9–27.

Orwell, George. "The Prevention of Literature." *Polemic* 2 (1946): 4–14.

Parsons, Lucy E., ed. *Life of Albert R. Parsons.* Chicago: Lucy E. Parsons, 1903.

"People v. Most." In *New York Criminal Reports: Reports of Cases Decided in All the Courts of the State of New York Involving Questions of Criminal Law and Practice,* 7:376–93. New York: Peloubet, 1889–90.

"People v. Most." In *Reports of Cases Decided in the Court of Appeals of the State of New York,* 171:423–32. Albany, NY: J. B. Lyon, 1902.

Pettenkofer, Max von. *Haupt-Bericht über die Cholera-Epidemie des Jahres 1854 in Bayern.* Munich, 1857.

Pettenkofer, Max von. *Untersuchungen und Beobachtungen über die Verbreitungsart der Cholera nebstBetrachtungen über Maßregeln, derselben Einhalt zu thun.* Munich: Literarisch-artistische Anstalt der J. Cotta'schen Buchhandlung, 1855.

Peukert, Josef. *Erinnerungen eines Proletariers aus der revolutionären Arbeiterbewegung.* Frankfurt: Verlag Edition AV, 2002.

Phillips, Adolf, ed. *Die Reichstags-wahlen von 1867 bis 1883: Statistik der wahlen zum konstituierenden und norddeutschen Reichstage, zum Zollparlament, sowie zu den fünf ersten legislatur-perioden des deutschen Reichstags.* Berlin: Louis Gerschel's Verlagsbuchhandlung, 1883.

Porter, Bernard. "The Freiheit Prosecutions, 1881–1882." *Historical Journal* 23, no. 4 (1980): 833–56.

Protokoll des Sozialisten-Congresses zu Gotha vom 19. bis 23. August 1876. Berlin: Allgemeinen Deutschen Associations-Buchdruckerei, 1876.

Protokolle der sozialdemokratischen Arbeiterpartei. Band I: Eisenach 1869—Coburg 1874. Glasshütten im Taunus: Verlag Detlev Auvermann, 1976, sections 1, 3, 4.

Prüfer, Sebastian. "Johann Most und die Berliner Kirchenaustrittskampagne 1878." *Internationale wissenschaftliche Korrespondenz zur Geschichte der deutschen Arbeiterbewegung* 41, no. 1–2 (2005): 126–36.

Quail, John. *The Slow Burning Fuse: The Lost History of the British Anarchists.* London: Freedom Press, 2017.

Ramm, Agatha. *Germany 1789–1919: A Political History.* London: Methuen, 1967.

Ravenstein, Ernest George. *Meyers Reisebücher. London, England, Schottland und Irland.* Leipzig: Bibliographisches Institut, 1880.

Reichard, Richard. *Crippled from Birth: German Social Democracy 1844–1870.* Ames: Iowa State University Press, 1969.

Reichesberg, Naum. *Handwörterbuch der schweizerischen Volkswirtschaft, Sozialpolitik und Verwaltung.* Bern: Verlag Encyklopädie, 1903.

Ribak, Gil. *Gentile New York: The Images of Non-Jews among Jewish Immigrants.* New Brunswick, NJ: Rutgers University Press, 2012.

Rocker, Rudolf. *Johann Most. Das Leben eines Rebellen.* Berlin: Verlag "Der Syndikalist," 1924.

Rocker, Rudolf. *The London Years.* Translated by Joseph Leftwich. Oakland, CA: AK Press, 2005.

Rolleston, J. D. "The Smallpox Pandemic of 1870–1874. President's Address." *Journal of the Royal Society of Medicine* 27, no. 2 (1933): 187.

Salisbury, William. *The Career of a Journalist.* New York: B. W. Dodge, 1908.

Sapir, Boris. "Liberman et le socialisme russe." *International Review of Social History* 3 (1938).

Schaller, Karlheinz. *Einmal kommt die Zeit: Geschichte der Chemitzer Arbeiterschaft vom Ende des 18. Jhd. bis zum Ersten Weltkrieg.* Bielefeld: Verlag für Regionalgeschichte, 2001.

Scheu, Andreas. "Erlebnisse eines Kämpfers. Aus den Erinnerungen Andreas Scheus." *Salzburger Wacht,* September 8, 1927.

Scheu, Andreas. "Johann Most." *Salzburger Wacht,* February 1, 1924.

Scheu, Andreas *Umsturzkieme: Erlebnisse eines Kämpfers.* 3 vols. Vienna: Volksbuchhandlung, 1923.

Scheu, Heinrich, ed. *Der Hochverratsprozeß gegen Oberwinder, Andr. Scheu, Most, Papst, Hecker, Perrin, Schönfelder, Berka, Schäftner, Pfeiffer, Dorsch, Eichinger, Gehrke, und Baudisch. Verhandelt vor dem k. k. Landesgerichte in Wien begonnen am 4. Juli 1870. Nach stenographischen Berichten bearbeitet und herausgegen von Heinrich Scheu.* Vienna: Selbstverlag, 1870.

Scheu, Heinrich. *Erinnerungen. Ein Beitrag zur Geschichte der österreichischen Arbeiterbewegung.* Vienna: Wiener Volksbuchhandlung Ignaz Brand, 1912.

Schlimper, Jürgen. "Vom Volksagitator zum Redakteur einer Tageszeitung. Johann Most und die Chemnitzer sozialistische Presse 1871/72." *Internationale wissenschaftliche Korrespondenz zur Geschichte der deutschen Arbeiterbewegung* 41, no. 1–2 (2005): 137–49.

Schmid, Christoph von. *Erinnerungen aus meinem Leben.* 4 vols. Augsburg: Verlag der Wolffischen Buchhandlung, 1857.

Schmidt, Axel W.-O. *Der rothe Doktor von Chicago—ein deutsch-amerikanisches Auswandererschicksal: Biographie des Dr. Ernst Schmidt, 1830–1900, Arzt und Sozialrevolutionär.* Frankfurt: Peter Lang, 2003.

Schneider, Erich. *"Die Presse ist das Herzblut unserer Bewegung": der Sozialdemokrat Franz Josef Ehrhart als Publizist und Zeitungsgründer und die "Pfälzische Post" Ludwigshafen in der Ära des "Roten Pfalzgrafen."* Sonderdruck: Mitteilungen des Historische Vereins der Pfalz, 1996.

[Schneidt, Karl]. *Die Hintermänner der Socialdemokratie: von einem Eingeweihten.* 2nd ed. Berlin: Conitzer's Verlag, 1890.

Schneirov, Richard. *Labor and Urban Politics: Class Conflict and the Origins of Modern Liberalism in Chicago, 1864–97.* Urbana: University of Illinois Press, 1998.

Schönchen, Ludwig. *Geschichte der Stadt Augsburg: (XXVIII S.) zur Geschichte der Volksbildung u. d. Unterrichts in Schwaben u. Neuburg.* Dr. C. Wolf & Sohn, 1863.

Schröder, Wolfgang. "Wilhelm Liebknecht und Johann Most. Eine Annäherung." *Internationale wissenschaftliche Korrespondenz zur Geschichte der deutschen Arbeiterbewegung* 41, no. 1–2 (2005): 67–92.

Shipley, Maynard. "Homicide and the Death Penalty in Austria-Hungary." *Publications of the American Statistical Association* 10, no. 77 (1907): 254.

Sperber, Jonathan. *Karl Marx: A Nineteenth-Century Life.* New York: Liveright, 2013.

Spies, August. "Autobiography of August Spies." In *The Autobiographies of the Haymarket Martyrs*, edited by Philip S. Foner, 59–72. New York: Monad Press, 1969.

Staats- und Adreß-Handbuch der freien Stadt Frankfurt 1852. Frankfurt: Krug's Verlag, 1852.

Steiner, Herbert. *Die Arbeiterbewegung Österreichs 1867–1889. Beitrage zu ihrer Geschichte von der Gründung des Wiener Arbeiterbildungsvereines bis zum Einigungsparteitag in Hainfeld.* Vienna: Europa Verlag, 1964.

Steiner, Herbert. *Die Gebrüder Scheu. Eine Biographie.* Vienna: Europa-Verlag, 1968.

Stenographische Berichte über die Verhandlungen des Deutschen Reichstags. Berlin: Verlag der Buchdruckerei der "Norddeutschen Allgemeinen Zeitung," 1871–1918.

Stöbe, Herbert. *Der große Streik der Chemnitzer Metallarbeiter zur Durchsetzung des Zehnstundentages im Jahre 1871.* Chemnitz: Stadtarchiv Karl-Marx-Stadt, 1962.

Stöcker, Adolf. *Christlich-Sozial: Reden und Aufsätze.* Bielefeld: Velhagen & Klasing, 1885.

Strauss, Rudolph. "Die 'Chemnitzer Freie Presse'-die Zeitung der 'Eisenacher' im Chemnitzer Industriegebiet." *Volksstimme*, Ausgabe B, nr. 95, vol. 24 (April 1958).

Strauss, Rudolph. "Die Sozialdemokratische Arbeiterpartei in Chemnitz im Kampf gegen den preußisch-deutschen Militärstaat 1870 bis 1872. Eine Untersuchung zur revolutionären Tradition von Karl-Marx-Stadt." In *Beiträge zur Heimatgeschichte von Karl-Marx-Stadt.* Heft 3 (1972), 10–56.

Sveida, George J. *Castle Garden as an Immigrant Depot, 1855–1890.* Washington, DC: Office of Archaeology and Historic Preservation, National Park Service, 1968.

Szmula, Volker, ed. *Johann Most: Dokumente eines sozialdemokratischen Agitators.* 4 vols. Grafenau: Trotzdem Verlag, 1988.

Taylor, A. J. P. *The Habsburg Monarchy 1809–1918: A History of the Austrian Empire and Austria-Hungary.* London: Hamish Hamilton, 1966.

Tcherikower, Elias, ed. *The Early Jewish Labor Movement in the United States.* New York: YIVO Institute for Jewish Research, 1961.

Thümmler, Heinzpeter. *Sozialistengesetz §28: Ausweisungen und Ausgewiesene, 1878–1890.* Vaduz: Topos Verlag, 1979.

Trautmann, Frederic. *The Voice of Terror: A Biography of Johann Most.* Westport, CT: Greenwood, 1980.

Umlauft, Friedrich. *Die Oesterreichisch-Ungarische Monarchie: geographisch-statistisches Handbuch mit besonderer Rücksicht auf politische und Cultur-Geschichte für Leser aller Stände.* Vienna: Hartleben, 1876.

U.S. Congress. *Report of the Select Committee of the House of Representatives to Inquire into the Alleged Violation of the Laws Prohibiting the Importation of Contract Laborers, Paupers, Convicts, and Other Classes.* 50th Congress, 2nd Session. Washington, DC: Government Printing Office, 1889.

U.S. Department of Labor. Bureau of Labor Statistics. *History of Wages in the United States from Colonial Times to 1928.* Washington, DC: Government Printing Office, 1934.

Venturi, Franco. *Roots of Revolution: A History of the Populist and Socialist Movements in Nineteenth Century Russia.* New York: Knopf, 1961.

Verzeichniß der Hausbesitzer in und um Augsburg. Augsburg: Verlag von J. A. Brinhaußer's Erden, 1844.

Verzeichniß derjenigen Schüler und Schülerinnen, welche im Schuljahre . . . in den deutschen Werktags-Schulen der Königlichen Haupt- und Residenzstadt München sich öffentlicher Preise oder rühmlicher Bekanntmachung würdig gemacht haben: nebst einem Vorbericht über den Zustand dieser Schulen. Munich, September 1831.

Wadauer, Sigrid. *Die Tour der Gesellen: Mobilität und Biographie im Handwerk vom 18. bis zum 20. Jahrhundert.* Frankfurt: Campus Verlag, 2005.

Waddington, Patrick. "Sleazy Digs and Coppers' Narks: The Fate of Russian Nihilists in Paris a Hundred Years Ago." *New Zealand Slavonic Journal* (1989):1–39.

Wagner, Joachim. *Missionare der Gewalt. Lebensläufe deutscher Terroristen im Kaiserreich.* Heidelberg: Kriminalistik Verlag, 1980.

Waldeck, Friedrich Meyer von. "Die russischen Nihilisten." *Unsere Zeit. Deutsche Revue der Gegenwart* 15, no. 2 (1879): 110–25.

Walter, Nicholas. "Joseph Lane." https://geocities.restorativland.org/~johngray/ joelane.htm.

Waltershausen, A. Sartorius Freiherrn von. *Der moderne Socialismus in den Vereinigten Staaten von Amerika.* Berlin: H. Bahr, 1890.

Wangemann, Hans. *D. Dr. Wangemann, Missionsdirektor: ein Lebensbild; dargeboten von seinem ältesten Sohne.* Berlin: Wiegandt & Grieben, 1899.

Welskopp, Thomas. *Das Banner der Brüderlichkeit: die deutsche Sozialdemokratie vom Vormärz bis zum Sozialistengesetz.* Bonn: Dietz, 2000.

Whelehan, Niall. "'Cheap as Soap and Common as Sugar': The Fenians, Dynamite and Scientific Warfare." In *The Black Hand of Republicanism: The Fenians and History*, edited by James McConnell and Fearghal McGarry, 105–20. Dublin: Irish Academic Press, 2009.

Wiedemann, Theodor. "Sechzehn Jahre in der Werkstatt Leopold von Ranke's. Ein Beitrag zur Geschichte seiner letzten Lebensjahre." *Deutsche Revue: eine Monatschrift* 18, no. 3 (1893): 227–36, 342–54; no. 4 (1893): 253–72.

Wish, Harvey. "Governor Altgeld Pardons the Anarchists." *Journal of the Illinois State Historical Society (1908-1984)* 31, no. 4 (1938): 424–48.

Wittke, Carl. *Against the Current: The Life of Karl Heinzen.* Chicago: University of Chicago Press, 1945.

Wurzbach, Constantin von. *Biographisches Lexikon des Kaiserthums Oesterreich.* Vienna: Verlag der k.k. Hof- und Staatsdruckerei, 1881.

Yecheved [pseud. Etta Byer]. *Transplanted People.* Chicago: Lider Organization of Chicago, 1955.

Zimmer, Kenyon. "Haymarket and the Rise of Syndicalism." In *The Palgrave Handbook of Anarchism*, edited by Carl Levy and Matthew S. Adams, 353–69. Cham: Springer, 2018.

Zimmer, Kenyon. *Immigrants against the State: Yiddish and Italian Anarchism in America.* Urbana: University of Illinois Press, 2015.

Zorn, Wolfgang. *Augsburg: Geschichte einer europäischen Stadt; von den Anfängen bis zur Gegenwart.* Augsburg: Wißner, 2001.

Dissertations and Theses

Devreese, D. E. "Militanten rond de Eerste Internationale in België, 1860–1880." BA thesis, Gent University, 1967–68.

Goodrich, Robert W. "On the Road to Wyden: The Expulsion of Johann Most from the German Socialist Democratic Party, 1878–1880." MA thesis, University of Wisconsin, 1994.

Luksch, Andreas. "Der Beitrag der 'Chemnitzer Freie Presse' zur Durchsetzung des Marxismus in der Chemnitzer Arbeiterbewegung, insbesondere untersucht an der propagandistisch-theoretischen Arbeit zwischen 1871–1878." Karl-Marx-Universität Leipzig, 1984.

Index

Index

TOM GOYENS is a professor of history at Salisbury University. He is the author of *Beer and Revolution: The German Anarchist Movement in New York City, 1880–1914*.

The University of Illinois Press
is a founding member of the
Association of University Presses.

———————————————

Composed in 10.5/13 Minion Pro
by Lisa Connery
at the University of Illinois Press
Manufactured by Sheridan Books, Inc.

University of Illinois Press
1325 South Oak Street
Champaign, IL 61820–6903
www.press.uillinois.edu